Multicultural Education

Multicultural Education

AN INTERNATIONAL GUIDE TO RESEARCH, POLICIES, AND PROGRAMS

Bruce M. Mitchell and Robert E. Salsbury

GREENWOOD PRESS
Westport, Connecticut • London

Library of Congress Cataloging-in-Publication Data

Mitchell, Bruce M.
    Multicultural education : an international guide to research,
policies, and programs / Bruce M. Mitchell and Robert E. Salsbury.
        p.   cm.
    Includes bibliographical references and index.
    ISBN 0–313–28985–9 (alk. paper)
    1. Multicultural education.   I. Salsbury, Robert E.   II. Title.
LC1099.M583   1996
370.19'6—dc20   95–37337

British Library Cataloguing in Publication Data is available.

Library of Congress Catalog Card Number: 95–37337
ISBN: 0–313–28985–9

First published in 1996

Greenwood Press, 88 Post Road West, Westport, CT 06881
An imprint of Greenwood Publishing Group, Inc.

Printed in the United States of America

The paper used in this book complies with the
Permanent Paper Standard issued by the National
Information Standards Organization (Z39.48–1984).

10   9   8   7   6   5   4   3   2   1

Contents

Preface

The decade of the 1990s is turning out to be one of the most exciting in world history. Many countries are composed of highly diversified, pluralistic peoples who cry out for independence and dignity. A growing demand for an egalitarian philosophy has emerged, and school systems around the world have been searching for ways to help engender better interpersonal relations among all persons within their borders. Achieving such goals has proven to be difficult when students have had limited cross-cultural experiences.

This book is a reference work which examines a sampling of the world's educational systems. The countries chosen for inclusion in the book consist of nations which participated in the authors' international study of multicultural education (see Appendix). In addition, other countries which did not respond to the survey requests were also included in order to provide a solid sampling of nations on all continents. An attempt was made to include both developing nations and industrialized countries, as well as nations with differing political systems and varying religious perspectives. The authors attempted to include countries from all parts of the world in the book, along with nations possessing a great variety of educational systems.

The idea for the book originated from a previous work, which examined gifted/talented education programs throughout the world. However, this time, the topic of multicultural education was the central theme since many countries have initiated such programs in an attempt to help young learners acquire more positive attitudes about their countries' pluralistic microcultures, acquire a strong sense of their own self-esteem, identify examples of stereotypical thinking and prejudice, acquire more enlightened attitudes about gender equity, and articulate understandings about their own microcultures in order to learn how such influences have shaped their own thinking and behavior. The survey results have been augmented by extensive research in order to create a book which provides information about the multicultural efforts around the world.

We felt that it was important to provide the reader with a brief history of each country in order to better understand the reasons for the basic structure of a nation's educational system. The second segment of each chapter includes a glimpse of the organizational structure of the country in order to comprehend how the educational system fits in. Finally, various types of multicultural education efforts were also described. This information was taken from the author's international multicultural education study (see Appendix). These findings were augmented with information from the literature. It should be pointed out that although only a sampling of all the earth's nations are included in the book, the reader can probably make use of the information about countries with similar characteristics.

The term "multicultural education" means many things to different people. However, in this study, it was defined as educational strategies which attempt to prepare youth to function constructively in a changing pluralistic society by providing teachers and students with the capacity to diagnose and work through racial, ethnic, cultural, and gender issues and misunderstandings, prejudice, and racial fears. Moreover, it also consists of educational experiences which positively reflect and embody the diverse nature of the national and international community.

Undertakings of this nature require a great deal of assistance, and this work was no exception. The authors are grateful to the Department of Education at Eastern Washington University for absorbing the costs of mailing in the initial survey. Also, we owe a debt of gratitude to Eastern Washington University's Chicano Education Program, particularly Mary Velez, for assisting us in some of the Spanish translations.

We give our thanks to Eastern Washington University students Nancy Atwood, Heather Grisham, Shannon Bryan, Carisia Burger, Pippin Rosebrook, Dawn Mertens, Brian Dickey, Jeff Mitchell, and Karen Grimm for their work as research assistants. Further thanks are due to Jeff Mitchell and Neil Groenen for assisting in the translation of the questionnaire responses during the international survey we conducted. We also thank Oletha Jernigan and Sherry Miller for preparing the manuscript.

The project has proven to be quite fascinating. Nothing is more interesting than the study of human efforts to understand the nuances of human cultures, and it has helped us to acquire a new understanding of intercultural life on the planet. Through our communications, we managed to obtain a number of international "pen pals," to whom we will always be indebted.

Introduction

Historians have sometimes characterized human history as a chronicle of the victors and the victimized. Throughout history, human beings often have searched for wealth and cheap labor at the expense of indigenous populations. At times, the conquerors have inflicted their cultural values on the conquered to the extent that entire microcultures have virtually disappeared, resulting in ethnocide. Whenever the conquered either have taken over a territory or colonized it, new educational systems often have resulted.

Most of these educational systems have had as their primary goal the inculcation of youth with the ideas and skills considered to be important to the dominant culture. For example, prior to the invention of the printing press, there was little need for the inclusion of reading in the curriculum. Gradually, this became of critical importance throughout much of the world. Other curricular elements have been introduced into educational systems as the need arose.

During recent decades, many countries have had a love affair with the notion of egalitarianism. Commencing with the French Enlightenment, extending through the Marxist revolutions and other democratic upheavals, including the American civil rights movements of the 1950s and 1960s, the world's communities have seen a steadily increasing commitment to human rights issues and the development of solid measures to ensure equal opportunities for all humans. Indeed, this has been a major goal of the United Nations.

Even though these lofty ideals have affected the prevailing philosophies of many nations, the educational systems have often been slow to change their practices in order to become consistent with existing attitudes. For example, during the American Revolution, even though the issues centered around the acquisition of individual freedom, the country still practiced slavery, and the schools of the time had no formal programs for the children of African slaves. Moreover, few educators were the slightest bit concerned over the creation of educational programs for Native American children. This condition has prevailed among many aboriginal populations the world over.

Throughout the world, educational systems at times have been limited to children of the wealthy classes, and separate schools were developed for the rich and the economically disadvantaged. Consistently, such school programs for poor children were decidedly inferior. For example, during the nineteenth century, Germany had its Volkschule (folk school) for poor children and the gymnasium for the upper classes. This structure finally commenced to change after World War II.

Eighteenth- and nineteenth-century England provided a separate school system for wealthy students. A ''pauper'' system was made available for poor children. Because of lax child labor laws, many young children from the culture of poverty did not attend school at all. This would not change until shortly after the beginning of the twentieth century, when the country began funding elementary and secondary schools. However, the private school still remained in place to serve the wealthy.

Until World War I, France maintained a separate system of schools. Elementary schools were available for the poor, and secondary schools for the rich. A common elementary school for both rich and poor was created after the war, but not until 1930 could all secondary students have access to free tuition.

These examples tend to illustrate that only recently have many of the world communities made serious attempts to provide an equal education opportunity for all of their people. This practice has had a dramatic effect on the nature of the curriculum. Since the persons of privilege were often the persons of power, it is understandable that the educational curriculum of the country seldom dealt with the judicious pluralistic treatment of the various microcultures in a nation. Textbooks focused on the activities of the dominant groups and tended to promote an ideology of elitism which neglected the achievements and national contributions of the poverty powerless. This deeply affected such groups as the Tasmanians in Australia, numerous indigenous groups in the African and South American countries, and the hundreds of indigenous tribes and clans in North America.

In addition to these problems, a number of countries encouraged the peaceful immigration of people from various parts of the world for economic, political, and religious reasons. Although many of these new immigrants were of the same racial background as the dominant culture, some of them differed ethnically, bringing diverse values, religions, and language patterns to various parts of the world. New arrivals were expected to assimilate into the dominant culture, giving up their original ethnicity in the process.

Surfacing during the American Colonial period, this ''melting pot'' theory of cultural assimilation became a prevailing concept in the emerging nation. Persons coming to the country were expected to rid themselves of their native language and speak English. Of course, Native Americans and African-American slaves were not expected to assimilate in the American melting pot

because of their perceived second-class status. Similar situations existed elsewhere around the world. However, multicultural education experts argue that a
"stew" or "salad" theory should replace the melting pot idea. This metaphor
means that all the humans in a macroculture contribute positively to the total
"stew" or "salad." To subscribe to such a philosophy might empower young
learners to be more successful if they understand the value of their own microculture and learn in their "mother tongue" before learning the official language
of the land.

Some have argued that too much emphasis on assimilationist philosophy
might engender racist and ethnocentric behaviors which could damage groups
of people who were not allowed to participate in decision-making processes.
Such persons were often destined to become part of the poverty cultures of their
various countries.

In the schools, this has meant that some poor children have not had access
to the same quality of education set aside for children of privilege. The dominant
ideologies and values promoted in the schools often means that children from
the "underclasses" acquire negative perceptions about their ability to think and
learn. Since many of these children have come from very poor families, this
also means that the ravages of poverty had a negative effect on their ability to
learn in school. Because of these poverty factors, many low-income students
often have not had a good syntactical knowledge of their native language, let
alone the instructional language used in school. Hence, it might be found that
such children fall further and further behind the longer they remain in the educational system. As their educational lives become more and more hopeless,
many of them may drop out of school and the education problems become
intensified.

As countries gradually began to understand that it was important to educate
all of their citizens, they began to seek solutions, and out of the search came
the concept of multicultural education, which was twofold: to help students from
all of a country's microcultures become better learners, and to help all children
in each nation's school system learn to celebrate the multiethnic and multiracial
uniqueness of all persons in their midst.

Obviously, such an approach has necessitated a new look at the historical
development of any country. In some cases it required brave admissions of past
errors. In the United States, it spawned a social revolution which sometimes
chastised the Eurocentric school system and cried out for major changes. United
States Supreme Court decisions such as *Brown v. Board of Education* and *Lau
v. Nichols* mandated major changes as did the 1960s demonstrations in local
communities such as East Los Angeles, which resulted in bilingual/bicultural
programs being put in place in many U.S. school districts in order to upgrade
the education of young students.

Gradually, many schools around the world instituted a multicultural educational thrust which had as its primary goal the elimination of racism and ethnocentric behavior. In America, one of the early pioneering efforts was carried

on by the Committee of Intergroup Education in Cooperating Schools appointed by the American Council on Education. Under the Direction of Dr. Hilda Taba, this group was established in the 1950s and was designed to reduce racial and ethnic prejudices and misunderstanding. Activities of this group utilized strategies which included (1) instructional units geared toward persons of color; (2) lessons on the damages of racial prejudice; (3) the organization of intercultural interaction, disseminating information on religious, racial, and ethnic backgrounds; and (4) screening the language in textbooks and other educational materials which might convey gender and/or racial bias. It was one of the first serious efforts throughout the world to address the issue in any systematic manner.

However, the multicultural education "movement" is not without its critics. Far-right groups in the United States have chastised this relatively new educational strand and have exhorted educators in that country to subscribe to a more "Eurocentric" philosophy and to "return to the basics." Moreover, some right-wing groups have claimed that such educational efforts are not part of the school's "basic education" parameters and they might undermine the family's values.

However, studies conducted by the authors have revealed that many countries of the world are concerned about the issues of multicultural education. For example, Brazilians have tried to provide specialized instructional programs for indigenous populations in the Amazon Basin, and Australians have attempted to do the same with theirs. In the United States, some states now require that all teachers must complete certain requirements in multicultural education before they can be certified to teach in the schools. Many new teachers are required to have a solid background about cultural pluralism in the country and utilize planning strategies which enable their students to acquire the same information. Moreover, such course requirements often necessitate the utilization of classroom activities which help defuse racism and sexism. Multicultural education experts argue that such components must be put in place in all school settings, regardless of the racial, ethnic, and socioeconomic nature of the students.

Exploitation, adventurism, religion, economic enhancement, and armed conflict have continuously caused many persons around the world to become nomadic or move permanently, thus becoming exposed to new groups of people with different language patterns, values, religions, and racial characteristics. Gradually, some nations have discovered that all persons are valuable members of the human race and have much to contribute. Unfortunately, this view has yet to surface in many countries. Nonetheless, many of the world's school systems have sought ways to provide better instruction for such groups regardless of their individual characteristics. Moreover, the world's peoples have begun to realize that racism, sexism, and ethnocentric attitudes have taken a heavy toll. It is the hope of educators everywhere that multicultural education programs will be able to help solve the problems of racial and ethnic minorities and majority cultures alike.

In the United States, the idea of multicultural education has grown steadily due to the efforts of such national leaders as James Banks, Pamela and Iris Tiedt, Ricardo Garcia, Ronald Takaki, Hilda Hernandez, and many others. The term has been defined to include any kind of instruction which helps students to value cultural pluralism and acquire more accurate and sophisticated concepts about the various microcultures which comprise the macroculture of a particular country. It deals with instructional efforts which concentrate on the improvement of instruction for all racial and ethnic groups within a country's school system. Finally, the term also relates to educational efforts which attempt to help all students become fully functioning human beings regardless of their race or ethnicity.

The research portion of this undertaking includes the following issues of the authors' international multicultural survey:

1. The extent of central direction for multicultural programs in the nation's schools.

2. Funding levels for multicultural programs.

3. Leadership in multicultural education programs provided by the central education offices.

4. Cultures which exist within the country.

5. Multicultural certification requirements for teachers.

6. The extent to which the official state position stresses a culturally pluralistic or assimilationist perspective in the educational curriculum.

7. Official languages of instruction in the country's school system.

8. Racial integration/segregation of the nation's schools.

9. The extent to which the history of indigenous peoples is consciously stressed in the curriculum of the schools.

10. National efforts to include bilingual/bicultural instruction in the schools.

11. Procedures for evaluating curriculum materials, library materials, and textbooks for racist and/or sexist content.

12. The biggest problems facing the country in the area of multicultural programs in the schools.

13. The most important improvements needed in the country's educational programs.

The results of this study can be viewed in the Appendix.

I

Afghanistan

HISTORY OF THE SYSTEM

Afghanistan's geographical location at the crossroads of central, west, and south Asia has had a major effect on the country's total history. During ancient times, hordes of migrating people went through the area, forming a fascinating multicultural patchwork quilt of people from different racial and ethnic backgrounds. In addition, many armies passed through the territory, causing a number of wars and sometimes controlling Iran and northern India as well. But even though there were many empires and much activity, Afghanistan did not become an independent nation until the twentieth century.

After World War II, archaeological digs were conducted throughout the country and a number of fascinating findings emerged. Based on these bits of archaeological research evidence, it is thought that the Iranian plateau, which includes most of present-day Iran and Afghanistan, could have begun as long as 3,000 to 2,000 years before the birth of Christ. Present-day Afghanistan consisted of several provinces (satrapies) of the Achaemenid Empire.

By approximately 330–327 B.C., Alexander the Great had conquered the areas which now comprise Afghanistan and some of the areas in the former Soviet Union. About 327 B.C., Alexander marched into the Indian subcontinent, where his progress was actually aborted because of a mutiny of his own forces. Even though the effects of his incursions into the area were minimal at best, he left cultural influences which lasted for several centuries. When he died in 323 B.C., his empire crumbled and his cavalry commander, Seleucus, gained control of the eastern lands and founded the Seleucid Dynasty. But the Seleucids were unable to hold onto the eastern end of their dynasty.

During the third and second centuries B.C., nomadic peoples who spoke the indo-European languages entered the Iranian plateau. The Parthians gained control of what constitutes present-day Iran as early as the middle of the third century B.C. Approximately 100 years later, the Sakas or Kushans entered present-day Afghanistan and started an empire which lasted for approximately 400 years.

The Kushans moved from the valley of the Kabul River to become victorious over a number of Central Asian tribes that had prevailed over other groups who had conquered segments of the north central Iranian plateau. By the third century A.D., Kushan control had dissipated into a number of smaller kingdoms, which became an easy target for a rising Iranian dynasty known as the Sassanians. But after approximately 100 years, both the Sassanians and Kushans became targets for the Hepthalites (White Huns) who swept out of Central Asia in the fourth or fifth century. Five years after the death of the Prophet Muhammad, the Arab Muslims defeated the Iranian Sassanians, and this Muslim conquest was a long-lived campaign in the territories which make up present-day Afghanistan.

During a 24-year period of peace under the leadership of Caliph Haran al Rashid, the ancestors of many present-day Afghanistan citizens settled in the Hindu Kush area in order to acquire better grazing land. These tribes assimilated a great deal of the language and culture of the Pashtun tribes who already lived in that region.

By about A.D. 850, semi-independent states began to emerge throughout the region. The best known was the Sammanid Dynasty, which endured until the tenth century. Its influence extended clear to India in the east and west into present-day Iran. But by the middle of the tenth century, the Sammanid Dynasty was terminated because of pressure by the Turks and the Ghaznavids to the south. Out of this dynasty came the first great Islamic empire in Afghanistan, the Ghaznavids. But by 1200, Turkish dynasties had come into power, with the Ghorids controlling most of present-day Afghanistan.

Invasions by the Mongols started in 1220 with dramatic victories by Genghis Khan. The Mongols sacked Baghdad in 1258, and the destruction had a disastrous economic impact on the entire area, including present-day Afghanistan. And about 160 years after the incursions by the Mongols, Timur-i-Leng, a Turko-Mongol invader, ferociously overran Afghanistan. Timur was of both Turkish and Mongol descent and claimed that Genghis Khan was one of his ancestors. The rule by the Mongols lasted until the early 1500s.

One of the next most influential figures in the area was Babur, who descended from Timur on his father's side and Genghis Khan on his mother's side. He was chased out of his father's kingdom in the present-day Russia. Eventually, his 12,000-man army captured Kabul, launching the Mughal Empire, which was powerful until about 1707, the year in which Babur's great-great grandson, Aurangzeb, died.

Kabul and Qandahar were captured in 1738 by Nadir Shah, known as the Napoleon of Persia. He also was famous for having defeated an excellent army in India, ravaging Delhi and massacring thousands of people. From Nadir Shah's death in 1747 until the communist coup of 1978, Afghanistan was governed by Pashtun rulers of the Abdali tribe. In fact, during the leadership of the first

Pashtun ruler, Ahmad Shah, the present nation of Afghanistan began to develop. During the reign of Ahmad Shah, the Mughal and Safaji empires, which were adjacent to the country, deteriorated. He finally died in 1772 in his mountain home east of Qandahar.

The successors of Ahmad Shah tended to be rather weak rulers who unfortunately were in power during a period of more than 50 years when Dost Mohammad took over the throne in Kabul in 1826. He achieved his power by using the support of his mother's Qizilbash tribesmen and his apprenticeship under the tutelage of his brother, Fateh Kahn.

Dost Mohammad repelled an invasion by ex-shah Shuja Dost Muhammad and contacted the British in hopes of securing assistance in dealing with the Sikhs, who had been attempting to increase their influence in the area by moving westward. The British, through the East India Company, had exerted their influence in the area, particularly in England. Britain and Russia were both interested in these lands. For the British, Afghanistan was an enticing plum, located just north of their interests in India. Indeed, they had been moving into Punjab, Kashmir, and Sind. They viewed the Russian incursions into the Caucasus and Georgia, Kirghiz, Turkmen lands, Khiva, and Bukhara. These conditions set the stage for a British invasion of Afghanistan in 1838. A manifesto was issued by Lord Auckland; the document argued that India's welfare required a trustworthy ally on their western frontier. After some initial successes by the British, their garrison suffered a major defeat which prompted wide-scale retaliations by the British against the Afghans. These conflicts would persist into the next century.

The reign of Abdur Rahman Khan resulted in Afghanistan's emergence as a modern state. He was willing to work with the British and accepted certain power limitations as a result of their influence. Nonetheless, he was able to consolidate the various entities into a state, modernizing it in the process. Moreover, the borders of the Afghan state were established during his reign. Another accomplishment during his period of leadership was the creation of a regular army and the country's first national governmental structure, which included a royal council and general assembly. However, they were only advisory in nature because of the autocratic nature of Abdur Rahman's leadership period. In addition, his modernization efforts included an interest in technological development through the work of foreign physicians, engineers, geologists, and printers. He also was successful in creating a number of small factories for the production of soap, leather goods, and candles.

Afghanistan managed to remain neutral during World War I in spite of pressure from Turkey to become involved when that country's sultan argued that it was a holy war. After the war, King Amanullah, Abdur Rahman's oldest son who had assumed the leadership of the country, was assassinated in 1919. This occurred right after the Russian revolution of 1917, and Afghanistan became a major player when the detente between Russia and Great Britain broke down. The new leader, Amanullah, attacked the British, who were taken by surprise.

However, during his reign, Afghanistan became a tool for both the Russians and the British.

Amanullah was followed by King Muhammad Nadir Shah, a deserter from the Afghan army who had a short nine-month reign. This new ruler abolished most of Amanullah's reforms, and during his four-year reign the army was fairly weak, allowing some of the tribal leaders to become stronger. During his rule, he appeased some of the country's religious leaders by establishing a constitutional emphasis on orthodox religious dogma.

The next Afghanistan monarch was in control longer than any of the Afghan leaders. King Muhammad Zahir Shah assumed power in 1933, and managed to maintain his position of leadership until 1973. During 1934 Afghanistan joined the League of Nations and the king issued a statement of neutrality in 1940, during World War II. Shortly after the war, Afghanistan began a relationship with the newly created state of Pakistan. The issue of whether there should be an independent or semi-independent state including the Pashtu and Pakhtu ethnic groups would have a major impact on Afghanistan politics for many years to come.

During 1953, Prime Minister Daoud became the first Western-educated member of the royal family to ascend to power in Kabul. He proved to be a dynamic leader who wished to correct a ''pro-Western'' bias in the country's policies. He fostered the Helmand Valley Project, which attempted to change life in southwestern Afghanistan. Taking rather cautious steps toward the emancipation of women, he had the wives of his ministers appear in public unveiled. And when religious leaders protested the action, he challenged them to find one single reference in the Quran that specifically required veiling. They were unable to do so.

During Daoud's period of leadership, relations with the Soviet Union started out well when the Soviets provided the country with an economic development loan. In spite of the improved relations with the USSR, Daoud also sought a relationship with the United States during the time when President Dwight Eisenhower was interested in solidifying an alliance with Turkey, Iran, Iraq, Pakistan, and Afghanistan. But border disputes with Pakistan plagued the country, and Daoud resigned his position in 1964.

Just two weeks after Daoud's resignation, a new constitution for the country was drawn up. A royal commission of multicultural members reviewed and revised the draft, which was finally signed by 452 members of the Loyal Jirgah of Afghanistan and by the king. The document barred the royal family, other than the king, from political and governmental involvement. It also designated the term ''Afghans'' as an official word which would be used in referring to all citizens of the country.

The new constitution also provided for a bicameral legislature, but the ultimate power still rested with the king. Religious judges were incorporated into the judicial system, but the constitution also established the supremacy of secular law. When the constitution went into effect, the literacy rate was low, voter turnout was minimal, and the country had no political parties.

In 1973 Daoud returned to power in Afghanistan because of the country's dissatisfaction with the leadership during the previous ten years. The Western countries believed that the coup was inspired by pro-Communist factions. In an attempt to develop a state-centered economy, Daoud drew up a seven-year economic plan in 1976. In order for it to work, an infusion of foreign aid was required, so he made several contacts with the Soviet Union. However, conditions between the two countries deteriorated and eventually the Soviets invaded Afghanistan in 1979 and were there until 1988. The Soviets were afraid that the United States might exploit the disorder in the country and install a pro-American government in Kabul with Pakistani assistance.

Change was also occurring in the country's educational system at this time. During the 1970s, Afghanistan attempted to modernize its elementary language arts curriculum, changing from the traditional materials, which tended to place a high emphasis on rote memorization, to a procedure that encouraged active inquiry and problem solving. New curriculum goals and objectives were established, which placed a greater emphasis on a whole language approach to the teaching of language arts in the schools. Special attention was given to the instruction of the two official languages, Dari and Pashto.

In an attempt to control Kabul and control the Salang Pass Highway, the USSR used a number of conventional tactics. The city had a population of about 2.5 million people, including many refugees, and the road was an important communication line with the Soviet hinterlands. European-style armored vehicles did not work in spite of the 115,000 Soviet troops who were in the country and supported by Turkish troops across the border. Due to repeated failures and intensified anti-USSR sentiment around the world, the Soviets finally withdrew.

STRUCTURE OF THE SYSTEM

Afghanistan became part of the world's state system after the second Anglo-Afghan War, which was fought between 1978 and 1980. It served as a kind of buffer between the English and Russian empires which actually drew up the boundaries that still exist to this day. Being surrounded by the USSR, Iran, and Pakistan has resulted in almost continual conflicts through history, and Afghanistan's foreign aid assistance has usually been politically motivated. This was the situation that existed during the Russian invasion. The United States, Saudi Arabia, and China started programs of aid through Pakistan. Also, world public opinion was generally directed against the Soviets.

The war had reached a stalemate by 1986 and the Soviets were looking for a way out. Finally, the Geneva Accords of 1988 paved the way for a Soviet withdrawal by 1989. At that time, Najibullah implemented a number of reforms in an attempt to make it appear that democratization was occurring in Pakistan. Najibullah and his Soviet backers established the Nicaraguan model, resulting in free elections that were internationally monitored. Najibullah requested that the Great Council of Afghanistan (Loya Jirga) approve a new constitution providing for an elected government and elect him president with nearly unlimited powers.

In an attempt to settle other Afghani disputes with Saudi Arabia and Pakistani political units, Perez de Cuellar of the United Nations (U.N.) issued a statement which he felt summarized an international consensus on Afghanistan. His political settlement would commence with the creation of a transition mechanism, which would begin with all parties terminating their arms supplies to the country. Moreover, all internal parties should start an immediate cease-fire. An interim authority would organize free and fair elections in accordance with Afghan traditions in order to choose a broad-based government.

Pakistan, Saudi Arabia, and Iran formally agreed to support a U.S.–Soviet agreement by January 1992. The new U.N. Secretary-General, Boutros Boutros-Ghali, announced a plan in which all Afghan parties would submit the names of candidates for an ''Afghan gathering,'' which would eventually lead to the development of an interim government and national elections.

Because of the conflicts in Afghanistan, new groups emerged. The Ubeks had received rather heavy Soviet backing, and the Shi'a Hazaras enjoyed the support of their Iranian neighbor. After the foreign military aid had been essentially terminated, the non-Pashtun groups asserted their military power and several new ethnic alliances emerged. The Pashtun alliance (backed by the Pakistani alliance) and the Hizbi were two of the new Afghani groups which would have an effect on future Afghanistan issues.

Finally, through the assistance of the U.N., a new organizational structure was created for the country of Afghanistan during 1992. Called the Islamic State of Afghanistan, this new, embattled government had to fight for control of its own capital, Kabul. Just six months after assuming authority, the new interim government of Kabul was still far from being solidified.

These inter-ethnic conflicts in Afghanistan do not have their roots in deep-seated hostilities among ethnic groups, but rather from the supplying of arms to the warring factions. Indeed, these power struggles seem to be primarily caused by the international system's propensity to define states as political communities with fixed borders.

The educational system in the country has suffered from a history of violent confrontations between ethnic groups and the military incursions of other countries. For children between the ages of 5 and 11 years, education is free and compulsory. However, in spite of the ''free and compulsory'' stipulation, only about 20 percent of the people over the age of 15 are literate.

The University of Kabul is the country's primary institution of higher education. Founded in 1932, the school had been considered to be a respected institution of higher education. Then, in 1962, the University of Nangarhar in Jalalabad was started by the University of Kabul's faculty of medicine. During the relationship with the Soviets, many Afghani students were able to attend schools in the USSR.

MULTICULTURAL EDUCATION EFFORTS

One of the big problems for developing countries such as Afghanistan has been the tremendous difficulty in establishing specialized programs in the schools. The Afghanistan educational system is no exception. Due to severe financial restrictions, it takes an enormous effort to supply even the most rudimentary educational programs for children. Moreover, given the history of interethnic strife, the schools are often the center of controversy, and are hard-pressed to provide suitable educational programs for young people.

Afghanistan has a number of major ethnic groups including about 6.5 million Pashtuns, 3.5 million Tajiks, 1 million Hazaras, 1 million Uzbeks, a large percentage of Shi', and a large number of Pakistani refugees. The education of all students, regardless of their ethnic heritage, is the responsibility of the country's Ministry of Education.

While the primary languages of instruction are Pushtu and Dari, instruction is sometimes provided in the mother tongues of Dari, Pushtu, Uzbek, Turkmani, and Baluchi. The Ministry of Education Department of Educational Publications prepares textbooks and translates them into the five languages. Since 99 percent of the population are members of the Muslim faith, the schools have a strong religious orientation.

Gender issues in the schools reflect the Muslim beliefs. The Islamic religion argues for the maintenance of as much difference as possible between the genders. Muslim school children are forbidden to wear clothing typically worn by the opposite gender. Male Afghans sometimes view women as being disruptive elements in the social milieu. Since most of the Afghan researchers have been males, there is a dearth of data regarding the status of Afghan women. The men are expected to be the leaders, protectors, and disciplinarians. Moreover, they must be brave. These attitudes are reflected strongly in the missions of the country's schools.

SUMMARY

Afghanistan has had a turbulent history. Surrounded by Iran, Saudi Arabia, and Pakistan, it has been forced to deal with a history of ethnic conflict and military intrusions by world powers such as the USSR and Great Britain. Being a Third World country, it has been forced to contend with severe financial restrictions, which have placed great limits on economic development and the country's educational system.

Consequently, Afghanistan has been able to develop very few programs in multicultural education. The ethnic strife has obviously created a tremendous need for such educational enterprises, but reality has made it virtually impossible to implement the types of multicultural education offerings which many educators in the country would like to adapt.

REFERENCES

de Cuellar, Javier Perez. Statement made through the United Nations Department of Public Information, May 21, 1991.

Dupree, Louis. *Afghanistan.* Princeton, NJ: Princeton University Press, 1932.

Fraser-Tyler, Kerr W. *Afghanistan: A Study of Political Developments in Central and Southern Asia.* New York: Paragon Books, 1967.

Gregorian, Vartan. *The Emergence of Modern Afghanistan.* Stanford, CA: Stanford University Press, 1969.

Hauner, Milan. *The Soviet War in Afghanistan.* Philadelphia: University Press of America, 1991.

Mayerson, Paul and Alimi, M. Zaher. "Developing a Language Curriculum in Afghanistan." Conference Presentation. ERIC No. ED 140232, August 1976.

Mitchell, Bruce and Salsbury, Robert. *Multicultural Education in the World Community.* Cheney, WA: Western States Consulting and Evaluation Services, Publication Division, 1991. (See Appendix.)

Nyrop, Richard F. and Seekins, Donald M. *Afghanistan: A Country Study.* Washington, DC: U.S. Government Printing Office, 1986.

Rubin, Barnett R. "Post–Cold War State Disintegration: The Failure of International Conflict Resolution in Afghanistan." *Journal of International Affairs* (Winter 1993).

Sykes, Percy M. *A History of Afghanistan.* London: MacMillan, 1940.

2

Australia

HISTORY OF THE SYSTEM

Geographical conditions have shaped the history of all countries around the world, and Australia is no exception. With a land mass quite similar in size to the United States, this island continent has enjoyed a substantial level of mineral wealth, relatively good agricultural surpluses, and a good, warm growing climate.

Prior to the arrival of the Europeans in 1770, approximately 300,000 aboriginal persons populated the country. However, during that year, Captain James Cook of the British Royal Navy gained control over the eastern coast of the country in the name of George III of England. This would eventually lead to the English control of the continent. This control lasted until Australia became a Commonwealth state with a parliamentary system of government after World War II.

It has been argued that human beings first populated the country about 30,000 years ago. During the late 1770s, a penal colony was constructed at Botany Bay. Two years after completion of the new facility, the first of many shipments of male prisoners arrived in Australia. A new place was needed for indentured servants and other types of English prisoners.

Consequently, during the year of 1788, about 1,500 people arrived in Australia. About half of them were prisoners from the British jails which were overcrowded. Eventually, some 160,000 British prisoners found their way to Australia. Some were freed because of good conduct. But while some were freed and returned to Great Britain, most remained in Australia.

As was usually the case in such ventures, aboriginal groups suffered severely at the hands of the new European settlers. Both the Tasmanian and Australian aborigines suffered greatly. In fact, the last Tasmanian aborigines died out about 1876.

The Australian Commonwealth was created in 1901. A constitution was approved by Australian voters and the British Parliament allowed the commonwealth to become part of the British Empire at the time. The political system was somewhat similar to that of the United States, with a cabinet, headed by a prime minister. Australia's six political subdivisions include Victoria, New South Wales, Queensland, South Australia, Northern Territory, and Western Australia.

By the latter part of the twentieth century, the organizational structure of the Australian Commonwealth's educational system was quite well solidified. The system was generally established around traditional and conservative principles. By and large, the Australian schools have been viewed as major institutions for conformity and social control.

STRUCTURE OF THE SYSTEM

Since 1901, responsibility of education has belonged to the six state governments, even though the federal government has exerted increased influences since the end of World War II. The Australian government is advised on educational matters by the Federal Department of Education. Even though the state systems function independently, they are quite similar in their administrative organization. All six states have a centralized department of education headed by a state cabinet minister. State departments control the fiscal management, curriculum, staffing, planning, and research.

When considering the structure of public education in this country, parallels can be drawn between Australia and the United States of America. Both countries have a firm belief that education is more a state than federal enterprise, resulting in more autonomy in the states' pursuits of educational agendas. A second similarity is the separation of secular and "moral" aspects of education, especially as the latter might be based on religious beliefs and practices. This type of system is seen in various ways by teachers from other countries who have observed Australian education up close. Some observations include the following: the school buildings are attractive; classloads are small; discipline is lax, at least by their standards; and teachers are not respected, again from the perspective of teachers from countries which practice a more formal and nationally controlled form of public education, often based on strong religious faith and practice.

Like many other major industrialized nations, Australia's public schools have been making an effort toward bringing technology, especially the computer, into the classroom. The Sunrise Experience Project, in particular, has been attempting to move student understanding beyond the learning of computer applications programming to levels at which learners use computers and related technology to meet their own needs and interests for seeking and manipulating information for a variety of individual and small-group generated projects.

MULTICULTURAL EDUCATION EFFORTS

Responses received during the initial survey indicated that the funding for formal multicultural programs was terminated by the Ministry of Education during the late 1980s. There is a National Advisory Committee on Multicultural Education (NACME), which functions as an advisory committee and also helps develop policy.

The country has a large population of English-speaking European-Australians. However, there are also indigenous microcultures, such as the aborigines, Tasmanians, and Torres Strait Islander cultures, as well as Asian, Pacific, and Latin American groups. Australian teacher certification procedures do not require any special preparation in multicultural education at the present time. There are over 100 languages in regular use, excluding more than 150 indigenous language patterns. The official language of instruction is English, although other languages are accepted and promoted in the schools.

Immigrant children are provided instruction in their native language along with strong English as a Second Language (ESL) programs. Also included in the curricular offerings are bilingual programs for immigrant and indigenous children, along with "community" languages. During the late 1980s, the country's educational system addressed the issue of language and instruction in hopes of adapting more formal national policies. While all children have the opportunity to attend fully integrated schools, some "ethnic" schools do exist. Such schools are fully supported financially by the Australian Education System.

The history of indigenous peoples is part of the Australian school curriculum. However, there are a number of curricular problems that are being addressed by the National Advisory and Coordinating Committee on Multicultural Education. According to the authors' survey, Australia's biggest problems in multicultural education are resource limitations and inadequate funding levels. It was felt that the greatest needs were more rigorous teacher preparation programs, adequate funding levels, and a greater emphasis on multicultural studies.

One recent issue regarding multicultural education in Australia has been the attitudes pertaining to the integration of migrants. The official view was that migrant families should conform as quickly as possible to Anglo-Australian standards, customs, and language, and intermarry with the British-Australian groups. This expectation is similar to the "Melting Pot Theory" which dominated multicultural issues in the United States until the American Civil Rights Movement.

However, during the 1970s, ethnic lobbying groups argued that the educational system should support the maintenance of their native languages. Consequently, Australian schools have moved to a more multicultural perspective. A study of multicultural issues in the schools revealed the following responses among 790 Australian educators:

1. Should non-English speaking migrant children be encouraged by the school to retain their ethnic language? 80% yes

2. Do you consider the maintenance of the ethnic language important for the migrant child? 85% yes

3. If there are large numbers of non–English-speaking migrants in a school, should the school play a significant role in teaching ethnic languages? 36% yes (56% of ESL teachers said yes)

4. Is it desirable for ethnic languages to be used as a medium of instruction for part of the day in schools having large numbers of migrant children? 49% yes

5. Is it the school's responsibility to help the children retain their ethnic language? 24% yes

6. Should schools work for the preservation of cultural differences among ethnic groups in Australia? 50% yes

7. Should a study of migrant cultures and histories be incorporated into the curriculum of Australian schools? 91% yes

8. Should Australian children attend special migrant language/culture classes to learn about the culture of ethnic groups? 52% yes

9. Should teachers be familiar with the customs and language of the migrant children in their classroom? 89% yes

10. Should migrant children be encouraged to appear ethnic at school by wearing ethnic clothes, eating ethnic foods, and playing ethnic games? 28% yes

11. Is the maintenance of cultural traits by migrants good for the social community of Australia? 74% yes

12. Should migrant groups live together in national communities? 11% yes

13. Does the existence of national groupings within schools hinder the child's integration into the school community? 76% yes

Of particular interest in this study were the responses to Items #3, #5, and #12. The issue of language maintenance is puzzling. While educators strongly encourage migrant children to maintain their native language (Item #2), they seem to feel that the schools should not play any significant role in seeing that it happens (Items #3 and #5). Evidently the responses did not consider the possibility that if the students quit using their language, they would probably lose it, along with their culture. Of further interest is Item #10, which seemed to reveal that teachers did not feel migrant students should display their ethnicity in the schools. These items seemed to suggest that Australian educators tend to subscribe to an assimilationist philosophy.

To shed light on the country's attitudes regarding the designing of curriculum materials for multicultural education, some messages seem clear in the examination of a recent project entitled "An Indian Ocean People," which sought to help Australian children take their role as members of a multicultural society. The project utilized a research and development model of curriculum construction. A total of eleven people participated in the project. The project team initiated the project and its four team members monitored its development.

The project team recruited a research group which conducted studies with local families. They were persons who had displayed a sensitivity to the various ethnic groups in the community. A design group was also recruited by the project team to develop curriculum materials which were in keeping with the results of studies conducted by the research group. As these three entities worked on their various segments of the problem, three basic questions guided the project decision making: (1) How could the content of multicultural education be defined? (2) How could the content be translated into a set of educational materials that would reflect not only the content but also its potential for multicultural education? (3) How could the materials be designed for use in the classroom so as to portray accurately the multicultural philosophy of the project?

The project team believed that all children should have access to multicultural education through the development of an appreciation for diversity and an understanding of how diversity enhances the macroculture of the country. Also, it should be noted that multicultural education was not seen as a subject unto itself, but rather a theme strand which teachers would find in all instructional topics.

Eventually, "An Indian Ocean People" became a set of multicultural education materials which were suitable for the upper-elementary and middle-school grades. The materials were included in a kit which had a teacher's guide. The families used in the materials were actual examples of the Than Htay and Devellerez from Burma; de Sousa, Singh, Chaterjee, and Arasu from India; the Sujatna from Indonesia; the Yow from Malaysia; the Dean from Pakistan; the Klass from Singapore; the Chandraratna from Sri Lanka; the Matires from Timor; the Adolphe from Mauritius; and the Benson from the Cocos Island.

This project included the actual families in order to avoid stereotyping. The selection of the family groups from throughout the Indian Ocean area was done deliberately so that Australian children could better understand the kind of cultural and racial diversity which existed in their midst.

Student response to the curricular materials included in this project was positive. They seemed to like the notion that the families depicted in the curriculum materials were real. They provided the students with an opportunity to become engaged in meaningful problem-solving activities which were conducted both in groups and individually.

One criticism of this type of multicultural educational study might be that it does not deal with the ethnic and racial diversity within the country's own borders, particularly the presence and (30,000 to 40,000 years) history of the Australian Aborigines. Observed across the 200 years of Euro-Australian history, the paucity of information about the Aborigines as an indigenous microculture might be seen within a context of internal colonialism. According to this theory, which describes the domination of one previously independent nation by another within the former's own borders, the Australian Aborigines have been seen as an inferior group within the white Australian macroculture, largely as a way to explain or rationalize the harsh treatment dealt to them by white settlers in the early days of the country. Consequently, there has been less of an interest in studying Aborigines as a cultural group.

One approach to the problem of making Australian education more responsive to cultural diversity and the opportunities to be found in increased multicultural understanding is through modifications in teacher education programs. Through courses such as one at the James Cook University of North Queensland titled "Issues in Cross Cultural Education," teachers-in-training study curriculum and pedagogy by focusing on race/ethnicity, class, and gender, and ways to meet the educational needs of disadvantaged. Although James Cook University is located in an area which is home to a large proportion of the indigenous population, namely, Aborigines and Torres Strait Islanders, a similar approach to cross-cultural education studies would be of equal value in locations serving a largely "all white" population. Statistically, 40% of Australia's population are of migrant backgrounds, second only to Israel in terms of this level of ethnic diversity.

SUMMARY

Australia seems to be taking the subject of multicultural education rather seriously, certainly in recent years. As the nation becomes more racially and ethnically diverse, educators seem to have acquired an increasing interest in ensuring that their students develop more positive attitudes about the new migrants who are moving there. Australia's acceptance of the 1978 Galbally Report, and the development of new initiatives in teacher education designed to strengthen multicultural education programs, provide encouraging testimony that the nation is serious about using the schools to help prepare future citizens for participation in a pluralistic, multicultural country.

REFERENCES

Australian Deputy Chairperson, National Advisory and Coordinating Committee on Multicultural Education (NACCME), 1992. (Survey responses.)

Bethell, Leslie (Ed.). *The Cambridge History of Latin America.* Cambridge: Cambridge University Press, 1991.

Donohue-Clyne, Irene. " 'Children Only Go to School to Colour In. . . . ' Overseas Educated Teachers' Perception of Australian Schools." *Multicultural Teaching to Combat Racism in School and Community,* Vol. 11, No. 3 (1993).

Galbally, F. *Review of Post-Arrival Services and Programs.* Canberra: Australian Government Printing Service, 1978.

Gunther, John. *Inside Australia.* New York: Harper and Row, 1972.

Kelly, G. and Altbach, P. *Education and the Colonial Experience.* New Brunswick, NJ: Transaction Books, 1984.

Kennedy, Kerry J. and McDonald, Gilbert. "Designing Curriculum Materials for Multicultural Education: Lessons from an Australian Development Project." *Curriculum Inquiry,* Vol. 16, No. 3 (1986).

Lynch, James. "Community Relations and Multicultural Education in Australia." *Comparative Education,* Vol. 18, No. 1 (1982).

McInerney, Dennis. "Teacher Attitudes to Multicultural Curriculum Development." *Australian Journal of Education,* Vol. 31, No. 2 (1987).

Neville, Liddy. "The Sunrise Experience: Theory and Practice in an Australian Educational Community." *Education,* Vol. 110, No. 4 (1990).

Singh, M. Garbutcheon. "Issues in Cross-Cultural Education: Inverting the Education Studies Curriculum." *Teaching Education,* Vol. 4, No. 1 (1991).

Welch, A.J. "Aboriginal Education as Internal Colonialism: The Schooling of an Indigenous Minority in Australia." *Comparative Education,* Vol. 24, No. 2 (1988).

Whitaker, Donald. *Area Handbook for Australia.* Washington, DC: Foreign Area Studies of the American University, 1978.

3

Austria

HISTORY OF THE SYSTEM

The territory surrounding modern-day Austria has been inhabited since the early Stone Age. The first known political unit in the region was the Kingdom of Noricum which was established by the Celts about 400 B.C. By 15 B.C., parts of the area were inhabited by the Romans. But by about 500 A.D., the Romans were forced to abandon the territory because of pressure by the Huns and German tribes.

A major change in the area occurred when Charlemagne defeated the Bavarians and Avars and established an administrative division (March) in 788 as a buffer against future invasions. The region consisted of Upper and Lower Austria which consisted of areas separated by the Enns River. But these Austrian lands finally came under the control of the Moravian kingdom and eventually the Magyars.

After the Magyar influence was terminated by Otto I, the Holy Roman Emperor Otto II gave the land as an imperial fief to the Babenbergs, the area's first important ruling family. But by 1246, the Babenberg lands were taken over by the Bohemian King, Premysl Otakar II. The Habsburg rule of Austria occurred after Rudolf I was elected Holy Roman Emperor in 1273. The Habsburg family controlled lands which were located in Alsace and in present-day Switzerland.

By the sixteenth century, considerable new territories had become part of the Habsburg Monarchy. As a result of marriage and sheer luck, the Netherlands and part of Burgundy became Habsburg possessions. In fact, the Habsburg Monarchy became a major world power because of the eventual control of other parts of Europe including Spain, Italy, and large segments of Eastern Europe. During the middle of the sixteenth century, the Habsburg lands were proving to be too difficult to govern so they were divided. Philip II took control of Spain, Italy, and the Netherlands, along with their possessions. Ferdinand I received the Austrian Hereditary Lands, along with the Hungarian and Bohemian areas. But despite this division, the House of Habsburg still managed to maintain a rather strong union.

The Habsburg leaders were subjected to constant threats which came from France, the West, and from the Ottoman Empire to the east. The eighteenth century was a period of time in which warfare was rampant. From 1716 to 1791, the monarchy was involved with warfare three different times—their enemy being the Ottoman Empire; and when the century came to a close, the enemy was France. After a series of defeats by the French, the Habsburg lands were partitioned. But by 1815, the Congress of Vienna resulted in a long era of peace as the Austrian Empire emerged. In fact, the next major conflict did not occur until 1914.

The European settlement which was finally negotiated in 1815 resulted. The Habsburg Empire lost the Austrian Netherlands, some scattered German territories, and some Polish lands. But Dalmatia, Venetia, Istria, and Salzburg all became part of the Habsburg Empire, which finally became known as the Austrian Empire.

Rapid improvements in transportation occurred between 1815 and 1867. Both private and state funding made the development of an Austrian rail system possible. Actually, Austria created Europe's first transcontinental railroad when a 78-mile line between Budiveis and Linz utilized a horse-drawn train, and Vienna was the center of the railroad network in the country. At the same time, the government also was heavily involved with the upgrading of roads and canals. By 1829, the Danube Steamship Company was started, and this commercial enterprise went on to become an important cog in Austria's trade and commerce undertakings.

As Austria experienced growth in its industrial development, the country's working class also expanded in numbers. But the new industrialization thrust brought on poor working conditions, long hours, overcrowded housing, and low salaries. Even though Vienna's population grew to some 400,000 by the middle of the century, the monarchy was still primarily an agricultural macroculture.

The middle-class segment of Austrian society consisted of teachers, doctors, merchants, lawyers, and manufacturers. Most of these people were native German speakers, and the reign of Francis the Good at least partially ended the period of radical reform and turmoil. But by the 1840s, the peasant population was forced to face a number of critical problems pertaining to the growth of the rural areas to provide enough jobs. This caused the peasantry to acquire a basic mistrust of the system. While these problems affected the peasant population because of their economic and social problems, other portions of the public were becoming increasingly interested in political reform. The growing middle class became interested in liberalism and nationalism. Moreover, this liberal middle class had access to books, magazines, and ideas which intensified their interest in liberal reform. Interestingly enough, the liberal element consisted mostly of

Germans. However, nationalism proved to be most attractive to non-German people, particularly the Hungarians.

Beginning in 1815, the Habsburg Empire had to deal with the possibility of a major revolt in the Italian peninsula, and in 1859 war was declared. The Italian state and Piedmont were invaded. But Napoleon intervened and supported the Italian side. Finally, the Seven-Weeks War of 1866 required Austria to surrender Venetia to Italy and pay nominal reparations. After the dust settled, the German Confederation was replaced by the North German Confederacy under the leadership of the Prussians. The new unit included all of the German states except for Bavaria, Baden, Wurtemberg, and Hesse-Darmstadt. So the Habsburg Empire experienced a major demise of power. At that time, Austria consisted of Bukovina, Galicia, Silesia, Bohemia, Moravia, Upper and Lower Austria, Syria, Carinthia, Tirol, and Carniola.

By 1867, a dual monarchy of Austria-Hungary emerged. Francis Joseph was the Emperor of Austria and the King of Hungary. Each country had a separate constitution, but they both collaborated in military, economic, and foreign affairs. Both countries were loyal to Francis Joseph. However, in spite of the agreement between them, a number of ethnic problems emerged, and one major issue pertained to the agricultural enterprises in Hungary which clashed with the industrial interests of Austria.

Finally, in 1878, a new Balkan map was created, including Romani, Serbia, and Montenegro, which became separate states. Also, north of the Balkan mountains, an autonomous Bulgarian state was created, while Serbia, Montenegro, Greece, and Romania all received additional lands.

In 1879, the Dual Alliance with Germany was negotiated with the Austrian Habsburg Monarchy. A second alliance materialized between the Habsburg Monarchy and Germany against Russia; and in 1881, the Three Emperors Alliance of Russia, Germany, and the Habsburg Empire was signed. Finally, the Triple Alliance between Italy, Germany, and Austria/Hungary was agreed upon in 1882. This agreement was a defensive pact aimed against France, and it was still intact in 1914.

But the leadership of Francis Joseph was becoming more difficult, and his family life also was experiencing major problems. In 1853, he had married his cousin, Elisabeth of Bavaria. But major conflicts arose over this union due to disagreements between his mother and his wife. Eventually, Elisabeth ran away and spent most of her life traveling. She was eventually assassinated by an Italian anarchist named Luigi Lucchini. Their son, Archduke Rudolph, committed suicide, and Francis Joseph's brother, Maximilian, became an emperor of Mexico. He was assassinated in Mexico by rebels who were never apprehended.

These family disasters and the other problems of the Habsburg Empire took their toll on Francis Joseph; and the Serbians and other ethnic groups wanted to become independent of the Habsburg Empire. The disagreements between Francis Joseph and the Serbs intensified greatly, and the Habsburg ministers believed force should be used against the Serbs. Another incident leading to major military conflict between the two factions was the assassination of Francis Ferdinand and his wife. Francis Ferdinand was the grandnephew of Francis Joseph. The assassination and the other hostilities led to the declaration of war on the Serbs by Francis Joseph. This helped trigger World War I.

One of Austria's historical dilemmas has been in coming to grips with the German ethnicity issue. If, indeed, the people were truly Germans, what did that really mean? Austria-Hungary was an ally of Germany during World War I. Their foes were the victorious allies, including the United States, Russia, France, and Britain. And while the Habsburg Empire had a population of more than 50 million people at the start of the war, the remaining entity, German-Austria, had approximately 6.5 million people. The country's industry was mostly in Vienna. Many people thought that Austria should become allied with Germany, but in 1919 the Treaty of Saint Germain contained a clause in which Germany guaranteed to repeat the independence of Austria. Moreover, the only way the agreement could be terminated was by special approval of the League of Nations.

Austria's first constitution was adopted in 1920, and three major political parties emerged, including the Social Democratic Party, the Christian Social Party, and the Austrian Nazi Party. By 1932, Englehart Dollfus had become the Austrian chancellor. In the following year, he was able to dissolve the Austrian parliament. At the same time, Adolf Hitler had assumed control of the German parliament and was successful in consolidating his absolute power. He attempted to suppress the Social Democrats and the Austrian Nazi Party while he sought to parlay his Christian Social Party into a national political unit which conveyed the true elements of Austrian ethnicity. A series of conflicts, coupled with alarming unemployment rates, finally resulted in a two-day civil war between Dollfus's ruling Social Christian Party and the Social Democratic Party. The fighting resulted in total defeat for the Social Democratic Party.

Meanwhile, enormous trouble was brewing between Dollfus and Adolf Hitler. The Austrian Nazi Party wanted to make the nation part of Nazi Germany regardless of the Treaty of Saint Germain. At the same time, Hitler grew increasingly concerned over the Austrian constitution, which in effect made it impossible for the Austrian Nazis to gain power in a free election. Amazingly, Hitler pressed for free elections in Austria. Finally, in July 1934, a group of Austrian Nazis broke into the chancellery in Vienna and captured Dollfus. In an attempt to escape, he was shot and left to die without seeing a priest or a doctor. Finally, the assassin was executed along with six others who were involved in the plot. Adolf Hitler denied any participation in the event.

Kurt von Schnuschnigg, Dollfus's successor, sought to develop close ties with Benito Mussolini in order to create a buffer against Hitler's Nazi Germany. But by 1936, Mussolini let it be known that Schnuschnigg should make direct contact with Berlin, and an Austrian-German agreement was signed in that year. The pact guaranteed Austria's full sovereignty. While there were some temporary advantages in industrial production increases and a substantial decrease in unemployment, it ultimately resulted in a two-year respite until the time when

German troops marched into Austria in 1938. Austria made no major attempt to defend itself, and no other nations stepped forward to intervene.

During World War II, there was an active Austrian resistance movement and close to 3,000 of the members were killed, while an estimated 22,000 died in prison. Austria was also involved in the failed German attempt to assassinate Adolf Hitler. Of the 220,000 Jews in Austria during the beginning of the war, only some 5,000 remained after its end.

The Austrian occupation by the Russians resulted in a period of violence and looting which not only created immense hardship on the Austrian people, but for the Austrian Communist party as well. As the Russians approached from the east, there was some resistance by the Austrians who were afraid of Russia's retaliation for the actions of the Germans in their country. However, as the Western allies approached from the west, the Austrians offered no resistance and even tended to provide a friendly welcome.

The occupation of Austria resulted in the nation being partitioned into four areas, which were occupied by the United States, Russia, France, and Great Britain, respectively. However, during the occupation period, Austria was able to keep its 1920 constitution. The first free election since 1930 occurred in 1945. While the People's Party won the most seats and the Socialists were a close second, the world was stunned when the communists only managed to get about 5 percent of the total vote. Nazi party members were prohibited from voting and holding most offices as a result of pressure from the Allies. The occupation lasted until 1955 when the allied forces finally left the country. The Allies and the Austrians agreed that the country should be a neutral nation and not take sides in any future conflicts. Indeed, Austria has remained neutral for many years, and has proven to be an excellent site for conducting various kinds of negotiation settlements between countries because of its neutrality and its central location. In 1955 Austria was allowed to become a member of the United Nations.

After Austria signed its neutrality agreement, the question was whether the country was a third German state along with the Democratic Republic and Federal Republic, or a truly independent nation which had no political connection with either East or West Germany. The first election after the treaty was signed addressed the issues of the administration of nationalized industries. The election was seen as a victory for Chancellor Raab of the People's Party, who was able to negotiate the treaty.

While Austria's constitution was structured around the notion of political neutrality, two actions by the Russians tested the document. These two actions were the Soviet intervention in Hungary in 1956 and in Czechoslovakia in 1968. Austria received refugees from both countries during the two confrontations. However, in spite of their assistance to the recipients of the Soviet aggression, Austria still maintained its connections with the Soviets and the Eastern Bloc countries. And the Austrian government took actions which were perceived as being sympathetic to the Soviets.

During the elections of 1966, the Austrian Socialists experienced a major defeat at the polls. However, in the 1970 election, the Socialists won a plurality of 81 seats. Later, in the 1975 elections, the same party maintained a previously won plurality of 93 seats. In 1979, the Socialists won another impressive victory in which they increased their plurality to 95.

During the 1970s, Austria was a participant in the Helsinki Conference on security and cooperation in Europe. The culmination of this act resulted in the agreement of all participants to accept the European map as it existed at the end of World War II.

During this same period of time, Vienna also became a center for terrorist activity. In September of 1973, Arab activists captured three Jewish emigrants from the Soviet Union along with an Austrian customs official. At this time, Vienna had become a staging center for Jews who had fled the Soviet Union in an attempt to reach Israel.

Austria has made an amazing transition from an enormous multinational empire to a small neutral state. In spite of its neutral status, Austria can be considered to be an integral part of western Europe; in fact, the country shares its economic, political, and cultural values. The Second Republic has been able to establish a prosperous economy in the modern world in spite of the country's rather limited resources. It has been argued that Austria has surpassed all countries in the world—except for Japan—insofar as industrial growth since 1960 is concerned.

STRUCTURE OF THE SYSTEM

Austria is a federal republic which consists of nine autonomous provinces known as Landers. These provinces are Burgenland, Carinthia, Lower Austria, Salzburg, Styria, Tyrol, Upper Austria, Voralberg, and the city of Vienna. All Austrian citizens over the age of 19 are able to vote in elections. Presidents are elected for six-year terms. The prime minister (also known as the chancellor) is appointed by the president and usually is the leader of the party which receives the greatest number of votes in the National Council.

Each of the ten provinces has a legislature, known as a Landtag, and a provincial governor for four- to six-year terms. The ten provinces are divided into communes which have their own councils. The bicameral parliament consists of an upper house (Nationalrat) with 183 members who are elected for four-year terms. The lower house (Bundesrat) is elected by the provincial legislatures who choose 65 representatives. The Austrian Supreme Court is the highest court of appeals, and there are also four lower courts which deal with such matters as labor disputes, juvenile cases, and constitutional and administrative issues.

Approximately 90 percent of the Austrian people are Roman Catholics, and the Jewish population is estimated to be about 12,000. The official language is German which is spoken by about 98 percent of the Austrian people. A number of different dialects are spoken in different sections of the country.

Austria has one of the highest literacy rates of all European nations, and one of the reasons for this has been the excellent system of education which the country has enjoyed throughout its history. Children between the ages of six and fifteen are required to attend school. Public schools are free and the minimum program requires eight years of elementary education and one year of either polytechnic or vocational education. Students who are interested in higher education can pursue a college preparatory program which can lead to enrollment in one of Austria's four major universities or any of the other institutions of higher education. Founded in 1365, the University of Vienna is Austria's largest. Educational programs are directed and evaluated by the Office of the Minister of Education. This office also coordinates the country's ambitious adult education system which includes more than 350 centers and 1,900 local institutions.

Like all other industrialized nations, except for the United States, Austria has a national health care program which meets the needs of all Austrian citizens. Public health is the responsibility of the Health Department which functions as an arm of the Ministry of Social Administration. The country's health system is one of the best in the world as can be seen by comparisons of worldwide infant mortality rates. In addition to its excellent health care system, the Austrian government also provides national social insurance, disability insurance, old age, sickness, survivors, and unemployment benefits.

The Austrian government operates the postal, telegraph, and telephone systems. The transportation system is largely controlled by the government, including the rail lines and the Austrian Airlines. There are more than 112,654 kilometers of highways and roads, two-thirds of which are paved.

MULTICULTURAL EDUCATION PROGRAMS

Austria does have a formal multicultural education program in the Ministry of Education's Department for International Contacts and Intercultural Learning (DICL). Special funds are budgeted for such programs. Another function of the DICL is to organize seminars for teacher training on intercultural education, and to support private groups which organize student exchanges with foreign countries.

In addition to the German Austrians, the major minority groups are the Slovenes, Croats, and Jews, even though they are small in number. In addition to these minorities are the Turks and the Yugoslovs who are two of the major migrant groups. One of the chief concerns of European educators in recent years has been the training of teachers who work with migrant children. Special programs have been developed in order to provide effective in-service training programs to meet that need.

In the authors' multicultural education study, the Austrian respondent stipulated that the country had no special teacher certification requirements in multicultural education. Cultural assimilation is stressed in the curriculum and instruction sequences, but some special programs have been implemented to help develop more positive attitudes about cultural pluralism. But the same survey respondent was concerned that there seemed to be a prevailing notion that foreign persons should become assimilated into the Austrian macroculture, and there did not appear to be much public support for the encouragement of pluralistic microcultures.

Austria's official language of instruction is German, but there are special programs for instructing some students in their mother tongue. The nation's public schools are free and can be attended by anyone. The Ministry of Education does have a formal procedure for the evaluation of texts, library holdings, and curriculum materials in order to make certain that they are free of racist and sexist content.

In regard to the issue of the country's multicultural history, one of the major concerns has been the specter of Nazism. Proportionately, there were actually more high-ranking Nazis in Austria than there were in Germany. Anti-Semitism is still a problem even though there are only a very small number of Jews left in the country (and most of them are quite old). Studies conducted during the 1980s showed that only 14 percent of the Austrian people were "largely free of prejudice" and 64 percent of those polled thought that Jews were "too powerful." Fifty-seven percent of the population thought that they shouldn't have to be reminded of the slaughter of Jews during World War II. About one in every four persons believed that Jews should not be allowed to be in influential positions in Austria.

SUMMARY

It has been said that the biggest historical problems for Austria have been caused by its location. Not only has the nation been situated in a tenuous physical location in central Europe, but it has had to learn how to make the adjustment from a powerful empire to a dual monarchy and eventually to an independent European nation.

As in most other countries, the educational system has tended to reflect the various changes occurring in the country, and develops in a way that makes the country work most effectively. The fact that Austria has always had a strong system of education has helped it to take its place as one of the most "western" European countries.

Austria's history has helped motivate its interest in multicultural education programs. The fact that the Ministry of Education has seen fit to identify a person who is responsible for such programs seems to suggest rather strongly that Austria is indeed serious about issues of equality which affect the country. Its historical relations with Nazi Germany have caused many debates over issues of racism against Austria's Jewish population.

It has been argued that because of the country's need for cheap labor, other groups of immigrants will move to the country, thus increasing the need for expanded programs of multicultural education. However, since such programs have already been started through the efforts of the Ministry of Education, it seems highly probable that the schools have an excellent chance of meeting the educational needs of new migrant populations in the schools.

REFERENCES

Barker, Elisabeth. *Austria 1918–1972.* Coral Gables: University of Florida Press, 1973.

Brown, Larry. "Hunger in the U.S." *Scientific American* (February 1987).

Elon, Amos. "Report from Vienna." *The New Yorker,* Vol. 67 (May 13, 1991).

Gonen, Amiram. *The Encyclopedia of the Peoples of the World.* New York: Henry Holt Publishing Co., 1993.

Jelavich, Barbara. *Modern Austria: Empire and Republic 1815–1986.* Cambridge: Cambridge University Press, 1987.

Katzenstein, Peter J. *The Political Economy of Austria.* Washington, DC: American Enterprise Institute, 1982.

Mayall, James and Navari, Cornelia. *The End of the Post War Era: Documents on Great Power Relations, 1968–1975.* Cambridge: Cambridge University Press, 1980.

Mitchell, Bruce and Salsbury, Robert. *An International Survey of Multicultural Education.* Cheney, WA: Western States Consulting and Evaluation Services, 1991. (See Appendix.)

Momatey, Victor. *Rise of the Habsburg Empire, 1526–1815.* New York: Holt, Rinehart and Winston, 1971.

Rey-von-Allmen, Micheline. *The Education of Migrant Workers' Children—The Training of Teachers.* Lisbon: Council for Cultural Cooperation, 1981.

Von Schuschnigg, Kurt. *The Brutal Takeover.* New York: Weidenfeld & Nicholson, 1971.

4

Bangladesh

HISTORY OF THE SYSTEM

What is now the country of Bangladesh was first a part of India—an area in the northeast of the country, known as Bengal. The people inhabiting this region were known as Bengalis, and are thought to have been originally migrants from Southeast Asia. Regarded as a lower caste in the Brahminical order of the Hindu religion, Bengalis have historically affiliated with more egalitarian religions (the most notable and recent being Islam). The conversion to the Muslim religion was not a smooth one—there was yet a new version of the caste, or at least "caste-like" system, with noble class and foreign-born Muslims viewing the indigenous Bengalis as not quite as orthodox in their faith. Even with these internal problems, the Bengal region, with its Islamic focus, became a natural partner in the efforts of the Muslim League to seek independence from India in 1947. In that year, the new country of Pakistan was created, comprised of the former Indian provinces of Sind, Baluchistran, North West Frontier Province, and West Punjab in the west and Bengal in the east.

Although this alliance, ostensibly bound by religious unification, lasted for 24 years, differences between the Punjabi-dominated west and the Bengalis in the east existed almost from the beginning. In a sense, it was Rudyard Kipling's "East is East and West is West and never the twain shall meet" played out in microcosm within a single country. Harking back to the belief that the Bengalis weren't as orthodox in their beliefs and practices, and possibly too Hindu in their customs, the Pakistani government sought to keep a geographically separated and culturally pluralistic nation together by strengthening its Muslim identity and minimizing or eliminating cultural traditions that did not fit the orthodox Islamic mode.

Over the next years, a series of government-sponsored assimilationist initiatives—met by East Bengali resistance—came to characterize the uneasy nature of the original union. Beginning with attempts to make Urdu the official national language as a means of downgrading the importance and use of the Bengali language of the eastern region, to attacks on art forms that seemed "too Hindu," to the rape of 30,000 Bengali women as an official strategy of the process of Islamization, the Pakistani government's attempts to unify the country through becoming monocultural eventually resulted in a period of bloody warfare which resulted in the creation of yet a new nation, Bangladesh. A new government was formed and India became the first nation to recognize its newly established independence at the end of that year.

An often-amended constitution was adapted in late 1972. This document required the state to reorganize society in order to create an equal citizenry and provide for the general welfare of all people. Moreover, the state had to perpetuate a free and equal citizenry, provide for everyone's welfare, and ensure that all persons receive adequate food, clothing, and shelter. Finally, it was the responsibility of the government to guarantee social and economic equity among all citizens and to see to it that all of the wealth of the land was distributed equally among the people. Thus, it can be seen that the country adapted many postulates of a socialistic notion of government and politics.

The constitution addressed a number of key issues, including equality before the law of both men and women; and the right to assemble, hold public meetings, and form unions. Also guaranteed in the document were the freedom of the press and freedom of speech. The Bangladesh constitution also guaranteed gender equity and prohibited discrimination based on religion, race, caste, gender, or birthplace. The Islamic religion has maintained a dominant role in Bangladesh society. In 1977, a phrase was inserted in the constitution which stipulated that a fundamental principle was "Absolute trust and faith in the Almighty Allah." This superseded the 1972 statement in the constitution which described the government as "secular."

STRUCTURE OF THE SYSTEM

During the early 1800s, a system of liberal schools utilizing the English language was created within the present boundaries of Bangladesh. This educational system was based on the British model, and eventually an elite class of the population would emerge. These people would become involved in clerical and administrative support services for the colonial administration needs of the British. They would be provided the necessary support services, and they acquired minimal practical skills and technical knowledge. This elite group was isolated from the masses who had access to the educational system of the country.

Literacy rates in Bangladesh were just 19.7 percent in 1981. However, rather large literacy rate disparities existed between men and women, as well as a sizable urban–rural discrepancy. The estimated teacher–student ratio was estimated at 54:1 during the 1987–1988 school year, but only 13:1 in universities. Some 10,000,000 children attended school in 1981. Primary education occurs for the first five years, and in 1986 there were nearly 3,000,000 students attending the secondary schools. Forty-nine primary school teacher-training institutions and ten secondary school teacher-education colleges prepare prospective teachers for the classroom.

The educational system has put a heavy emphasis on liberal arts education. However, toward the end of the 1980s, greater attention was given to technical education. The nation has four engineering colleges, eighteen polytechnic institutes, four law colleges, two agricultural colleges, a graphic arts institute, an institute of glass and ceramics, a textile college, a college of leather technology, sixteen commercial institutes, and fifty-four vocational institutes. There are also ten medical colleges, one dental college, and twenty-one nursing institutes. The country also has one physical education college and a music college.

A free and inexpensive system of tertiary education has not been without its problems and its detractors, however. Because of severe budgetary problems and a history of Bengali student activism, public higher education is often perceived as being of low quality and unnecessarily prolonged in duration. As an alternative to sending young people abroad for higher education, two private universities have been created in Bangladesh. Spear-headed by Dr. A. Majed Khan, former education minister and first president of the new institution, the Independent University of Bangladesh (IUB) is modeled on international academic standards, but a lesser cost. The second private university is known as the North-South University.

As hard as the Bangladesh government has striven to create and maintain a program of free and accessible education, it has done so in the face of frequent and recurring natural disasters, including approximately 10 percent of the world's cyclones (which originate in the Bay of Bengal). As a result of the most recent disaster, the cyclone which struck southeastern Bangladesh on May 1, 1991, in and around the Bay of Bengal, thousands of schools and public buildings were destroyed along with approximately one million houses.

MULTICULTURAL EDUCATION EFFORTS

Responses submitted by the Bangladesh respondent during the authors' international survey of multicultural education revealed that the country consists of five ethnic groups, namely, Muslims, Hindus, Christians, Buddhists, and various tribal groups. There is a multicultural education program in the country even though they have few colonial minorities and no linguistic minorities. The Ministry of Religion and Culture is responsible for multicultural education programs.

The country does not require special multicultural certification for teachers. The official language of instruction in the country is Bengali, and there are no special programs to teach immigrant or indigenous children in their native ethnic language. Children attend racially and ethnically integrated schools, and the respondent to the research instrument reported that there was no discrimination due to the color of students' skin. The Ministry of Education evaluates curriculum, library, and textbooks for racist or sexist content.

Taking the point of view that the overall concept of multicultural education embraces and provides for elements of cultural diversity in addition to race, ethnicity, and language, there are at least five other microcultures that seem pertinent to Bangladeshi multicultural education efforts. Based on the idea that each person is the product of a combination of each of a number of different microcultures or cultural elements, the following five microcultures also seem important as they relate to the presence or absence of equitable educational opportunities for individuals and groups in the Bangladeshi educational system. These five are: exceptionality or special needs; gender; socioeconomic levels of children and their families; religion; and geographic residence, as related to rural or urban locations within the country. Holding the concepts of race, ethnicity, and language constant, in that none represents patterns or evidence of discrimination, it is the interaction of these latter microcultural elements that hold the key to understanding of the state of multicultural education in Bangladesh.

As one of the poorest of the developing countries, Bangladesh has serious health problems among its children. One example, which has an effect on learning, is serious hearing loss. Affected by a combination of climatic conditions or malnutrition, it is estimated that up to two million people in Bangladesh suffer a significant hearing loss. Half a million are children—up to 100,000 need full-time special education. This is compounded further by the fact that while doctors practice in large cities like Dacca, approximately 80 percent of the population, many poor, live in rural areas. While this refers to just one health problem, others such as malnutrition, blindness, and mental retardation stand in the way of educational equity for many Bangladeshi children.

Perhaps the most important challenge to Bangladesh from a multicultural point of view is the education of girls and young women. Here the microcultures of gender, socioeconomic level, place of residence, and religion combine to create a set of conditions which markedly affect educational opportunities for Bangladeshi females.

If there is a generalization that can be made of the results of these interactions it might be that urban females, of middle to high socioeconomic class, and living in urban areas, have the best opportunities for educational opportunities. At the base of this is the influence of the Islamic religion. As the history of Bangladesh is bound up with religion, so is the whole issue of gender equity in the school and workplace likewise related to Muslim doctrine and practice.

Ironically, where originally the Bengalis, particularly those in small towns and the countryside, were seen by urban Muslims as too Hindu in their cultural practices and embracing of a philosophy of inclusion, it is now the urban followers of Islam who are less doctrinaire and more inclined to support a more secular point of view in matters of public policy, including educational and employment opportunities for girls and women.

In rural areas of Bangladesh, the influence of the Islamic religion is most prevalent, to the extent that religion and public policy and law are often virtually intertwined. Local mullahs, through the issuance of religious sanctions called fatwas, enforce a more traditional and militant form of religion, particularly with respect to the proper conduct of girls and women. A result of this emphasis is that educational and employment programs targeted for girls and women at the national level have less impact in the Bangladeshi countryside.

A further example of the interaction of Islamic religious customs with future educational and employment opportunities, again, mainly in low income rural areas, is the practice of purdah or separation of girls at puberty. This, combined with the patriarchal family structure, and the proximal space of family compounds and villages, has resulted in a situation in which poor rural girls and women are spatially constricted to a degree that works against the more liberating and financially rewarding aspects of education and employment. As the condition of landlessness increases in rural Bangladesh, it will be necessary for girls and women to increase their space to include the possibility of working outside the home. This situation is resulting in some gains, but the government recognizes the need to provide more opportunities and official support for educational and employment initiatives for girls and women, particularly those from small, impoverished, rural communities.

A 1985 study sponsored by UNESCO, through the Bangladesh National Commission for UNESCO, investigated the status of education for girls in the country. Based on the findings of the study, the following recommendations were made:

1. Measures for increasing the interest of girls in schooling should be addressed to childhood personality factors as well as the school situation.

2. Young girls from the lower classes should be treated with special care; and older girls should be treated in a culturally appropriate manner.

3. Learning activities should include skills in solving day-to-day problems in their immediate environment.

4. Learning exercises should be combined with recreation within and outside the class setting.

5. Teaching/learning materials should be diversified, enriched, and further developed through special projects.

6. Teachers should make home visits, as a part of their job, to help girls overcome any difficulty experienced in connection with schooling.

7. Measures for the improvement of the school situation should include adequate classroom seating accommodations for girls so that they do not have to compete with boys to get seats; a target of 50% female teachers; suitable recreation facilities for girls; separate toilets for girls; and class hours suited to local conditions, thus enabling girls to help their families in household activities.

8. Measures for improving family conditions should aim at creating effective support and motivation of the parents for girls' education.

9. Providing stipends to girls, especially of poor families, enabling them to continue their schooling in the higher classes.

10. Formation of a special community fund to assist poor children to attend school.

11. Training and motivation of religious leaders to popularize school education for girls.

12. Taking necessary legal and administrative steps to enforce compliance with the minimum age for the marriage of girls.

13. Measures for the improvement of teachers' quality and teaching shall be concerned with training and retraining of teachers, training of trainers, developing and making use of appropriate teaching materials, placement of teachers outside their own locality, and increasing the number of trained female teachers.

14. Financial, administrative, and supervisory measures should be addressed to ensure adequate coverage of school-age population, equality between genders through special provisions for girls' education, proper implementation of policy and programs, and improvement of the quality of teachers' conduct.

15. Experiences, policies, and programs for the promotion of girls' education in the neighboring countries should be utilized in Bangladesh as far as practicable.

The extent to which these recommendations are carried out for the future, especially in the poor and rural sections of the country, will determine the success of the national policy of providing equal educational and employment opportunities to girls and women.

SUMMARY

The country of Bangladesh appears to be making a solid attempt to address the issue of gender equity. This might be characterized as a first step toward establishing a multicultural frame of reference. Given the economic constraints of this nation, it would seem that other basic education issues probably will be consuming the time of the education institution. However, the major changes within the education system during recent times, coupled with the new reforms in education for young women, provide hope for more positive actions in the future.

REFERENCES

Blood, Peter. *Bangladesh: A Country Study.* Washington, DC: Department of the Army (D.A. Pam. 550-175, Headquarters, Department of the Army), 1992.

Gollnick, Donna and Chinn, Philip. *Multicultural Education in a Pluralistic Society.* New York: MacMillan College Publishing Company, 1994.

Kabeer, Naila. "The Quest for National Identity: Women, Islam, and the State in Bangladesh." *Feminist Review,* No. 37 (1991), pp. 38–56.

Kamaluddin, S. "Malthusian Nightmare." *Far Eastern Economic Review,* Vol. 51, No. 20 (1991), p. 12.

Kamaluddin, S. "Top Degree, Top Dollar." *Far Eastern Economic Review,* Vol. 55, No. 21 (1992), p. 27.

Lowe, Armin. "Early Intervention Programs in Bangladesh." *The Volta Review,* Vol. 95, No. 5 (1993), p. 137.

Mitchell, Bruce and Salsbury, Robert. *An International Survey of Multicultural Education.* Cheney, WA: Western States Consulting and Evaluation Services, 1991. (See Appendix.)

Papanek, Hanna. "Class and Gender in Education-Employment Linkages." *Comparative Education Review* (August 1985), p. 317.

Paul, Bimal Kanti. "Female Activity Space in Rural Bangladesh." *The Geographical Review,* Vol. 82, No. 1 (1992), pp. 1–12.

Rahim, Enayetur. In *Bangladesh: A Country Study.* Washington, DC: Department of the Army (D.A. Pam. 550-175, Headquarters, Department of the Army), 1992.

UNESCO. *Primary Education for Girls.* Bangkok: UNESCO Principal Regional Office for Asia and the Pacific, 1987.

Weaver, Mary Anne. "Letter from Bangladesh: A Fugitive from Justice." *The New Yorker* (September 14, 1994), pp. 48–60.

5

Belgium

HISTORY OF THE SYSTEM

Many historians have referred to the history of Belgium as a saga of conflict and accommodation. The area in which the country is located has been viewed as a battlefield which has seen numerous confrontations throughout the history of the European continent. The area now called Belgium has enjoyed a rather brief history—as recently as 1830, a parliamentary monarchy was created, allowing Belgium to become an independent nation. Since that time, the country has managed to live through economic turmoil, sectarian conflicts, protest movements, foreign occupation, and other problems.

Prior to 1830, the area consisted of autonomous provinces and municipalities. Throughout the years, the residents of these rather isolated areas acquired a strong sense of independence. It was this spirit of independence that prevailed when the surrounding countries attempted to impose a centralized state. Thus, the pre-1830 history can be characterized as a constant tug of war between the independent states and those countries which were interested in imposing a centralized state.

Since independence, the country has been forced to deal with three primary issues. The first has pertained to religion and the efforts of Roman Catholics to impose their faith on the Belgiums. The anticleric group wished to have no officially sanctioned religion. This battle raged on for about five decades, from the mid-1830s to the mid-1880s. The issue was finally resolved in 1884 when both public and free Catholic schools became part of the nation's primary and secondary school system.

Second, Belgium's labor movement had attempted to better the lives of average workers by social actions, mutual aid societies, and strikes. But these activities seemed able to only make slight changes and couldn't totally change the conditions. In 1885, the Belgium Workers Party was founded in an attempt to secure social legislation which would be to their benefit.

The third major issue, which involved a conflict between French and Dutch speakers, slowly but surely became a major political problem. While Flemish leaders had argued for equal recognition of the Dutch language during the 1800s, the issue really did not get dealt with on a truly serious basis until World War I, when a series of threats and near mutinous acts on the part of the Flemish soldiers occurred at the front.

However, in spite of the problems created by these three issues throughout the years, Belgium has been a relatively stable country for the most part. Some have argued that the reason for this was the rather placid countenance of the people as well as the role of the political parties which have tended to champion causes after they have become popular. The leaders of the Social Christians, the Liberals, and the Socialists (the country's three major parties) have been able to limit political conflicts to a few demonstrations and the normal tactics of parliamentary politics. In all cases, these causes have related to the ultimate control of the Belgium parliament.

One unique characteristic of Belgium's history has been traced back to the Roman period of 57 B.C. to A.D. 431. Many Europeans were concerned about Julius Caesar and his written record of the geographical area which included present-day France, Belgium, Luxembourg, and parts of Germany. The area was inhabited by a number of independent tribes which may have been Celtic. The Romans felt that the southern Belgians were important because they served as a barrier against Germanic invasions.

Roman cultural influences had a huge impact on the region. Latin gradually became the language of commerce; and about A.D. 300, Christianity appeared and eventually became the dominant religion in the area. In the third century, Germanic tribes from the east and north cut a wide path of mayhem and destruction, thus threatening the control enjoyed by the Germans. But by the fifth century, the Roman Empire was falling apart. Many of the Germanic tribes migrated throughout Europe during the Frankish period which lasted from about 430 until nearly 1,000. However, the Franks did not migrate, and slowly expanded the areas which came under their control. They were able to make peace with the Roman Empire, and in some ways they actually became part of it.

The dukes of Burgundy gained control of the Lowlands from the late 1300s until midway through the sixteenth century. During this period of time, the economy was strong and the area experienced a great deal of growth in culture, commerce, and scholarship, and a great level of cultural growth accompanied the economic boom. The Flemish school of art was born, and painters such as Pister the Elder commenced to create this new school of art.

During the midst of the sixteenth century, the Burgundian period came to an end. The Spanish dominated most of present-day Belgium when Philip II of Spain assumed the leadership of the Burgundian territories. A devout Catholic,

Charles V opted to enter a monastery and gave the Spanish Netherlands to his son, Philip II, who died in 1598. At this time, Spain was experiencing a gradual decline which left the Spanish Netherlands in a vulnerable position. During this time, two ethnic groups, the Walloons and the Flemings, inhabited the area. The linguistic differences between these two groups became quite pronounced during the seventeenth and early eighteenth centuries. Also during that time, French started to become the dominant language of the area.

During the reign of Isabelle and Albert (1598–1621), only painting seemed to be a significant part of Belgium's cultural milieu. Pierre-Paul Rubens and others worked in Belgium for some time, but a number of other artists and intellectuals left the country for other areas such as Holland. Early in the next century, the War of the Spanish Succession plagued the country for a period of twelve years. The Treaty of Utrecht in 1713 tended to restore a balance of power among France, Spain, Austria, and Britain. For the remainder of the eighteenth century, the Spanish Netherlands became the Austrian Netherlands.

Up until the end of the eighteenth century, Belgium was an innocent victim of European politics. The country endured an attempt to restore Belgium trade, which was only partially successful; an escape from the Seven Years War because of the diplomacy of Maria Theresa; and the failed attempt by her son and successor (Joseph II) to completely end Dutch occupation. Finally, during the latter 1700s, Belgian patriots began to organize. They were motivated by the French Revolution, and the resulting Brabant Revolution was a heterogeneous mixture of differing ideas and age groups. However, due to a great deal of internal confusion, the rebellion was put down by the Austrians in December 1790.

But when the revolutionary armies of France rolled through Europe, the Austrian Netherlands ultimately were annexed to France in 1795, and the French control lasted until 1815 when Napoleon's empire fell apart with the Battle of Waterloo, just south of Brussels. The European map was redrawn at the Congress of Vienna from 1814 to 1815. The Kingdom of United Netherlands was then established, and William of Orange was named king. Few people in Belgium actually opposed the creation of the new state.

After being controlled by other countries for so many years, the Belgians finally reached the point where public demonstration became common, and violence erupted in 1830 when workers attacked factories and the homes of some of the leading citizens of Brussels, Liege, and several other cities. Finally, on September 25, 1830, the provisional government of Belgium was formed and Belgium independence was declared on October 4. Elections were held, and 299 delegates were chosen among an equal number of Catholics and Protestants. Then a constitution was written and ratified on February 7, 1831. A constitutional monarchy was formed with a bicameral parliament, direct elections, and personal liberties. The first elected Belgium king was Prince Leopold of Saxe-Coburg, a German principality.

Actually, the revolution which was responsible for the creation of Belgium was a political rebellion as opposed to a social one. The new state was really created for the elite who were mostly French speakers. The new nation was primarily right wing, and the only franchised people in Belgium were about 11 percent of the white males. This small percentage was determined by a property ownership requirement. A political alliance of Catholics and leftists helped the country's economic development, but the alliance was terminated after hostilities between the two groups intensified when they began accusing each other of abusing the constitution.

The Treaties of 1839 saw Belgium become a fully sanctioned European power, even though official recognition by the Russians was not granted until the spring of 1853. However, these treaties had dealt a major blow to some of Belgium's industries which had been organized to meet the basic needs of the Dutch provinces between 1813 and 1815. After independence, capital disappeared, salaries dropped, and economic depression became a major national problem. The Dutch king hoped that a total economic collapse would allow him to regain his lost provinces. The French also hoped to capitalize on the country's economic misfortune, but the Treaties of 1839 helped to stave off that threat.

Belgium's educational system historically has caused a great deal of controversy. During the mid-1800s, Catholics and Protestants were involved in a large number of educational squabbles. In 1847, the Liberals believed that there should be limited church influence in the operation of state government. Primary school legislation in Belgium strengthened a relationship between church and state which had really occurred since the country was founded. It legitimized the dominance of the church over primary education. However, leftist groups, under the leadership of Charles Rogier, believed that the church's influence over education had to have more limitations. So, in 1850, a state-run secondary school system was started which competed with the Catholic system. The secondary schools tended to be populated by middle-class children.

But both in Rome and Belgium, the church reacted as one might expect. The move was denounced soundly, but in 1854 a compromise was reached which required that two hours per week be set aside for religious instruction while the church made no attempt to influence the hiring of state school teachers. Finally, the Education Act of 1879 excluded all religion from the public schools.

The Europe surrounding Belgium during the decades of the 1850s and 1860s was quite different from the Europe which existed before Belgium became a nation. The map of Europe changed with the advent of a United Italy and a brand new North German Confederation under the militant leadership of Prussia. Also, Russia and Austria became weaker because of their defeats.

One thing that Belgium always viewed with a great deal of pride was the country's rail system. Having been the first European nation to construct a rail line, the complex was owned partly by the state, yet it was also partly controlled by private entities.

The ocean has always been of critical importance to Belgium. Since 1830 and before, Belgian ships have carried many manufactured items to all parts of the world. Antwerp has been one of the more active seaports in the entire world, situated on the right bank of the Scheldt River, 53 miles from the ocean. It is a deep river, so ocean-going ships have been able to navigate the long distance in order to take advantage of Antwerp's 30 miles of docks. The barges, used in the river traffic, are a basic part of Belgium's economy.

After the defeat of Napoleon III's army in 1870, the map of Europe made no more major changes until World War I. At that time, only a small section of the African continent had been colonized. This race over colonialization was quite competitive with Britain and France leading the way until Germany entered the fray later. In retrospect, it seems amazing that Belgium entered the competition with world powers such as these. However, King Leopold II won an African colony for the Belgian government through the founding of the Congo Free State in 1908 because of his interest in personal gains, high-level diplomacy, and adventure.

Africa had been an intriguing prospect for Leopold II because of the European interest in the African Continent as a result of the popular interest in the colony, which was precipitated by Henry M. Stanley's famous meeting with the missing Livingstone in 1871. After a number of challenges by other European countries, Belgium's hold on the African Congo became well solidified. Some of the most important raw materials used in Belgian industries came from the mines of Katonga, a Belgian colony until the colonial period for Belgium ended in 1960.

Belgium's primary strength throughout the years has been the nation's high level of industrialization. Probably no other European country was impacted by the Industrial Revolution like Belgium. Its extensive coal fields produced power for manufacturing and transportation. The previously discussed railroads, canals, and the proximity to the sea have made it possible for Belgium to create a flourishing export business which also enhanced the manufacturing industry.

The nation's metal-making industry has employed a large number of Belgian workers. One of the major factors for the amazing success of Belgium has been the nation's access to large amounts of cobalt, zinc, lead products, steel, and iron. Cobalt and tin have been refined in Belgian plants along with uranium, which is used in the production of fissionable atomic material. Some of the country's finest coal has already been mined, but new mines in Limburg were later opened and alternate sources of energy have been initiated in Belgium.

When the nineteenth century ended, Europe was experiencing a new balance of power. Britain, France, and Russia found themselves in a confrontational position with Germany and Austria/Hungary for the control of Europe. Although neutral, because of the treaty of 1831, Belgium was closely allied with Britain. Leopold II signed a piece of legislation on his deathbed which established a military draft; and a new defense bill designed to increase the size of the army to 340,000 men was passed in 1913. But the Belgian army was no match for the powerful German forces who invaded the country in August of 1914. The Germans occupied all of the country except for a tiny strip which managed to stay in Belgian hands. The remainder of the Belgian army and the king stayed in that area for the remainder of the war.

From the outset of the German occupation, there was confusion about whether occupied Belgium should be a strong or a weak Belgium as part of Germany's sphere of influence. The period of German occupation took a heavy toll on the country. The four and one-third years resulted in Belgian losses totaling 46,000 dead and 50,000 seriously wounded. Moreover, the infrastructure was in a shambles and the heavy industry was nearly destroyed.

During the two decades between the two world wars, Belgium worked diligently to repair the economy without incurring an oppressive level of inflation. They entered the French alliance system under a Franco-Belgian military agreement in 1920, became a League of Nations member, and joined the Lacarno Treaties with France and Germany which guaranteed the borders of these three nations. While there was some significant improvement, the situation was less than satisfactory for the working class which saw a decrease in their per capita income level during the reconstruction period. During the same period of time, their taxation rate jumped 70 percent. Universal male suffrage was initiated in 1919.

The German occupation during World War II was even more troublesome than the first had been. Thousands of Belgian citizens were deported and would never return to the country. Nazi demands for supplies and materials created severe shortages in Belgium. Also, during the intervening two decades between wars, the Germans had recruited a number of collaborators among both the Flemish nationalists and the Walloons. During the war, many young Belgian males escaped and joined the Allied forces.

To make matters worse, King Leopold III surrendered to the Germans, thinking that this would make life better for his people. Toward the last part of the war, he was taken to Germany and there was a great deal of opposition to his interest in returning to Belgium and maintaining his leadership of the country. So, finally, Leopold III was persuaded to turn over the leadership of Belgium to his son.

After World War II, Belgium's recovery was impressive. Both agriculture and industry rebounded nicely. At the San Francisco United Nations (U.N.) Conference of April–June 1945, in which the U.N. Charter was drafted, the Belgians fought to disallow the use of the veto. Even though they were outvoted, Belgium signed the U.N. agreement because they were convinced that the U.N. was of critical importance for keeping peace around the world. After all, the country had been involved in two back-to-back world wars, and was occupied by the Germans both times. So, even though the country was not totally satisfied by the U.N. Charter, Belgium signed.

Another part of the Belgian recovery was the restoration of social stability. This was accomplished through the enactment of measures which attempted to reform the position of labor in the nation's economy. The Social Christian Party (CUP/PSC) was established in 1945. This action resurrected the Catholic Bloc and dropped the previous requirement of being limited only to avowed Catholics and admitted anyone who adhered to its conservative political philosophy. The Belgian Workers Party was reorganized in 1945 after being disbandoned for five years. It was renamed the Belgian Socialist Party.

In 1950, the educational system was again in the national spotlight. The problem of funding resurfaced when the Catholic-supported Social Christian government announced a new plan in which the free schools were mostly Catholic financial subsidies with very few restrictions. But the supporters of the state schools (mostly Socialists and Liberals) argued that the manner in which the subsidies were carried out gave the Catholic schools an unfair advantage. Finally, the national elections of 1954 returned the leadership to the Socialist-Liberal coalition and, ultimately, a system was established which was favorable to the state school system. Once again, the religious problem was managed, even though it was far from being solved.

Charles de Gaulle made his Brazzaville speech in 1958. He offered French colonies the choice of membership in the French community or immediate independence. This was troubling to some Belgian leaders who believed he was trying to provoke a conflict between the Congo and the Belgians. Moreover, Belgium had initiated a number of reforms in their African colony, and it would probably be necessary to accelerate the pace of the changes. Finally, serious rioting at Leopoldville in January of 1959 caused the Belgians to finally agree to the creation of a state in the Congo. It was decided that independence would be granted by 1963.

However, Belgium had concerns that they could become involved in a situation similar to that encountered by the French in Algeria. The Socialists argued against sending Belgian troops to the Congo, and the Belgian cabinet began hinting that perhaps some sort of self-government should be instituted in 1960. Ultimately, it was decided that the Belgian Congo would become an independent nation on June 30, 1960. It was hoped that a gradual transfer of control could be consummated in such a short period of time. However, on just the third day in the life of the newly independent Republic of Congo, serious violence occurred in Leopoldville, the capital, and Luluabourg. The outbreaks terrorized the Europeans who were still present in the new nation. Despite the protests of Patrice Lumumba, the new nation's first prime minister, Belgian troops were sent to bases at Kitona and Kamina. Lumumba, supposedly under communist control, appealed to the United Nations for help in restoring the rioting Congalese army to order. On July 14, 1960, a U.N. resolution called for the withdrawal of Belgian troops from the Congo. Subsequent U.N. resolutions of July 22 and August 9, 1960 requested Belgium to quickly withdraw and remove all of its troops from Katanga. The U.N. resolutions plus mounting international pressure forced the Belgians to evacuate the country.

The Social Christian Liberal government, under the leadership of Gaston Cyskens, proclaimed the single law (loi unique). This referred to a budget packet of money-saving measures which were extremely harsh. The single law included decreases in public expenditures, increased taxation, and also a five-year plan for industrial development.

In the parliamentary election of 1965, major gains were made by the nationalist parties. A government coalition consisting of the Socialists and Social Christians accounted for about 78 percent of the vote in 1961. However, this plurality experienced a 15 percent drop which was shared about evenly between the two parties. The reorganized Liberal Party, stressing the importance of the country's language issues, gathered 22 percent of the vote. In March 1968, a general election was held over a resolution to the language problem. But it took a Social Christian-Socialist coalition to extract an agreement which stipulated that equal numbers of Dutch-speaking and French-speaking participants would be represented on the cabinet ministries. Constitutional reforms of 1971 recognized four linguistic regions—the French, Dutch, and German-language regions, and the bilingual capital. General elections were held again in 1977, and Leo Tindemans, a Flemish Social Christian, crafted a coalition which eventually created a five-tiered system of government in which the central government controlled foreign affairs, defense, justice, economic policies, and fiscal policy.

STRUCTURE OF THE SYSTEM

Located across the North Sea from Britain between France and Germany, Belgium is a small, densely populated European country with a well-developed social security system and a high standard of living. The regions of Wallona and Flanders are unique in several ways. Flanders, which is more densely populated than Wallona, is rather flat and partly coastal. It has been able to provide the resources necessary for the country's industrial growth. Belgium's small size has tended to obscure its complex nature. For example, the Belgian educational enterprise essentially has separate Dutch and French systems in addition to nonsectarian public schools and private Catholic schools. But the country still seems to have a language cleavage on the order of Canada. As previously stated, French is spoken in Wallona, and Dutch in Flanders, while both languages are commonly spoken in Brussels.

Politically, Belgium has a constitutional monarch who reigns but does not really rule. The prime minister and cabinet ministers are selected from members of the parliament. Like many other nations, the powers of the state are divided into the legislative, executive, and judicial branches. The administration and political divisions are under the edicts of the nation's constitution. The multiparty system essentially has three dominant political parties, consisting of the Social Christians, Socialists, and Liberals. The Belgium parliament consists of the senate and house of representatives. The constitution contains a number of provisions which are designed to safeguard the personal rights and liberties. Freedoms of religion, speech, assembly, education, and equality of law are also guaranteed. Protection of minorities, due process of law, education, and the right to use the language of choice are also guaranteed by the Belgian constitution.

A parliamentary democracy under a constitutional monarchy, Belgium bases succession on the direct line of male heirs of the first king. If there are no male heirs, the monarch nominates a successor who must be approved by the parliament. The Belgian king is the head of state and in charge of all the armed forces.

For the entire history of the country, education has been held in high esteem. Prior to 1794, the Catholic Church was in control of the Belgian educational system. But a secular system along with state control replaced the control by the church. It has been said that the nation's school system actually reflected a kind of "linguistic apartheid." The system has been controlled by two separate ministers of education and two community councils. Since the mid-1800s, Belgium has been noted for its progressive approaches to preschool education. Even though the compulsory age for beginning school is six, most Belgian youth start their schooling much earlier. Froebelian and Montessorian philosophy is quite common for the country's pre-school education programs. Normally, the curriculum and teaching strategies have been based on the interests of the child, a strong tenet of the American educator, John Dewey. The teaching emphasis has been on helping students becoming self-functioning, highly motivated learners.

Belgium has been known for its progressive approaches to education. Although the compulsory years do not start until the age of 6, 90 percent of children from 2½ to 5 are in pre-school kindergarten schools. Pre-school classes do not allow formal instruction. Instead, the curriculum is based on the interests of the child and stresses the development of self-discipline, observation powers, and manual dexterity.

The primary grades include first through sixth, and the compulsory school ages are from six to eighteen. There are three cycles of two years each, and students have one teacher for each cycle. The primary-level goals are to teach self-expression in the mother tongue, reading, writing, arithmetic, and to emphasize practice in spelling and multiplication. The curriculum also consists of natural sciences, music, art, physical education, hygiene, and moral or religious instruction. Some subjects are incorporated into theme units, and, in recent years, Belgium has attempted to make the instruction more child-centered rather than fact-centered. Also, there has recently been more group problem-solving activities.

The traditional secondary school consists of two cycles of three years each— the first cycle being comparable to the middle schools which are found in some countries. Students not starting in an academic high school can transfer to one after completing the middle school portion. The academic high schools offer Greek and Latin studies, a core of classical or modern humanities, economics, modern languages, and science. The second cycle of the academic schools includes specialized areas of study which can be chosen by the student. Usually these choices depend on the areas of study a student wishes to pursue at the university later on.

However, Belgium also has other types of special-need high schools such as the International School of Brussels which was designed to meet the needs of "at risk" students. The school is a nonprofit, private, nonsectarian day school. There are approximately 400 students in grades 10 to 12. To the school's credit, about 95 percent of their graduates go on to college. Moreover, many of the students have various kinds of learning disabilities. Of special interest is the research arm of the school. A curriculum-based assessment model was adapted by the school. The strategy was developed by the school staff who reviewed curriculum offerings, examinations and activities, enabling objectives/minimum competency skills, and multinational approaches to special needs.

Prospective pre-school teachers, primary school teachers, and secondary school teachers attend separate normal schools which focus on the specific needs of the three levels. Teachers in upper secondary schools are required to obtain a special teaching certificate as well as a university degree in their specialty subjects. Supplementary training is provided by study circles which are sponsored by the director general of teacher training.

Belgium's complete universities all include faculties of medicine, law, philosophy, science, and applied science. Tuition is not free, but about one-third of the students receive grants and loans. Even though tuition is charged, the fees are quite nominal. Admission to a university is based on the courses which students studied in their secondary school programs. All majors generally require four years of study, with the exception of dentistry (five years), veterinary medicine (six years), and medicine (seven years).

MULTICULTURAL EDUCATION EFFORTS

Belgium's multicultural education program is part of its basic education offerings. One reason for the strong emphasis on multicultural education has been the large number of foreign students in the nation's schools. About 10 percent of Belgian students come from other countries, including Italy, Spain, Israel, Portugal, Morocco, Algeria, Tunisia, Turkey, France, Holland, Germany, and the British Isles. Starting in the kindergarten years, a supplemental teacher can be employed whenever an immigrant population reaches 30 percent or more. This person then develops a language program which is designed to meet the needs of students who do not speak one of the primary languages of instruction.

Special elementary school courses can be organized for foreign students in order to meet their specific needs. In order to qualify, each school must have at least ten foreign students. The classes meet three times a week. Also, in certain schools with a large population density of children, a special project called *"Greeting Each Other"* is employed. This project makes it possible for children from a given microculture to obtain instruction in their own native language and culture. Many ideas have been brought forth to help children of migrant workers from Europe adjust to frequent moves. Some of the strategies have included reception teaching, teaching about the culture and language of the native country, educational reintegration, development and distribution of teaching materials, and teacher training.

In the secondary schools, an attempt is made to provide instruction in the student's native language whenever possible. Also, special programs focusing on Dutch as a second language are created in order to help the students reach the point where they become bilingual. This program also requires a minimum of ten students.

Multicultural education programs are a part of the Belgian in-service training sequences for teachers. In many of the programs, the focus is on the education of migrant children. Seminars normally have six primary objectives in multicultural seminars and/or workshops; the six goals are to make teachers aware of the: (1) historical, social, economic, cultural, and socio-psychological effects of migration; (2) various forms of cultural expressions present in the migrant workers national cultures and in the culture of the host country; (3) differences existing between the migrants' countries of origin and the host country, not only in the cultural field but also in their historical and economic dimensions; (4) the fact that in teaching to migrant children, their parents' mother tongue requires an appropriate methodology; (5) the basic principles of multicultural education; and (6) procedures for using instructional material for teaching a language as a second language.

Multicultural education in-service programs for teachers are an integral part of Belgium's total in-service program efforts. Since 1986, an informational workshop for international education is attended by the nation's teachers, and the topic of multicultural education has been incorporated into the teacher preparation sequence in the country's normal schools.

In Belgium, all students attend racially integrated schools and they are subject to the same compulsory attendance requirements regardless of their race, religion, or ethnicity. The schools try to instill the notion that all persons are citizens of the world. This philosophy requires all people to be responsible citizens in their local community and in the world as well. Consequently, all subjects taught in the schools (geography, language, history, morality, etc.) utilize this philosophical strand. Moreover, given the numbers of immigrants to the country, a great deal of national attention is given to issues such as the transition from school to working life and other areas such as: (1) problems relating to the education of migrant workers' children; problems concerning access to vocational training; and (3) the links between school success, vocational training success, employment success, and access to the labor market. It has been found that migrants have stayed on the fringes of the job market because of the notion that they probably would be going back home. It also has been found that many Belgian immigrants are at risk for unemployment because they tend to lack job training and do not seem to possess the same kind of work ethic as their parents.

The Belgian Ministry of Education has a procedure for screening all teaching materials to ensure that they are free of racist and sexist content. In the authors' initial multicultural survey, the Belgian respondent argued that the biggest problems facing multicultural programs in the country were the language barriers. The predominant language patterns (French, German, and Dutch) have provided difficulties for immigrants which has necessitated a decision as to which national language to learn. Historically, most Flemish parents send their children to Catholic schools, while most French speakers utilize the public schools. The fact that Belgium has had two separate ministers of education underscores the sort of linguistic apartheid which has caused some difficulties for migrant children. Also, these language barriers have impacted teacher-student interaction and parent-school communication as well. The Belgian respondent to the previously mentioned survey also felt that too many of the nation's teachers were not sensitized to multicultural education issues. It was argued that Belgium needed to improve the relationship between the schools and the growing number of immigrant students by finding ways to break down the language barrier and conditioning new students in order to meet the needs of all Belgian students more effectively.

SUMMARY

It is indeed interesting that Belgium's sophisticated multicultural education programs have been motivated in part by the influx of immigrants during recent years. Belgium, like so many other countries, has had a history of conflict between language groups. So the language issues have also played a major role in the development of multicultural education efforts. One of the country's interesting multicultural programs, called *"Meeting Each Other,"* has been developed in order to help students learn to appreciate racial and ethnic diversity. The project also makes it possible for Belgian students to have bilingual/bicultural instruction. The program's goals also hope to overcome this disruption of communication. If bilingual instruction is necessary, the instruction is provided in the student's native language. But students also receive instruction in Dutch or French so they can become fluent in both languages, and the need for bilingual instruction disappears. Most countries seem to use this model whenever possible.

In order to sensitize students to the pluralistic macroculture, several steps have been taken. Each year, informative workshops have been organized for the Worldwide Formation in Education. In the new normal school teacher preparation programs for elementary and secondary teachers, the topic of multiculturalism is part of the training sequence. Finally, the Center for Worldwide Education of State Universities in Ghent organizes international conferences centered on the subject of education for international understanding.

Thus, it can be seen that the issue of multicultural education is viewed quite seriously in Belgium, and other countries could learn from the interesting programs which have been created in an attempt to help young people acquire positive attitudes about the country's increasingly pluralistic society.

REFERENCES

Bastenier, A. et al. *Vocational Training of Young Migrants in Belgium*. Berlin: European Centre for the Development of Vocational Training, 1986.

Belgium. Ministry of Education. *Education in Belgium*. Brussels: Ministry of Education, 1984.

Cammaert, Marie France. *Interculturalism: Theory and Practice*. Seminar on the Education and Cultural Development of Migrants, Limbourg, Belgium, April 1987. (Council for Cultural Cooperation, Strasbourg, France.)

Fitzmaurice, John. *The Politics of Belgium: Crisis and Compromise in a Plural Society*. New York: Martens, 1983.

Gerson, Noel. *Belgium*. New York: The Macmillan Company, 1964.

Helmreich, Jonathan E. *Belgium and Europe: A Study in Small Power Diplomacy*. The Hague: Mouton, 1976.

Janietz, Patricia L. "Developing Collaboratively on International School Special Needs Plan for Multicultural, Multilingual, and Multinational Secondary Students." Paper presented at the Council for Exceptional Children Symposium on Culturally Diverse Exceptional Children. Albuquerque, NM, Oct. 18–20, 1990.

Kossman, E.H. *The Low Countries: 1780–1940*. Oxford: Clarendon Press, 1993.

Mezerik, A.G. (Ed.). *Congo and the United Nations* (3 vols.). New York: International Review Service, 1960–1963.

Mitchell, Bruce and Salsbury, Robert. *An International Survey of Multicultural Education*. Cheney, WA: Western States Consulting and Evaluation Services, 1991. (See Appendix.)

Strukelj, I. *Socio-Cultural and Linguistic Integration of the Children of Migrant and Farmer Migrant Workers*. Meeting of Specialists, Final Report. Proceedings, Bled, Yugoslavia: Sponsored by the U.N. Education Scientific and Cultural Organization, June 1989.

Vander Linden, H. *Belgium: The Making of a Nation,* trans. Sybil Jane. Oxford: Clarendon Press, 1920.

Wickman, Stephen B. *Belgium: A Country Study*. Washington, DC: Department of the Army, 1984.

6

Brazil

HISTORY OF THE SYSTEM

The Portuguese controlled the country of Brazil for approximately 300 years. However, by the year 1822, Portugal was not able to offer resistance to an independence movement. By that time, the Portuguese forces were quite small and independence was won rather easily. King Joao founded the royal press in 1808 and started publishing the *Gazeta do Rio de Janeiro*. The country's naval academy was founded in 1808, and the Royal Military Academy during 1810. While the first university would not be established until the 1900s, the country saw several higher education institutions being started in Rio and Bahia from 1809 to 1813. Featuring courses in surgery, anatomy, and medicine, these early institutions provided a beginning for the training of Brazilian doctors.

The Royal School of Sciences, Arts, and Professions was begun in 1816. Thus, for the first time in the country's history, an educational system was developing for the education of a people who had survived colonialism and were becoming yet another of the world's independent nations. However, at this time in history, only about 10 percent of the adults in the nation were literate. Moreover, progress toward a liberal education was quite slow; in fact, this progress was much slower than in North America and in the countries of Europe.

The Brazilian Declaration of Independence occurred during 1822, and this act freed the country from a history of exploitation by the Portuguese trade monopoly. At the time when Brazil achieved its independence, Europe was involved in many industrial ventures, but the newly independent country did not yet have the experienced persons who were skilled enough to participate in such entrepreneurial ventures. In fact, after independence, the country continued to be an exporter of tropical products and an importer of manufactured goods for about a century.

During the early 1920s, sentiment against the country's history of slavery grew more pronounced, particularly in the urban areas. Consequently, in 1826, 1827, and 1830, the country took steps against the importation of slaves, a practice which had been carried on by the Portuguese for years. Other countries were also commencing to terminate their trading policies during this general period of time.

Following Brazil's independence from Portugal, the country attempted to create a system of free education which could foster the cultural development of the country. However, the good intentions were overshadowed by the impoverished status of the new nation as well as the great lack of qualified persons who could become classroom teachers. These two problems were exacerbated by a lack of interest in a public education system by the Brazilian people. At this time the illiteracy rate was approximately 85 percent.

During the new period of independence, the first efforts were to train teachers for the primary level. So the first Brazilian normal school was founded in 1836. A second one opened in 1837, and a third in 1845. At first they became known as colleges for girls, rather than teacher preparation institutions. By 1889 there were about 3,500 public schools in Brazil with approximately 116,000 students. But by 1876 there were 6,000 public schools with about 200,000 students.

World War I provided a tremendous boost to the Brazilian economy. During this time, Brazilian manufacturing was stimulated because it was more difficult to receive manufactured goods from Europe. Moreover, there was an increased demand for Brazil's raw materials which provided the country with badly needed capital to help with its economic expansion.

By 1920 Brazil had some 13,336 factories which employed more than 275,000 people. Many small factories were started during the war years. Some of the newly manufactured products included knitted goods, soap, beer, wine, canned items, tin cans, footwear, iron utensils, soap, and candles. In addition, the war had the effect of urbanizing the country as a result of these new economic ventures which had sprung up in the cities. In fact, when it was over, approximately 1.5 million Brazilians earned their living in the country's industrialized factories.

Sao Paulo was viewed as a model for Brazilian education. Many teachers were sent there to observe the teaching learning process. The educational philosophy was based on the work of Herbart, who at that time was popular in the United States. Also, Sao Paulo would allow its teachers to go to other parts of the country in order to instruct teachers in new pedagogical methods.

One of Brazil's major problems during the mid-1900s was how to deliver good educational programs to the rural areas. During the late 1950s, two-thirds of the Brazilian school children resided in such locales. Teachers in the rural portions of the country encountered difficult problems, such as those articulated by Almeida:

There are fazendeiros and farm managers who consider the teacher to be an employee of the fazenda under the orders of the master and subject to the general discipline of the laborers. . . . Frequently the girl must find shelter in the house of the caipira, where the mistress of the house, although an excellent person, cooks the beans badly with no fat. Cleanliness is unknown. . . . The teacher is given a room, with the walls full of holes, which is also used for keeping saddles and harness.[1]

African-Brazilian slavery lasted in the country until 1880. By that time, approximately 25 percent of the country consisted of African-Brazilian persons. Brazil's social integration of the racially mixed populations of the country has created an excellent level of cultural pluralism. Moreover, it has been argued that the ethnic and cultural mixing of Europeans, South American Indians, and sub-Saharan Africans has helped to provide Brazil with a unique type of cultural stability which few other countries enjoy.

Beginning about 1900, Brazil was able to slowly start modeling the French system of education. The pre-primary years were mostly privately supported and served the needs of children between the ages of four and six. The primary grades were for children between ages seven and eleven. They were primarily funded by state and municipal monies. Supplementary education was for students from age 11 to 13. These three sections comprised the elementary division of education. Secondary education programs served the needs of children up through the age of 18.

Brazilian education has been controlled by the central government and/or state governments according to the country's constitution. The country's education system has contained a number of constitutional articles concerning education. All Brazilians are entitled to an education based on the principles of freedom. The various branches of education have been provided by public authorities, but can also be provided by private persons in accordance with the law. Instruction in the primary schools is compulsory and is conducted in Portuguese.

STRUCTURE OF THE SYSTEM

A 1971 reform law led the country's educational system through a restructuring process. It consisted of a major change in philosophy and a reassessment of goals. These new goals saw the country improving access to education, retaining students in school for longer periods of time, making vocational training a major focal point of the curriculum for all students through middle school, and attempting to provide equal educational opportunities for all children. The latter goal meant that many children who never attended school before would commence to do so. This became a key factor in Brazil's economic development. It was looked upon as a vehicle to help develop human resources for the country's rapidly growing labor market as well as preparing students to become university scholars.

One of the major new changes was the abolishment of the country's rigid system of terminal examinations which kept many low-income children from advancing to the next grade level. Critics also have argued that the education

of low-income children was so poor that many of them were forced to drop out
of school by the fourth grade. The problems encountered by low socio-economic
children have been most pronounced in the more rural parts of the land. They
have been attributed to the need for children to work, health problems, and
inadequate nutrition.

The restructuring legislation of 1971 organized the country's educational system into four "grades," which included an eight-year primary school period; a
three- to four-year middle school cycle; and two higher education levels including undergraduate and graduate programs. These changes meant that grades five
through eight, which had formerly been considered part of a lower-middle concept, were then part of the primary level. The Brazilians felt that making this
change would encourage students to remain in school for a longer period of
time.

The administration of Brazilian schools is decentralized. While the rural
schools are normally operated by the state, urban schools are generally administered by the state and municipal governments. The Ministry of Education and
Culture is responsible for operating schools in the federal territories along with
special vocational and adult education programs and public higher education.
This body also has the responsibility of estabilishing national guidelines. There
is a large private school segment of the Brazilian educational system. Most
private schools are sponsored by the Roman Catholics. These private schools
are eligible for federal subsidies and tuition tax is deductible.

In Brazil there is also a Federal Council of Education which functions under
the Ministry of Education and Culture. This body is charged with the responsibility of creating minimal national standards for federal, state, and municipal
systems and proposing syllabi for subject areas at each grade level.

Since the major reforms of 1971, the country's greatest changes have occurred
in the middle schools. This phase of the Brazilian education system has consisted
of two educational tracks—vocational and academic. As the term implies, the
primary function of the academic track is to prepare students for the higher
education level. The vocational track includes about 60 percent of the country's
students, and is designed to provide them with marketable skills for the Brazilian
workforce.

In both of these middle school programs, the school year is divided into a
number of class hours. There is a common nucleus of 1,000 class hours for
courses in Portuguese language and Brazilian literature, history, social studies,
mathematics, and science. The vocational track includes 130 specialized areas
of training in industry, agriculture, primary education, service occupations, and
commerce.

Entrance examinations for admission to higher education programs are highly
competitive. In fact, they have been so competitive that many students enroll
for *curzinhos* (mini-courses) in order to prepare for them. These courses have
been offered by private educational enterprises and there is a great deal of competition for students.

Primary and middle school teachers are certified by the state education authority, and completion of a comprehensive pedagogical preparation program is required for certification. However, provisional certification can be acquired by completing a normal school program. More than 90 percent of the primary school teachers and over 50 percent of the middle-level instructors are women. And while teaching is considered to be a highly acceptable occupation in Brazil, salaries tend to be low and consequently the country is faced with a problem of high turnover.

MULTICULTURAL EDUCATION EFFORTS

At one time, Brazilian people consisted of three primary ethnic groups: native Brazilians, Portuguese, and African-Brazilians. However, it has been argued that none of these three groups was ethnically homogeneous during the first 200 years of Portuguese occupation. Portuguese peoples themselves were a composite of ethnic Iberians, Arabs, Celts, Romans, Goths, and Suevi. All of these groups occupied the portion of Europe which would eventually become known as Portugal. At the time of the first incursions of the Portuguese-Europeans, the native Brazilians consisted of many different microcultures with their own distinct characteristics. When the Portuguese-Europeans came into contact with these indigenous groups, they appropriated much of their material culture, particularly the weaving of vegetable fibers and other native materials. Eventually, the European-Portuguese and the native Brazilians became the ''pioneer race'' who conquered central-western Brazil in the name of Portugal.

The Portuguese failed in their attempt to enslave the aboriginal Brazilians and make them work the land, so they imported African slaves from western Africa to do the heavy agricultural work and other forms of labor which the Portuguese did not wish to perform. Consequently, three main racial/ethnic groups became part of the present day Brazilian macroculture. It is important to consider that, even today, the African immigrants constitute the greatest proportion of Brazilians (80 percent) who find themselves in the lower-income classes of Brazilian society.

The Brazilian educational system is not segregated, and both the public and private schools admit children from all racial and ethnic backgrounds. However, the private schools are able to exclude children for other reasons (usually the inability to pay the tuition which is sometimes rather expensive).

Portuguese is the language of instruction in Brazilian schools. However, the educational system has been wrestling with the issue of equity education, and many schools are attempting to provide instruction in the student's native language if it is needed. This has been a problem for many children from remote regions of the Amazon basin who are now seeking an education for the first time in the country's history. Consequently, Brazil has been attempting to improve the instruction of such youth through the use of bilingual instruction.

A major problem in Brazil is the issue of educating the poor. While the country's constitution requires an education for all citizens, the education of low-income children has presented a major problem as it has in many other countries. Freire, one of the country's major educational leaders, has expressed grave concerns over the number of poor children of school age who are allowed to enter school and then are "expelled" under the guise of having "dropped out." The illiteracy rate among such Brazilian youth has escalated in recent years, creating a major problem for Brazilian educators.

Another concern of Brazilian educators has been the recent tendency to provide insufficient funding for the nation's schools. Some educators have argued that much of the problem is attributable to an attempt by the far right to encourage participation in private schooling which might lead to the demise of equal education opportunities and an elitist system of education in Brazilian schools. Moreover, there is a concern over the democratization of access to school. Particularly in Sao Paulo, there is a migrant population for whom schooling is a somewhat precarious commodity. Thus, the educational system is hard pressed to provide equal educational opportunities for these exploited persons. Moreover, some critics fear that the recent attempts to decentralize education may further exacerbate the problem.

An attempt to rectify some of the major problems of the educational system has rested in the country's Literacy Movement of Sao Paulo (MOVA). This is a current effort to create 2,000 literacy centers which would serve the needs of more than 60,000 people. The objectives of this movement are to reinforce and expand the work of popular groups which already work with adult literacy in the outskirts of Sao Paulo; develop a literacy method that enables students to think critically; contribute to the development of political consciousness in the students and teachers involved; and stimulate grass-roots participation and the struggle for the social rights of citizens, emphasizing the basic right to public and progressive education.

SUMMARY

Like most of the other South American countries, Brazil has had a history of colonial exploitation by European adventurers. These historical exploits have not only had an effect on the general history of the country, but on the educational system as well. Many of the native languages have disappeared, and the language of the conquerors (the Portuguese) is now the language of the land and of the educational system as well.

Since the country is struggling to shed its status as a "developing nation" and secure a more well-established economic posture, the educational system is trying hard to provide the kind of instructional programs which will allow the nation's youth to become competitive in the international economic marketplace.

This nation has been blessed with an adventuresome spirit, in addition to the extraordinary leadership of well-recognized educators such as Paulo Freire. It is expected that the educational system will be successful in helping Brazil to take its place as one of the world's leaders in the twentieth century.

NOTE

1. Thomas E. Weil (Ed.), *Brazil, A Country Study* (Washington, DC: U.S. Government, Department of the Army, 1983).

REFERENCES

Dossantos, J.C. "The Recent Process of Decentralization and Democratic Management in Brazil." *International Review of Education,* Vol. 39, No. 5 (1993), pp. 391–403.

Freire, Paulo. *Pedagogy of the City.* New York: Continuum Press, 1993.

Gonen, Amiram. *The Encyclopedia of the Peoples of the World.* New York: Henry Holt Publishing Co., 1993.

Havighurst, Robert and Moreira, Roberto. *Society and Education in Brazil.* Pittsburgh: University of Pittsburgh Press, 1965.

Hutchinson, Bertram. *Trabalho, Status, e Educacao.* Rio de Janeiro: Centro Brazileiro de Pesquaisas Educacionais, Ministry of Education and Culture, 1989.

Weil, Thomas E. (Ed.). *Brazil, A Country Study.* Washington, DC: Department of the Army, 1983.

Williamson, Edwin. *The Penguin History of Latin America.* London: Penguin Books, Ltd., 1992.

Wirth, John (Ed.). *State and Society in Brazil: Continuity and Change.* Boulder, CO: Westview Press, 1992.

Wong, P.L. "Constructing a Public Popular Education in Sao Paulo, Brazil." *Comparative Education Review,* Vol. 39, No. 1 (1995), pp. 120–141.

7

Bulgaria

HISTORY OF THE SYSTEM

The early history of Bulgaria is traceable to the Bulgar control of the region between the Balkans and the Danube. This Bulgar control was granted in 681 by the Byzantine empire which was the eastern half of the Roman Empire. By 1908, Ferdinand had declared Bulgaria fully independent of the Ottoman Empire which had ruled the Bulgar region for more than five centuries. In 1941, the country signed the Tripartite Pact which allied it with Nazi Germany during World War II. However, during the war, Bulgaria was never involved in actions against the Soviet Union. Following the war, the new Republic of Bulgaria became part of the Soviet Bloc, under the leadership of Georgi Dimitrov. At this time, the state confiscated all private property. Then, during 1948 and 1949, the state restrained or banned Muslim, Orthodox, Protestant, and Catholic religions. From that time until the late 1980s, the Communist regime reigned supreme. However, dissident groups began to address a number of environmental and human rights issues during 1987 and 1988.

Starting with a general strike during the late Fall of 1990, the country began to see the demise of the Communist regime. Finally, a new constitution was approved by the Bulgarian National Assembly in 1991. Bordered by Turkey on the southeast, Greece on the southwest, and the Black Sea on the east, Bulgaria is a part of the Shatter Belt, which is a narrow strip of land between the USSR and Western Europe. It is an area which historically has been occupied by disorganized, weak nations. The Bulgarian nation has a population of nearly nine million people with a small percentage of Turks, Gypsies, Romanians, and a few other ethnic groups.

Controlled by the Turks for 500 years, commencing with the end of the thirteenth century, the Bulgarian monastery schools were able to preserve the Bulgarian alphabet and literature. By 1870, the Bulgarian Orthodox Church had become a powerful force in the development of the country's educational system. When the nation was finally liberated from the Turks in 1870, there were nearly 1,500 primary schools, 50 secondary schools, a university, and also a number of reading clubs.

Between the two world wars, Bulgaria's school system was quite slow in materializing. Due to the country's industrial development, the emphasis was on vocational education during that period of time. Entry examinations for admission to secondary schools were also instituted during that time frame. The war years saw a general curtailment in the development of the nation's schools since most of the country's resources were committed to the country's military involvement. During 1944, a Communist *coup d'etat* was responsible for many changes in the Bulgarian educational system. A publishing house, Narodna Prosveta, was created for the purpose of preparing new books and other teaching materials for the nation's schools. Marxist/Leninist concepts were utilized, and teachers who were not sympathetic to these ideas were replaced with instructors who subscribed to the Communist doctrine.

A new constitution was based on Communist ideology. It declared that all citizens had the right to a secular education, and it contained a democratic and progressive spirit. The study of Bulgarian was mandatory even though national minorities had the right to be educated in their own language. The schools were operated by the state, and elementary education was compulsory and free.

Following World War II, Bulgarian education began to adapt many of the programs and policies connected with the Soviet system. Indeed, much of the pedagogical philosophy emanated from the Soviets. Moreover, the influence can be seen in the curriculum, educational objectives, and extra-curricular activities. The teaching methods used in the two countries have also been rather similar, with the lecture technique being commonly used.

Between 1960 and 1980, the number of students in higher education increased quite dramatically. In 1960, government figures showed that 54,795 students were enrolled in institutions of higher education. The number jumped to about 220,000 by 1980. One of the major reasons for this increase was the country's need for engineers in mechanics, power, electricity, and chemicals.

Post-World War II objectives for the Bulgarian system of education have been consistently articulated by Communist Party leaders, government officials, and the Ministry of Education. Since education in Bulgaria has been highly centralized, these objectives are valid for the entire country and have been stipulated in the "Law for Closer Ties between School and Life." The Bulgarian objectives for schools have been to prepare young people for life in socialist and communist societies. They attempt to link the education of young people with social and productive labor, and to develop the principles of communism in love of toil and in the spirit of socialist patriotism and proletarian internationalism. Moreover, these objectives were designed to prepare well-educated and well-rounded people by providing youth with a good understanding of science, teaching them the tenets of the Marxist-Leninist ideology, and helping them to acquire productive moral, aesthetic, political, and professional training. This had to be accomplished through the provision of a balanced combination of academic education and labor. In other words, the country's schools had two major purposes: to develop students who were competent in a trade or profession, and train them to be loyal to the Communist state and to the Communist party.

The curriculum for the country's elementary and secondary schools consisted of Bulgarian language and literature, Russian language and literature, western European languages, mathematics (including algebra and geometry), chemistry, biology, geography, history (including history of the constitution of Bulgaria), elements of communism, physical culture, drawing, singing, labor training, and general technical subjects.

A viable portion of Bulgaria's educational efforts stemming from Marxist doctrines consisted of training in labor. Grades one through four focused primarily on crafts activities. Children were instructed in the use of scissors and pasting. However, in grades five through seven, the emphasis shifted to the use of equipment, such as hammers, saws, sewing machines, and stoves. In some schools, students tended gardens on plots of land called *trudovoopitno poles.* In these experimental plots, students would raise fruits and vegetables and also conduct agricultural experiments.

A third portion of the elementary school curriculum included extracurricular activities, even though many of them were considered to be part of the regular school program. Some of these functions consisted of hobby groups such as history clubs, geography clubs, hiking clubs, chess clubs, etc. Such activities were a part of the Pioneer program in each school. A Pioneer leader was responsible for coordinating the activities of the clubs. These clubs were also an arm of the Pioneer Palace in Sofia.

Teaching methods for social instruction in the country's schools did not differ greatly from the strategies used in other types of classroom instruction. In general, they followed the same patterns as those instructional strategies used in other traditional European schools. Thus, the traditional method was still the lecture, with little opportunity for questioning by the participating students. Other strategies such as laboratory experiments, individual projects, and the like were rarely used. However, cooperative efforts were used as a means of encouraging capable students to assist those for whom learning was difficult.

Bulgarian teachers during the 1950s and 1960s were usually products of two-year normal schools. These schools admitted persons who were graduates of secondary schools. Preparation in the normal schools was for elementary teachers who took courses in the history of the Communist Party, specific courses on Marxist/Leninist theory, and pedagogical courses. Teachers also received a steady diet of in-service courses which were designed to improve their competency and their pedagogical skills.

STRUCTURE OF THE SYSTEM

The year 1979 was one of major educational reform in the Bulgarian system of public education. In fact, the fall of Zhikov ushered in a sweeping reformation of Bulgaria's educational system. Bulgarian educators rejected the socialist system of education as being boring, impersonal, and not focused on the rights of individual students. A new system of educational councils was ushered in. This allowed teachers to elect delegates to the National Council of Teachers. The primary goal of the new structure was to de-politicize the schools through a spirit of cooperation with the Ministry of Education.

Since 1991, Bulgaria has had three different types of schools: state, municipal, and private. Some of the private schools are religious in nature. Primary schools serve the needs of children in grades 1 to 4; basic includes grades 5 to 7; and secondary covers grades 8 to 12. First grade children are usually six or seven years old, and parents have the option of enrolling their children in kindergarten before that. The nation's private schools usually are on the secondary level. However, there are also a number of specialized high schools which teach foreign languages, music, and math. Other special schools have attempted to meet the needs of children with various types of handicaps. Moreover, children with chronic illnesses have been able to receive educational instruction in hospitals or sanitariums.

During the 1990–1991 school year, new textbooks had been printed for the nation's schools, but some of them still contained socialist ideology. For example, one math book had a problem which asked the student to count the number of words in a sentence. The sentence was as follows: "I am grateful to the Party, for it leads my country to beautiful, radiant life and vigilantly protects us from war." In addition, many of the nation's school teachers continue to espouse the same Marxist doctrines that they taught throughout the 1960s through the 1980s.

The country's educational reform movements also reached higher education circles. During 1990, a new law pertaining to academic freedom focused on the notion of an intellectual market in which colleges and universities along with teachers and students maintained high performance levels in order to remain competitive. This academic freedom legislation led the way for institutions of higher education to deal with issues of teaching and instruction without any interference from the central government. This not only pertained to the nature of the curriculum, but also to student enrollment, admission requirements, etc.

Bulgaria's university system has been criticized as lacking in the technical fields. So in 1991, France and Germany made technical commitments to help the country carry out a number of educational reforms, and the United States began planning for a new American college. The instruction would be carried out in English, and American teaching methods would be used. It was hoped that these forms of assistance would help move Bulgaria into the European mainstream from which the country had been isolated since the end of World

War II. However, the educational system of Bulgaria can be viewed as a highly successful enterprise since the country claims a 95 percent literacy rate. Presently, Bulgaria is moving from its former status as a member of the Eastern European Communist Bloc to a new and more independent role. During most of its history, the country has been a small, agricultural nation which is now moving toward a market economy. The transition to a market economy has been a bit difficult due to a lack of appropriate legislation; and the modern Bulgarian economy is badly in need of cash.

MULTICULTURAL EDUCATION EFFORTS

Bulgarians make up 85 percent of the country's population, with Turks comprising the largest minority group at 9 percent. The remaining 6 percent includes Armenians, Greeks, Macedonians, and Romanians. The primary language of instruction is Bulgarian, but Turkish children have been allowed to learn in their native tongue at the primary level. However, the Turkish language instruction was eliminated for a ten-year period of time starting in 1960. While the study of the Bulgarian language is compulsory, minorities still have the right to further their own cultural traditions.

Gypsies have lived in Bulgaria since the fourteenth century. The largest group was Orthodox and spoke Bulgarian, while the next largest group of Gypsies were also Orthodox but spoke either Romanian or Romany (the Gypsy language). Another 22 percent were Muslim, spoke Turkish, and considered themselves to be ethnic Turks. The Gypsies have long been viewed as one of the country's most disadvantaged minorities, and there is little evidence that the educational system has attempted to deal with that issue through carefully crafted multicultural education programs. But one of the reasons for this particular problem probably stems from the Gypsy microculture itself which has tended to be relatively isolated from the Bulgarian macroculture.

Religious groups in Bulgaria have tended to get along with only minimal friction, compared to other countries. Most Bulgarians are at least somewhat connected to the Bulgarian Orthodox Church which was the state church until after the decline of the Communist regime. When the church became separated from the states, it was unable to participate in the political activities of the country.

Islamic groups in Bulgaria have lived primarily in the northeastern portion of the country and in the Rhodope Mountains. During the latter years of the Zhikov regime, Bulgarian Muslims had rather difficult times because they were considered to be foreigners even though they were actually ethnic Bulgarians. After the fall of the Zhikov regime, new mosques were built and the Muslims started to publish their own newspaper.

In the early part of the thirteenth century, Roman Catholics formed a brief union with the Bulgarian Orthodox Church. It was a political ploy designed to balance the religious power of the Byzantine Empire. However, Rome declared war on Bulgaria, and the Catholic Church had no influence in the country until diplomatic relations were established between the Vatican and Bulgaria in 1925. In 1991 about 44,000 Roman Catholics resided in Bulgaria.

Protestantism came to Bulgaria during the mid-1800s through the work of United States missionaries, primarily Methodists and Congregationalists. The Protestants were subjected to severe persecution under communism. During 1949, 31 Protestant clergy were accused of running a Bulgarian spy ring. As a result of these charges, all church properties were confiscated and the legal status of Protestant churches was terminated.

During the Communist years, Jews were declared to be a nationality rather than a religion. Moreover, during World War II, Bulgaria did not follow the anti-Jewish behavior of their Nazi allies. One reason for this is that, in general, most Bulgarian Jews tended to be urban and had adapted a secular posture. After World War II, 90 percent of the country's Jewish population migrated to the new country of Israel.

SUMMARY

Like the other Eastern European countries, Bulgaria has gone through major and sometimes traumatic changes as a result of the breakup of the Iron Curtain countries. Moreover, the nation is relatively homogeneous in its cultural composition. Consequently, the schools have yet to decide that major efforts in multicultural education pursuits are necessary.

At this point in their development, the schools are struggling to implement the necessary changes in the school curriculum which will empower the country to become a major player in the economic marketplace of Europe and the rest of the world. The massive ideological changes have made it difficult for educators.

REFERENCES

Bulgaria. Ministry of Education. *Law for Closer Ties Between School and Life.* Sofia: Ministry of Education, 1954.

Curtis, Glenn E. (Ed.). *Bulgaria: A Country Study.* Washington, DC: Library of Congress, 1989.

Din'o Koev, Za. *Concerning Party Partisanship in Education and Instruction.* Sofia: Narodna Prosveta, 1964.

Directives of the Eighth Congress of the Bulgarian Communist Party for the Development of the People's Republic of Bulgaria During the Period 1961–1980. Sofia, 1961.

Georgeoff, Peter. *The Social Education of Bulgarian Youth.* Minneapolis: University of Minnesota Press, 1968.

Gotchev, A. "Education and Research in the Social Sciences: Transition Dilemmas in Bulgaria." *East European Politics and Societies,* Vol. 7, No. 1 (1993), pp. 43–58.

Meyer, W.D. "Remnants of Eastern Europe's Totalitarian Past: The Example of Legal

Education in Bulgaria.'' *Journal of Legal Education,* Vol. 7, No. 1 (1993), pp. 43–58.

Peasley, Amos J. (Ed.). *Constitutions of Nations,* vol. I. The Hague: Martinus Nijhoff, 1956.

8

Canada

HISTORY OF THE SYSTEM

An examination of the early beginnings of Canada's educational system reveals a number of similarities between its history and that of the United States and Australia. Native Canadians had their own forms of education prior to the arrival of the Europeans. But these educational patterns changed dramatically during the post-Columbian era. In addition to the numbers of European immigrants during the earlier years, the country was also populated with freed African-American slaves who were able to find refuge beyond the United States borders by virtue of the Underground Railway. Canada's social institutions have tended to be open and democratic throughout the years. With the arrival of the French-Canadians and the English-Canadians came major changes in the concept of education that a rapidly changing society like Canada's really needed.

The issue of language and ethnicity has been a topic of great controversy throughout the history of the country's educational system. Two powerful European countries fought for control of that portion of the world, and the question has always been whether English or French should be the language of instruction employed in the schools. While both languages have been used throughout the land, it is probably safe to say that, as a general rule, English has dominated in the western portions of the country, while French has been used more frequently in the eastern part, particularly in Quebec and Montreal. But the issue of language use in the schools has always caused a number of problems for the country's educational system. These issues will be addressed in the final section of this chapter.

The European involvement extends back as far as John Cabot's voyage in 1492 and the Jacques Cartier expeditions which commenced in 1524. Explorers, such as La Verendrye and Mackenzie, managed to cross the continent during the 1700s on their journeys to the Pacific. These ventures and others opened up the vast natural resources of the country and paved the way for the involvement of many Europeans who came to the country for economic reasons or pure adventurism. As a result, trappers and traders helped develop trading enterprises with European countries as well as the United States. Moreover, the Canadian water routes made transportation relatively easy. River routes, such as the MacKenzie, Columbia, and St. Lawrence, made it possible for adventurers to settle into parts of Canada which would eventually become choice sites for agricultural enterprises and industrial developments, due to the country's rich supply of natural resources.

Canada's transcontinental railway was completed in 1885. As had been seen in the United States, this rail system would open up additional territories for future expansion and provide the motivation for even more European-Canadians to move into the new areas. The nation relied on Chinese laborers, many of whom had already worked on the transcontinental rail systems in the United States. This would eventually add to the multiracial/multiethnic composition of the Canadian schools.

It is useful to trace the present educational system back to the British North America Act of 1867. This piece of legislation clearly established the responsibility for the education of Canadian youth in each province. Each provincial legislature has organized a department of education which is headed by a minister of education. These departments of education are responsible for the administration of the elementary and secondary schools within their respective provinces.

STRUCTURE OF THE SYSTEM

Canada's primary and elementary schools are either publicly controlled or administered by private agencies, although schools for native Canadians and schools for overseas personnel are run by the federal government. While most Canadian schools have adequate facilities for providing children with excellent educational opportunities, some schools in the rural areas are not as well equipped.

The nation's school system employs more than one-quarter million teachers to staff its elementary and secondary schools. Due to a decline in student population since the "baby boom" years of the 1970s, the country enjoys a ratio of about one teacher to eighteen students. The median years of schooling in the country ranges from 10.5 in Newfoundland to 12.3 in British Columbia and Alberta. The national median is 11.8 years.

Nearly 70 percent of the funding for Canadian schools comes from the provincial governments, while about 29 percent of the nation's education budget is provided by municipal budgets. Only 3 percent comes from the federal level. These percentages reflect a dramatic increase in the levels of funding by the provincial governments since the middle of the century. It also reveals an equally substantial decrease by municipal governments during the same time period.

Canada's educational policies are determined through the minister of education in each province. The provincial department of education is responsible for teacher certification and the supervision of teacher competency. Courses of study and textbooks are also approved by that body. These provincial education departments are also responsible for the provision of financial assistance, establishing various educational rules, regulations, and guidelines, and determining the roles and responsibilities of school administrators and teachers.

Local school boards actually operate as quasi-corporations and function under the School Acts and Regulations of each province. These School Acts usually consist of both permissive and compulsory regulations which affect the functioning of the province's schools. As is the situation in many countries, these local boards of education turn over the various educational duties to professional educators who are responsible for seeing that they are carried out.

Private schools in Canada normally are required to comply with provincial regulations. Only a very small percentage of the country's schools are private, and only Alberta, Saskatchewan, and Quebec provide any sort of public financial system to these private sector schools. However, tax support is provided for separate schools with a certain denominational philosophy.

Ministers of education approve the appointment of education officers who might be hired by a local school board. Superintendents are appointed by the department of education in some provinces. However, the most common practice appears to be the hiring of such administrators by the local board of education. The funding for Canada's schools comes from provincial government grants from general revenue sources and from local property taxes. Equalization formulas create a situation where expenditures for the operation of the nation's schools are not related to local wealth or lack of it.

During recent years, Canadian educators have debated a number of issues pertaining to the operation of private schools. While their neighbors to the south have been quite clear about the constitutional separation of church and state on a national level, these national issues have been mostly left up to the provincial governments. For example, the country's Roman Catholic separate school system has been publicly funded in Ontario, Alberta, and Saskatchewan. Moreover, independent or private schools may exist in all the provinces and receive public funding in British Columbia, Alberta, Manitoba, and Quebec.

Another question debated among Canadian educators is the issue of whether the private schools foster elitism. While the issue has often led to a disparity in per-capita income levels of public and private school parents in such countries as the United States, this does not seem to be as true in Canada. In fact, it has been found that when comparing public and private schools in British Columbia, socioeconomic variables, particularly per-capita income levels, were about the same between public and private school parents.

MULTICULTURAL EDUCATION EFFORTS

Compared to many other nations around the world, Canada has fared rather well economically, enabling the country to generate special programs which are sometimes not found in other countries. The province of New Brunswick provides a useful opportunity to examine some of the basic issues of multicultural education efforts. This province has more than 70 microcultures, including native Canadian groups, Greek-Canadians, Jamaican-Canadians, English-Canadians, French-Canadians, Vietnamese-Canadians, Egyptian-Canadians, and Sri Lankan–Canadians. There are two official languages of instruction—French and English.

The language of instruction used in Canadian schools has long been a point of contention. While the province of New Brunswick has no special programs for providing instruction in the students' mother tongue, the French versus English issue has occupied much of the time and energy of Canadian educators. In order to help maintain national unity and to enforce a francophone phenomenon outside of Quebec, the Canadian Parliament passed the Official Languages Act in 1969. However, this attempt to encourage the use of both English and French in the schools did not seem to have any great effect in countering the pressures on French-speaking Canadians to give up their language and culture in predominantly English-speaking parts of the country.

One key issue regarding the language dispute in Canada has been Section 23 of the Canadian Charter of Rights and Freedom which guarantees French- and English-speaking Canadians the right to be educated in their mother tongue. Section 23 of the Charter is worded as follows: "Citizens of Canada whose first language learned and understood is that of the English or French linguistic minority population of the province in which they reside have the right to have their children receive primary and secondary school instruction in that language in that province." During 1982, a group of French-speaking parents in the predominantly English-speaking provinces sued the schools, and their case went all the way to the Canadian Supreme Court which ruled that the francophone parents in Edmonton had the right to manage and control French-speaking schools. Moreover, the schools could be funded with public funds.

It should be noted that French appears to be losing ground in Canada as a "mother tongue." In 1871, 31 percent of Canadians cited French as their "ethnic origin." However, census figures in 1986 disclosed that just 24 percent of all Canadians cited French as their "mother tongue." In fact, the language issue in Canada's schools has become so volatile throughout the years that the country appointed a new language "czar" during 1991. Victor Goldbloom, the new language commissioner, is a Quebec anglophone who has defended the country's bilingual policies. The new commissioner is upset over Quebec's "French only" posture, adopted in the Quebec Bill 178 which banned the use of "English only" commercial signs in 1988.

New Brunswick has no formal procedure for the evaluation of curriculum materials, textbooks, and library holdings for the inclusion of racist/sexist content. Cited in the authors' questionnaire returns as reasons for the lack of such a procedure were a lack of understanding about the importance of including strong multicultural education components in the curriculum and instruction, and inadequate funding which would enable educators to address this issue.

Additional insights into multicultural education in Canada can be acquired by examining the results of a study conducted by the Saskatchewan League of Educational Administrators, Directors, and Superintendents (LEADS) during the 1987–1988 school year. Some of the findings related to the conceptual elements of multicultural education are as follows:

1. Heritage language instruction as part of multicultural education was considered very important by over 70 percent of the respondents.

2. English as a Second Language (ESL) was considered very important or important by nearly 80 percent of the respondents.

3. Native/Métis education was considered very important or important by more than 93 percent of the respondents.

4. Social equity concerns were considered very important or important by 89 percent of the respondents.

5. A multicultural education curriculum was considered very important by over 86 percent of the respondents.

6. Helping students develop an awareness of the similarities and differences of various cultural groups was considered very important or important by nearly 98 percent of the respondents.

7. Helping students develop an awareness of the importance of their own cultural identities was considered very important or important by 96 percent of the respondents.

8. Teaching students about their own community and their cultural groups was considered very important or important by 98 percent of the respondents.

9. Teaching students about human rights and legislation was considered very important or important by 85 percent of the respondents.

10. Teaching students about intercultural and interracial relations was considered very important or important by 97 percent of the respondents.

11. Helping students examine and analyze their own attitudes, biases, and stereotypes was considered very important or important by 93 percent of the respondents.

12. Encouraging minority group members to become assimilated into mainstream society was considered very important or important by only 35 percent of the respondents.

13. Enabling minority group students to participate in mainstream society as they choose was considered very important or important by 87 percent of the respondents.

14. Encouraging minority group students to have a positive self-concept about being different in some ways was considered very important or important by 96 percent of the respondents.

15. Educating all students about the multicultural realities of Canadian society was considered very important or important by 93 percent of the respondents.

16. Promoting an egalitarian, harmonious society in Canada was considered very important or important by 84 percent of the respondents; 10 percent of the respondents viewed it as unimportant.

The study is significant because it shows that multicultural education is a deep interest among the key school administrators in this Canadian province. It would be useful for other studies of this type to be conducted in the other provinces and in other countries as well. At this level, educational policies are controlled by school administrators, and these results show a great deal of enthusiasm for multicultural education programs.

One interesting controversy in Canada pertaining to the multicultural education theme is a dispute over the "mosaic versus the melting pot." Some Canadian writers have argued that when comparing the educational systems of Canada and the United States, it can be seen that Canada subscribes to the "mosaic" philosophy, while the United States has adapted a "melting pot" philosophy. However, it is questionable that one can describe the multicultural milieu in the schools of these two countries in such terms.

It has been argued that, in Canada, each constituent part retains its color, identity, and separation, but at the same time fits into a larger picture which social scientists would refer to as the Canadian macroculture. While the implications of this concept are still being worked out in educational circles, the strength of the philosophy throughout the country stems from the legal adoption of "multiculturalism" as a way of life during the administration of Pierre Trudeau in the late 1960s. This legal action is one of the more unique features of the Canadian educational system, and might serve as a useful model for other nations, particularly its neighbor to the south.

SUMMARY

It can be seen that Canada has made major strides during the past four decades of this century in developing multicultural education programs. Much of the new interest in multicultural education can be attributed to the rapid increase in immigrants during recent years. The rather lax immigration policies have made it possible for immigrants to come to Canada and become citizens in just three years. Presently there is a growing number of Hong Kong residents moving to the country due to the loss of control by the British in 1997. New groups of immigrants include the Hungarians after 1956, Chileans after 1973, the French-speaking Haitians in Montreal, Salvadorans, and Indians who were expelled from Uganda.

But other multicultural education issues have created difficulties for Canadian educators. Like the situation in the United States, native Canadians also have been embroiled in a number of land disputes with the Canadian government. Native Canadians have struggled in the country's schools, and some are now operating their own schools in an attempt to provide a better education for their children.

However, despite these problems, the Canadians can be looked upon as world leaders in the multicultural education movement. Educators around the globe could do much worse than to study the Canadian programs to improve their own educational systems.

REFERENCES

Easton, Stephen. *An Analysis of Elementary, Secondary, and Vocational Schooling.* Vancouver, BC: The Frasier Institute, 1988.

Erickson, T. et al. *Characteristics and Relationships in Public and Independent Schools, COFIS Baseline Survey Interim Report.* British Columbia: Center for Research in Private Education, 1979.

Gayfer, Margaret. *An Overview of Canadian Education.* Toronto: The Canadian Education Association, 1974.

Goldbloom, Victor. "The New Language Czar." *Macleans* (July 8, 1991).

Katz, Joseph. *Society, Schools, and Progress.* Oxford: Permagon Press, 1969.

Kindler, Anna M. "Children and the Culture of a Multicultural Society." *Art Education,* Vol. 47, No. 4 (July 1994), pp. 54–60.

Kuehn, Larry. "Education vs. Melting Pot." *School Policy* (Summer 1992), pp. 65–68.

Legge, Eric. "Beyond Two Languages." *Macleans* (April 22, 1991).

Lingard, John. "Multicultural Education: Perception and Implementation at the School Division Level in Saskatchewan." Unpublished Paper, Saskatoon, Saskatchewan, 1987.

McConaghy, Tom. "French Education Rights Upheld by Supreme Court." *Phi Delta Kappan* (October 1990).

Mitchell, Bruce and Salsbury, Robert. *An International Survey of Multicultural Education.* Cheney, WA: Western States Consulting and Evaluation Services, 1991. (See Appendix.)

Wilkinson, Bruce W. "Elementary and Secondary Education Policy in Canada." *A Survey, Canadian Public Policy* (December 1986).

9

China

HISTORY OF THE SYSTEM

In examining the Chinese educational system, it is necessary to analyze the work of Confucius as a starting point. His influence permeates the entire educational system of the country. Confucius died in 479 B.C. While he lived, he established his famous school at Lu, which is now the Chinese city of Qufu in Shandong Province. Confucius opened his private school when he was about 30 years old, and his educational philosophy consisted of five primary elements: (1) to train young people who are loyal to the government; (2) that education was utilitarian in the sense that it aided those in power at a particular time in history; (3) the curriculum content consisted of "the classics," and students must master these classics; (4) the success of endeavors should always be measured in terms of "mastery of the classics for utilitarian purposes"; and (5) the measurement standard for judging the skill in "classical techniques" was the ability to draw analogies from sacred sayings of the classical texts.

Twenty years later, Confucius entered the government of Lu and soon became the minister who was responsible for the public security of the kingdom. Ultimately he was forced into exile for a period of fourteen years; he was 68 years old at the time. Prior to his death, he enjoyed a five-year period during which his private school prospered. By this time, some of his students had become involved in government, and Confucius felt that these highly regarded disciples had not allowed him to interfere in governmental issues.

Among the works of Confucius were the *Four Books,* which were viewed as vessels for the systematic transmission of his ideas. However, these works only represent the ideas and work during the final years of his life.

Confucius believed that there were just two types of people: the superior person (junzi) and the ordinary person (xiaoren). During his later years of teaching, he argued that people must become superior Confucians and not just ordinary ones. He argued that the concept of the ordinary person related not only to the social class but also to social class (chusen) and character.

Confucius's students represented all socio-economic echelons of Chinese society. However, tuition fees were a pre-condition for study, and he reserved the right to choose the students who would study with him. One of the essential elements of his educational philosophy was ritual. His notion of ritualistic learning was that through this process one could create superior individuals who also could perform rituals. Thus, this became the central thrust of his school curriculum. He insisted that his pupils not only master the inner cultivation in accordance with the rituals, but they also outwardly express their words and action in keeping with the ritual. It was thought that this combination of nature and culture made the superior person (weenzhi binbin ranhou junzi).

During this time in China's history, schooling procedures generally involved strict regulations, corporal punishment, and rigid compliance with the rules and regulations of the schools. There was much emphasis on rote learning. One reason that Confucius became so popular was that he made major reforms in existing teaching methods because of his interest in developing "superior persons."

The Confucian ethic was primarily humanistic, and individuals were expected to develop to their fullest potential in order to serve their communities more effectively. Thus, the function of education in China has been to serve the needs of society as a whole rather than to enhance the growth of the individual for the sake of a single person.

Beginning in the twentieth century, Chinese students who had gone abroad to study in the United States, Europe, and Japan had started to return home. Many of them were interested in replacing the Confucian ethic with some elements of Western culture and political thought. About the same time, Sun Yat-Sen, a Western-trained doctor, organized a movement which was designed to overthrow the Ch'ing Dynasty. One of the goals of this movement was to promote policies of national strength.

Between 1906 and 1922, students returning from Japan helped to reform the Chinese educational system, bringing about separate schools for academic, pedagogical, vocational, and technical education. However, by 1922, Chinese interest in the Japanese educational system was replaced by a fascination with the merging educational influences in the United States. At this time, the Chinese educational system was restructured, using many of the basic concepts employed in the United States. Primary education would be of six years duration, and middle school would consist of two three-year segments.

During 1924, the Kuomintang (KMT) was reorganized along Soviet lines of 1924. By 1927, the KMT military forces, which were then led by Chiang Kai-shek, embarked on the Northern Expedition which defeated the warlords, enabling the party to maintain its control over the country's educational enterprises. The greatest span of the KMT's influence was during 1927–1937. During this period of time, Western education influences peaked in the country. This created an emphasis on higher education, a concentration on science and technology, and an increasing use of foreign ideas in the curriculum.

The communist takeover in the country created enormous changes in China's educational system after 1949. The new Marxist movement stressed socio-economic change, resulting in a temporary sacrificing of egalitarian social goals in favor of a developing economy. This caused a reorganization of the higher educational system along the order of the Russian system, Chairman Mao Tse-tung's Cultural Revolution, and a modernization program stressing the study of science and technology after Mao's death in 1976. China's first Five-Year Plan (1953–1957) resulted in the creation of a number of key elementary and secondary schools which had superior facilities and outstanding students and teachers in an attempt to upgrade the level of science instruction in the schools. While these schools were deemed to be quite successful at first, they were closed down in 1966 when they were portrayed as elitist institutions by various proponents of China's cultural revolution. Moreover, it was argued that they tended to promote ideals which did not coincide with the basic tenets of communism.

However, after the demise of the "Gang of Four," the key schools plan was revived when Deng Xiaoping argued for the need to further develop the country's high-ability students to their fullest potential. During 1978, the Ministry of Education published a document which argued that the re-establishment of the key schools was an absolute necessity. These efforts by the Ministry resulted in the creation of 20 new elementary and secondary schools which were operated by the Ministry itself. Ordinary schools could become key schools as long as they produced a substantial number of students as measured by their scores on examinations. Consequently, the Chinese schools became more competitive.

STRUCTURE OF THE SYSTEM

After the end of the "Gang of Four" influence, China faced a major teacher shortage which threatened to hinder their attempts at modernization and teacher reform. Because of these shortages, China has been forced to utilize the services of teachers who sometimes did not fully meet the preparation requirements.

During recent years, the country has also found itself in the midst of major structural changes which have affected students, teachers, and principals. Designed to correct past problems resulting from rigid bureaucracy, central decision making, and inefficient management, these changes have resulted in a number of interesting changes in the Chinese educational system.

Currently, schools in China tend to be selective, characterized by a uniform curriculum for all students, driven by the nation's testing program, and heavily influenced by social and political issues. At the national level, there has been an emphasis on expanding the curriculum to include vocational education in order to meet the new demands of international economic competition.

The funding of the education enterprise increased during the late 1980s when it increased from 2.51 percent of the gross national product, which was well below the 4 percent average which was found in developing countries around the world.

Presently, decisions made by the nation's school principals do not require the approval of other agencies, in contrast to previous years. It is no longer necessary to consult ideological units about some financial issues, hiring practices, admission policies, or teacher assignments.

China has struggled historically with the education of its children who dwell in the more rural parts of the country. However, one of the characteristics of the recent reforms in the country's educational system has been the attempt to improve education in the rural portions of the country. The good news has been that from 1985 to 1989, the average education level increased 7.7 percent to 6.03 years. At the same time, the illiteracy rate dropped.

One characteristic of the country's primary school system is the 1981 version of the ''Rules for Primary School'' pupils. The list reads as follows:

1. Ardently love the motherland, the people, and the Chinese Communist Party. Study well and make progress every day.

2. Go to school according to schedule and don't miss classes without reason. Give undivided attention to the lessons; earnestly complete tests.

3. Persist in physical exercise; actively take part in extracurricular activities.

4. Pay attention to hygiene; be neatly dressed and clean; don't spit everywhere.

5. Ardently love labor; do yourself what you are capable of doing.

6. Lead a thrifty and simple life; use grain sparingly; don't be fussy about food or clothing; don't indiscriminately spend money.

7. Observe school discipline; observe public order.

8. Respect the teacher; unite with classmates; be courteous to people; do not swear or fight.

9. Be concerned for the collective; protect public property; hand over to the state things you pick up.

10. Be honest and courageous; don't tell lies; if you have faults, correct them.

The curriculum of the schools reflects the country's attitudes toward patriotism and the Communist party. Textbooks used in the schools have a decided socialistic slant. The following story is an example of the kind of writing which could be found in a Chinese textbook.

Not All Orphans Suffer the Same Fate

Six years ago, in Shandong, Tai'an County, Manzhuang Gongshe Beixiao Brigade, the father and mother of brother and sister Li Zhangshan died one after the other. The children became orphans. Immediately, the brigade provided them with relief grain, and relief money. The brother and sister felt indescribably happy. The previous year when Li Zhangshan had become ill, uncle and auntie had taken them to the hospital and been charged more than 100 yuan for medicine, the brigade paid everything. In the summer, one time when it was raining, the Party secretary came to them, saw their house was leaking, immediately cleared out two storerooms and let them move there to live. Winter had still not arrived when the brigade also gave them new padded clothes and a new quilt. At the spring festival the pair wore the new clothes, ate *jiaozi,* and played happily with their little friends in the village.

But in capitalist countries rich people only look after their own pleasures, basically do not take care of their children, and the fate of orphans is really miserable. In France there was a two-year-old child with five cigarette burns on his body and twenty bite wounds. He was bleeding from twenty places and swollen. Why had he suffered like this? It turned out he was an orphan with no one to take care of him.

Finally, it is important to note the emphasis on early childhood education which has been occurring during recent years. Generally, pre-school programs meet the needs of three- to six-year-old students. The programs are child-centered, and involve a great deal of ''let's pretend'' play to stimulate the development of the imagination. Some of these programs are actually boarding kindergartens which date back to the 1950s when they were highly influenced by the Soviets. Children live at the school for six days a week, staying home from Saturday night until Sunday night or Monday morning. Free medical care is provided at the school.

MULTICULTURAL EDUCATION EFFORTS

While no specific funding for multicultural education programs exists within the Ministry of Education, China does have an office for the promotion of minority affairs with the Ministry of Education. In the schools, students take a high school course which provides them with information about the different minority cultures which reside in the country. Also, the failure of the ''Great Leap Forward'' and the split with the Soviet Union created a period of difficulty for the nation's minorities. The official language of instruction is Han, the language of the dominant culture in China.

The major goal of Chinese educational policy is for national minorities to become assimilated into the dominant (Han) culture, but substantial gaps exist between the educational achievements of the Han majority group and the various minority microcultures. For example, as of 1982, only 85 percent of the minority-group children completed their primary education and the figure dropped to 70 percent at the high school level.

Modern China has five official religions, including Buddhism and Taoism, deemed the native religions of the country. Newer religions include two forms of Christianity (''Protestantism'' and Catholicism) and Islam. While Marxist ideology has deemed none of these to be desirable, they have nonetheless been tolerated. In addition to these five religious factions, an ethnic minority within the country is the Chinese Jews around the ancient city of Kaifeng (Henan). Other ethnic minorities include the Uighur (Central Asian Turkic) and Tibetans.

In spite of these factions, however, little is being done in the school curriculum to address the various problems of pluralism in China, and no formal multicultural education programs seem to be in place.

However, the country has created some changes in its educational policies toward minorities. Primary schools and adult education programs have been crafted in hopes of raising the cultural standards of the population. Ma Xulun noted that there were several main requirements for minority education: (1) it must be scientific, popular, and reflect the characteristics of the nationalities; (2) special departments must be established, and leadership must be nurtured in the field of minority education, and teacher education must be improved; (3) political education programs must nurture equality, unity, fraternity, and cooperation among nationalities, and preserve the minority cultures; (4) the curriculum must be modified to meet local conditions; (5) indigenous languages should be used in the schools; and (6) the People's Government must make appropriate monetary appropriations for special educational programs.

SUMMARY

Even though China's questionnaire responses in the authors' original study did not specify a strong multicultural education program, it is interesting to note that education for minority students consists of legitimate efforts to address many of the multicultural issues which were articulated in the survey instruments which were used in the study. Minority education has been viewed as a critical part of the Chinese educational system. However, in spite of the attempts to provide a better education for minority students, a rather substantial gap still seems to exist when one attempts to compare the education of minorities and the Han majority group.

REFERENCES

Ching, Julia. *Probing China's Soul.* San Francisco, CA: Harper and Row, 1990.

Delaney, Brian and Paine, Lynn. "Shifting Patterns of Authority in Chinese Schools." *Comparative Education Review* (February 1991), p. 33.

Gardner, Howard. *To Open Minds: Chinese Clues to the Dilemma of Contemporary Education.* New York: Basic Books, 1989.

Gonen, Amiram. *The Encyclopedia of the Peoples of the World.* New York: Henry Holt Publishing Co., 1993.

Jiaoyu, Zhongguo. *Beijing: Chinese Education Yearbook,* 1984, vol. 1.

Jinfang, Qian and Kexiao, Huang. "On the Contemporary Reform of Secondary Education in the Eighties." *Canadian and International Education,* Vol. 16, No. 1 (1987), pp. 86–102.

Mayhoe, Ruth (Ed.). *Education and Modernization: The Chinese Experience.* Oxford: Pergamon Press, 1984.

Price, R.F. *Chinese Intellectuals and the West.* London: Oxford University Press, 1970.

Rosen, Stanley. "Editor's Introduction." *Chinese Education,* Vol. XVII, No. 2 (1984).

Smerling, Louis. "Admissions." In Jay Henderson and Ronald N. Montaperto (Eds.), *China's Schools in Flux.* White Plains, NY: M.E. Sharpe, 1979.

Taylor, Robert. *China's Intellectual Dilemma.* Vancouver: University of British Columbia Press, 1981.

Wang, Y.C. *Chinese Intellectuals and the West, 1872–1949.* Chapel Hill: University of North Carolina Press, 1966.

Ximin, Pan. "A Preliminary Discussion of Problems Involving Several Aspects of Key Schools." *Chinese Education,* ed. and trans. Stanley Rosen, Vol. XVII, No. 2 (1984).

Zhongguo, Xingzheng. "Should a Government Be 'Large' or 'Small?' " *Beijing Review* (April 8–14, 1991).

10

Colombia

HISTORY OF THE SYSTEM

Some historians are convinced that aboriginal groups first settled in present-day Colombia as early as 20,000 B.C. It is reasonably well documented that Mesoamericans arrived about 1200 B.C. and introduced the cultivation of corn. A second wave of Mesoamericans reached the same area in about 500 B.C. Then, between 400 and 300 B.C., the Chibchas traveled from Nicaragua and Honduras and reached Colombia just before the Arawaks commenced migrating from coastal South America to the Caribbean. Finally, near the end of the first millennium A.D., the Caribs arrived in the Caribbean Islands.

By the 1500s, the Chibchas and the Tairona arrived in the area. They were considered to be quite advanced culturally. These were the indigenous Colombian groups who encountered the European Conquistadors when they first made their incursions into Colombia. Figuring prominently in expeditions to the Colombian interior were Gonzalo Jimenez de Quesada and Nikolaus Federmann, and Sebastian de Belazcar. In 1536 Jimenez de Quesada went on an expedition to see if he could find a route to Peru. On the trip he founded present-day Bogota. This and other expeditions played a significant role on the future development of the country.

The colonial period in Colombia occurred from about 1550 to 1810. Historians have referred to this time in history as a period of social stratification. At the top of the pyramid were the elites who were referred to as the Peninsulares; they were Spaniards who were born in Spain but they opted to settle in Colombia. Next came the Criollos, Spaniards who were born in the colonies. The mestizos (mixed Indian and Spanish blood) came next, while the African-Colombian slaves (zambos) were considered to be at the bottom of the social ladder.

The colonial economy was structured so as to take advantage of the cheap native labor. However, the Spaniards came to Colombia and the rest of South America in search of quick wealth in the form of precious metals and jewels. Consequently, gold and copper mining became the backbone of the country's economy. However, by the end of the 1700s, sugar and tobacco had become important exports and agriculture acquired a greater level of importance.

By 1812, individual provinces in Colombia began to declare their independence as the Spanish empire found it more and more difficult to sustain itself. Finally, in 1919, a republic was formed known as Gran Colombia, and Simon Bolivar became its first president. However, this alliance crumbled and throughout its history, unlike other South American countries, Colombia was able to enjoy a relatively long history of civilian rule. The most recent military rule occurred in 1953 when General Gustavo Rojas Pinilla overthrew a conservative government which was not able to quell major incidences of rural violence. The level of confrontation between liberals and conservatives abated between 1958 and 1974 due to the National Front agreement to share the power between these two factions.

STRUCTURE OF THE SYSTEM

Colombia has had central direction of education through their ministry of education during most of the twentieth century. It has been the responsibility of this office to direct the various functions of the nation's educational system. During the second quarter of this century, both liberals and conservatives defended elite class interests by nurturing an educational system which professed to help students advance socially through education, but in actuality severely limited the opportunities for social advancement by the underclass. Consequently, this has had the effect of promoting the interests of the elite class.

There is a faulty distinction between public and private schools because the secondary schools have not been free and often were run by clerics. Moreover, the funding for public schools has been insufficient, creating a perfect climate for a private school system which has served the educational needs of elite students.

An example of such an educational enterprise is a school for able learners, sponsored by the Rotary International of Baranquilla through the Humbolt Foundation. The school is for children between the ages of nine and eleven and one-half. Most of the participants are from affluent families.

Throughout the country, the educational patterns have been dictated by the Ministry of Education. So not only do class differences exist throughout the land, but regional ones are also in evidence. During the middle of this century, urban schools tended to grow dramatically as peasants migrated to the cities. This phenomenon was responsible for a proliferation of upper-class students in private schools, while the public school student population became gradually poorer.

In Columbia, the middle class has been relatively small and never has been powerful. In fact, it is only a recent entity in Colombian society. Persons in the new middle class have arrived at that station of life through education. Most of them tend to live in the more urban areas of the country. Even though they have started to become politically active, their small numbers have not allowed them to become a major voice in decision-making processes.

The great majority of the people are from low socio-economic classes, and the country has always had a relatively low literacy rate. The upper classes have represented about 5 percent of the country's population. They have tended to be a rather closed group which has generally sustained itself through birth and intermarriage.

During the country's history, ministers of education often were selected by virtue of political factors rather than their professional expertise. Consequently, during the critical mid-portion of this century, program continuity was often a problem. In fact, in one four-year presidential period, as many as eight different ministers of education have served.

Ministers of education in Colombia are the major administrative authorities for all levels of education. The ministry exercises control over private and public schools in both the private and public sectors, including the school system of the Catholic Church, which is extremely influential. There are also secretaries of education in each of the nation's 23 states. Appointed by the governor of each state, they come under the jurisdiction of the nation's Ministry of Education.

Providing funding and the establishment of needed new schools is the responsibility of state legislatures. However, the Ministry of Education must determine the types of curricula, minimum course requirements, the school calendar, and qualifications for teachers. Another responsibility of the Ministry of Education is to inspect both public and private schools for compliance with national laws and decrees.

All institutions from primary through higher education (with the exception of the university level) operate under one of the nation's educational calendars. School is in session for 198 days per year, and all students receive one week's vacation during Easter.

Kindergartens in Colombia are available for children from ages four to six. Most of them are free schools which are under the control of the state governments; however, they also receive assistance from the Ministry of Education.

Most of the classes are self-contained and the teachers spend about six hours per day working with the students. Grades are based on a five-point scale, and a grade of 3 (a C) must be attained to pass a course.

School attendance in the country is compulsory for the first five years of primary school. However, only about 75 percent of the children actually enter school, and only about one-third of this group actually finishes the primary schooling process.

Higher education institutions, for the most part, have been modeled after the European universities which were prevalent in the countries of the Spanish-

Colombians who migrated to the country from Europe. Colombian universities have a long history—the oldest one is Santo Tomas, founded in 1573 in Bogota. Entry to any type of higher education program is predicated on students' scores on state examinations administered through the National Testing Service.

MULTICULTURAL EDUCATION EFFORTS

Colombia does have a program for multicultural education with an office in the Ministry of Education. Although modestly funded ($37,000 U.S. during 1987), leadership in specific multicultural programs is provided. There are nearly half a million indigenous people represented by 80 ethnic groups speaking 60 different languages. Teachers in special multicultural programs require certification, and the curriculum stresses a cultural pluralistic approach rather than an assimilationist model. Although Spanish is the official language of instruction, there are a number of bilingual instruction programs throughout the country. Students attend racially integrated schools, and the history of indigenous people is part of the regular curriculum. The Ministry of Education provides no screening of curriculum, texts, or library materials for sexism or racism. A 1982 document entitled "General Limitations of Indigenous Education" outlined a policy of intercultural education.

Even though 95 percent of the Colombian population considers itself to be Roman Catholic, the Colombian constitution guarantees religious freedom to all people in the land. Throughout the history of Colombia, the Catholic Church has made its influence felt in a number of ways. During the time of the Spanish colonization of America, the Vatican and the king of Spain agreed to put the Church under the authority of the king of Spain. Consequently, the government and the Church mutually supported each other in the colonies.

Missionaries also played a major role in the historical development of the country. However, in 1767 the Jesuits were expelled from Latin American by King Charles III because of their increasing influence and also because their allegiance to the Pope superseded their allegiance to the throne. Finally, in 1853, Colombia became the very first Latin American country to pass legislation which separated church from state. Finally, in 1973, Catholicism was no longer an official state religion.

The role of women in the educational system has also been a difficult problem for the country. Until 1933 they were unable to enroll in higher education institutions. In fact, the Church took the position that women should be relegated to domestic roles. However, the situation has changed rather dramatically during the past two decades. The proportion of female university students has improved significantly.

In the 1970s, Colombian ethnic groups began a series of efforts to become citizens, with all the rights and responsibilities enjoyed by the nation's power structure. In responding to the demands of these seventeen groups which represented the various indigenous factions, the Minister of Education addressed the issues in Decree #1142. Influenced somewhat by the American Civil Rights Movement, Colombian ethnics sought to improve their quality of life through equal rights, better education, and full participation in the Colombian political system. Decree #1142, issued in 1978, recognized the plurality of Colombian peoples and established the right of indigenous communities to have an education that was in keeping with their interests, characteristics, and requirements for program implementation.

SUMMARY

Colombia has experienced rather dramatic changes in its multicultural education efforts during the last three quarters of the twentieth century. Most significant and quite encouraging have been the recent attempts to change the educational offerings for indigenous groups. Including the history of such populations in the school curriculum has heightened the national awareness of the country's original residents and has helped all students acquire a more comprehensive view of the country's history.

The nation also has been making significant improvement in its attempts to establish new programs which address gender issues more extensively. In comparison with other countries, Colombia has been forced to deal with rather severe economic problems, which has made it somewhat difficult to address specific issues such as multicultrual education.

Thus, it is extremely encouraging that Colombia has seen fit to establish a multicultural education program through its Ministry of Education. Moreover, Colombian schools have adopted a pluralistic approach to instruction as opposed to a more assimilationist posture. Trying to deal effectively with an indigenous population of 80 ethnic groups speaking 60 different languages has created an enormous pressure on the country's educational infrastructure, and Colombia has responded to the challenge with verve and imagination.

REFERENCES

Bethell, Leslie (Ed.). *The Cambridge History of Latin America.* Cambridge: Cambridge University Press, 1991.

Hanratty, Dennis M. and Meditz, Sandra W. (Eds.). *Colombia, A Country Study.* Washington, DC: Department of the Army, 1990.

Helg, Aline. *La educacion en Colombia, 1918–1957: Una historia social, economica y politica.* Bogota: Fondo Editorial CEREC, 1987.

Lucio, Ricardo and Serrano, Mariana. "The State and Higher Education in Colombia." *Higher Education,* Vol. 25, No. 1 (January 1993), pp. 61–72.

Mitchell, Bruce and Salsbury, Robert. *An International Survey of Multicultural Education.* Cheney, WA: Western States Consulting and Evaluation Services, 1991. (See Appendix.)

Psacharopoulos, George and Velez, Eduardo. "Schooling, Ability, and Earnings in Colombia, 1988.'' In *Economic Development and Cultural Change*. Chicago: University of Chicago Press, 1992.

Wellington, Stanley. *Colombia: A Study of the Educational System of Colombia and a Guide to the Academic Placement of Students from Colombia in Educational Institutions of the United States*. Stockton, CA: National Council on the Evaluation of Foreign Education Credentials, 1984.

11

Cuba

HISTORY OF THE SYSTEM

From the best available evidence, Columbus was one of the first Europeans to hear the name "Cuba" when local Indians spoke of that large island. Believing it to be a legendary place known as Cipango, flowing with precious minerals and spices, he finally named the island Juana, in honor of the prince Don Juan, son of Isabella of Castille and her husband, Ferdinand of Aragon. Columbus was extremely impressed with what he saw on the island. However, it was not colonized until later. Originally, it was inhabited by three main groups of aborigines, including the Ciboneys, the Guanahacabibes, and the Tainos. The Ciboneys and Guanahacabibes were nomads, hunters, and fishermen. Although the Tainos were more advanced culturally than the other two groups, they had not advanced as much as the native groups in Peru and other Central/South American regions.

After the island was explored and captured by the Spaniards, there was an interest in gold seeking, and the artisans, tradespersons, and planters thought they could make a good living because of the large number of miners who were in need of such services. However, the gold fields were not particularly extensive and they actually played out in about 1535. By 1820, the Cuban people learned of the uprisings in Spain against Ferdinand's despotic rule, and a new atmosphere for freedom began to emerge in the country.

Part of Cuba's history is a history of slavery. As the agricultural pursuits became more prominent throughout the country, African slaves were imported to be used as a primary source of cheap labor, particularly in the tobacco and sugar cane industries. They were imported from West Africa and, according to the census of 1791–1792, Cuba's population consisted of 96,440 Whites, 31,847 free African-Cubans, and 44,333 African slaves. (At the time, "Whites" included Spaniards and the indigenous groups.)

The Spanish-American War in 1898 resulted in Cuba becoming independent from Spain. By 1901, the country had drafted a new constitution which provided for universal suffrage, separation of church and state, a popularly elected president who could be re-elected for a second term, and a fairly weak senate and chamber of deputies. In 1952, Fulgencio Batista overthrew President Carlos Prio's regime in a bloodless coup; but by 1959, the leadership of the country changed hands again with the dramatic revolutionary victory of Fidel Castro.

STRUCTURE OF THE SYSTEM

An examination of Cuba's educational system requires one to consider the dramatic changes due to the Cuban revolution under Castro. During the pre-revolutionary years under Batista's regime, there was a general lack of strong leadership in the nation's education program. In fact, there was also widespread corruption and structural obstacles which were problems for Cuban education. Before the revolution, nearly 24 percent of the population couldn't read or write, and there were about 1.03 million illiterate adults.

The regional differences also constituted major problems for the country's educational system. While the illiteracy rate in Havana Province was just a bit over 9 percent in 1953, the poorer and underdeveloped provinces of Oriente, Pinar del Rio, and Camaguey averaged about 31 percent. Moreover, just prior to the Cuban Revolution, half of all primary-age Cuban children had no education, and the overall Latin American average was 36 percent. Also, less than half of the needed classrooms in the country were available.

Batista's educational policies seemed to negate education as a vehicle for social mobility. For example, in 1953, 52 percent of Cubans had not gone beyond the third grade. Moreover, fewer than 1 percent of the population had four years of higher education.

The revolutionary army of Cuba took over Havana on New Year's day, 1959. The conquering body viewed education as a critical vehicle for creating economic and political mechanisms which would nurture the new socialistic system. Post-revolutionary Cuban reforms stressed the mobilization of the people into productive activities and helped citizens acquire the ideological framework being espoused by the new regime. One of the new education strands was an all-out war against illiteracy. Fidel Castro, in his famous 1960 speech to the United Nations, announced that his country would reach the goal of establishing a totally literate society. He wanted Cuba to become the first nation in the Americas to become completely literate. During 1961, an enormous fleet of literacy workers attacked the problem. Nearly one million Cuban people were involved in the effort to help all Cubans learn to read at a minimum first grade level.

Included in the huge cadre of teachers and tutors were 100,000 "Conrado Benitez Brigadistas." These people were mainly young volunteers who were quickly trained and served mainly in the more rural sections of the country. A second large group consisted mostly of adults who served in the urban areas.

In this manner, many were able to keep their jobs and serve as reading tutors in their spare time.

That the literacy campaign was closely allied with the revolution can be seen from this quote by Richard Fagen:

Our campaign has put the youth of Cuba in direct contact, on a daily and prolonged basis (almost a year), with the peasants and mountain folk, the poorest and most isolated people on the island. Thus, almost 100,000 scholars and students, aided by more than 170,000 adult volunteers, produced a very real growth of national fusion. This extensive experience in communal life cannot but greatly increase understanding among the classes and strata of the population. But in our view there is something more; during the campaign, the entire populace could participate in the tasks of the revolution. The revolution was no longer a phenomenon reserved for a small group, zealous and active; it was converted into a true mass movement. (Fagen, 1964, pp. 12–13)

The formal program of reading instruction was based on a number of consistent steps which were to be followed by the reading instructors:

First Step: CONVERSATION

Conversation between the brigadista and the pupil in regard to the photograph in the primer . . .

(a) To find out what the pupil knows about the subject of the photo.

(b) To provide oral expression.

(c) To clarify the concepts.

Second Step: THE READING

A complete reading of the text (block letters) that appears beside the photo:

(a) First, by the teacher: slow and clear.

(b) Second, by the teacher and the pupil at the same time.

(c) Third, by the pupil all alone.

Third Step: PRACTICE AND EXERCISE

(a) Recognition of a phrase or sentence that has been selected . . .

(b) Breakup of that phrase or sentence into syllables.

(c) Examination of each syllable within an exercise.

The methodology contained unmistakable political bias as can be seen from the following quotes by Jonathon Kozol in the same primer:

"The campesinos now at last are owners of the land."

"The campesinos cultivate the land."

"The Cuban land is rich."

Later in the book, the sentences become longer with more sophisticated syntax.

"The campesino buys his needs both good and cheap within the people's store."
"In the people's store there are all kinds of things."
"The people's store is a cooperative too."
"We now have more than 2,000 people's stores."

As can be seen quite clearly, the Great Campaign (to establish a literate society) involved much more than pedagogy alone. For many members of the group, it was an education in political and moral issues which coincided with the Castro version of Marxist dogma.

During the revolution, private schools were nationalized—a practice which was declared to be unconstitutional in the United States as a result of the famous Kalamazoo case. At this time, education became free and compulsory. Elementary school enrollment jumped from 717,000 in 1959 to 1,666,267 in 1961. The primary school year was increased to 1,080 hours in urban communities, and 900 in the rural sections of the country. During this same time frame, the number of teachers increased from 17,355 to 33,916. Secondary schools experienced an enrollment growth of more than 60,000 students. The number of secondary teachers grew from 5,120 to 8,620.

Fidel Castro believed that the most important facet of education was the political education of the people. Moreover, he believed that education and revolution were the same thing.

Cuba's literacy campaign yielded impressive results. At the beginning of 1961, it was estimated that the official illiteracy rate was 21 percent. By December 22, 1961 (the end of the literacy campaign), the illiteracy rate was reported to be just less than 4 percent. However, it should be pointed out that "literacy" was defined as reading competence at only the first-grade level, which is the lowest definitive level in Latin America.

Polytechnic education was introduced to the Cuban system in 1965 as part of a Marxist philosophy which stressed the importance of students doing work which was educational, productive, and of some social value. The primary goal of Cuban education has been to upgrade the productive power of young people. The intent was to help young people grow up thinking of themselves as producers rather than as only consumers of goods.

Cuba is still spending millions of dollars in health care and education for revolutionaries, so one of the nation's education missions has extended beyond the usual function of many ministries of education. At a time when leftist regimes the world over have been falling, Cuba still clings to its Marxist principles, and its educational enterprises reflect this phenomenon.

MULTICULTURAL EDUCATION EFFORTS

According to Cuba's Ministry of Education, there are no specific multicultural education programs in the land. On the contrary, such programs are built into the regular curriculum units utilized in the schools. Moreover, there is no special funding from the Ministry of Education for such efforts. The educational approach tends to emphasize an assimilationist approach, although egalitarian principles guide the nation's educational system.

There are no cultural pluralism strands in the teacher preparation sequences, and the official language of instruction is Spanish. No other languages of instruction are provided since Cuba is a monocultural society. The Ministry of Education is responsible for ensuring that all textbooks and teaching materials are evaluated for racist/sexist content. The history of present inhabitants is studied, but the indigenous population is not dealt with in the curriculum.

In looking at Cuba's multicultural education efforts, it is necessary to examine the national efforts to move from racism to equality. The country has made noble efforts to alter the pattern of relationships between people of differing racial origins. According to Cole, the racial prejudices which still exist in Cuba will eventually cease, due to the efforts of education. But the elimination of racism requires the integral participation of all people through a process of revolution. However, as encouraging as it sounds, it would appear that without the special funding for multicultural education through the Ministry of Education, it could be difficult for this to occur.

SUMMARY

Cuba is unique. As one of the few Marxist systems left in the world, the educational community still subscribes to a philosophy which requires the sort of educational approaches commonly employed throughout the world.

The emphasis on literacy has become a crucial benchmark. Indeed, the Cuban strategy has become a kind of role model for other developing nations to emulate. The loss of valuable financial aid from the USSR has recently created a great fiscal strain on the educational infrastructure.

REFERENCES

Carnoy, Martin and Werthein, Jorge. *Cuba's Economic Change & Educational Reform.* Washington, DC: World Bank, 1979.

Cole, Johnetta. "Race Toward Equality: The Impact of the Cuban Revolution on Racism." *The Black Scholar* (November/December 1980).

Comision Economica para America Latina (CEPAL). *La evolucion de America,* 1980.

Fagen, Richard. *Cuba: The Political Content of Adult Education.* Stanford, CA: Hoover Institution, 1964.

Foner, Philip S. *A History of Cuba.* New York: International Publishers, 1962.

Gonen, Amiram. *The Encyclopedia of the Peoples of the World.* New York: Henry Holt Publishing Co., 1993.

Kozol, Jonathon. *Children of the Revolution.* New York: Delacorte Press, 1978.

Mitchell, Bruce and Salsbury, Robert. *An International Survey of Multicultural Educa-*

tion. Cheney, WA: Western States Consulting and Evaluation Services, 1991. (See Appendix.)

Mtonga, H.L. ''Comparing the Role of Education in Serving Socioeconomic and Political Development in Tanzania and Cuba.'' *Journal of Black Studies,* Vol. 23, No. 3 (1994), pp. 382–402.

UNESCO. *Metodos y medios utilizados en Cuba para la superacion del analfabetismo.* Havana: Editora Pedogogica, 1965.

United Nations. *Compendium of Social Statistics.* New York: United Nations, 1963.

United Nations. *Official Records of the General Assembly, Fifteenth Session, Part 1,* Plenary Meetings, Vol. 3, Verbatim Records, New York (September–October 17, 1960).

U.S. News and World Report (June 1, 1992).

Valdez, Nelson. *The Cuban Revolution: A Research Study Guide (1959–1969).* Albuquerque: University of New Mexico Press, 1971.

12

Egypt

HISTORY OF THE SYSTEM

When discussing Egypt, it is necessary to go back about 6,000 years and examine the nature of life on the shores of the Nile. One of the most significant incidents in the country's history was the unification of the upper and lower Nile people which occurred some time during the third millennium B.C. These ancient peoples were among the first known groups of humans to believe in life after death. They were also able to use stone in construction and to erect arches made out of brick and stone. The Egyptians were also excellent sailors and shipbuilders. In learning how to predict floods on the Nile, they became adept at charting the skies, and have been referred to as the first astronomers. In fact, Egypt's history is recorded in stone, and much of it has been understood through the analysis of pyramids and rock tombs.

People first began to settle along the banks of the Nile from 6000 to 2686 B.C., during the first and second dynasties. During this period of time, people in the area were developing the first religion, language, and social institutions which made it become one of the oldest organized societies. Throughout the history of the country, a bond has existed between the Nile River and the residents. Indeed, the Nile has been responsible for the fertile silts which have allowed the people to develop one of the world's earliest agriculture economies.

During an 1,100-year period from 2686 to 1552 B.C., two major "kingdoms" and one "period" came and went. The Old Kingdom and Middle Kingdom were times of unification and rather strong central government. The political and economic systems were based on the notion of an incarnate god who was able to control the Nile floods for the good of the country. The Middle Kingdom ended with the conquest of Egypt by the Hyksos, known as the Shepherd Kings. During this time, the first pyramid was erected, consisting of over two million blocks of limestone which weighed up to fifteen tons each.

Around 1552 B.C., the period referred to as the New Kingdom commenced, lasting until about 664 B.C. During this time, Egypt reached the peak of its influence and acquired the most extensive territories up to then. The government became a military state and was ruled by a pharaoh and a prime minister. During this era, there was a new movement toward the creation of many elaborate tombs for the pharaohs and the upper classes. Perhaps the most famous is the tomb of Tutankhamen, who ruled between 1347 and 1337 B.C. These tombs have proven to be invaluable to the work of historians who were able to provide the world with an understanding of the brilliant art and amazing skills of the artisans.

During the Late Period (664–323 B.C.), Egypt was able to effectively maintain its status as a centralized state. However, from 525 to 323 B.C., a Persian invasion force dethroned the last pharaoh, and Egypt became a Persian province until 335 B.C. when the Persian occupation of the country ended with their defeat at the hands of Alexander the Great in the Battle of Issus. The Egyptians looked upon Alexander's victory with great delight, since they despised the Persians and resented being ruled by their forces. However, Alexander died just twelve years later in 323 B.C., but Ptolemy, who was the son of one of Alexander's bodyguards, secured the provincial governorship of Egypt.

The Ptolemaic period lasted from about 323 B.C. to about 30 B.C., when Cleopatra committed suicide. At that time, the country came under the control of the Romans. The early Ptolemies were tough business persons. Under the leadership of the Ptolemies, the culture was Greek, and so was the language of the court, the army, and the administration. They founded the library, the university, and the museum. Cleopatra was the last of the Ptolemies. She was the wife of Julius Caesar and later Mark Anthony. As the records show, she decided to commit suicide through the bite of an asp rather than see Egypt become part of the Roman Empire.

When Emperor Augustus established Roman rule, it began a period of six centuries during which the country was under the control of the Romans. Egypt was once again a province, as it had been under the Persians. Egypt under the Romans had a strong centralized administration under the protection of a large military force which was powerful enough to protect the country from marauding nomads. There was a rather elaborate bureaucracy and a social hierarchy which was based on caste and privilege. Under the Romans, Egypt's exploitation led to economic and social decline.

When looking at the history of Egypt, it is necessary to examine the parallel events in the history of the Roman Empire. Egypt was affected by the introduction of Christianity in A.D. 37. By the third century A.D., the demise of the Roman Empire had a great effect on the Roman administration of Egypt, and in the middle of the fourth century Egypt had become essentially a Christian nation.

One of the most important events in Egyptian history was the conquest of the country by the Arabs. Under the command of Amr ibn al As, a Muslim hero, Egypt became transformed from a Christian country to a Muslim nation, and the Arabic language and culture became dominant. After the Arab conquest in 641, Egypt was ruled by eastern caliphs for about two centuries. During that time, Egypt's history was heavily influenced by the Arabs. Egyptians were able to choose whether to adopt Islam as their primary religion as opposed to maintaining their own religion (usually Christian) and paying a poll tax.

After Al Fustat in 868, a new era began in the country. Four dynasties with varying degrees of control by Baghdad saw Egypt gradually become the center of an enormous empire which at one time included North Africa, Sicily, Syria, Palestine, the Red Sea coast of Africa, the Hijaz in Arabia, and Yemen. This phenomenon occurred during the Fatimid Dynasty, which also established Al Azhar in Cairo as an intellectual center where teachers and scholars provided significant educational leadership. The Fatimid Dynasty also was influential in fostering significant commercial expansion and industrial production. The Fatimids realized the importance of trading with India and Europe. Egyptian ships were sent to Sicily and Spain, and the Fatimids established close ties with the Italian city states, especially Amalfi and Pisa. However, the ambitious attempts by the Fatimids to become a world power were unable to withstand the incursions by the Crusaders.

After Palestine was captured by the Crusaders in 1099, the Fatimids were eventually driven out of Jerusalem by the famous Kurdish general Salah ad Din ibn Ayyub (known in the west as Saladin) who eventually became the master of Egypt. During this era, Egypt returned to Sunni orthodoxy, and Egypt again became closely allied to eastern Islam.

After the Mamluk Empire, during which time the Mamluk sultans ruled an empire encompassing Egypt and Syria (including the holy cities of Mecca and Medona), the Ottoman sultan Selim I conquered Egypt in 1517. By this time, Cairo had become the most important religious center of the Muslim world. The roots of the Ottoman Empire go back to the Turkish-speaking microcultures who crossed the frontier into Arab lands during the early part of the tenth century. These Turkish tribes were prominent in Baghdad and Anatolia, but met their demise because of the Mongols in the thirteenth century. The Ottoman Empire was founded by Osman. By the thirteenth century, his and other amirates had become an empire which actually spread to eastern Europe by the fourteenth century. After capturing Constantinople in 1453, this Byzantine capital became the Ottoman capital, and the name was changed to Istanbul. From the middle of the seventeenth century, political clout in Egypt had been passed to the beys, and from that time forward, it has been argued that the history of Ottoman Egypt can probably be best characterized as a struggle between the Ottomans and the Mamluks for the revenues of Egypt and the control of the country as well.

A major change came to Egypt with the occupation of the country by Napoleon Bonaparte in 1798. Initially, the intention was to establish a French colony. However, when faced with French cannons, the Mamluks retreated to the Sudan and other remote areas. The French invasion force included a contingent of scholars and scientists who wished to study the Egyptian culture, including ancient and contemporary Egyptian life. The French looked upon the country as a potential source of grain and raw materials. Also, the French viewed the area as a strategic acquisition in terms of its potential as a threat to Britain's commercial interests.

The French had little difficulty in conquering Alexandria; they defeated the Mamluk army, and entered Cairo just 24 days after they landed. But Napoleon's troops in Egypt became isolated because of a decisive victory over his navy at the hands of Lord Nelson. After the people of Cairo rioted against the French occupation forces on October 21, 1798, the French suffered a number of defeats. Finally, on August 22, 1799, Napoleon and a small number of his men secretly left the country, leaving most of his forces behind. By the end of September 1807, the last French forces had vacated the country after their surrender in Cairo during the previous May. Unfortunately for Egypt and the rest of the region, Napoleon's invasion served notice on Europe as a whole that the Middle East had great potential as a strategic resource for the European countries. It exacerbated the rivalry between the Anglos and the French, and stimulated an interest in the region by the British.

By the beginning of the nineteenth century, a power struggle for the leadership of Egypt occurred. In addition to the Ottoman government and the Mamluks, the Albanian contingent of Ottoman forces also because a main player in the quest for power. Their leader, Muhammad Ali, eventually became known as the "father" of modern Egypt. He possessed extraordinary leadership talents. He was able to defeat the Mamluks, and actually had 64 of them executed in the citadel. From that time onward, he was Egypt's only ruler. He realized the importance of the country's agriculture enterprise, and he had crops planted according to their use in trade exports. The surplus funds generated by crops such as indigo, rice, cotton, and sugar cane were used in the public works enterprises such as canals, dams, and irrigation projects. Peasants were told which crops to plant, in what location, and how much. Under Ali's leadership, Egypt also expanded its industrial development, establishing modern factories for the weaving of silk, wool, cotton, and jute. The looms were controlled by the government. In fact, the country's production reached the point where it began to constitute a threat to the British.

When Egypt invaded Syria and came close to Instanbul, Britain, Prussia, Russia, France, and Austria allied themselves with the Ottoman government to drive the Egyptians out of the country. Because of the intervention by the Europeans, Muhammad Ali and his Egyptian forces retreated to Egypt, and Muhammad Ali was forced to comply with British demands. He eventually became senile, and his son, Ibrahim, assumed the leadership of the country for six months, due to his tuberculosis illness. He was followed by Abbas Hilmi I, who was actually the grandson of Muhammad Ali. During his administration, a railroad was constructed between Alexandria and Cairo that facilitated Britain's communication with India.

The most important waterway in Egypt is the Nile River. The fourth son of

Muhammad Ali, Said, was a friend of Ferdinand de Lesseps, a French engineer. While he was Egypt's ruler, he granted a contract to de Lesseps to construct a canal between the Red Sea and the Mediterranean. The Suez Canal Company was given a strip of land which linked the canal site and the river.

During the nineteenth century, Egyptian peasants gradually changed from independent producers who were able to use the land to peasants who were landless and forced to work as common wage earners. Their other choice was to move to the cities where many of them became part of an urban microculture.

Probably no ruler in the history of the country (with the possible exception of Abdul Nasser) has created such a controversy in western Europe as Khedive Ismail, who ruled Egypt from 1863 to 1879. His goals for Egypt were the same as his grandfather, Muhammad Ali. He wanted Egypt to become a military power in the eastern Mediterranean. During his time in office, Egypt built more than 100 canals, 400 bridges, 480 kilometers of rail lines, and some 8,000 telegraph lines. But Ismail's ambitious construction projects cost more money than the country had, and by 1875 Egypt had incurred a debt of one million pounds, forcing him to sell his shares in the Suez Canal Company, making the British government the largest shareholder in the company. As a result, Ismail was deposed and replaced by his son, Tawfiq. In 1882, Britain occupied the country, promising to withdraw its troops in the near future. During the time of occupation, Egypt was actually part of the British Empire, although it never was a true colony.

By 1914, cotton comprised approximately 90 percent of Egypt's exports, and the British were heavily involved in the economic fruits of the cotton industry. But opposition to European interference in the country's economy caused a strong nationalist movement in Egypt, culminating in a 1919 revolution. Some observers believe the drive for independence was at least partly motivated by President Woodrow Wilson, who argued for self-determination in all countries after World War I. Marches and demonstrations by various women's groups led to the revolution which finally resulted in Egyptian independence in February 1922.

The era of independence following 1922 was a period of time during which Egypt dealt with the continual British power with a triangular approach which relied on the king, the Wafd, and the British. The British army of occupation was allowed to remain in the country after the termination of the 1919 revolution. However, just one year after the 1919 revolution, a number of British officials were assassinated, and by 1936, an Anglo-Egyptian treaty made it possible for the British to maintain a force of 10,000 troops in the Suez Canal Zone. The agreement was known as the Anglo-Egyptian Treaty of 1936.

When World War II started in 1939, Egypt became a critical part of Britain's wartime defense, and after the war the country became an unwilling participant in the Cold War because of the Canal Zone. Winston Churchill argued about Britain's ''rightful'' position in the war zone. By December 1945, Egyptian students were involved in a series of riots in Cairo and Alexandria. Finally, the

British agreed to remove its troops by September 1949. However, a dispute over the self-government of Sudan resulted in a number of major conflicts eventually leading to a revolution and self-governance after a major Egyptian victory.

The Suez Canal Company was an international corporation with headquarters in Paris. July 26, 1956 would be a critical time in Egypt's history because Abdul Gamal Nasser formally announced that the Suez Canal would be nationalized. This action enraged Britain and France who depended on the canal for the transportation of their oil supplies. But Egypt promised to compensate all stockholders of the Suez Canal Company and to guarantee the right of all ships to pass through. Nonetheless, Egypt was invaded by France, Britain, and the new state of Israel. The invasion goal was for France and Britain to gain control of the canal, and for Israel to attack across the Sinai Desert. However, because of mounting world pressure, the three countries finally withdrew, with the Israelis carrying out a scorched-earth policy of destruction on their way out.

During the mid-1960s, tensions between Israel and the Arab states intensified, and by 1966, Egypt and Syria had signed a five-year defense pact. In November of that year, Israel threatened to invade Syria if the guerrilla raids across the Syrian border did not stop. After more hostilities during the next number of months, Israel launched a major assault on Egypt, Jordan, and Syria on June 5, 1967. In only three hours, about three-fourths of Egypt's combat aircraft were destroyed. The Israeli ground forces charged into the Sinai, and in only three days were able to reach the Suez Canal. Just six days later, by June 11, the Israelis had achieved complete victory. At that time, the four nations accepted a U.N. resolution for a cease-fire. But by that time Israel held all of Palestine, the West Bank, and the Gaza Strip. They also held the Old City of Jerusalem, the Sinai, and part of Syria's Golan Heights.

The Egyptian losses were enormous. About 10,000 soldiers and approximately 1,500 officers were killed, and 80 percent of the country's military equipment was destroyed. The Sinai was controlled by the Israelis, and the Suez was blocked and closed to shipping. Nasser took the entire responsibility for the country's terrible losses.

In November 1968, the Security Council of the United Nations adopted Resolution 242 which created a process for settling the 1967 war. The resolution stipulated that the acquisition of land by force was unacceptable, and it also called for Israel to withdraw from territories occupied in the recent conflict. Also, the freedom of navigation through international waterways in the region was guaranteed, and a ''just'' settlement of the refugee problem was to be worked out.

Finally, fighting between the Egyptians and Israelis was terminated along the Suez Canal in 1970, and a 90-day truce was agreed upon. But during 1970, Nasser died, and the new Egyptian leader, Anwar Sadat, was convinced that the answer to Egypt's problems was through the encouragement of Western financial investment. Moreover, he realized that these investments would not materialize until the climate in Egypt was more favorable to Western capitalism,

Soviet influence was diminished or eliminated, and peace was established between Israel and Egypt. When he assumed the leadership of Egypt, Sadat decided to tread lightly and continue the policies of Nasser. By December 1975, a disengagement was signed by Sadat and Golda Meir after a series of hostile engagements between Egypt and Israel.

In 1977, Sadat decided to form his own political party which was called the National Democratic Party (NDP). This action was actually a movement which favored the two-party system of the United States and a move away from the Soviet Union which had a major sphere of influence in Egypt. Moreover, Sadat believed that the United States was the only country which could force Israel into a peace settlement. Finally, at Camp David in the United States, a peace agreement between Israel and Egypt was signed in 1979. Israel agreed to withdraw from the Sinai within three years of the new agreement. A multinational force, headed by the United States, was established, and Israeli ships were granted uninhibited access to the Suez Canal.

Sadat was viewed as a hero in the United States and Europe, and the reaction in Egypt was generally favorable. But in the Arab world there was immense disfavor. The Arab states terminated diplomatic relations with the country and Egypt was expelled from the Arab League. While the Camp David Accords brought peace to Egypt, it did not bring economic prosperity. Finally, worsening economic times and other problems finally led to the assassination of Sadat by the Al Jihad movement, which was actually a group of religious extremists. In a 1981 national referendum, Husni Mubarak was elected by a huge margin. After his election, Mubarak allowed more political activity and many of Sadat's political opponents were released from prison. More overt political activity has been allowed, and many of the defunct newspapers finally reappeared. During April 1982, the agreed-upon withdrawal of the Israelis took place. By 1983, Egypt's isolation in the area began to change after a meeting with Mubarak and Yasir Arafat. Finally, in 1987, the Arab states voted to resume diplomatic relations with Egypt.

STRUCTURE OF THE SYSTEM

Modern Egypt operates under the country's constitution of 1971, which gives executive authority to the president. Since Nasser, the incumbent vice president has twice succeeded to the country's top position of leadership. Both vice presidents were military officers. Egypt's president is able to appoint vice presidents, prime ministers, and the council of minister, which includes a minister of justice, foreign affairs, economic ministries, service, interior, and defense.

Under Egypt's central government, there are 26 governorates which are subdivided into districts, villages, and towns. However, Egypt is a highly centralized state, and the local units have relatively limited powers. A two-chamber legislature consists of the Lower People's Assembly and the Upper Consultative Council. The power of the People's Assembly is essentially in the hands of the leadership, an elected speaker, and the chairs of the specialized committees into which the assembly is divided. The president is above parliamentary authority and is able to legislate by decree when the parliament is not in session. Also, the president is able to bypass parliament in certain situations.

Egypt's legal system is based on Islamic law (sharia) and the Napoleonic Code which was used after the French occupation. The executive is prohibited from interfering in lawsuits or other affairs of justice. It is extremely difficult to remove judges who are appointed and serve for life.

When Mubarak took office, he restored freedom to Egypt's secular press. Prior to that time, the press was controlled by the government. Until Mubarak, newspaper editors were appointed by the government, and under Anwar Sadat, there was an increasing curiosity about interest-group politics. But Egypt's system of government is built around the notion of the Dominant Party System. This involves a large ruling party which straddles the political center, and opposition parties from the left and right are also active in the nation's political arena. Before the nineteenth century, the clergy controlled Egypt's system of education. Theological seminaries, mosques, and churches taught boys to learn how to read and write in Arabic, to do arithmetic, and to memorize passages from the Quran or Bible. The country's system of secular education was begun by Muhammad Ali in the early part of the nineteenth century. His educational goals were to develop a trained cadre for the military units and for his civil administration. The educational system was expanded by his grandson, Ismail, who set up a system of primary, secondary, and higher level schools which were public in nature. His wife finally established the country's first school for girls in 1873. There was no expansion of the Egyptian educational system between 1882 and 1922 when the country was under British control. After the direct rule of the British, Egypt's new constitution required the country to ensure adequate primary schools for all of the nation's school-age youth. However, in spite of this educational mandate, less than 50 percent of the primary-age children in Egypt were attending school. Nearly all were boys.

Moreover, at this time in the country's history, the literacy rate was only about 25 percent; and the literacy rate for females was only about 10 percent. But educational opportunities were greatly expanded during the third quarter of the century. The expenditures on school construction increased dramatically, and the operational budget of the Ministry of Education jumped to a level which constituted about one-fourth of Egypt's annual budget by the mid-1970s. During this time, enrollment in the nation's schools escalated rapidly. From the mid-1950s to the mid-1960s, the attendance rates doubled and experienced the same kind of growth in the next decade at the primary level and, since that time, primary enrollments have increased about 4 percent each year. During the third quarter of the twentieth century, Egypt also experienced major gains in the school enrollment of intermediate school students, secondary school students, higher education participants, and the number of women involved in higher education.

By the 1985–1986 academic year, about 84 percent of all the country's primary-age students were enrolled in school. However, on a less encouraging note, only about 30 percent of all eligible intermediate and secondary level students were enrolled in Egypt's schools. But in spite of these major efforts to improve the general educational level of Egyptians, the country's literacy rate is still less than 50 percent.

During 1981, Egypt passed a compulsory education law which required all students to receive nine years of school. But in spite of the legislation, a large number of parents remove their children from school before they have attended for the full nine years. The basic school cycle includes the six years of primary school and three years of intermediate school (grades 7, 8, and 9). In order to be admitted to the three-year secondary program, students must achieve adequate scores on special examinations. Once admitted, students may opt to participate in either a college preparatory program or a technical program.

Throughout the modern history of Egyptian education, there has been a general shortage of teachers, especially in the rural schools. Teaching in Egypt has been viewed as a relatively low-status career, with correspondingly low salaries. This was particularly true during the years of British occupation.

The higher education system also experienced rapid growth during the same period of time. During the first ten years after the 1952 revolution, the funding for higher education increased about 400 percent while student enrollment in public universities grew about 1,400 percent. Presently there are sixteen public universities with more than 750,000 students enrolled. Presently, women constitute about 35 percent of the Egyptian students enrolled in higher education programs.

MULTICULTURAL EDUCATION EFFORTS

The authors' international survey of multicultural education revealed that Egypt did not have a formal multicultural education program emanating from the Ministry of Education. But in examining issues of pluralism in Egypt, a look at the national attitudes pertaining to family structure offers a good beginning. As in many countries, the family is the most important element of Egyptian society. In Egypt, a husband and wife are not thought to be a true family until the birth of the first child. Older members of the family are held in higher esteem.

Throughout the country's history, most Egyptians have thought that women were inferior to men. New wives usually lived near their husband's family and were expected to help out with the chores. The early days of marriage tended to place a great deal of pressure on the new wife to produce children, specifically a son. Muslim husbands could have several wives, but women were allowed just one husband at a time. In the case of divorce, the husband was usually awarded custody of the child, and men were only required to pay alimony to their divorced wives for a period of one year. However, very few penalties are encountered by divorced men who fail to pay the designated monies to their ex-wives.

Egypt was Christianized during the first century when the country was part of the Holy Roman Empire. But for the past 1,000 years, Egypt has been mostly Islamic. Among the religious minorities, the Copts (an indigenous religious minority) account for nearly 9 percent of the population. Other religious minorities include about 750,000 followers of several denominations, and some 1,000 Jews still reside in the nation. However, the primary religion in Egypt is Islam.

The primary language used in Egyptian schools is Arabic, and there has been a major effort to improve the literacy level of the country in recent years. There are almost no known bilingual education efforts in the nation's schools, and foreign language instruction in the public schools has been minimal compared to some other nations.

On an encouraging note, the education of women has increased dramatically in recent years, particularly at the university level. Nonetheless, only about 45 percent of the primary-level students are girls and only 75 percent of girls between the ages of six and twelve are enrolled in primary school compared with about 95 percent of the boys. In addition, girls drop out of primary schools more often than boys. When considering all Egyptian girls from the age of twelve to eighteen, less than 50 percent are enrolled in school.

Finally, an examination of the nation's system of higher education reveals that after the Persian Gulf War, these institutions have returned to normal. However, critics have argued that returning to "normal" has meant returning to some basic issues that have been afflicting Egypt for many years. The immediate issue seems to be the general problem of overcrowding. Some educators argue that the rise of Islamic fundamentalism and intellectual timidity is having a negative effect on the pursuit of intellectual attainment. It has been argued that Islamic fundamentalists have sought to impose their ideas on the universities where many social and cultural activities have been terminated if they have been deemed to be decadent and frivolous by this increasingly verbal religious right. It has also been argued that the Islamic dogma has resulted in an approach to teaching which has emphasized rote learning with little classroom discussion, resulting in the education of students who are virtually unable to engage in critical thinking.

SUMMARY

At first, it might seem that Egypt has chosen to ignore the issue of multicultural education because of a lack of such efforts from the Ministry of Education. Also, the country's history of inattention to the education of females has been apparent. However, in spite of the bleak history of education for females, there are some encouraging signs.

For example, more girls and women are participating in the nation's schooling efforts from the primary grades onward. It must also be remembered that Egypt, like some other nations, has experienced a long history of viewing education for women as a relatively unnecessary pastime. But as Egypt seems interested in making certain changes in its political system and economic structure in order to keep pace with international economic competition, so does it appear certain that the country will continue to improve its educational enterprise in order to facilitate the country's successful participation in the international marketplace.

REFERENCES

Aldred, Cyril. *The Egyptians*. London: Thames and Hudson, 1984.

Bollay, Burton. "Enrollment Boom, Rise of Fundamentalism Put Egypt's Universities Under Pressure." *The Chronicle of Higher Education* (June 12, 1991), pp. 31–33.

Burnstein, Stanley M. "Introducing Kush: A Mini-Guide to an Ancient African Civilization." *Social Studies Review* (Fall 1993), pp. 22–30.

Crecelius, Daniel. *The Roots of Modern Egypt*. Minneapolis: Bibliotheca Islamica, 1981.

Dupuy, Trevor N. *Elusive Victory: The Arab-Israeli Wars, 1947–1974*. New York: Harper and Row, 1978.

Goldschmidt, Arthur, Jr. *Modern Egypt: The Formation of a Nation State*. Boulder, CO: Westview Press, 1988.

Kamil, Jill. *The Ancient Egyptians*. Cairo: American University in Cairo Press, 1984.

Marsot, Afaf Lutfi Al-Sayyid. *Egypt in the Reign of Muhammad Ali*. Cambridge: Cambridge University Press, 1984.

Marsot, Afaf Lutfi Al-Sayyid. *A Short History of Modern Egypt*. Cambridge: Cambridge University Press, 1985.

Metz, Helen Chapin (Ed.). *Egypt: A Country Study*. Washington, DC: Department of the Army, 1991.

Waterbury, John. *The Egypt of Nasser and Sadat: The Political Economy of Two Regimes*. Princeton, NJ: Princeton University Press, 1983.

13

England

HISTORY OF THE SYSTEM

One suitable starting point for the study of the present English educational system is the initiation of Christianity in Kent in A.D. 597, when St. Augustine established a cathedral church at Canterbury for training ministers of the Church. At the time, religion and education went hand in hand. Gradually, Christianity spread throughout England, and bishops taught in "schools" which were merely groups of students, usually with no buildings.

Originally, "grammar" referred to the Latin language and literature, and was the first of the seven liberal arts. Actually it was considered to be the foundation for the others. Eventually, the country established reading and writing schools in order for students to become literate in their native language.

English grammar schools usually were responsible for the teaching of rhetoric, grammar, and sometimes dialectic. In the eighth century, a York grammar school became a college of theology and university, with a curriculum which dealt with nearly all of the basic subjects taught during the Medieval era. But after Oxford University opened its doors during the twelfth century, the English grammar schools reverted back to being focused on grammar instruction alone—a practice which has persisted through the years. After that time, many other grammar schools were founded for the same purpose.

Throughout the history of English education, the Church has controlled organized education. With few exceptions, teachers were clerks in the order of the Church. However, during the English Reformation, major participation was seen on the part of the laity.

During the 1700s, there was a general decline in grammar school and university education. At the end of the eighteenth century, many grammar schools had closed. Oxford and Cambridge had become more like social clubs than institutions of higher education.

Another issue of the century was the polarization of the classes. The wealthy subscribed to the tenets of the established Church, while followers of John Wesley tended to come from the ranks of the poor as well as the burgeoning middle class. The latter two groups tended to reject the curricula of the grammar schools and universities because they felt it was not in keeping with their needs. As a result, there was an influx of students from these two groups into private schools which tended to offer more modern and more efficient educational programs for their children. Moreover, "dissenting academics" were attracted to this group, since they offered courses of university caliber which were not reserved for members of the established Church.

At the same time, the wealthy class commenced sending boys to elite boarding schools, such as Eton, Marrow, and Winchester, which were becoming known as the "public" schools. The thinking was that for children of the lower classes, only a very rudimentary education was really necessary. In fact, the wealthy classes believed that to overeducate the lower classes was an unsavory pursuit which could damage society.

During the late 1600s, several groups sought to better the lot of the lower classes. Their religious dogmas stipulated that there was indeed a moral obligation to improve their well-being. One such group was the Society for Promoting Christian Knowledge (SPCK). The goal of that organization was "to further and promote Catechetical schools in each parish in and about London." This design was successful in improving the literacy quite dramatically during the eighteenth century.

However, the Industrial Revolution would motivate still greater educational needs. Consequently, the Sunday Schools were provided for children and adults who were toiling in the mines and factories in ever-increasing numbers. Industrialists liked the Sunday Schools, since they didn't keep children out of work like the weekday schools did. However, it was clear that these one-day a week schools were inadequate. By 1802, Sir Robert Peel attempted to secure better schooling and shorter working hours for children, but he was unsuccessful.

The tutorial system of education was introduced by Joe Lancaster and Dr. Andrew Bell at the close of the nineteenth century. The model was cheap and it appealed to the ruling classes. Then, finally in 1833, the House of Commons appropriated 20,000 pounds to aid the National and British Societies to build schools. By 1839, the funding was increased to 30,000 pounds and an education committee of the Privy Council was created to supervise this new educational funding which had become an annual occurrence. By this time, the English government had assumed the responsibility for funding public education.

Passed in 1870, the Elementary Education Act was a major attempt to create a statutory system of public education in England. The act was approved in the midst of intense opposition, and the final resolution made it illegal for the schools to impose any religious catechisms—a characteristic of English schools which has persisted down through the years. This act maintained the voluntary notion of English education, even though it empowered the English government to assist the school systems in the event that the schools were deemed to be inadequate. The document also stipulated that school boards *could* make attendance compulsory if they so chose.

In spite of these efforts, the country paid relatively little attention to the issue of secondary education. In fact, it was not until 1894 that the Bryce Commission helped the English create a blueprint for establishing secondary schools throughout the land. Just before World War I, the new educational system was developed more extensively. A large number of endowed grammar schools were accepted into it, along with other advanced secondary schools. A short time later, during the World War I years, the system of public education became quite well established, and the English educational system would include the secondary portion from that time forward.

The 1918 Education Act was designed to improve the education of all English children and, in so doing, the compulsory attendance age became fourteen. It also required a compulsory part-time education before that age. However, due to economic difficulties, this portion of the act was not always fully implanted. Then, six years later, the "Hadow Report" recommended that at the age of eleven, the primary (first) stage should end and the secondary stage would commence.

During the early part of World War II, the educational climate was ripe for reforms. Finally, during 1944, the Education Act resulted in a number of major educational changes in England. The Office of the Minister of Education was created as an alternative to the old President of the Board of Education. Local Education Agencies (LEAs) became equally responsible for acquiring suitable facilities for educational programs. Religious worship and instruction was required. LEAs were required to provide free health and medical care for all children between the ages of two and eighteen. LEAs were also required to craft special programs for children with special physical or psychological needs. Finally, teachers' salaries had to be approved by a legal negotiating group (consisting of teachers, employers, and LEAs) and approved by the Minister of Education; and no female teachers could be terminated for being married. Since that time, many sections of the act have been created because of actions by Parliament.

After World War II, an emergency training program was initiated in order to prepare an adequate number of teachers. Many countries around the world experienced teacher shortages at this time in history. Another addition to the education programs in England during that time were the television services by the British Broadcasting Company and the Independent Television Authority.

The preparation of teachers was an issue which was investigated during the late 1960s. Inquiries were conducted by a select committee which was appointed by Mrs. Margaret Thatcher. The chair of this committee was Lord James, president of York University. The resulting report, published in 1972, proposed a new program of teacher education which incorporated a new blueprint for the education of the country's teachers.

Also, during the 1950s and 1960s, England experienced an enormous increase in the number of colleges and universities. The "open" university opened its doors in 1971. It was a school which focused on the use of correspondence courses and radio and television broadcasts. However, after 1970, the economic problems precipitated cuts in supplies and the requests for higher education waned dramatically. Moreover, the school population declined as the birthrate commenced to decline during the mid 1960s.

Throughout the twentieth century, two entities have had a major role in the preparation of English teachers. Universities and colleges have viewed themselves as being the main parties in teacher preparation, while the local agencies have monitored the administration of schools, in-service training programs, and the professional development of the teachers. An experimental program has been instituted which involves the Leeds and Bradford local education agencies, along with Leeds Polytechnic, and Bradford and Ilkley Community College. The Council for Academic Awards, a national body which monitors the various processes involved in the awarding of degrees and diplomas, supervises this new project. The initiative for this new program came from teacher complaints about in-service programs offered by colleges and universities. One of the major complaints was that the in-service offerings did not translate to course credits which would lead to an academic degree.

The key characteristics of the new model are freedom and self-direction. It is primarily directed by students who submit their plans which can include prior learning, courses, and independent learning projects. Each plan must demonstrate that the work is of a sufficient level of difficulty, and that it exhibits an acceptable degree of professional relevance. Professional and academic standards must be in keeping with national norms.

STRUCTURE OF THE SYSTEM

Responsibility for the control and direction has been in the hands of the Minister of Education. Public education is financed by Parliament. These revenues are derived through a process of national taxation. Funds are also provided through local sources of taxation and are distributed by the LEAs.

The system of public education is divided into the primary education stage (ages five to eleven or twelve), and the secondary stage (eleven or twelve to eighteen). Nursery school education (ages two to five) is voluntary. The classes are all co-educational. The curriculum is focused around the acquisition of effective social interaction skills.

The grammar school serves the educational needs of bright children. It provides a special educational program for the top 20 percent of the school population. This program helps children prepare for the General Certificate of Education (G.C.E.) and for entrance to colleges and universities.

In addition to the country's public schools, there are a large number of independent schools. These schools are not able to receive any public funds. All of these schools must be registered in accordance with the Education Act of 1944. This act provided for the special education treatment of exceptional children.

Children from ages two to eighteen have been provided free health care, along with a comprehensive range of integrated health services for children. English children also receive daily cooked noon meals and other appropriate refreshments for a minimum cost, free milk, special school programs, various cleaning services, transportation to and from schools, and services designed to help children's career choices.

The Education Act of 1944 requires the provision of "further education" for persons who left a secondary school at the age of sixteen. The three types of further education programs include vocational studies, nonvocational studies, and recreational/social activities. Local educational agencies provide most of the vocational education programs along with the colleges of education. Since the late 1950s, the English efforts in further education have experienced continous change and modification.

Ultimate control of the English educational system has rested within the hands of Parliament. This body has been responsible for ensuring that laws pertaining to education were enacted and that the various laws were being observed. However, Parliament has not prescribed what should be taught in the schools and colleges. One exception to this basic tenet occurred in 1944 when religious instruction became compulsory in all of the country's maintained schools.

A Curriculum Study Group, established in the Ministry of Education in 1962, offered consultant services in the nation's schools and technical services to the Secondary Schools Examination Council (SSEC). This council has represented the entire spectrum of English education. However, teachers have tended to dominate the organization. The primary role of the council has been to encourage curriculum development and promote research endeavors.

Much of the assistance to the Secretary of State has emanated from the Department of Education and Science. This body has provided the bulk of information which has led to national policies that have guided England's educational programs throughout the years.

Also prominent in the nation's system of education has been the HM (Her Majesty's) Inspectorate of Schools. Appointed by the Crown, it is the responsibility of Her Majesty's Inspectors to monitor the general effectiveness of English schools. England has been divided into nine geographical sectors to facilitate the process.

Primary education in England has addressed the learning needs of students before the age of twelve. Children have been able to enter nursery schools at the age of two, and nursery classes when children are at the age of three. Usually, education for English youth has been divided into two stages. An infant stage ends when the youngster is seven or eight years old. The junior stage is somewhat longer, sometimes lasting for up to four years. Many primary schools have been organized around an open plan system.

Infant schools have looked something like the nursery schools, but the curriculum has tended to be a bit more pedagogical in nature. The education of five-year olds has attempted to expand on the world in which they live. For example, there have been opportunities for young students to work with water, clay, paint, wood, etc. In addition, the curriculum has focused on story/music enjoyment, working with clay, sand, and water, and exploring music, writing, reading, and story-telling.

The middle school curriculum for students from ages nine to thirteen has consisted of foreign language; science courses which include laboratory stations; educational specialists, who have the expertise for teaching crafts; and an appropriate number of educational specialists who are capable of crafting sound educational programs.

Secondary education in England has been organized around a format of grammar, technical, and modern schools. The grammar school is the oldest and has provided a curriculum which sought to teach classical and modern languages, mathematics, and science. The usual subjects are computer education, English language and literature, foreign language, history, geography, mathematics, chemistry, physics, biology, art, music, wood/metal work, and home economics. Physical education is also included as an integral part of the curriculum. Some grammar schools supplement the curriculum with offerings such as engineering, technical drawing, architecture, economics, and sometimes philosophy, psychology, and/or sociology.

Special education programs constitute an important segment of England's educational system. The Education Act of 1944 required local education agencies to establish special programs which would meet the needs of exceptional children. Since that time, the schools have put programs in place for the blind and partially sighted, deaf and hearing impaired, learning disabled, epileptic, physically handicapped, emotionally disturbed, and speech disabled. To the fullest extent possible, all English children are to be educated with "normal" children.

Another basic part of the English educational system is the health component which is provided by the local education agencies. Since 1907 it has been the responsibility of these education agencies to provide for free medical examinations and, since 1918, for treating minor ailments, improper vision, and dental problems. School meals are also provided for English students at a very modest cost. Most of the nation's schools have cooking facilities, and all meals must conform to established nutritional standards. Originally, both the provision of meals and the country's milk and nutrition programs were carried out through the use of volunteers.

Independent schools in England are administered by boards of trustees and are financially self-supporting. In general, such schools receive no public funds. However, all such schools must adhere to the national dictums which guide the country's educational efforts.

Further education refers to the country's efforts to provide continuation for students who have left school at the age of sixteen. All local education agencies must provide adequate education offerings for such persons. These programs are carried out in polytechnics, major colleges, evening institutes and colleges, and centers of adult education. Colleges of Advanced Technology (CATs) have been available for advanced studies leading to diplomas in technology.

In addition to the vocational offerings, further education efforts have also included nonvocational classes for adults. Most lectures and courses are open to the general public. During 1975, an Adult Literacy Resource Agency was established at the request of the Secretaries of State for Education and Science.

MULTICULTURAL EDUCATION EFFORTS

A suitable starting point for discussing multicultural education efforts in England is the Swann Report of 1985. The report proposed that the nation's teachers should demonstrate an appreciation of the diversity of lifestyles and cultural, religious, and linguistic backgrounds which are part of the nation. Nine basic issues were addressed in the report:

1. Have the key multicultural issues been treated comprehensively throughout the curriculum?
2. Does the curriculum address the diversity of the students' cultural experiences?
3. Does the curriculum pertain to the affective lives of students and allow them to share their feelings and ideas which reflect their cultural background?
4. Does the curriculum help students to acquire positive attitudes about the country's pluralistic populations?
5. Are students taught that all microcultures have their own integrities which should be shared and enjoyed by everyone?
6. Do school activities focus on the many contributions of England's pluralistic microcultures?
7. Does the curriculum help students learn to appreciate the nation's various microcultures?
8. Do educational programs help students understand the migrational tendencies of humans throughout history?
9. Do the schools help students understand the severe damages to people which can be caused by stereotyping?

The Swann Report was sent to all schools through actions taken by the Secretary of State for Education and Science. The English government, through the Secretary of State, announced three major policies which the schools were directed to follow. The first policy addressed the school performance of all students. This was to be improved through the removal of learning obstacles. Second, minority students were to have access to equal opportunities for learning in the schools. Finally, the country's national values would be preserved and transmitted in a manner which would promote racial harmony and tolerance while accepting the country's ethnic diversity.

Some English educators have argued that multicultural education should help to alter the pervasive Eurocentric bias found in the production and dissemination of knowledge which has tended to promote a type of subconscious racism. It has been suggested that mathematics should not be overlooked as a vehicle for fostering multicultural values. Several strategies have been suggested for incorporating multicultural strands into the curriculum. It has been suggested that the mathematical contributions of Arabs, Chinese, Indians, Mayans, and Persians should be stressed in the classroom; for example, it could be shown that the word for "algebra" was taken from "Al-jabr w'al Mugabala," who was a famous Arab mathematician during the Islamic Renaissance. Another way to illustrate the multicultural influences of math could be to have students discuss the accomplishments of Chinese mathematicians such as Ch'in Chiu-Shao, who solved simultaneous equations using Horner's method in A.D. 1247—500 years before Horner! There are many other similar examples which could help young students learn that mathematics can become a very pluralistic topic.

During recent years, cultural pluralism has been increasing in England. In addition to the British themselves, Irish, Pakistanis, West Indians, Chinese, Cypriots, Italians, Ukrainians, Vietnamese, Liverpool Blacks, and Scottish groups now comprise the English macroculture. In order to address the issue of English pluralism, teachers are required to take basic training in order to meet the needs of students from diverse backgrounds. According to questionnaire responses in the original survey, cultural assimilation still prevails, meaning that an Anglo-Saxon perspective still prevails and is promoted in the school curriculum.

While the official language of instruction is English, special programs have been put in place for immigrant children. They consist primarily of classes in English instruction. The country has a formal multicultural education program, even though there is no specific office in the Ministry of Education for the development of such efforts. Most children attend racially integrated schools. The curricular offerings attempt to promote understanding and tolerance of culturally different persons whether or not ethnic and racial minorities are present in a given school setting.

According to the authors' survey responses, the history of indigenous peoples is not normally taught in the regular curriculum. The Ministry of Education evaluates all curriculum materials for racist/sexist content. Finally, the same respondent indicated that one of the biggest problems in English schools was perceived to be the lack of teachers of color in the nation's schools.

Another problem plaguing the English school system has been the underperformance of some ethnic minorities in the schools. The Swann study examined the educational levels of West Indian children. It was found that they performed substantially lower on their examinations compared to their white counterparts. However, it was found that Asian children performed on about the same level as their white peers.

Many countries around the world have struggled with the problem of low school performance for some of its microcultural populations, and England is no exception. Professor Bhiku Parekh has attempted to suggest six factors which might cause such a disparity between West Indian students and their white counterparts:

First, the low attainment of West Indian children is, according to some commentators, easily and adequately explained in terms of their generic intellectual inferiority. This view is more widely held than is realized. A second explanation accounts for West Indian children's low attainment in terms of the structure of their family. Third, some commentators explain the fact of low attainment in terms of the materially and culturally disadvantaged West Indian home. While the previous explanation blames the parent and the traditional structure of the family, this one blames their economic condition and the character of the wider social structure. Fourth, some explain low attainment in terms of racism both in society at large and in the school. Fifth, some hold the structure and ethos of the school responsible because many a school has renounced its traditional task of educating its pupils and helping them achieve basic intellectual skills, in favor of dabbling in social work and psychotherapy they underplay the value of formal methods of teaching, hard work and discipline. Sixth, some explain the low attainment of the West Indian child in terms of the failure of the educational authorities to identify and meet his educational needs.

Interestingly, these six reasons for the low academic achievement of West Indian children are not unlike the reasons put forth for the underachievement of Native Americans in the United States, the Tasmanians of Australia, or the Maoris of New Zealand. While some have argued that genetic inferiority has caused the trouble, it now seems clear that the primary barrier to solid school performance is poverty. Malnourishment, a byproduct of poverty, is capable of doing physical damage to the brain cell structure of the infant. The fact that a preponderance of persons of color were members of low-income groups has misled many persons to think that the low performance was due to basic genetics rather than the crippling ravages of poverty itself. These actions have done a great disservice to many minority groups all over the globe.

Such beliefs about racial inferiority have caused many arguments over the proper approaches to be taken in multicultural education (MCE) programs. Indeed, some have argued that the very topic itself is misleading, and that multicultural education should be replaced in the curriculum with instructional approaches which stress antiracist education (ARE). However, the authors contend that a viable part of multicultural education should be the so-called ARE efforts. Such instructural strategies seem to be a logical part of a total instructional approach to multicultural education. This view is corroborated by Banks, who has generated an inclusive definition of multicultural education which contains many properties of antiracist education.

Part of this broad view of multicultural education is that one of its purposes is to educate teachers to become multiculturally sensitive. Specifically, it has been presupposed that Europe, the United States, and Australia have had a monopoly on the creation and perpetuation of scientific knowledge. According to one educator, this has created an unconscious racism on the part of teachers. Part of a valid multicultural education approach would be to include educational components which help both teachers and students to understand that mathematics and science has always been a worldwide phenomenon, and that the end product has resulted because of the intercultural/interracial involvement of peoples all over the world.

However, in spite of the multicultural education efforts of some English educators, it appears that assimilation may still be the primary foundation of multicultural education in predominantly white English schools. For example, the York schools seem to have no systematic attempt for a formal multicultural education program other than a kind of "travel guide" attempt. In addition, interviews with English teachers reveal that few serious attempts to promote the value of pluralism, racial equality, and a racist-free society are being carried out in the English schools in spite of the strong positive multicultural pronouncements of English educational institutions.

SUMMARY

England's long history of public education has placed the nation in a position of leadership among educators the world over. Although critics of the English system have accused it of being dualistic for the rich and poor, attempts have been made to provide equity education for all children since the 1960s. An interview with a history teacher prompted the observation that it was very important to have minority students assimilate the English language and customs in order to compete effectively. The same interview yielded the response that there was no problem with racism in their schools because there were almost no minorities in the schools. The interviewer also felt that racial issues in the primary schools tended to be dealt with in about the same way as manners and morals were. In some western countries, this might be referred to as being "politically correct."

But the 1985 Swann Report has indeed altered the attitudes of English educators about the issue of multicultural education. The nine topics which were addressed have created new discussions about the role of multicultural education in the school curriculum. As has been true in other countries, the concept has been quite controversial, even appearing radical and threatening to some. Hence, it is understandable that the idea is still incubating and has not completely blossomed.

REFERENCES

Adult Education: A Plan for Development. London: HMSO, 1973.

Antonouris, George. "Multicultural Perspectives." *Times Educational Supplement,* Vol. 30, No. 9 (1988).

Banks, James. "Multicultural Education and Its Critics: Britain and the United States." In S. Modgil et al. (Eds.), *Multicultural Education: the International Debate.* Lewes: Palmer Press, 1990.

Dent, N.C. *Education in England & Wales.* Great Britain: Linnett Books, 1977.

Education Act of 1944, Section 5. London, England. Original regulations are from Section 33(2) of the Education Act of 1944 and Circular 276, Provision of Special Schools, dated June 25, 1954, London, England.

The Education of the Adolescent. London: HMSO, 1926.

Elementary Education Act of 1870, Section 14(2). London, England.

Freedman, Darlene. "There Aren't Many of Them Here So There Isn't a Problem." Unpublished Paper, Eastern Washington University, 1990.

Gonen, Amiram. *The Encyclopedia of the Peoples of the World.* New York: Henry Holt Publishing Co., 1993.

The Handicapped Pupils and Special Schools Regulations (SI 1959, No. 365). London, England, 1959.

Joseph, George. "The Multicultural Dimension." *Times Education Supplement,* Vol. 30, No. 9 (1988).

Lord Swann. *Education for All London.* London: Department of Education and Science, HMSO, 1988.

"The Multicultural Dimension." *Times Educational Supplement,* Vol. 3562 (October 5, 1984), pp. 45–46.

The Schools Regulations (SI 1959, No. 365). London, England, 1959.

Troyna, Barry. "Beyond Multiculturalism Towards the Enactment of Anti-Racist Education in Policy and Pedagogy." *Oxford Review of Education,* Vol. 13, No. 3 (1987).

Williamson, Graham. "A New Approach to Teacher Education in England." *Educational Leadership,* Vol. 49, No. 3 (1991), pp. 61–62.

14

Finland

HISTORY OF THE SYSTEM

Compared to many other nations, Finland has experienced one of the longer periods of human inhabitation. Archaeologists claim that its human history can be traced back to the end of the latest ice age—some 10,000 years ago. The country eventually became home to the Finno-Urgic linguistic group, which was not related to the Indo-European group. Recorded history for the country extends back to the twelfth century when Finland was conquered by Sweden. It was controlled by that country for more than six centuries. Under the Swedish influence, Finland adopted the primary characteristics of the western European countries in regard to politics, religion, culture, and economics. However, the Finns did maintain their native tongue which is quite different from most other European language patterns. After a number of conflicts involving the Finns, Swedes, and Russians, Russia took over the country and Finland remained under Russian control from 1809 to 1917.

The early beginnings of Finnish nationalism appeared during the eighteenth century. Originally, it started as a kind of academic movement, incorporating studies of history, folklore, and linguistics which helped to define a Finnish macroculture. After the 1809 takeover by the Russians, the country was allowed to maintain its Finnish culture because Russia viewed this as a healthy situation for them since it provided a cushion against Sweden. Russia and Sweden had been involved in many violent conflicts throughout the years. The Russians also opted to move the capital to Helsinki because it made their control of the country much easier since it was closer to St. Petersburg. After the University of Turku was moved to Helsinki in 1827 (because of a fire), that institution became a primary influence on the Finnish nationalist movement.

However, a counter-nationalist movement (Svecoman movement) was mounted by Finland's native Swedish speakers who felt that they should be a separate nation in order to maintain their native language and culture.

Toward the end of the nineteenth century, the Russian empire was facing a number of difficult issues. Since it had remained rather isolated, the country tended to become more ethnocentric and intolerant of non-Russian minorities within its empire. Consequently, attempts to "Russify" the other groups intensified. After a series of Russian manifestos—including making the Finnish army part of the Russian army—these Russification attempts were temporarily terminated with the Russian Revolution of 1905. But Finland finally became ruled from St. Petersburg as a subject province of the Russian empire. However, the Russian Revolution of 1917 changed Finland. The country became independent and a parliamentary democracy emerged.

However, Finland soon became involved in its own civil war which resulted in the death of some 30,000 Finns. The end of the Finnish Civil War in 1918 resulted in the re-seating of Prime Minister Svinhufvud in Helsinki. During 1919, a constitution was created which included a republican form of government, a six-year presidency term, and a guarantee of basic human rights.

Although the Finns won the admiration of the world by fending off Russian attacks during the early stages of World War II, the Russians finally prevailed and the countries signed the Peace of Moscow in March 1940. Finland was forced to cede important territories. By the Spring of 1941, Finland allowed Germany to send its troops through Finland in an invasion of Russia. The Finns sided with the German invasion because they were convinced that they would have a chance to regain their territories which had been lost in the Peace of Moscow agreements. Finally, after a number of major conflicts between Finland and Russia, an agreement was signed between the two countries in 1947. The country was successful in not being occupied by the Germans.

Another significant agreement with the Russians was the Treaty of Friendship, Cooperation and Mutual Assistance (FCMA), signed on April 6, 1948. This agreement actually became a building block for future relations with the Soviets. This called for military cooperation between Finland and Russia. It also guaranteed the Russians that the Finns would never become a military threat to Russia. Moreover, the two countries required cooperation between Finland and the Soviet Union if Germany or any country allied with it attempted to invade Russia through Finnish territory.

During the two decades following the termination of World War II, a number of critical domestic developments occurred in the country. Industrial disputes were reconciled because of a general agreement made in 1946 between the Confederation of Finnish Trade Unions (Suomen Ammattiyhdistysten Keskusliitto-SAK) and the Confederation of Finnish Employers (Suomen Tyonantajain Keskusliitto). This agreement mandated compulsory negotiations between labor and management and was successful in settling many industrial disputes.

The northern part of Finland had been lagging behind the rest of the country, and by 1966 special ways were being investigated for the promotion of economic development in that portion of the country. Therefore, the 1966 concerns were focused on domestic issues, and the results of the elections were major victories for the socialist parties of Finland. These victories constituted a growing consensus in Finnish politics, and the decades through the late 1980s provided a high level of presidential stability since there were only three presidents during that period of time.

Economically, Finland is considered one of the more highly industrialized countries of the world because of its emphasis on manufacturing. Main products and services include wood, metals, and engineering. Finland is actively involved in trade on a global basis, with exported goods comprising about 25 percent of its GNP. Because of the country's geography, agricultural production is limited to meeting domestic needs and does not constitute a component of Finland's export economy.

STRUCTURE OF THE SYSTEM

Finland has an executive, legislative, and judicial branch, and the Eduskunta is Finland's highest governing body, since it represents the people who have sovereign power. Neither the president nor the cabinet is able to carry out many actions without the support of the Eduskunta, so there is generally a close working relationship between the three bodies.

Universal suffrage for national Finnish elections began in 1906, and all Finns over the age of 18 are able to vote (election turnouts average about 80 percent). Presidential elections are held in January every six years.

Finland has had a long history of high literacy, originally motivated by the Lutheran Church which wanted its members to read the Bible. A Comprehensive Education Act was passed in 1921, requiring free, compulsory education. Passed in 1968, the School System Act created a nine-year school for students between the ages of seven and sixteen. Academic high schools serve the needs of students from ages sixteen to nineteen. Students not involved in the academic high schools attend three- to five-year programs in vocational institutes. The curriculum of the schools is set by law; and the Ministry of Education, the National Board of General Education, and the National Board of Vocational Education are responsible for seeing that the schools comply. Local educators are able to make some decisions about how the subjects are to be taught.

All teachers are now required to have a college degree. Teachers involved in the first six years are required to have a masters degree in education, while the others need a masters degree in their teaching field. As a general rule, students with special needs are kept together with their peers and special services are provided on an individual basis.

As of the late 1800s, Finland had ten universities in its higher educational system. These institutions grant a masters degree which requires between four and six years of study, the licentiate which requires an additional two years, and a doctorate which usually requires about four years to complete.

As a consequence of this strong emphasis on education as a national priority, Finland has a literacy rate of 100 percent, high newspaper circulation rates, and 1,776 public libraries throughout the country.

MULTICULTURAL EDUCATION EFFORTS

Results of the authors' international study indicated that Finland had no formal multicultural education programs. The country tends to be quite culturally homogeneous. The Swedish-speaking minority lives in the coastal part of the country and has its own schools. Presently, they number about 250,000. Many children from this minority group live in the more coastal parts of the country and they have their own schools. The Finnish constitution stipulates that both Finnish and Swedish are national languages, making the country officially a bilingual nation.

In addition to the Swedish population, there are other minority groups in the country. Another minority group in Finland is the Samis. Actually, this is one of the smaller minority groups. The language of the Samis is a legitimate language pattern and it has become a second national language of the country. Of the four million persons in Finland, only about 1 percent are Samis. The Sami language is related to the Finno-Ugric languages. The present Sami population is spread through a huge region stretching from the Kola peninsula to the coast of northern Norway. Anthropologists believe that the Samis have been in the area for about 11,000 years. Whenever possible, the Samis are provided instruction in their native language in order to improve their access to equal education opportunities. However, sometimes it is not possible to provide bilingual instruction for the Samis or the country's other ethnic minorities.

Other minority groups in Finland include the Gypsies and the Lapps. This group is very small (estimated at about 6,000 persons). As a group, the Gypsies have kept to themselves and have generally lived apart from other Finnish groups. The Lapps arrived in the southern part of Finland approximately 2,000 years ago. The oldest inhabitants of the country, they gradually moved to the northern part of the country as the Finns arrived.

Most Finnish children attend racially and culturally integrated schools. Since Swedish is the second language of the country, some of the schools are Swedish speaking. The history of indigenous peoples is taught in the regular curriculum. In fact, at the VII Nordic Sami Conference in 1971, decisions were made on the following mutual goals in the field of cultural policy:

We are Samis and we will remain Samis, without, for this reason, being neither greater or less than other peoples in the world. We are a people with a territory of our own, a language of our own, and a cultural and social structure of our own. In the course of history we have gained our livelihood and lived in Same-Atnam (the land of the Samis) and we wish the culture which we possess to develop and live on.

Guarantees of religious freedom are part of the multicultural education notions of the Finnish educational system. The right to worship freely is guaranteed in the Finnish constitution; however, the country's religious bodies are dominated by *one* of its two state churches—the Lutheran Church of Finland, which has about 90 percent of the population in its membership. The Orthodox Church of Finland is the other state church, and has a membership of only 1 percent of the population. While about 7 percent of the people belong to no church at all, the remaining 2 percent are either Jews, Muslims, Roman Catholics, Protestants, Mormons, or Christian Scientists.

A final issue pertaining to multicultural education relates to gender factors. Recently, the country has become concerned over "feminization of society" and the democratic ideal of a society of equal civil, social, and political citizens, regardless of gender. One of the main concerns rests with the percentage of Finnish teachers who are female. Since 60 percent of the country's teachers are females, the concern is that boys do not see the proper kind of role models in the schools.

In 1989, Finland served as the host country for a conference titled "The CDCC Teacher Bursaries Scheme. A European Teacher's Seminar on the Teaching of Linguistic and Cultural Minorities." The seminar had a multicultural focus and emphasized the instruction of linguistic and cultural minorities with an eye toward integration of these students into both school and society in a way that would foster the retention of both language and culture. In addition, teachers from both Sweden and Finland worked together to focus on intercultural needs and interests, with an emphasis on the importance of teacher education in the process of building better understanding and promoting educational equity for all learners.

SUMMARY

Although the respondent to the authors' international survey specified that Finland had no formal multicultural education program, it can be seen that some interesting efforts are currently taking place in the schools. The Finns attempt to provide instruction in the students' native language whenever possible. While this has not been a major issue compared to some countries, it constitutes an honest effort to meet the needs of minority students.

Also, the Finnish constitution provides students with access to equal educational opportunities which seem to be absent in some countries. Moreover, the history of indigenous populations appears to be a substantial part of the basic curriculum. Finally, it is encouraging to note that the very small ethnic minorities are not forced to assimilate into the dominant culture. The Samis feel strongly that the inclusion of the Sami language in the teaching programs of Finland has had a positive effect on the development of the students' identity and their attitudes toward their own cultural background.

REFERENCES

Gonen, Amiram. *The Encyclopedia of the Peoples of the World.* New York: Henry Holt Publishing Co., 1993.

Gordon, Tuula. "Citizens and Others: Gender, Democracy and Education." Unpublished Paper, University of Helsinki, 1992.

Kosonen, Liisa. The Teacher Bursaries Scheme. A European Teacher's Seminar on the Teaching of Linguistic and Cultural Minorities. Vaaksey, Finland, 1990.

Mitchell, Bruce and Salsbury, Robert. Responses received from the authors' international multicultural education study. Cheney, WA: Eastern Washington University, Unpublished Monograph, 1991. (See Appendix.)

Pietila, Asta (Ed.). *Education of the Samis in Finland.* Helsinki National Board of General Education Research and Development Bureau, 1981.

Solsten, Eric and Meditz, Sandra (Eds.). *Finland: A Country Study.* Washington, DC: U.S. Government Printing Office, 1990, pp. xxiii–26.

Sundquist, J. "Ethnicity, Migration, and Health: A Population-Based Study of 338 Refugees from Latin America, 396 Non-Refugee Immigrants from Finland, and 161 from Southern Europe and 996 Age-Matched, Sex-Matched." *Scandinavian Journal of Social Welfare,* Vol. 4, No. 1 (1995), pp. 2–7.

15

France

HISTORY OF THE SYSTEM

According to some historians, there has never truly been a French race. None-theless, it has been argued by some that a few thousand years ago, in the area comprising present-day France, Celtic tribes of warriors and shepherds moved into the valleys of the Rhine and Rhone. Belonging to the Indo-European group, these new migrants came from the Danube area and they were able to forge the two-edged iron sword, which was considered to be the finest weapon of the time.

These early Celts migrated to Asia Minor, crossed the Rhine and the Alps, eventually becoming the overlords for the areas which now make up France and Spain. Celtic societies were divided into clans, while a group of the clans formed a tribe. Several clans sometimes would band together in order to form a nation.

The villages in that area have been described as looking like some of the dwellings which could be found in central Africa. Mud-wattle huts were thatched with straw. The people worshipped local and rural divinities such as Borvo, the god of hot springs. They also practiced a more secret cult which included ele-ments which were taught by the secret fraternity of the Druids who believed that the human spirit survived death and dwelled in a new body.

The culture was barbarous but not really savage. The people were intelligent, sensitive about the mysteries of life, had an interest in the use of words, and were good craftspersons and good soldiers. Eventually, Caesar captured the area and treated the people quite severely. For 500 years, this area remained a Roman province. But by A.D. 476, the western segment of the Roman Empire ceased to exist and became a cluster of Barbarian kingdoms. No organized state existed, but local warrior bands existed, and eventually the chieftain of the Franks, Clo-vis, dominated the other Barbarians throughout Gaul.

By the start of the sixth century, monasticism had been reformed by Saint

Benedict who founded the monastery of Saint Cassino in Italy and published his famous *Rule of the Monastic Life*. But by A.D. 725, Arab invaders moved up the Rhone valley, eventually in the southern portion of modern-day France. Later in that century, Charlemagne had motivated an intellectual renaissance which would exert a profound influence on the country for many years to come. However, by 888 seven kingdoms emerged, including France, Navarre, Provence, Burgundy, Lorraine, Germany, and Italy.

During the eleventh century, present-day France experienced a rebirth of the cities and the formation of a third estate. New fortified towns grew up to protect marketplaces, and the residents of these new boroughs were referred to as bourgeois. During the development of these new towns, rules were drawn up and leaders were selected. As a matter of fact, this practice was being carried on throughout most of Europe.

The new bourgeois class supported the king. One of the most influential kings of the time was Louis VI. Referred to as "Louis VI, the Fat," he attempted to establish a strong communication system between the royal and episcopal cities. He also was the self-appointed defender of French customs. He was often praised for defending churches, watching over the peace of the realm, and succoring the poor.

One of the most famous French kings was Louis XIV. He was a man with a rather violent temper but he also had a great sense of piety. He was canonized later and actually became Saint Louis. He was a courageous soldier who participated in two crusades. In fact, he eventually died in Tunis, the victim of the plague. During his reign, he respected the legitimacy of the feudal system but was quick to suppress its excesses and abuses.

During the Middle Ages, the French civilization began to unfold. The Middle Ages was a period of time during which the development of a moral and social equilibrium would affect Europeans and others for years to come. Moreover, it was a time of creation. In fact, some of the greatest art works of the western part of the world came into existence during this period of time. The imposition of Latin by the Catholic Church provided a communication system which made it easier for people on the European continent to interact. The development of the French Renaissance helped to spread many of the arts which would influence that part of the world so profoundly.

It was the Church that commenced to develop quasi-schools for privileged children. Priests taught children their catechism, consisting of reading, writing, and simple arithmetic. Bishop's schools were able to provide licenses for people who wished to become involved in the teaching enterprise. The University of Paris became an important university, and Robert de Sorbon founded the Community of Poor Masters and Scholars, the first college in the University of Paris. Moreover, the University of Paris was utilized by the Pope to spread sound doctrine.

Another important intellectual during this era was Saint Thomas Aquinas, who spent the better part of his career reassuring the faithful that it was possible to reconcile Aristotle's philosophical doctrines with the Scriptures, and intelligence with faith. Because of Saint Thomas, faith was confirmed, but at the same time, scientific research was legitimized.

During the Hundred Years War, a nationalistic spirit in France was beginning to surface. Edward III attempted to lay claim to the crown of France. The war became an imperialist way. It was popular in England because it led English soldiers into the wealthy countryside of western France where English soldiers came across rather lucrative spoils. As a result of the conflicts, France almost ceased to exist as a free nation. An English regent governed in Paris. But perhaps the most significant event during that period was the death of Joan of Arc, a peasant's daughter and shepherd. In the eyes of the English, Joan was a witch and a heretic, and of course she was ultimately burned at the stake. The incident served to create France's moral unity; and for the French, Joan's assassination became the utmost symbol of patriotism. However, the Hundred Years War practically bankrupted the country. Also, it weakened the status of the king and provided hope for the landowners who attempted to develop states within the states.

Following the Hundred Years War, France experienced a gradual transition from the middle ages to modern times during the fourteenth and fifteenth centuries. Because of the evolution of the printing process, more people were becoming literate. Universities were becoming more prominent, and the country began to value education more than ever before. Of course, this interest in education was intensified dramatically during the Renaissance.

For France, the Renaissance was a time during which the "good things of life" came into prominence. It was also a time of discoveries and explorations. French explorers reached Newfoundland and Guinea, and Cartier had ventured to Canada. Moreover, the court was most favorable to artists and writers, particularly poets. After Martin Luther nailed his 95 theses to the door of the castle church in Wittenberg, the Protestant Reformation would exert its influence on France and the rest of Europe as well. Toward the end of the sixteenth century, Henry IV found himself a Protestant king in a primarily Catholic country.

During the eighteenth century, the emerging political and religious philosophy actually began to take shape as a political entity. Voltaire spoke of a country in which people could think freely and nobly. Rousseau's writings articulated the kind of world which young children required if they were to become properly nurtured. Even artists were making significant changes. Tiring of the grandeur of previous works of art, they turned to a format which tended to stress the peace and honesty of average persons' lives.

Perhaps the most significant event during the eighteenth century was the French Revolution. Eventually, King Louis XVI attended the meeting of the National Assembly on February 4, 1790 in order to announce his acceptance of the principles of the Revolution. He also promised to prepare people to accept the new changes which this set of circumstances had brought about. A new constitution was drawn up which created a legislature. In general, the King was cooperative in the new venture.

In the nineteenth century, the military exploits of Napoleon resulted in France conquering an enormous portion of the European continent. He believed in force, and argued that if you wished to govern you should first and foremost be a soldier. A person could only rule with spurs and boots. By 1805, he decided that he wanted peace in order to reorganize France and build the country a great navy. However, England had other ideas and was bent on revenge. Moreover, his foray into Russia resulted in major supply problems. The Europe which had once been sympathetic to Napoleon turned against him, and the country of France became war weary.

After Napoleon's defeat, a provisional government was established, but this second republic had only a short duration. The Constitution of 1852 created a president who was elected for ten years. The president had the power to make treaties, war, and appoint all officials. The president held all the executive power, and neither the president nor the ministers were bound by any of the decisions of the chambers. The president could propose all legislation, and a senate included 150 life members who were appointed by the president. Obviously, this was a very authoritarian empire, and the War of 1870 brought about its collapse.

An election held in 1871 returned a national assembly which consisted mostly of moderates and conservatives. Historians have argued that this particular election was essentially a signal for peace by the French citizenry. A conservative, Adolphe Thiers, was chosen to head up the provisional government which established its headquarters in Versailles. Paris was outraged over the decision. By 1875, the Third Republic was established. The philosophical principles underlying the latest of the French republics were monarchism, republicanism, radicalism, reaction, Bonipartism, and clericalism.

During the era of the Third Republic, France built the Eiffel Tower, presented the Statue of Liberty to the United States as a gift, and, after 1870, the country emerged as Europe's cultural inspiration. Indeed, during that period France saw the brilliant artistic works of Gauguin, Lautrec, Picasso, Degas, Van Gogh, and many others. In addition, brilliant music was created by Bizet, Debussy, and Ravel. In addition to the artistic works were the accomplishments by scientists such as Curie (radiology), Poincare (mathematics), and Pasteur (bacteriology).

By 1914, France, Great Britain, and Russia had formed the Triple Entente as a buffer against the Triple Alliance (Germany, Italy, and Austria). During the first four months of World War I, France suffered an estimated 850,000 casualties. The United States entered the war in 1917 and, eventually, the Treaty of Versailles was signed which terminated the hostilities. But France paid dearly for its wartime role. The country lost 1,322,000 young men, one-fourth being under the age of 18. In addition, there were three million wounded. These losses placed serious limitations on the country's available workforce after the Armistice. The war nearly ruined France economically, and by 1919 the country had generated a debt of 175 billion francs.

The Bloc National acquired the political power first. A Nationalist–Catholic alliance, it was formed to protect the interests of the right wing and the Church. When Germany defaulted on its reparations payments in 1923, Marshal Foch occupied the Ruhr Valley in order to enforce payment. During this period, all the Socialists would do was to help the Radicals fend off the bloc. In 1929, the United States stock market crashed and France was deeply affected when the unemployment rate shot up to 1,300,000. By 1932, the Nazis took control of the German Reichstag and Hitler assumed control in 1933.

After Munich in 1938, France signed a pact with Germany which agreed to let Germany expand in the east. By that time, the French appeared to have an army equivalent to that of Germany, but Germany prevailed and established the German-controlled Vichy government. Charles de Gaulle persuaded the Americans and British to let him be the head of the free French forces and, inside France, a strong resistance movement beleaguered the Germans with acts of sabotage. In 1944, the allies landed in Bordeaux, and France was ultimately liberated from Germany.

After the war, de Gaulle established a provisional government with the argument that he had saved the country from communism, although some historians have argued vigorously that he did not. During 1946, a new constitution was drawn up and the Fourth Republic of France came into existence. But by 1947, communists and socialists discovered that they could not coexist, and a third party evolved, consisting of radicals, socialists, and a new party called the Popular Republican Movement. Between 1947 and 1958, governments in France lasted an average of only about six months.

By 1958, another new constitution was drawn up and the Fifth Republic emerged. The president was recognized as the national sovereignty and the assembly continued to function as a parliament, but with its powers of government curtailed and its sessions limited to six months out of the year. Legislative power was given to the premier and cabinet, which was no longer responsible to the assembly. The president was able to choose the premier. de Gaulle became the new leader, and his policies included tax increases, reduction of state expenditure in veterans' pensions and food subsidies, a wage-price freeze, and devaluation of the franc. By the early 1970s the policies appeared to have positive benefits, but the gap between the "haves" and the "have-nots" was widening.

STRUCTURE OF THE SYSTEM

Presently, France is still governed by the Constitution of 1958. Elected by citizens over 18 years of age, the National Assembly shares legislative and amending powers with the upper house. The French constitution and its corresponding laws have established strict rules of conduct for individual representatives as well as for parliament as a total body. The extent of the parliament's law-making powers is clearly articulated in the national constitution. According to the current working constitution, the executive was to be a two-headed body with power distributed between the president and the premier. The president is the head of state and also the executive leader of the government. Elected by direct popular vote, the president can run for re-election once. The president then appoints the premier who offers advice on the appointment over the team of ministers. The president is able to dissolve the parliament once in any twelve-month period. The president is also able to submit bills for special vote by the people, in the event that a need is perceived for going over the head of the parliament.

Furthermore, the president is able to invoke special powers and rule by dictatorship in the event of a serious crisis. The procedure was crafted by de Gaulle, and for the most part it is viewed favorably by the people. Critics of the procedure argue that the French constitution allows the president too much power and, indeed, the French parliament does seem to have less influence on government than its British counterpart or the United States Congress.

Local government in France consists of a three-tiered structure. The country is divided into about 36,000 communes, each guarding its autonomy. These communes are run by a mayor and municipal council which are elected by popular vote. Some mayors are quite powerful and actually double as national politicians in Paris. The middle tier of government includes 96 "departments" which are usually named after some specific geographical feature such as a river.

One of the commonalties between the French people and those who populate other democracies around the world is that citizens enjoy making use of their rights in order to address their specific interests. A great number of pressure groups exist in France. Rather than attempting to influence the parliament, it seems that the greatest efforts to create pressures for their pet issues are directed toward the personal staffs of the various ministers.

Electoral participation is high in the country. Typically, about 80 percent of the registered voters go to the polls, which compares favorably to other European democracies. It is much higher than the normal turnout in the United States where the voter turnout sometimes fails to reach the 50 percent mark.

Like the other Western countries, except for the United States, France has benefits of health insurance for employees. This coverage is provided by employers and workers contributions, and these benefits are available for sickness, injuries at work, maternity, disablement, and old age. The national health care system has made enormous improvements in recent years, and is considered to be among the best systems found anywhere in the world.

France has one of the world's more uniform systems of public education. This is due to the supremacy of the central government. The Ministry of Education has the power to appoint teachers, allocate resources, make curriculum decisions, and administer examinations for elementary and secondary students throughout the entire country. Moreover, the Ministry decides where schools should be located. While the country has a system of local school councils, consisting of officials, parents, teachers, and local community representatives, they have little power due to the centralized nature of the nation's school system.

Education is compulsory for all children between the ages of six and sixteen, and early childhood education has also become an integral part of the French school system. A large number of three-year old children and practically all four- and five-year olds are enrolled in *ecole maternelles*. Only Belgium has a more comprehensive system of pre-school education than France.

The French elementary schools have five grades which lead up to matriculation in the secondary schools. Pupils are required to meet fixed standards at the end of each grade. The curriculum consists of a core of French and mathematics which is supplemented by "curiosity awakening" subjects such as history, geography, civics, moral education, science, art, and music. A four-year secondary school program is then provided up through the compulsory attendance age of 16. The *lycees* serve as upper secondary schools.

French school teachers are civil servants employed by the central government. Teachers are paid at different rates according to the grade they teach and the ability of the students with whom they work. Some of them teach for different periods of time, and the teachers have various levels of training according to the grades they teach.

Most of the private schools are Roman Catholic and they receive only minimal government support. They enroll about 20 percent of the nation's school children. In general, the Roman Catholic schools provide education for lower-income children in schools which tend to be rather poorly equipped compared to those in the public sector.

MULTICULTURAL EDUCATION EFFORTS

The French people are from a variety of racial backgrounds. The Latin background is probably the most pronounced. There seems to be heavy influence from the southerly Mediterranean areas, but other strains include rather tall, fair descendants from Denmark's Vikings; the shorter, darker people of Celtic origin; and people from the old Germanic tribes. In recent years, the country has experienced an increased number of immigrants. Because of its liberal policies, immigrants have entered the country from southern Europe, North Africa, and Algeria. Moreover, France has always had a liberal policy of welcoming political refugees which allowed many people from places such as Indo-China and Communist Europe. While the Europeans have been readily accepted and assimilated, unemployment problems have sometimes made life rather difficult for the North Africans.

Because of its egalitarian philosophy throughout the years, France has been long known as a haven for people who were subjected to racism in other countries. For example, African-American jazz musicians such as Sidney Bechet spent much of their careers in France because of their acceptance by the French. Interviews with such musicians revealed that they were treated better and were more appreciated than in the United States.

While there was a time when certain languages were discouraged by the

French, presently they are used in the schools. In general, there has been a rather striking change in the country's tolerance for the use of different languages. In fact, since World War II, many English words have crept into the French language. However, such language changes have been attacked by language purists as has been the case in many other countries. While French is the official language of instruction in the schools, other languages are sometimes used in order to ensure that students receive the best education possible.

France is predominantly Catholic, with 90 percent of the population still belonging to the Catholic Church. However, the historical domination by the Catholic Church has waned recently with the country adapting a more secular posture. The Catholic Church hierarchy has not attempted to impose its authority over the new diverse trends in Catholicism. Also, the country has a number of religious minorities, with Protestants and Jews comprising the largest group. While anti-Semitism was a problem before the end of World War II, it still exists to some degree, but the incidents seem to be diminishing in number.

The role of women in the country has become much more liberalized since 1945 when they received the right to vote. Prior to that time, their role was primarily that of homemaker. Recently, women have been moving ahead in the workplace, coming closer to receiving equal compensation for equal work compared to men. The percentages of women in the professions has also been rising. Now, about 30 percent of the nation's young doctors are women.

However, French women still seem to be reluctant to enter politics. Since the end of World War II, less than 10 percent of the members of the 480-member National Assembly were women. The Women's Movement, so pronounced in the United States, did not quite catch on in France, and the concept of *vive la petite difference* seemingly has had an effect.

SUMMARY

Perhaps the biggest problems encountered by France have resulted from its location in the continent of Europe. Like the rest of Europe, France has been forced to participate in two of history's greatest wars in the same century. The country has successfully made the transformation to a strong, independent European republic.

Its education system, like many of the systems of Europe, has historically maintained a strong central direction, led by a minister of education whose office is able to make decisions which affect the educational futures of children and teachers from all parts of the land. This has resulted in a uniform educational effort all over the country.

Perhaps France can best be characterized as a nation with a strong egalitarian spirit which has made it possible for immigrants and minorities to live with dignity and peace. The country is also famous for its unique contributions to Western culture. The philosophical principals of democracy have had profound influences on such countries as Canada and the United States.

Finally, the strong system of public education in France has helped to serve as an example to the rest of the world. The example is that in order for a country to become truly great, it must make every effort to initiate educational programs which attempt to provide a solid education for all children regardless of gender, race, ethnicity, or level of affluence.

REFERENCES

Ardlagh, John. *France in the 1980s.* New York: Penguin, 1983.

Barnard, H.C. *Education and the French Revolution.* Cambridge, MA: Harvard University Press, 1969.

Brinton, Crane. *The Americans and the French.* Cambridge, MA: Harvard University Press, 1968.

Gonen, Amiram. *The Encyclopedia of the Peoples of the World.* New York: Henry Holt Publishing Co., 1993.

Guerard, Albert. *France, A Short History.* New York: W.W. Norton, 1946.

Lebovics, Herman. *True France.* Ithaca, NY: Cornell University Press, 1992.

Lewis, H.D. *The French Education System.* New York: St. Martin's Press, 1985.

Maurois, Andre. *A History of France.* New York: Farrar, Strauss, & Cudahy, 1956.

Peyrefitte, Alain. *The Trouble with France.* Tom Bishop and Nicholas Wahl (Eds.), trans. William R. Bryan. New York: NYU Press, 1986.

Schlesinger, Philip. "On National Identity: Some Conceptions and Misconceptions Criticized." *Social Science Information,* Vol. 26 (1987), pp. 219–264.

Talbott, John E. *The Politics of Educational Reform in France, 1918–1940.* Princeton, NJ: Princeton University Press, 1969.

16

Germany

HISTORY OF THE SYSTEM

The history of present-day Germany has been traced back to prehistoric times by writers such as the Roman author Tacitus (A.D. 55–116), who described the Germanic tribes' political and social organization, modes of warfare, notions about crime and punishment, and other social mores. However, the history is even older than that, since anthropologists have placed the Neanderthals in the region. Moreover, stone-, bronze-, and iron-age civilizations have been described.

The Roman Empire extended to the areas which presently comprise the German nation, and profound influences were felt by the people who lived under Roman control in the Germanic areas. By the fifth century, the Roman Empire began its famous decline, and medieval Germany under the Saxon and Salian dynasties was characterized as a dominating military aristocracy with a feudal organization of society and politics. Most people resided in small villages, hamlets, and isolated farmlands which were surrounded by large forests. Houses were rather primitive, and only the castles were built to last for long periods of time. The average life expectancy was thought to have been only about 30 years, even though the figures were much higher for the wealthy.

The feudal system became the major form of socio-political organization, with the vassal swearing allegiance to the lord who in turn promised protection. By the eleventh century, a conflict erupted in Germany between subvassals, non-heritable fiefs, and major vassals. This dispute led to the development of a feudal law code called the Constitutio de Feudis, which was issued in 1037. About this time, the knights started to emerge as a class which would find itself between the peasants and the higher nobility.

The church was responsible for the revival of intellectual life because of the monasteries, episcopal churches, and cathedral schools. Many of these entities were either founded or revived during the tenth century. The Salin dynasty, beginning with Conrad II in 1024, was a period of time during which there was a great deal of construction. Palaces and cathedrals were erected, but a decrease in the consolidation of the imperial monarchy and a temporary union of church and state also occurred.

During the later middle ages, the size and number of towns increased rather dramatically. By the mid-thirteenth century, there were about 3,000 towns which were mostly rather small but enjoyed considerable importance. They also were mostly self-governed. They led to a greater level of urbanization throughout the country, and their main features can be observed throughout Germany today in the form of town walls, castles, fortifications, churches, rather elaborate town halls, guild halls, and burgher houses.

Between 1200 and 1300 B.C., the population of present-day Germany increased from about eight million to fourteen million people. Peasants who colonized the eastern territories were able to take advantage of a considerable level of personal freedoms compared to other European peoples. But during the fourteenth century, dramatic decreases in population occurred as a result of the Black Death (Bubonic Plague). It is during this period that Jews, who migrated to Germany from elsewhere, were often made scapegoats for the plague and were even accused of poisoning the water.

By the year 1500, the geographical area comprising present-day Germany was referred to as the ''Holy Roman Empire of the German Nation.'' Its political map consisted of dynastic and ecclesiastical territories which included free cities and castles of knights. The Reichstag was in operation and consisted of three chambers which were regularly summoned. Historians have described this time as the beginning of the German Reformation. One significant religious change occurred in 1517 when an academic theologian named Martin Luther wrote his set of 95 theses which he posted on the door of the Castle Church in Wittenberg. In fact, some historians look upon this single action as the beginning of the Reformation. Luther's primary quarrel about the existing Church was that salvation could be achieved by good works, including donations to the church, and that indulgences were sold to buy time off from purgatory. Out of this action, the German Lutheran church would provide a strong influence on the social and moral climate of the country.

During 1524–1526, a number of peasant revolts eventually led to the German Peasants War. Starting in the southern Black Forest and Lake Constance areas, the ultimate suppression of the uprisings resulted in about 100,000 peasants losing their lives while many more were maimed and blinded. Some of the leaders of the peasants were actually clergy, while many members of lower-ranking urban dwellers, artisans, and peasants were supporters of the rebellion.

Also during the Reformation, a series of major conflicts occurred between the Catholics and Lutherans. The Peace of Augsburg in 1555 helped to resolve some of the hostilities, but many of the problems were still left unresolved.

The German counter-Reformation occurred after the Council of Trent (1545–

1563). Catholics attempted to win back the ground they had lost. Thus, the Society of Jesus (Jesuits), founded by Ignatius Loyola, initiated an aggressive campaign through the schools, seminaries, universities, and the courts. Protestantism was not united, and Calvinism became more powerful during the latter sixteenth and earlier portion of the seventeenth centuries.

The seventeenth century also saw a complex set of situations in the Holy Roman Empire and the European states which eventually led to the Thirty Years War (1618–1648). By 1630, the conflicts had become quite international. The Jesuit-educated Archduke Ferdinand of Austria attempted to establish control of Germany. However, his efforts were thwarted by the intervention of Swedish king Gustavus Adolphus. A settlement of hostilities was finally consummated in the Peace of Westpahalia which was negotiated in 1648.

The Thirty Years War was a significant episode in German history. It constituted an important stage in the decentralization of the Holy Roman Empire. After that time in history Germany became a series of small- and medium-sized principalities, courtly nobilities, and bureaucracies. There was a general loss of self-confidence in German culture and a need for a general renewal after a long period of instability and suffering. The situation created a condition which generated an age of absolutism which existed from 1648 to 1815. But the Peace of Westphalia did not end the long period of warfare which occurred during the seventeenth century. Various wars were fought on German soil in the latter half of the century, and in the eighteenth as well.

From 1648 to 1815, there developed a court-oriented military aristocracy and a new, educated middle class which often held positions as civil servants and minor court officials. The literacy and education of the people was expanding and new ideas were being discussed. The issue of religion no longer would precipitate warfare; rather the topic became part of the country's history and their tradition of absolute authority came into question. There was a vigorous literary revival and German became a literary language once again.

The same period of time also saw the creation of some of the world's great classical music. The musical work of Johann Sebastian Bach, Franz Joseph Haydn, and Wolfgang Amadeus Mozart would make an enormous impact on the world's music. Also, during this period of German Enlightenment, the philosophical work of Immanuel Kant did a great deal in framing the patterns of thought which emerged during this time in history. Indeed, Kant defined enlightenment as the courage to use one's reason to think independently and critically. It also related to the refusal to accept the tutelage of somebody else's authority. Kant also developed important notions about universal morality, peace, and world citizenship.

Military expansion also impacted Germany during this time frame as the French armies invaded the turf of the Holy Roman Empire. France captured all of the German territories west of the Rhine River. Under the occupation of the French, administrative, judicial, and legal systems were reorganized. Also, serfdom and feudal social relations were abolished.

The year 1815 ushered in a 100-year period of industrial growth and development. While there definitely was a liberal faction in the country during this time, the prevailing political force consisted of the reactionary conservative movement. The liberals were primarily members of the professional middle classes; and the system of idealist philosophy was developed by Friedrich Hegel and would affect human beings all over the world.

The 100-year period saw Germany change from a feudal, rural state to an increasingly industrialized society. After a rather slow start, the industrialization process grew steadily and finally erupted into a volatile transformation by the end of the century. Some of the main improvements were more sophisticated communications, programs of road building, the improvement of navigability on Germany's rivers, the construction of canals to link rivers, and, finally, the introduction of steamboats on the Rhine River. The first German train to be developed was a line connecting Leipzig and Dresden. Rails greatly facilitated the transportation of many new German goods to the market.

However, German industrial development was not without its critics. German doctors warned of problems related to traveling at high rates of speed. In spite of this concern, the rail system was greatly expanded in subsequent years. However, in spite of the great increase in industrial output, the largest proportion of Germans continued to make their livings as farmers, small-scale traders, artisans, and handicrafts persons.

Other socio-economic changes were occurring in Germany which would lead to political upheavals. In Europe, a general population expansion had been taking place, and in Germany, as in other parts of the continent, people were affected by the Revolutions of 1848 which were motivated by the French Revolution.

During the 1850s and 1860s, there was a general expansion of education which often manifested itself in the form of museums, zoos, theaters, and art galleries. The economy was becoming increasingly powerful which helped to motivate a stable bourgeois culture. However, a lack of certainty seemed to prevail in respect to national identity. Unification of the country in 1871 resulted because of Prussian expansionism and the colonization of non-Prussian Germany. This unification excluded Austria which had been weakened because of the Crimean War and a number of difficulties in Italy.

Otto von Bismarck, the son of a Prussian Junker, was appointed the Prussian Prime Minister. After the termination of the Franco-Prussian War in 1871, the German empire was proclaimed in a ceremony at Versailles. Many historians have argued that the new German Empire was actually an extension of Prussian power rather than a manifestation of a nationalistic demand for a united Germany. While Germany under Bismarck enjoyed two years of nearly unbridled economic success, a collapse of confidence led to an economic crash during 1873. A general economic depression gripped the country for several years. The 1870s led to the division of the liberal factions and a gradual movement toward a more conservative socio-political posture. Also during this time, Jews commenced to assimilate in the country, many becoming prominent in the nation's various banking enterprises.

This new conservatism of the 1880s was also accompanied by a new increase in a growing membership of the German Social Democratic Party. Viewed as a threat by Bismarck, he successfully pushed through an anti-socialist law through the Reichstag. In effect, the law banned socialist meetings, periodicals, newspapers, organizations, and associations. The legacy of Bismarck was twofold. On one hand, he was responsible for the unification and nationalization of the country. However, he was also the architect of a state with great authoritarian characteristics.

From 1871 to the start of World War I in 1914, Germany went through a period during which the general character of the country would be forever changed. While the population of France only increased by four million during this time, Germany's population grew from 41 million in 1871 to 67.7 million in 1914. During this period of time, Germany experienced dramatic population increases in its towns and cities. Anxious to participate in new industrial centers, young Germans left the farms in hopes of bettering themselves economically.

However, the cultural life of Imperial Germany consisted of many different strands. This diversity in cultural values was also existent in the popular culture of the land. While the bourgeoisie tended to adopt certain aristocratic manners and customs, many of the constraints of a rather stuffy, bourgeoise psyche were rejected by a burgeoning youth movement throughout the land. The writings of Nietzsche had a lasting but rather ambiguous impact with significant influence on scholars such as Weber. He developed a set of social and political concepts which forever left a profound influence on the country.

World War I, starting in 1914, was precipitated by the assassination of Archduke Franz Ferdinand, the Austrian heir to the throne. His murderer was a young Bosnian who killed him during a visit to the capital of the annexed Bosnia-Herzegoniva, Sarajevo. Early in the conflict, the German people experienced a great deal of enthusiasm. However, the war became a long series of trench-warfare battles with extremely high casualties. Moreover, the German economy was not suited for withstanding a long war of attrition. Splits developed within the ranks of the German Socialists and the Independent Socialist Democratic Party. Eventually, there were major food riots, and the United States entry to the war in 1917 was the beginning of the end for Germany. Finally, in 1918, the German empire collapsed and Germany's first parliamentary republic ensued. It became known as the Weimar Republic, since it was conceived in that German town. Hampered by an unstable economy, it was rather short lived, ending when Adolf Hitler assumed control of the country in 1933 after a clash between Communist and Nazi factions.

During March 1936, Hitler's armies had militarized the Rhineland. During this year, Hitler announced that Germany needed to prepare for war within the next four years. At this time, a Four Year Plan under Hermann Goering was announced. The Spanish Civil War, which broke out in 1936, helped create a

Berlin–Rome "Axis" which brought the two countries closer together. During 1938, a bloodless invasion of Austria occurred when German troops marched into Hitler's native land.

After taking control of Czechoslovakia, partly because of the appeasement efforts of England's Neville Chamberlain, Hitler invaded Poland after negotiating a pact with Joseph Stalin of Russia. Both countries had an interest in dismantling Poland, and Germany was able to defeat the country in just three weeks. However, this action precipitated a declaration of war on Germany by both England and France. Nazi conquests of France, Norway, Holland, and Belgium led to a feeling of invincibility, and Hitler proceeded to attack Yugoslavia and Belgium. Moreover, Goering convinced Hitler that Britain was also vulnerable, and the German Luftwaffe started the air attacks on that nation.

During the summer of 1941, Hitler began his disastrous invasion of Russia. As a result of the Japanese attack on the American fleet at Pearl Harbor, Germany declared war on the United States. However, Germany's disastrous defeat at Stalingrad, the relentless air attacks by the Americans and the British, the Russian offensive to the east, coupled by the invasion at Normandy, ultimately led to defeat in 1945.

When the wartime atrocities came to light, it was reported that more than six million Jews, a great number of Europe's Gypsy population, and many other opponents of Nazism had been murdered as a result of World War II. These mass murders, which occurred in the same highly "cultured" country that had produced folk heroes such as Bach and Goethe, have never been fully understood or adequately explained by the world community. To this day, the issue has provided great debates the world over.

Following the termination of the war, the country was in ruin, and two Germanys (East and West) existed until 1990. The United States, Russia, and the Soviet Union agreed that Germany should be denazified, demilitarized, and democratized. The new Federalist Republic (known as West Germany) was a capitalistic democracy. It evolved into a politically stable and economically prosperous state. The German Democratic Republic (East Germany) became arguably the most productive state in the Communist bloc and a reliable supporter of the Soviet Union until the Gorbachev era of the late 1980s. Berlin was partitioned into east and west sections as well. This condition prevailed until October 3, 1990, when the unification of the two Germanys finally took effect.

STRUCTURE OF THE SYSTEM

The first freely elected all-German parliament in 57 years met in the Reichstag building in December 1990. Reunited as the Federal Republic of Germany, Berlin was designated the capital in place of Bonn, the ex–West German capital. Two treaties were negotiated by the two Germanys, and the four World War II allies (Russia, England, France, and the United States) granted full sovereignty to the newly united Germany and suspended all of their own residual rights.

Executive authority continued to be vested in the federal chancellor and cabinet. The president's powers as chief of state were unchanged. The Bundestag (the lower house of parliament) was expanded from 519 to 663. The West German federal system was continued in the new republic, and the national government shared power with the constituent states. The states increased in number from 10 to 16, and Berlin became a full-fledged city state with voting rights. The upper house of parliament (the Bundestrat) increased from 41 to 69 members. The most populous states had six votes while the smaller ones had between three and five.

New German parties evolved due to the upheaval in the German Democratic Republic. In order to give these new political entities a chance for Bundestag representation, the electoral law was amended for the first all-German elections of 1990. It stipulated that a political party needed at least 5 percent of the total votes in eastern or western Germany rather than in all of Germany. The once-powerful Socialist Unity Party (SED) was renamed the Party of Democratic Socialism. Formerly it had governed the German Democratic Republic. In the first all-German elections of 1990, it won enough votes to give it seats in the Bundestag. Another east German party to win seats was Alliance '90, a coalition of citizen groups, the Greens, and the Independent Women's Association. However, the bulk of the seats were controlled by western Germany parties and their merged eastern German counterparts: the Christian Democrats, the Social Democrats, and the Free Democrats.

In eastern Germany's new states, a number of ministries and agencies were established with the help of civil servants from western Germany. Treaties between the two Germanys provided for the creation of a social service establishment that would provide social assistance, pension plans, unemployment and sickness compensation, and accident and health insurance. Problems of unemployment in east Germany were met with huge vocational retraining programs and a modernization of the infrastructure. These problem solutions were funded from the central government, western German states, and the European community.

The legal system and law enforcement agencies in eastern Germany were altered so they were similar to those of western Germany. Court decisions handed down before unification were valid unless they were not in compliance with the newly developed laws. Victims of persecution under the German Democratic Republic received compensation. However, the entire legal system was suffering from a lack of judges and trial lawyers in eastern Germany which greatly hampered the judicial process. East Germany's army was combined with the West German army, but the two states had pledged to reduce the number of armed forces in the next few years.

Some scholars have argued that when Adolf Hitler took over the country in 1933, Germany had the most highly educated population in the entire world. The country's educational system had become the primary source for disseminating the Nazi philosophy. The Nazi notions about Aryan supremacy were part of the school curriculum, and the schools were even stripped of Jewish teachers during this period of time. The same situation was true in the nation's universities, when Jews were purged from the faculties of higher education throughout the land. Physical education became a major part of the curriculum, and the country's humanistic traditions were rejected in favor of racist philosophies and a glorification of violence.

After reunification, immense political, economic, and educational problems confronted the newly united nation. Immediately, the curriculum question addressed was how to purge the east German schools of their communistic philosophy. Although most of the civics courses were abolished and many school principals and teachers who had been active members of the Communist party were dismissed, there was still a great deal of confusion about how far the purging should go. The structural and administrative organization of the nation's schools would consist of a number of decisions about the new educational system which should exist in each of the German states. Generally, the legislatures abolished the east German polytechnic school models in favor of the west German models. Moreover, the reconstruction of the German universities, particularly the east German ones, began in earnest.

MULTICULTURAL EDUCATION EFFORTS

Following reunification, one of the overriding issues was how to change an educational system that had created a rather monolithic world view into a system that addressed local issues as well as the needs of the new state, and promoted pluralistic attitudes as well. The latter issue was further complicated by the notion of "Aryan supremacy" which was promoted so vigorously during the Hitler regime. A further problem was presented by the changing cultural milieu. The Federal Republic became an increasingly multicultural and multiethnic society. Historically, the Germans had dealt with ethnic minorities (particularly the Jews) by suppressing them in a number of ways. Moreover, the east German attempts to create a "classless society" had failed, resulting in a number of new socioeconomic groups. These were the issues facing the reunified German school system during the early 1990s.

Still another problem for the new German republic has been the resurgence of a neo-Hitler youth movement. The newly unified country has been hard pressed to address the number of "skinhead" youth who seem bent on reverting to the old notions of Aryan supremacy which have plagued the country for part of the twentieth century. How effectively this problem can be addressed in Germany's educational system remains to be seen. Since the country did not respond to the authors' request for information in the original multicultural education survey, it is unclear as to how the schools are actually addressing this and other issues pertaining to specific multicultural education programs.

SUMMARY

Throughout modern history, the German educational system has been looked upon as a world leader. The creation of the kindergarten concept has prompted other countries to develop their own early-childhood educational programs. The work of outstanding German educators such as Froebel has profoundly influenced many educators the world over. Perhaps, much of this influence can be traced directly to the invention of the Gutenburg Press which helped people in this part of Europe become literate long before persons in other parts of the world had access to extensive printed materials. Moreover, the influence of the German Gymnasium has had an enormous influence on educational scholars.

However, the newly unified country is beset with two key problems relating to its multicultural enterprises. First, Germany is no longer a monocultural society. New groups of ethnic workers have required the schools to examine their educational efforts in order to assure that the needs of these newer groups of students are being met. Second, the re-emergence of German youth who have chosen to subscribe to the old notions of the "Hitler Youth Movement" has bewildered educators, law enforcement officials, and social workers. Whether these new problems can be solved by aggressive multicultural education programs in the schools remains to be seen.

REFERENCES

Brady, T. *Turning Swiss: Cities and Empire, 1450–1530.* Cambridge: Cambridge University Press, 1985.
Bramsted, Ernest K. *Germany.* Englewood Cliffs, NJ: Prentice-Hall, 1972.
Carr, W. *A History of Germany 1815–1985.* London: Edward Arnold, 1987.
Craig, Gordon. *The Germans.* New York: Putnam's Sons, 1982.
Fulbrook, Mary. *A Concise History of Germany.* Cambridge: Cambridge University Press, 1990.
Gill, Anton. *A Dance Between Flames.* New York: Carroll & Graff Publishers, 1993.
Grunberger, Richard. *A Social History of the Third Reich.* Harmondsworth: Penguin, 1979.
James, H. *The German Slump.* Oxford: Clarendon Press, 1986.
Noakes, J. and Pridham, G. (Eds.). *Nazism* (3 vols.). Exeter: Exeter Studies in History, 1988.
Planck, Max. *Between Elite and Mass Education* Albany, NY: SUNY Press (Institute for Human Development and Education), 1983.
Tent, James F. *Mission on the Rhine.* Chicago: University of Chicago Press, 1982.

17

Ghana

HISTORY OF THE SYSTEM

The history of Ghana is part of the history of the Gold Coast, a West African area which was a prime target for entrepreneurial Europeans who were searching for gold some 500 years ago. By that time, the need for cheap labor had surfaced, and soon after, the slave trade began. As a result of these two enterprises, a string of forts and castles was constructed. The slaves were branded with hot irons and crammed into damp dungeons where they were chained up in preparation for their journeys.

Some anthropologists argue that there is evidence of settlements along the coast of Ghana between 30,000 and 40,000 years ago, but the ancestors of today's Ghanaians probably migrated from the north. The Portuguese came during the late fifteenth century. Fortunes were made during the slave trade by Portugal, Spain, Holland, Britain, and Denmark. When the slave trade was finally outlawed, the British took over the forts and castles, and treaties were signed with some of the coastal chiefs. In 1873, the British attacked the Ghanaian city of Kumasi, capturing it after a year-long siege. They then declared it to be a Crown colony. However, resistance to the British by the Ashanti persisted in Kumasi through the turn of the century.

During the first few decades of the twentieth century, the British allowed few outsiders to have access to the Gold Coast area. Cocoa, gold, and timber were responsible for the region becoming one of Britain's most economically successful African colonies. Later in the century, the Gold Coast became the world's leaders in the production of manganese. Diamonds and bauxite were also popular exports.

Ghana has always had a reputation for having some of Africa's best schools. Indeed, the Cape Coast University, established in 1948, made it possible for young Ghanaian scholars to receive a higher-education degree at home. Prior to that time, it was necessary to go abroad for advanced studies.

One famous Ghanaian student who received his education abroad was Kwame Nkrumah. He studied and taught at Pennsylvania's Lincoln University where he developed his revolutionary ideas which he wished to apply to his native country. After his return to Ghana, he helped form the Convention People's Party (CPP). After calling a national strike, he was sent to prison by the British. However, after his party won the general elections in 1951, he was released by the British to form a new government. After agreeing to ban his slogan "Self-Government Now," he worked with Britain's colonial administrators and, in 1957, the British government granted independence to the country. Ghana thus became the first of the British colonies in Africa to become independent.

However, the early years of independence were turbulent. Within the first three decades following independence, Ghanaians experienced the birth and death of three republics, four successful military takeovers, six national development plans, a number of aborted overthrow attempts, and a major economic decline between 1976 and 1983.

One of Nkrumah's objectives was to promote pan-Africanism. As a result, he was instrumental in assisting other countries in acquiring their independence and exploring the possibility of developing a union of African nations. Nkrumah plotted to become the prime spokesperson for Africa but economic problems at home hastened his demise. Finally, after dismissing the Chief Ghanaian Justice and three Supreme Court Justices, Nkrumah was overthrown by army officers who assumed control through military rule in 1966.

The subsequent Ankrah administration tried to suppress national references to Nkrumah. It became a criminal offense to possess any of his writings or photographs. Moreover, it was illegal to spread his ideas. During this period of time, the Ankrah administration established the Centre for Civic Education whose purpose was to educate the people about Ghanaian politics. The Centre was headed by Dr. K.A. Busia who used his title to launch a political party, the Progress Party (P.P.), which won the 1969 national election.

During his three-year tenure, he liberalized trade to improve the supply of wage goods and promoted private ownership of businesses by local people through the granting of small business loans. However, a combination of student and labor opposition, and a general feeling of unhappiness, led to his overthrow by Colonel I.K. Acheampong in 1972. At that time, the cedi was de-valued, some debts were rescinded, and a national development levy was terminated. But foreign aid dried up and the country had a new slogan, "self-reliance."

Eventually, the regime was overthrown in 1979, ushering in the short administration of Flight Lieutenant Jerry Rawlings; but his leadership only lasted three months. However, inflation was out of control, and Dr. Hilla Limann's People's National Party (PNP) won the 1979 election. It, too, was beset with difficulties and, in 1981, another military takeover ensued which brought Rawlings back to the helm. From then to the present, the nation has been governed by a Provi-

sional National Defense Council (PNDC) which includes both military and civilian members. The goals have been to terminate corruption, create a more
equitable procedure for distributing the national wealth, and promote democracy
at the grass-roots level. Its methods have been generally authoritarian in regard
to many of its policies and practices. Although several unsuccessful military
takeovers have been recorded, the PNDC held district elections in 1989.

Ghana, like the other African countries, had an educational "system" which
was deeply rooted in the Ghanaian microcultures. Although different from the
European models, the traditional Ghanaian education efforts focused on the
tribal taboos, mores, and other functions of the microculture. In the child's
environment, adults helped young children become knowledgeable in history,
music, environmental studies, rhetoric, and philosophy. Both in the home and
community, young children have been taught about moral qualities, honesty,
sociability, courage, endurance, ethics, and honor. Dances, gymnastics, and
games comprised the physical education curriculum. Such educational undertakings are crucial in all cultures and can serve as prerequisites for the more formal
kinds of educational efforts. However, the more formal efforts are relatively
recent.

Western education came to Ghana during the early 1500s in order to facilitate
Europe's evangelistic efforts. The earliest schools were connected with the forts
and castles which were used by the European merchant companies for trading
centers. There was a school in 1529 at the Elmina castle which was operated
by the Portuguese. Similar schools were also run by the Dutch at the same site.
Founded in 1644, one Dutch school was in operation for some 200 years. While
the pupils in early schools such as these were largely the sons of the European
merchants and local women, there were also a few children of the wealthier
African traders in the urban areas.

Weslyan Methodists were among the most active missionaries in Ghana for
the 100-year period stretching from the mid-1800s to the mid-1900s. Actually,
the Weslyan Methodists had schools in about eighteen towns from Accra to
Cape Coast by 1844. German missionaries near the Volta region were also
influential. They established a school at Peki which eventually would come
under British control. But the north German (Bremen) missionaries were successful in putting Ewe (ev-vay), Twi (Twee), and Ga (gha) into written form.
After translating the Bible, they printed instructional pamphlets in the languages
of the various microcultures.

Finally, in 1882, the British colonial administration attempted to regulate West
Africa's struggling education efforts. It was decided to model the Ghanaian
schools after the British system. By 1890, a director of Ghanaian education was
appointed. Frederick Guggisberg became governor of the Gold Coast in 1919
and attempted to reform the educational system. After increasing the budget for
the area's education programs, he wrote his "sixteen principles" which became
the foundation for the Education Ordinance of 1925. He argued that literacy

alone was not an adequate education effort. His reforms included character building, thrift, temperance, etc.

The Great Depression of the 1930s affected Ghana as it did the rest of the world. In spite of the economic instability, the interest in education increased so much that by 1937 the colonial government appointed a committee to revise the system in keeping with the basic needs of the Ghanaian people. By 1950, the colonial government operated over 40 percent of the 2,904 primary schools. In the same year, Ghana had a total of nineteen teacher preparation institutions in operation which spurred more interest in the country's rapidly expanding system of education. The first university was founded in 1948. Located in Kumasi, it was established in order to provide courses in the humanities and sciences. By 1950, the British colonial government spent about 10 percent of its budget on education. However, the amount was not enough to provide universal primary education.

Shortly after achieving its independence from England, Ghana embarked on a plan to improve its higher education efforts. So in 1961 full university status was granted to the University of Ghana and the University of Science and Technology in Kumasi. After first being allied with the University of Ghana, the University of Cape Coast became one of the country's major universities.

Another milestone in Ghanaian education was the Education Act of 1961 which established the legal framework for compulsory education. The act also clarified the role of local education authorities (LEA), as well as the roles and positions of classroom teachers. Consequently, the number of primary and middle school children doubled, and the number of students in teacher education programs tripled. However, despite the increases in student population, an apparent decrease in the quality of the elementary and secondary school programs seemed to occur.

After Ghana became independent in 1957, Dr. Nkrumah became Chancellor of the University of Ghana where he deported a number of foreign lecturers, detained economics professor J.C. deGraft Johnson, and promoted lecturers to be professors. Morale was low due to an atmosphere of fear which his policies promoted. Many of the faculty members decided to leave the country in search of better teaching situations.

After Nkrumah's 1966 overthrow, the National Liberation Council named two bodies to investigate the country's educational system. The Mills-Odoi Commission recommended that secondary schools be redesigned in order to become decentralized. Moreover, it proposed the creation of a Teaching Service Division of the Public Service Commission and better salaries for educators. The Education Review Committee streamlined education according to the British system and insisted that private schools be inspected like the others.

During the Busia administration, a one-year development plan was created. The goals were to expand the number of secondary schools, diversify the curriculum, and open secondary schools which would specialize in technical and agricultural courses. The Busia regime also introduced an educational student loan plan which was designed to help students defray the costs of their education. However, a military takeover, led by Colonel I.K. Acheampong in 1972, would create yet one more education reform plan. Acheampong's administration helped mobilize students to become involved in community projects such as the construction of irrigation canals and the harvesting of sugar cane and other crops.

In December 1981, Flight Lieutenant Jerry Rawlings returned to power and established the Provisional National Defense Council (PNDC). These new reforms are particularly interesting in regard to curriculum reform. The concept of "basic education" was expanded in order to include the notion of a national macroculture in the school curriculum.

STRUCTURE OF THE SYSTEM

The Ghanaian educational system is organized around a 6-3-3 plan. The first six years are taken up with the primary school. Children then attend a three-year junior/senior school (J.S.S.), and then move into senior secondary schools which can either be technical, vocational, general, business/communication, or agricultural. The programs of the senior secondary schools are three years in duration.

Curriculum content for the junior secondary school curriculum includes a native Ghanaian language, a second Ghanaian language, general science, cultural studies, religion, music (including drumming and dancing), drama, arts and crafts, English, French, social studies, mathematics, youth program (including community service), physical education, agricultural science (including poultry and livestock keeping), home science, and pre-nursing. In addition to the required subjects, each student chooses two courses from the following list: woodwork, masonry, metalwork, technical drawing, pottery, commercial subjects, marine science, automobile practice, crafts, beauty culture (including hairdressing), tailoring, dressmaking, and catering.

The senior secondary upper course offers a specialization in the arts, sciences, Ghanaian languages, music, physical education, and dancing. Technical and vocational courses include electrical engineering trades, fashion, dressmaking, and tailoring. After graduation from senior secondary school, students perform one year of government service. In order to attend a university after the service year, it is necessary to pass a national test. The competition is quite keen and there are not enough slots in the universities, therefore, the passing level is quite high. In fact, Cape Coast University admits less than 10 percent of qualified applicants.

The recruitment and preparation of teachers has been a major problem in most developing countries and Ghana is no exception. In fact, the country is presently unable to provide senior secondary school placement for all Ghanaian students due to a shortage of teachers and classrooms, particularly in the rural parts of the land.

Secondary teachers in Ghana have always received their professional preparation programs in the country's universities. During the past three decades, the University of Cape Coast has been offering four-year undergraduate courses which include the usual subject matter areas, professional studies, and supervised practice teaching. Students who complete the program successfully receive a first degree and a diploma in education. Transfers who have graduated from other universities with one year's postgraduate teaching experience are required to take the Postgraduate Certificate in Education courses at the university.

Ghana has a total of seven colleges which offer admission to experienced teachers who are certified. The college then prepares the persons for teaching at the junior secondary and senior secondary levels. Ghana's academic secondary school teachers have traditionally received their preparation at the university.

Ghanaian schools are classified in two separate cycles. First-cycle schools are primary and middle schools. At this level, the Ministry of Education has been forced to employ teachers who were not certified. Second-cycle teachers include those persons who teach in secondary schools, technical institutions, training colleges, and vocational/commercial colleges. While the ministry attempts to hire persons with graduate degrees at this level, a large percentage of second-cycle teachers do not have their graduate degree.

While Ghana has experienced steady growth, most of the country remains rural even though some people have moved to the urban areas in search of better employment opportunities. Many people moved to the city because they were convinced that there were more higher paying jobs which carried a greater level of prestige. If the exodus continues, it is predicted that eventually there will be more urban than rural residents. But the Ghanaians are not only worried about the statistics of the rural issues. Formal education programs have tended to do a rather poor job of adapting to the needs of rural areas. Often, school programs have been too theoretical instead of addressing the specific needs of the young people in the more remote parts of Ghana. Consequently, some rural students tend to acquire the notion that agricultural occupations are of less value.

Social change in society occurs everywhere, and the Ghanaian educational system, like others, has been forced to change quite rapidly in order to keep pace. However, financial restrictions have made this difficult. One of the authors had occasion to visit two Ghanaian university libraries. Neither one had access to computer databases, ERIC, or journals of adequate professional quality. Moreover, the books were very old. In fact, there were only two texts on educational research—both published in the 1950s. The lighting was of very poor quality, making it difficult for students to work.

Because Ghana was subjected to the many problems generated by the colonial years, the country was exploited by the colonists (mainly British), and the educational system which was put into place by the British colonizers was designed to meet their own needs rather than the needs of Ghanaian people themselves.

On a more encouraging note, the self-esteem level of Ghanaian children is high and stable. The Ghanaian people themselves are optimistic about life and they live it to the fullest. To the observer of Ghanaian society, it seems clear that the educational system of the country will continue to flourish and improve.

MULTICULTURAL EDUCATION EFFORTS

Ghana's attempts to address the issue of multicultural education have been overshadowed by the struggle to provide a basic education for everyone. The national language is English, but the preferred languages of communication are Ga (gah), which is used around the capital area of Accra; Ewe (ev-vay) in the east; and Twi (twee), which is the language of the Ashanti and the Fonti. This language is spoken all over Ghana, particularly around Kumasi and in the southern part of the country.

English became the official language because of the long colonial period when the British brought their English language to the land. However, as is the case in many developing countries, the preferred languages of communication are the tribal tongues rather than English. Consequently, only the most highly educated people reach the point where they are able to read, write, and speak in English as well as they can in their tribal languages.

During the first three years of instruction, the language of use is the local language (depending on where the particular school is situated). English is taught as a second language subject, and it is heavily emphasized during the fourth year so that students are able to use it as the main instructional tongue. In addition to mastering their own language, Ghanaian children learn one other Ghanaian language. While English eventually becomes the language of instruction for the children, there seems to be a tendency to rely on the native Ghanaian languages more often than not.

The junior secondary curriculum includes instruction in a second Ghanaian language or a modern classical language. Also included are cultural studies, consisting of religion, music (drumming and dancing), drama, arts, and crafts. Senior secondary requirements include Ghanaian language, cultural studies, dancing, and crafts.

Communication is a major educational problem in developing countries insofar as educational pursuits are concerned. Given the problems of rural communication in Ghana, the country has explored a number of strategies to solve the problem. One recent attempt to address the issue has been the use of the radio for educational purposes. Long-distance education has been a popular area of inquiry for educators the world over. However, some have argued that the technique has not been overly successful, at least in Ghana, due to a number of political, economic, and social factors which tended to render it ineffectual. Ethnic communication systems involved information exchange through unstructured conversations. Conversation venues included shade trees, verandahs, and artisans' workshops. It was also found that ceremonies such as Kwafie afahye (local annual festival) and bragro (girls' rites of passage) created communication patterns which became part of the ethnic learning structure, which became part

of the indigenous communication system. Because of these unique ethnic communication patterns, it also has been argued that radio, as a linear one-way
communication mode, was not particularly effective as a means of education in
rural Ghana.

Textbooks utilized in the schools are not systematically screened for racist
and sexist content. Because of Ghana's poverty, many textbooks and curriculum
materials are dated. Some of them display gender biases. For example, there is
a tendency to use the masculine pronoun when referring to both genders. Interviews by one of the authors with Ghanaian educators have indicated that such
concerns have not become major issues in Ghanaian education circles.

SUMMARY

Ghana has long been known as one of the leading African nations in education. But faced with major financial problems, the country has found it difficult
to install the kinds of comprehensive programs it feels are necessary. While
some of the best schools in Africa exist in Ghana, they are only financially
accessible to a relatively small number of school-age youth. For example, the
tuition for one University of Cape Coast employee's seventeen year-old daughter
is 50,000 cedis a term, adding up to 150,000 cedis per year. (One U.S. dollar
was worth 9,150 cedis). The father only earns 360,000 cedis a year. Yet, the
parents believe so strongly in the education of their oldest daughter that they
are willing to make the sacrifice.

During May 1994, the junior staff members at the University of Cape Coast
went on strike to improve their maximum salaries of 40,000 cedis per month.
In fact, even top lecturers at the same institution can earn only about 120,000
cedis per month (approximately $131). Actually, the Ghanaian government
promised a 100 percent increase during 1992, but by the end of 1994 it had not
materialized. These examples provide good illustrations of the severe problems
which the world's developing nations must solve.

Finally, as is the case in most countries, Ghana is wrestling with the issues
of nationalism versus ethnicity. The national boundaries are artificial, and Ghana
has several major ethnic groups, as previously stated. With few exceptions, the
nation has been spared the bloody tribal massacres which countries such as
Somalia and Rwanda have been forced to endure in recent times. In spite of
some recent tribal hostilities in northern Ghana, people with different ethnic
backgrounds tend to get along rather well.

However, the country has yet to launch a sustained multicultural program in
the schools in which students are taught the value of having pluralistic populations within the national boundaries. As visitors travel through the country, it
is quite obvious that the preferred languages are tribal, even though English has
been the "official" language since the late 1950s.

Progress may best be analyzed from an evolutionary framework; and in doing
so with Ghana, it appears that since the country is only into its fourth decade

as an independent nation, there has been remarkable progress which should encourage Ghanaian educators.

However, major problems are still apparent. The country's infrastructure is still in need of development. For example, the highway from Cape Coast to Kumasi begins as a very nice two-lane road; but after reaching the Toradi intersection, it becomes so full of potholes that it is sometimes necessary to drive on the dirt shoulder in order to keep from breaking the springs in the automobile. In fact, some young men earn money by filling in the potholes and then pleading with the driver to give them some cedis for their efforts.

The Ghanaian people have a fervent desire for knowledge. In spite of their difficulties, they are eager learners; and their spirit and intelligence should empower them to compete successfully in the world's educational marketplace.

REFERENCES

Alawiye, Osman and Alawiye, Catherine. "Comparative Self-Concept Variances of School Children in Two English-Speaking West African Nations." *The Journal of Psychology,* Vol. 124, No. 2 (1990), pp. 169–176.

Andam, A.A.B. "Towards a Gender-Free Science Education: A Situational Analysis from Ghana." *Discovery and Innovation,* Vol. 6, No. 1 (1994), pp. 25–28.

Ansah, P.A.V. "Broadcasting and Multilingualism." In E.G. Wedell (Ed.), *Making Broadcasting Useful: The African Experience: The Development of Broadcasting in Africa in the 1980s.* Manchester: Manchester University Press, 1986.

Ansu-Kyeremeh, Kwasi. "Cultural Aspects of Constraint on Village Education by Radio." *Media, Culture, and Society,* vol. 14. London, Newbury Park, CA, and New Delhi: Sage, 1992, pp. 111–128.

Antwi, Moses. *Education, Society and Development in Ghana.* Accra, Ghana: Unimax Publishers Ltd., 1992.

Asiedu, Akrofi A. "Education in Ghana." In A. Babs Fafunwa and J.V. Aisiku (Eds.), *Education in Africa.* London: George Allen & Unwin, 1982.

Asiedu, Akrofi A. *Ghana, The New Structure and Content of Education for Ghana.* Accra: Ministry of Education, 1974.

Austin, D. *Politics in Ghana.* London: Oxford University Press, 1964.

Bartels, F.L. *The Roots of Ghana Methodism.* Cambridge: Cambridge University Press, 1965.

Conversation with employees at Cape Coast University, Cape Coast, Ghana, May 1994.

Conversations with school administrators at a USAID Grant Meeting at Cape Coast University, Cape Coast, Ghana, May 1994.

Fafunwa, A. Babs and Aisifu, J.V. (Eds.). *Education in Africa.* London: George Allen & Unwin, 1982.

Fage, J.D. *Ghana: A Historical Interpretation.* Madison: University of Wisconsin Press, 1959, p. 106.

Fitch, B. and Oppenheimer, M. "Ghana, End of an Illusion." *Monthly Review* (July–August 1966).

Ghana. *One-Year Development Plan.* Accra: Publishing Corporation, 1970, p. 159.

Ghana. *Report of the Commission on University Education.* Government Printing Department, 1961.

Ghana. Ministry of Information. *Report of the Educational Review Committee.* Accra: Tema, State Publishing Corporation, 1967.

Graham, T. "The Fourth Republic?" *West Africa* (March 16, 1987), p. 507.

Groves, C.P. *The Planting of Christianity in Africa. Vol. 1.* London: Lutterworth Press, 1958, p. 152.

Interviews between the author and advanced education students (graduate level) at University College of Education of Winneba, 1994.

Manoukian, M. *The Akon and Ga-Adangme Peoples of the Gold Coast.* London: Oxford University Press, 1950, p. 21.

Mitchell, Bruce. Visits to Ghanaian libraries were conducted in 1994 through participation in a USAID grant with Eastern Washington University and the University of Cape Coast.

Nimako, S.G. *Ghana Today: Education in Ghana 1930–1973.* Accra, Ghana: Information Services Department, 1976, pp. 5–6.

Williams, T.D. "Sir Gordon Guggisberg and Education Reform in the Gold Coast 1919–1927." *Comparative Education Review* (December 1964), pp. 290–306.

18

Honduras

HISTORY OF THE SYSTEM

Honduras became free from Spain in the early 1800s. Its early years as an independent nation were marked by many local rivalries and ideological disputes, which resulted in considerable political chaos and economic instability. In fact, this instability created an invitation for individuals both inside and outside the nation to exploit Honduras. Moreover, the co-terminal boundaries with Guatemala, El Salvador, and Nicaragua created the potential for conflict. Finally, liberal and conservative regimes in the area tended to become paranoid about governments which espoused positions which adapted an opposite political viewpoint from theirs, and exiled leaders tended to gather in states which shared their philosophy. These factors kept the nation in a period of turmoil which persisted throughout most of the nineteenth century.

Pre-Columbian Honduras was populated by a heterogeneous mixture of human beings from a very complicated mix of microcultures with a plethora of linguistic patterns. Some of these microcultures were related to the Yucatan Mayas. After the Mayan period ended, present-day Honduras was subjected to the influences of many different indigenous groups, including the Charateya and enclaves of Papils who were ethnically related to the Mexican Aztecs.

In 1849, the port of Trujillo was occupied by a British naval force which destroyed property and extorted money from the local governing bodies. Eventually the British agreed to a treaty which granted the country sovereignty over the Bay islands.

During the nineteenth century, the country viewed mining as a means of improving the nation's economy. However, due to a lack of adequate transportation, bad health conditions, and constant civil disturbance, the mining efforts gradually diminished and eventually most Hondurans were involved in agricultural pursuits. Some tobacco, cattle, and hides were exported to neighboring countries.

Geography has also impacted the country's history. Honduras can be characterized as being quite mountainous. This factor has made it difficult for rail and road construction. Numerous arable valleys have tended to entice many people to farm these lands, resulting in a situation which has made Honduras quite rural in nature. In fact, many Hondurans seldom have contact with some of the major national centers.

The United States and Great Britain were involved in the nation's development during the nineteenth century. British subjects were active in Belice, the Bay of Islands. British mahogany companies fashioned a number of territorial claims along the Caribbean coasts of eastern Honduras. This control peaked in 1848 when the British seized San Juan del Norte and renamed it Greytown. However, the British influences in the country moved in 1859 with the Wyke-Cruz Treaty at Conayagua.

Along with this decline in British influence came a new interest in the country from the United States. After a failed attempt to construct an interoceanic rail line, private U.S.-owned corporations commenced to play key roles in the country's economy after the mid-nineteenth century. The first economic venture was in mining, followed by involvement in banana plantations after the mining industry declined. Also, the United States was interested in Honduras as a possible location for an Atlantic–Pacific Ocean canal route.

Throughout the last six decades of the nineteenth century, Honduras developed into an independent nation. During this period of time, the country was consumed with local rivalries and ideological disputes which resulted in significant levels of political chaos.

The country was ruled by General Ferrera from 1840 to 1852. However, in 1847, a conservative ally of his, Juan Lindo Zeyelo, assumed the presidency and a constitution was adopted. During this time, there was a minor effort made to develop a system of education, but the poor economic conditions of the country made this impossible. Lindo turned over the governmental reins to Trinidad Cabanas, a liberal. His term of office was short, however, because the conservative government of Guatemala invaded the country, giving the leadership to Santos Guardiola, a conservative.

Following Guardiola's assassination in 1862, another period of turbulence ensued. During this time, there were several invasions by neighboring countries, coupled with a number of different presidents, including Ponciano Leiva and Marco Aurelio Soto, two liberal leaders.

During the last half of the nineteenth century, Honduras improved its educational system somewhat; even so, there were only 411 teachers in the country. More improvement was made in the last decade of the century, resulting in 851 primary schools and about 600 students involved in higher education.

Illiteracy in Honduras has always been a big problem, due to the poverty problems encountered throughout the country's history. In 1950, the illiteracy rate for all people over 10 years of age was 65 percent. While it has declined since that time, there are pockets of extreme illiteracy which exist throughout the land. Moreover, during the early 1970s, about three-quarters of the rural population had limited access to reading materials, which made the dissemination of information about nutrition and health extremely difficult.

STRUCTURE OF THE SYSTEM

Formal schooling in Honduras has been the responsibility of the government. During the twentieth century, the number of students attending school has increased along with the financial support from the government. However, the high incidence of illness has jeopardized school attendance for many children. Also, many parents from the rural parts of the country tend to believe that school participation is not particularly important, except for the schooling which is available in the village. Thus, few children from rural Honduras actually go away to the better schools, and only about 6 percent of the campesinos complete six years of primary education.

In the more urban parts of the country, the schools have been more successful and the literacy rate has reached about 70 percent as of 1980. But prior to the middle part of the 1900s, education in Honduras was mostly limited to affluent Hondurans who could afford to send their children to private schools. Ramon Villeda Morales actually solidified the notion of publication through his various reform movements during the late 1950s and early 1960s. The Honduran constitution requires children between the ages of seven and fourteen to attend school.

As a general rule, the quality of instruction in the country suffers because of inadequate teacher training, low teacher pay, and inadequate facilities and instructional materials. Some teachers are actually paid for their service in food. Instructional strategies usually consist only of rote memorization. There is a teachers' union in the country which has argued for a 400 percent increase in teachers salaries, but these requests seem to be generally ignored.

Gender differences seem to affect Honduran children due to the country's severe poverty problems. The jobs which are available in the cities are usually for boys. This means that young boys have tended to leave school at the age of eleven or twelve to seek work. This has resulted in an inflated school population of young girls.

Honduras also has experienced a growing private school movement in recent years. This has been due to the underfunding of the public school system which has caused a lack of public school classrooms for young children. However, even the private schools have experienced problems since many of them seem to be only money-making ventures and little attention is given to sound principles of pedagogy.

Higher education in Honduras has been viewed as including both high schools and universities. The central higher education institution in the country is the

National Autonomous University. The school was founded in 1847 and has 30,000 students enrolled in all of the campuses, which include branches located in San Pedro Sula and La Ceiba. There are also three private universities, including Jose Cecilio del Valle University, the Central American Technological University in Tegucigalpa, and the University of San Pedro Sula (USPS). The United States Agency for International Development (AID) began funding USPS in order to "provide a political counterweight to the traditionally leftist-dominated National University."

MULTICULTURAL EFFORTS

In order to understand the multicultural issues in the Honduran educational system, it is first necessary to examine the cultural pluralism which exists throughout the land. Ladinos, who comprise the predominant ethnic group, have descended from both the sixteenth century Spanish colonists and the native Hondurans they found when they arrived. The Lencas live in the municipalities of the southwest highlands.

Other aboriginal groups of Hondurans are the Miskitos, Sumos, and Payas, who are native Hondurans from the northeast. Because of their isolation, these three microcultures were able to maintain their native cultural values despite the Spanish and British influences.

African Caribs have descended from Carib aborigines of the Antilles and escaped African slaves. They were converted to Catholicism after settling on the southern coast of Honduras. They retained many elements of their own culture, even though they adopted many elements of the Ladino culture. Bay Islanders include both African and European racial/ethnic groups and may be the least assimilated of the Honduran microcultures. They reached Honduras in the 1830s from British Honduras and Grand Cayman Island.

Spanish is the official language of Honduras. It is the language of the schools as well as the language of government, newspapers, and radio. However, a number of other languages are spoken in Honduras, including Lenca, Jicaque, and the Hokan-Siouan language group. Mayan descendants speak the Charti language.

The religious preference throughout Honduras is Roman Catholic. However, religious freedom is guaranteed by the Honduran constitution. The 1965 constitution stipulated that the Church was independent of the state, and the Catholic Church has remained outside of politics. However, the Catholic Church has maintained over 60 schools. The 1965 constitution also stipulates that the state must provide education for the preservation, development, and dissemination of culture. This educational system also has to promote education through the use of libraries, cultural centers, etc.

The Honduran educational system is operated by the country's Ministry of Public Instruction. This body sets policies and establishes standards. Educational funding comes from the state, and secular education for all children aged seven to fourteen must be provided.

Curriculum in the pre-primary schools consists of reading, number readiness, simple arts and crafts, songs, and games. Socialization was deemed to be an important part of the educational system along with learning how to get along with others. Secondary education is divided into two parts. Stage one includes a program of general education which has language and literature, mathematics, science, music, handicrafts, and several elective courses. Then, during the second stage, students have a specialized education which leads to diplomas in industrial, commercial, agriculture, and teacher preparation. Several specialized programs are also available in fine arts and music. Private schools must attain the same standards as public schools in order to be accredited. Both private and public schools must submit to regular inspections.

Public school teachers are civil servants. They must be Hondurans by birth, except for teachers with certain areas of expertise. Honduran teachers enjoy a high level of prestige and are often the most highly educated persons in the community. Teachers in higher education must have a university degree.

SUMMARY

Multicultural education in Honduras is virtually nonexistent in terms of formal programs which are sponsored by the Ministry of Education. However, according to some Honduran educators, such programs are very important and should be initiated within their educational system.

In conclusion, it would appear that Honduras suffers from the same problems as some other developing countries. Financial constraints force them to focus entirely on a rather narrowly defined program of basic education. As a result, while the Ministry of Education may desire to create special multicultural curriculum strands, financial restrictions may prevent this from occurring.

REFERENCES

Barry, Tom and Norsworthy, Kent. *Honduras.* Albuquerque, NM: The Inter-Hemispheric Education Resource Center, 1990.

Blutstein, Howard et al. *Area Handbook for Honduras.* Washington, DC: U.S. Government Printing Office, 1971.

Gonen, Amiram. *The Encyclopedia of the Peoples of the World.* New York: Henry Holt Publishing Co., 1993.

Kurian, George. *Encyclopedia of the Third World,* 3rd ed. New York: Facts on File, 1987.

Mitchell, Bruce and Salsbury, Robert. *An International Survey of Multicultural Education.* Cheney, WA: Western States Consulting and Evaluation Services, 1991. (See Appendix.)

Rudolph, David. *Honduras, A Country Study.* Washington, DC: U.S. Government Printing Office, 1984.

19

India

HISTORY OF THE SYSTEM

India derived its name from the Indus River which flowed through one of the world's oldest civilizations. Long before the dawning of Christian, Islamic, and Buddhist religions, India became an enticing challenge for the adventurers and entrepreneurs from Macedonia to Central Asia. These opportunists viewed India as a source of great wealth and artistic potential.

In Mesopotamia, Egypt and Persia (India's western neighbors) made the transition from a hunting and food-gathering culture to crop raising. Ecologically, these sections of south Asia are often considered to be a single region which has trouble supporting a semi-arid agricultural and herding economy. Receiving less than ten inches of rainfall each year (almost all of it occurring in the winter), the area has had to rely on dry farming. There are a large number of village sites with homes made out of mud brick. The people used tools of stone and bone, and probably domesticated sheep, goats, and oxen. No metal or pottery have been discovered in the earliest sites; however, handmade pots of yellowish-red clay were produced a bit later in this area.

Excavations at the ancient Punjab city of Harappa have added valuable information which has upgraded the historical understanding of ancient India. Radiocarbon dating has confirmed that a great wall at Harappa protected the citadel from possible invasions as well as from the waters of the Ravi River. The ramparts were constructed of brick, and the base of the wall was 40 feet thick. The city itself flourished from about 2300 to 1750 B.C.

The Aryan conquest of the northern India region was a process of assimilation and socio-cultural integration between barbarians and pre-Aryan slaves. The Aryans had mastered the metallurgy of iron, probably from their Indo-European cousins who dominated the Iranian plateau during Sialk VI. They were able to clear ground through the use of iron axes and iron ploughs which were hitched to oxen.

The Mauryan Empire was one of India's most significant eras of unification. It existed from approximately 269 to 232 B.C., and was divided into districts which consisted of the earlier tribal boundaries. A Mauryan army included four major corps of approximately 600,000 infantry, 30,000 cavalry, 8,000 chariots, and 9,000 elephants.

India's Classical Age occurred from about A.D. 320 to 700. The Guptan Empire (A.D. 375–415) collapsed when the eastern areas of Bengal, Assam, and Orissa, along with the northern territories of Nepal and Kashmir, broke free. But in 606, a young leader named Harsha Vardhana came to power and tried to unify northern India, which he did during his 40-year reign. During these 40 years, Hinduism grew in popularity. The classical form of Hindu worship (puja), devotion (bhakti), and a number of secret rituals connected with female power (shakti) became part of the Hindu traditions. The secret rituals connected with female power became known as Tantric. The Tantric concepts seem to have emanated from ancient mother-goddess worship and Shaivite forms of worship.

The birth of Islam in Saudi Arabia in A.D. 622 eventually would change the course of Indian history. The religions of Islam and Hinduism are vastly different. Islam (meaning ''surrender'') requires each Muslim to surrender at all times to Allah's will as revealed in the prophet Muhammad. On the other hand, Hinduism relied on the yogi powers of self-control, suffering, abstinence, and meditation.

During the next 800 years, the Islamic influences increased dramatically. The Muslim world traveler, Ibn Battuta, who traveled through Africa and Asia from 1325 to 1354, was a judge at Muhammad's court, and described how strict the Sultan was about requiring the people to master the ordinances for absolutions, prayers, and the principles of Islam.

During 1498, Vasco da Gama sailed around the Cape of Good Hope. By that time, the Portuguese had become the world's navigational leaders, and Prince Henry's school of navigation had been motivated by both economics and Christian zeal. It was hoped that discovering a direct passage to the East would help the Christians win a victory against Moorish Arabs, Turks, and Mongols. His arrival in India started a period of European exploitation which would last for about four and one-half centuries. During the 1500s, approximately 800 Portuguese galleons would dominate the Indian Ocean. Holland and England then followed the lead of the Portuguese which created enormous influences on the country from that time on.

Calcutta was a bustling port when Vasco da Gama arrived there. But by that time, it had already become an important trading port for Arab, Hindu, and Chinese merchants who came there to buy pepper and ginger in return for gold, ivory, silk, and jewels. The architect of Portugal's Indian empire was Don Affonso d' Albuquerque, Portugal's Viceroy in the East from 1509 to 1519. A religious fanatic with a loathing of the Islamic religion, he dreamed of diverting the Nile in order to dry up Egypt. Albuquerque wrote his king, Don Manoel: "I do not believe that in all Christendom there will be so rich a king as Your Highness, and therefore, do I urge you, Senhore, to strenuously support this affair of India with men and arms, and strengthen your hold in her, and securely establish your dealings and your factories; and wrest the wealthy of India and business from the hand of the Moors."

During the fifteenth century, the English had started to search for a northern passage to India. One of the English attempts was made during 1551 by the cartographer Sebastian Cabot. During 1588, the Spanish Armada was quite badly defeated, and the Dutch also started to join the race around the Horn. They entered the competition so effectively that they established bases in the archipelago of Southeast Asia. The Great Mughals' rein spanned the entire seventeenth century. This period of dominance symbolized power and affluence, tenderness and cruelty, ferocity and sensitivity, and a love for luxury. Indeed, the Indian lifestyle known as Mughlai epitomized the cultural system of which Mughlai was a part. During this period of time, Aurangzeb became known as one of the most pious and the most ruthless of the great Mughals. Aurangzeb had hoped to win control of the entire country of India through his policy of love. He created an alliance of differing religious groups which focused on tax reduction, and tolerance for different socio-economic groups. But Aurangzeb (also known as Akbar) exhibited keen administrative skills and was also a clever statesman. One of his key letters stated that: . . . "If your majesty places any faith in those books by distinction called divine, you will be there instructed that God is the God of all mankind, not the God of Mussalmans alone."

The Seven Year War (1756–1763) stimulated Anglo-French conflict in India and helped to solidify the position of the British, particularly in Bengal. Lieutenant Colonel Clive was successful in defeating the French. Clive eventually governed Bengal in 1765. While he entertained thoughts about conquering Delhi, he thought better of it. After Clive's reign as the governor-general came a series of well-known British leaders including Lord Cornwallis, Sir John Shore, and Richard Colley Wellesley.

British missionaries also began arriving in Bengal before the end of the eighteenth century. Wellesley considered several of the Baptist missionaries to be subversives, and there was a running conflict between the missionaries and British officials who wanted tranquility to prevail. They were afraid that the missionaries might precipitate unrest and hostilities.

The Charter Act of 1833 opened India to unrestricted British emigration and enterprise. Soon after this time, the British had successfully extracted a treaty with Punjab Sikh factions which essentially made the entire country of India an English colony. However, a second war with the Sikhs was not terminated until 1849.

During 1858, the British government passed the Government of India Act through which one of the Crown's secretaries of state was vested through the cabinet with full responsibility for ruling India. The Indian army had a ratio of 140,000 Indians to 65,000 British soldiers. The Indian members of the army consisted of men who had already proven to be loyal to the British cause.

By 1859, 432 miles of rail track had been laid in India. But just ten years later, this figure escalated to 5,000, and by 1900 it had expanded to 25,000 miles of track. British industry also invested some 150 million pounds in public works projects, including irrigation canals which greatly increased the country's agricultural yield.

India has always been a country of great caste, religious, class, and regional variations. Much of the growing spirit of nationalism was due to the consolidation of British power. Also, during the 1800s, an elite cadre of young men had been receiving a British education. In Bombay City, the greatest early national leaders came from a small, elite group of mercantile entrepreneurs from Paris. Originally they had fled Persia in the seventh century, in order to avoid becoming converted to the Islamic religion. One of these grand old men of Parsi nationalism was Parsi Dadabhai Naoroji who established the first Indian business firm in London and Liverpool in 1855. Parsi leaders in Bombay became urban magnates because of their mercantile wealth and political clout.

After the turn of the century, the early 1900s saw a small but rigorous reaction against the concept of British rule in colonial India. British goods were boycotted, especially the cotton piece goods. Calcutta merchants complained that they were unable to even give away British goods. Some merchants tried changing the labels so they said "Made in Germany."

World War I saw the arrival of Mohandas Karamchand Gandhi, who went to London after a 20-year exile in South Africa. Born in the Kathiawad State of Porbandar, he was 19 years old when he left for London to study law. He accepted an offer to work for a Muslim firm in Durban, South Africa, in 1893. At that time, there were more than 40,000 Indians in Natal, most of whom had originally been sent to Africa as part of a new system of slavery. The abolition of slavery by the British empire in the 1830s had created a need for cheap labor. Hence, the Natal sugar planters commenced to use the services of cheap "coolie" labor from India.

The racism and bigotry of Natal's British-European community stirred up the acutely sensitive spirit of Gandhi. In due time, Ghandi was able to transform himself from a middle-class British barrister into a more traditional poor but serenely self-contained spiritual leader of the Indian people.

When Britain declared war on Germany in 1914, Lord Hastings notified India that she was also at war. However, the armistice brought something other than peace to India. The influenza epidemic of 1918 took about twelve million Indian lives. Ghandi looked on this tragic dilemma as a failure of the western civilization and the incapacity of British rule. The termination of World War I brought a general feeling of depression to India. Gandhi became the undisputed leader of the Indian Congress which dropped its policies of cooperation with the British Raj in order to follow Gandhi's pleadings for nonviolent cooperation.

He won a large Muslim following, and his popularity had a diverse appeal. This period of time (1920–1939) saw the country becoming more politically aware. The Communist Party developed in India, and Lenin's rise to power made an impact.

As a leader, Gandhi was a man with intelligence and personal charisma. He became a hero among India's youth because of his disinterest in power. He was also highly respected by the older generation. It was a following which he found to be extremely valuable in later years.

While World War I had been a catalyst to unify India's nationalistic movement, World War II proved to be the major motivational force for independence. Gandhi's hunger strikes had a profound effect on world opinion and finally, in 1947, Prime Minister Clement Atlee announced that His Majesty's government had decided to transfer its power by June 1948. So, by this action, the British divested themselves of their Indian responsibilities. By 1947, the House of Commons decreed that two independent dominions would be created in India. They would be known as India and Pakistan.

The first two decades of Indian independence were controlled by the brilliant leadership of Jawaharlal Nehru, the country's prime minister. A lawyer, Nehru was intelligent, cosmopolitan, erudite, and charming. In fact, India was indeed blessed to have a leader of his stature during the country's early days of independence.

Throughout its history, India has had a myriad of social groups that were involved in intense competition for goods, services, power, and even basic existence. Differences in language, religion, and caste have created enormous social problems for the country; and being the critical social institution of India, education has always had a difficult time providing the kind of schooling which the country had to have.

While Gandhi relied on certain Judeo-Christian beliefs in his personal philosophy, his social mores seemed to be based on ancient Indian traditions and beliefs. On the other hand, Nehru tended to advocate a society which was industrialized, socialist, democratic, secular, egalitarian and, most importantly, modern. Because of his enormous popularity with the common person, his policies were extremely important to India even through the 1980s.

STRUCTURE OF THE SYSTEM

Today, India is an enigma. It is a country of numerous microcultures, beset with major poverty problems which are far from being solved, yet there is an encouraging spirit of national unity. Suffering from crippling population problems in years past, India now has had an aggressive contraception program in which one-fourth of the reproductive-age couples have been using some form of birth control.

Indians have a life expectancy of about 57 years. But one of the country's problems has been the high infant mortality rate. There has been a major problem with diseases such as malaria and leprosy. On an encouraging note, however, smallpox essentially has been eradicated. People in several Indian states also have had problems with goiter and a number of nutritional disorders.

Attendance in school has been compulsory between the ages of 6 and 14, but the rural attendance rates have been far below the levels of attendance in the more urban areas. Moreover, the school attendance of females has been much poorer than the attendance of males. One of the country's major problems has been its enormous population. The 1990 census estimated the country's population at more than 700,000,000.

India has had a history of educational elitism. Since early times, education has been tailored to the needs of Brahman boys who were taught to read and write by Brahman teachers. Muslim education has also been elitist in a similar manner. But the Muslims added primary schools to the mosques, and Muslim boys learned to recite the Quran. Muslim colleges provided male students opportunities for studying the Arabic language, literature, Islamic theology, law, history, and the sciences.

Under British rule, Indian education was viewed as a way of preserving civilization, particularly Christianity. Thus, English became the official language of instruction. However, the British system tended to reinforce the elitist nature of Indian education which was generally accessible to only the privileged classes. But by 1980, the country attempted to change the more elitist portions of their educational system and to broaden the base of students. Funding was increased for both primary and adult education, and changes were made in secondary education in order to focus more heavily on the students who did not plan to attend college. This was part of India's sixth five-year plan which was carried out between 1980 and 1984. Another part of the plan was a major revision of the school system's vocational education programs in order to make them more directly related to the marketable skills needed in the workplace.

A major educational problem in India has been the high illiteracy rate of women. During the early 1980s, the rate of illiteracy among women was about 75 percent. As bad as this seems to have been, it was much worse during the early part of the century. It has been argued that high levels of female literacy helps to create lower infant mortality rates.

India's constitution gives the states the authority to legislate their own educational programs. However, a 1976 amendment determined that education was actually a joint responsibility of both the central and state governments. During recent years, the central government has spent a great deal of its energies to create the country's five-year plans. The central government has also set the standards for research enterprises.

The Ministry of Education provides funding for special programs and also serves as the major coordinating body in educational matters. But the states have their own ministries of education which are responsible for the local boards of education. This is a shared responsibility with the municipal governments. The funding of schools is also a major responsibility of the states. However, in recent

Table 19.1
School Enrollment as a Percentage of School-Age Children, 1950–1951 to 1984–1985

School Year	Primary School (Ages 6–11)	Middle School (Ages 11–14)	Secondary School (Ages 14–17)
1950–1951	42.6	12.7	5.3
1955–1956	52.8	16.3	7.4
1960–1961	62.4	22.3	10.6
1965–1966	76.7	30.8	16.2
1975–1976	83.8	36.7	18.3
1981–1982	83.7	41.9	28.2
1984–1985	93.2	50.3	n.a.

years, the central government has been forced to assume more of those responsibilities. When this happened, India started to receive more complaints from the states about the increased role of the central government in the schooling of Indian youth.

One major problem in Indian education has been the great diversity of educational programs. Coastal areas such as Tamil, Nadu, Maharashtra, and West Bengal, which were among the earliest parts of the country to be ruled by the British, made the fastest educational progress. Unfortunately, some of the interior areas such as Pradesh, Rajasthan, and Uttar Pradesh lagged behind. Like most other countries, the portions of the nation which have had the oldest, most well-established educational systems have the highest per-capita income levels.

In general, education is compulsory for Indian youth between the ages of six and fourteen, and in recent years education has provided a major impetus in improving the lives of India's "untouchables." The literacy rate of scheduled castes and scheduled tribes had risen to 18.82 percent by 1985. While this percentage is well below the national figure of 41 percent for the nation at large, it constitutes a rather dramatic increase.

Children entering first grade tend to span a rather large number of ages, and the country has a high dropout rate. Of every 100 children entering first grade, only about 40 are expected to reach the fifth grade, with just 25 completing the eighth. This high dropout rate is usually attributable to poverty which leads to overcrowded classrooms and poor instructional equipment—the availability of which varies a great deal from place to place. Through the incorporation of the five-year plans, the number of educational facilities has expanded greatly in recent years. Table 19.1 shows the enrollment of school age children from 1950–1951 to 1984–1985. As can be seen, the primary school enrollment improved from 42.6 to 95.2 percent.

In addition to the public schools, various forms of private schools have been common in the country. While some schools were totally "private" (in that they were given no public funding), others received various kinds of governmental grants in aid. Among the best private schools are the English-language mission schools, and there is a general tendency for the schools housing older children to be private rather than public. For example, 10 percent of the primary schools are private, while 20 percent of the middle schools and 60 percent of the secondary schools are also private.

Indian education traditionally has been dominated by a system of examinations. They are given at the end of secondary school in order to determine admissions to college. Since the college degrees have been necessary for the acquisition of most white-collar jobs, the competition on the tests has been fierce. Due to this high level of competition, cheating has been a problem, and the critics of this procedure have argued that the testing program is little more than a screening device to filter out students from low-caste backgrounds.

MULTICULTURAL EDUCATION EFFORTS

According to the country's original responses to the authors' multicultural education study, India does have a multicultural education program. From childhood on, children are exposed to the country's many microcultures which have a variety of values, as well as religious, language, and ethnic differences. Even though there is a Minority Commission in the Ministry of Education, there is no special funding for multicultural education.

When examining the multicultural education status of India, religious preferences become a significant issue. Over the years, Hinduism has been the major religion of the country. Moreover, the daily life in India is highly charged with religious symbolism. One of the world's most tolerant religions, Hinduism practices are affected greatly by geography, social position, family custom, and social preference. But the options for religious practice open to given individuals are directly related to their social positions. Other religions are also prominent in the country. Buddhism, Jainism, and Sikhism grew from indigenous populations. Islam is the second largest religion in the country, including about 11 percent of the people. Christians are one of the minority religions and constitute approximately 2 percent of the population.

No special multicultural education requirements are in the teacher education course sequences in the country. The Ministry of Education stresses cultural pluralism in the curriculum utilized in the schools. India's official language of instruction is English at the university and secondary school levels. However, the regional languages are normally used at the primary and elementary school levels. While separate schools are provided for children who wish to be taught in their native language, there has been no history of forced racial segregation in the nation's schools. In the school curriculum, the history of indigenous people is stressed so that students can learn to appreciate the vast ethnic and cultural differences which the country enjoys. India does evaluate textbooks and curriculum materials in order to ensure that they are free of racist and sexist content.

The Ministry of Education feels that the biggest problem to be dealt with is trying to maintain a proper balance between unity and diversity. Also, the Ministry would like to see the schools find ways to do a more thorough job of inculcating the positive values of secularism, democracy, and socialism.

One of India's biggest educational problems has centered around the need for more gender equity. The participation of women in the workforce has been limited by both customs and public policies. As mentioned earlier, there is still a gap in the literacy rate between the two genders. For example, in Kerala, considered to be a model state for high educational attainment, the male literacy rate is 75 percent and the female literacy rate is 66 percent. But Rajasthan, Bihar, and Uttar Pradesh all had literacy rates of less than 40 percent for males and under 15 percent for females.

Another factor affecting the education of Indian women seems to be the general level of family health. The issue is particularly important to the children. Women are generally in charge of health in Indian families, and better feeding, sanitation, and precautionary health care seem to be associated with better education for women.

Women also are viewed as the primary custodians of the culture, since they are the first teachers of children. The poverty factors which women must face have a dramatic impact on the educational attainment of women and their daughters. Thus, because of historical religious, cultural, and socioeconomic factors, the educational levels of Indian women—compared to men—still continue to suffer.

As already mentioned in this chapter, India has struggled to provide an education for some of its neglected microcultures. The republican constitution of 1950 stipulated that it was necessary for the country to promote the economic, social, and educational advancement of these groups. Two of these microcultures were the "untouchable" castes and people of distinctly tribal origin called Advisas. A quota of enrollment spots in colleges and schools was set aside for them in order to help correct centuries of overt neglect and blatant discrimination. If they could meet the minimum admission requirements, they could receive stipends for textbooks, school or college fees, and even board and lodging funds if they lived away from home.

SUMMARY

Given India's history of poverty, colonial exploitation, and cultural diversity, it is easy to see the problems of providing suitable education programs, but the ambitious goals which seem to be motivated by a very mature and forward-looking constitution have made it possible for the country to improve its educational system quite dramatically. However, India has also been forced to move from a general notion of "education for the elite" to a philosophy of "education for all," regardless of socio-economic status; but old ways are always hard to change, particularly when the funding potential is so limited. The country's attempts to make changes can be used as examples for other countries as well. The courageous quota system for upgrading the educational needs of "untouchables" and Advisas is commendable and serves to frame the good intention of the country's educational system.

The one factor that could be India's greatest obstacle to improvement is its population explosion. It is estimated that by the year 2000, the country should have about one billion people. Some have been concerned that should that prediction come to pass, the nation's precious resources will have to be centered on major problems of health care and famine, which could be an enormous setback for the country's struggling educational system.

REFERENCES

Agrawal, D.P. *The Copper Bronze Age in India: An Integrated Archaeological Study of the Copper Bronze Age in India in the Light of Chronological Technological and Ecological Factors.* New Delhi: Munshiram Manoharlal, 1971.

Banerjee, N.R. *The Iron Age in India.* Delhi: Munshiram Manoharlal, 1965.

Bayly, C.A. "Local Control in Indian Towns—The Case of Allahabad: 1880–1920." *Modern Asian Studies,* Vol. 5, No. 4 (1971), pp. 289–311.

Birch, de Gray. *The Commentaries of the Great Affonso d'Albuquerque, Second Viceroy of India.* London: Hakluyt Society, 1884.

Desai, L.P. "Western Educated Elites and Social Change in India." *Economic and Political Weekly* (Bombay), Vol. 19 (April 14, 1984), pp. 639–647.

Dunn, D. "Gender Inequality in Education and Employment in the Scheduled Castes and Tribes of India." *Populations Research and Policy Review,* Vol. 12, No. 1 (1993), pp. 53–70.

Futu'hu-l, Bulda'n in, Elliott, H.M., and Dowson, J. (Eds.). *The History of India, As Told by Its Own Historians: The Muhammadan Period: Historians of Sind, 1,* Vol. 25. Calcutta: Susil Gupta Ltd., 1955.

Gibb, H.A.R. *Ibn Battuta's Travels in Asia and Africa, 1325–1354.* New York: Robert M. McBride & Co., 1929.

Gonen, Amiram. *The Encyclopedia of the Peoples of the World.* New York: Henry Holt Publishing Co., 1993.

Grousset, Rene. *In the Footsteps of the Buddha.* London: George Routledge & Sons Ltd., 1932.

Heston, Alan. *Poverty in India: Some Recent Policies.* India Briefing, 1990.

India. Ministry of Information and Broadcasting, Research and Reference Division. *Statistical Outline of India.* Bombay: Ministry of Information and Broadcasting, 1984.

Joshi, Barbara R. *Untouchable! Voices of the Dalit Liberation Movement.* London: Zed Books, 1986, p. 14.

Malcolm, J. *Life of Clive, vol. 2.* Manchester: Manchester University Press, 1923.

Mitchell, Bruce and Salsbury, Robert. *An International Survey of Multicultural Education.* Cheney, WA: Western States Consulting and Evaluation Services, 1991. (See Appendix.)

Nyrop, Richard et al. *India, A Country Study.* Washington, DC: Department of the Army, 1986.

Saini, Shiv Kumar. *Development of Education in India: Socioeconomic and Political Perspectives.* New Delhi: Cosmo, 1980.

Sarkar, Judanath. *History of Aurangzeb.* Calcutta: M.C. Sarkar and Sons, 1952.

Sinari, R.A. *The Structure of Indian Thought.* New York: Oxford University Press, 1989.

Tinker, Hugh. *A New System of Slavery: The Export of Indian Labour Overseas, 1830–1920.* London: Oxford University Press, 1974.

Whitcombe, Elizabeth. *Agrarian Conditions in Northern India.* Berkeley: University of California Press, 1922.

Wolpert, Stanley. *A New History of India.* New York: Oxford University Press, 1982.

Zachariah, Mathew. "India." *Education and Urban Society,* Vol. 18, No. 4 (August 1986), pp. 487–499.

20

Iran

HISTORY OF THE SYSTEM

According to some present-day Iranian historians, prior to the second millenium B.C., Iran was occupied by a myriad of microcultures. Archaeological digs have revealed ancient cultures which made use of sun-dried bricks for their dwellings and revealed an old history of pottery making. Moreover, the artifacts have suggested strongly that these ancient peoples practiced rather sophisticated agricultural techniques for that time in history. The Sumerian influences in religion, art, and literature became pronounced when the Elamites came under the influence of Ur and Akkad (two Mesopotamian cultures).

Toward the beginning of the first millenium B.C., small groups of persons who probably used the Indo-European languages began to infiltrate the Iranian lands from Central Asia. They are thought to have been nomadic, and transported themselves to that part of the world on horseback. Hostile incursions by their neighbors may have motivated their migrations.

During the middle of the first millenium B.C., Croesus, the fabled king of enormous wealth, had been defeated by Cyrus, who was able to establish control of the Aegean coast of Asia Minor, Armenia, and the Greek colonies in the Levant area (lands of Jerusalem and Damascus). Cyrus was successful in his capture of Babylon and released the Jews who had been held captive there. (One account of this episode is described in the Book of Isaiah.) When Cyrus died, his land holdings stretched clear to Afghanistan.

The successors to Cyrus were known as the Achaemenids, who have been described as enlightened despots who were responsible for a small amount of administrative structure through the utilization of governors (referred to as satraps) who were responsible for administering their regions. At that time, the language of use was Aramaic.

However, the Achaemenids were eventually ousted by Alexander the Great of Macedon. By 334 B.C., he had advanced to Asia Minor, which was an Iranian satrapy. He captured Egypt, Babylonia, and, finally, the main portion of the Achaemenid Empire which by that time was in the process of disintegration. Ultimately the lands controlled by the Achaemenids were controlled by the Sassanids, who reigned supreme from A.D. 224 to 642. They attempted to re-invigorate the Iranian traditions which had been obscured by the Greek cultural traditions for many years. They were known for their rather advanced ideas about urban planning, agricultural improvements, and technological advances. Most historians seem to believe that they divided the people into four classes which included the priests, warriors, secretaries, and commoners. Zoroastrianism became the state religion, and the Zoroastrian priests were enormously powerful.

Probably the most well-known Sassanid ruler was Chosroes I (531–579), who was also known as Anushirvan the Just. He reformed the tax system and reor-ganized the army and bureaucracy. Chosroes I was also known as a great builder. He constructed new buildings and started new towns. Also, 'it has been stated that he brought in many books from India and had them translated into Pahlavi. Some of these books eventually became part of the Islamic literature.

Unfortunately, the rule of Chrosroes II suffered from wastefulness and a long drawn-out series of battles with the Byzantines. These wars and the economic decline of the Sassanids created a perfect climate for the invasion of the bedouin Arabs who were interested in conquests, and were also motivated by the Prophet Muhammad who was able to win over the city of his birth, Mecca, to the new religion. The Arabs were successful in controlling the entire area, and the new state religion, Islam, imposed its own system of moral values and social phi-losophy.

The conquering Arabs also brought another religion to the area. Known as Shia Islam, it originated with the Arab Muslims, but since that time it has become closely identified with Iran. Another group, known as the Shiat Ali faction, believed that following the death of Muhammad, the leadership of the religion should go to Muhammad's son-in-law, Ali, and to his descendants. This group became known as the Shiat Ali.

By A.D. 820, Iran experienced another ruling dynasty which descended from Nomadic, Turkic-speaking warriors who had been leaving Central Asia. They were recruited by the Abbasid caliphs and used for slave warriors during the ninth century. Gradually, the power of the Abbasid caliphs began to wane and, eventually, the Samanids ruled an area from central Iran to India.

By 1092, Iran began to experience a number of smaller, fragmented dynasties. During this period of time, Genghis Khan was able to unite a number of Mongol tribes, and they embarked on an extended invasion of China. Then, the Mongols attacked Iran which resulted in major problems for the country. Along with the destruction of irrigation systems, Iran suffered huge losses among its male pop-ulation, causing dramatic decreases in the country's total population.

The followers of Genghis Khan failed to rectify the poor situation in the country. In fact, it was finally Ghazan Khan who managed to provide Iran with some badly needed relief. This relief was partially in the form of lower taxes for artisans, the encouragement of agricultural enterprises, rebuilding, and an expansion of the irrigation system.

In 1541, the Safavids had come to power in Iran. They were leaders of a military order and were able to trace their ancestry back to Shauykh Safi ad Din, the founder of their order. During the mid-1400s, they adapted Shia Islam, and by 1501 they seized power in Tabriz, which eventually became their capital. Their leader, Ismail, became the shah of Iran. The rise of the Safavids marked the re-emergence of Iran as a country with national boundaries governed through a system of central authority. The Safavids established Shia Islam as the state religion and forced most of the Muslims to become converted to the Shia sect. Thus, Iran became a theocracy in which the state and its religion were closely interconnected. Finally, this empire began a decline which resulted in a series of victories over the Safavids by the Afghans who managed to take control of the capital, Tabriz, in 1722.

However, domination by the Afghans was short-lived and they were defeated. By 1736, Tahmasp Quli, a chief of the Afshar tribe, was successful in driving away the Arabs. In 1736, he became the leader and renamed himself the Nader Shah. He was successful in pushing out the Ottomans from Georgia and Armenia, and the Russians from the Iranian coast on the Caspian Sea. Ultimately, he went into India, attacking New Delhi before his armies left the country.

During the late 1800s, another Iranian power struggle ensued and the normal life of the country was thrown into a state of disarray. Aga Mohammad Qajar became the country's ruler, and this Qajar dynasty persisted until 1925. The concept of the shah was reinstated under the Qajar dynasty, and an element of unity, stability, and order returned to the country. But early in the nineteenth century, Russia and England commenced to show an interest in Iran, placing a great deal of pressure on the Qajars. The interest in Iran occurred because of a need to protect trade routes to India. The two countries also dominated Iran's trade and interfered in the country's internal affairs.

During World War I, Iran attempted to remain neutral, but the country became a battleground for Russian, Turkish, and British troops. By the end of the war, Tehran found itself dominated by the British because of Russia's involvement in its own revolution. By 1921, a new Iranian leader had surfaced, and the "modern era" of Iranian history got underway.

The new leader was Reza Shah, who was in power until 1941. With the help of a group of army officers, he inaugurated a program which addressed a need for broad, sweeping changes. These changes were designed to bring Iran into the modern world. It was thought that the country needed to extend government control and promote westernization. He created a new system of secular primary and secondary schools, and in 1935 established a European-style university in Tehran.

These European-style institutions of higher education became the preparation sites for a new bureaucracy and a new middle class was in the process of development. Also, the shah improved the rail system, completed a trans-Iranian railroad system, and built a number of factories which produced consumer goods such as cigarettes, textiles, matches, and sugar products.

The shah was interested in breaking down the religious powers and a lot of his measures were designed to accomplish that purpose. His reforms of the country's educational system were also designed to break the power of Iran's religious bodies in order to terminate their monopoly of the country's system of education. Gradually, the shah acquired enormous masses of land throughout the country. His taxation policies created a great hardship for the lower classes, and the living conditions for peasants worsened during his time in power.

During the beginning of World War II, Iran declared its neutrality. But after the country refused to expel all German nationals from the country, the British invaded. Later in 1941, Russians also invaded Iran as a result of a need for the allied forces to transport goods across Iran to the Soviet Union. Also that year, the Iranian leadership was transferred from Rezah Shah to his son, Mohammad Reza Shah Pahlavi.

By 1953, Iran had reestablished diplomatic relations with Britain and a new oil agreement was negotiated. The shah was worried about incursions from the Soviet Union, and closer ties with the United States and Britain were established. By 1955, Iran had joined the Baghdad Pact, which brought together Iraq, Turkey, and Pakistan in an alliance with Great Britain. While the United States was not a member of the pact, it was a strong supporter of the concept.

Elections in 1963 resulted in a new political party, the Iran Novin Party, which was committed to administrative and economic reforms of various types. The new party drew its support from senior civil servants, business leaders, and western-educated technocrats. Later, it also included bureaucratic professional, and business persons. The Iran Novin Party appointed Hasan Ali Mansur as its Prime Minister.

By 1959, the shah had married again and the new queen gave birth to Rezah, who was the male heir. In order that the crown prince would be able to take over the throne before he came of age, a special constitutional amendment was passed which would automatically make him his father's successor.

One of the more positive steps taken by the shah was in the field of education which was always one of his major concerns. A literacy corps was established in which young men were allowed to satisfy their military service requirements by participating in a reading program in some of Iran's most remote villages. The literacy of rural residents had long been a major Iranian problem and the shah was determined to correct it.

In order to enhance the shah's influence in the gulf, he expanded the country's military units through the use of oil profits, and during a 1972 visit to Iran by President Richard Nixon of the United States, the country was allowed to purchase conventional weapons of defense. Consequently, Iran was able to become one of the strongest military governments in the entire region.

During the middle 1970s, the shah also embarked on a major campaign to revitalize the country's industrial and construction infrastructure. While there were some available resources for these activities, the collective, military/industrial enterprises created a major strain on Iran's institutional and human resources which led to major problems. The public became disenchanted with these policies which they felt were causing the country to experience a high level of inflation, corruption, and a growing gap between the "haves" and the "have-nots." During this time, Iran nationalized all the private secondary schools and guaranteed all school-age children a free education. A free meal program was also made available for school children. In addition, the government took over the private community colleges and lowered income taxes. An ambitious health plan was also initiated.

But many of the new programs were not well administered and the country commenced to experience major difficulties. By 1977, the shah decided it was necessary to embark on a number of strategies to address major domestic and foreign criticisms of the country's human rights record. Political prisoners were released, and a number of new legal regulations were initiated in order to guarantee the legal rights of civilians who were being tried in the military courts. But the country was still restless, and by that time the Ayatollah Khomeini was becoming much more popular. Matters in Iran worsened when the Iranian government was forced to declare martial law in Tehran and eleven other cities on September 7–8, 1978 as a result of antigovernment demonstrations. By the end of December 1978, a national front leader named Shapour Bakhtiar agreed to form a government if the shah would leave the country.

However, Bakhtiar was unable to win the support of Khomeini who declared that the Bakhtiar government was illegal. Finally, Khomeini arrived in Tehran from Paris on February 1, 1979, and in a short time became the supreme leader of the country. In this position, he did not consider himself to be bound by the government and he made a number of unilateral policy pronouncements, named personal representatives to key government organizations, established new institutions, and announced decisions without ever consulting with his prime minister, who seemed to be little more than a figurehead.

Shortly after the dramatic governmental changes, a national referendum was held in order to determine the nature of the new political system which should be established. But the sole form of government appearing on the ballot was an Islamic republic, which Khomeini proclaimed for Iran on April 1, 1979, and the new constitution did not differ markedly from the last one which was drawn up in 1906.

STRUCTURE OF THE SYSTEM

The country of Iran possesses a specific geographical character, historical tradition, and a unique human culture which has helped its survival throughout history. Its society has successfully preserved its ancient beliefs and customs.

Visitors are usually struck by the mixture of old and new traditions in everything from the styles of architecture to the clothes that are worn by the people.

The Islamic Revolution of 1979 saw the replacement of the Iranian monarchy by the Islamic Republic of Iran. At the head of the government structure is the faqih who is the primary decision maker. The country's constitution specifically named Khomeini as the faqih for life and provides a procedure for choosing the successor of the faqih. The executive branch includes an elected president who chooses a prime minister and cabinet which must be approved by the elected legislative assembly. The prime minister is responsible for appointing the 24 ministers who must be approved by the president and the elected parliament (Majlis). The judiciary is independent of the Majlis and executive. In recent years, Iran has been divided into 24 provinces which are subdivided into several counties headed by governors who are appointed by the Minister of the Interior.

Up until the middle of the 1800s, educational pursuits were carried out by the religious institutions of the country. Instruction in basic literacy was the responsibility of the clergy. It was felt that instruction in reading and writing was not necessary for everyone in Iran, and so education was restricted to the sons of the economic and politically elite. Those who seemed to have the aptitude for higher education pursuits sometimes continued their education in a religious college. By 1851, the country felt that there was a need for a limited amount of instruction in military science, European languages, accounting, and technology, leading to the first government school which was opened in 1851.

By the early 1900s, a few schools commenced providing instructional programs in foreign languages and science. Some schools (but not many) were open to girls. These schools were operated by foreign missionaries, private Iranians, and the government. Their primary mission was to educate the children of the elite.

The Iranian educational "system" is said to have emerged during the Pahlavi era. While only 10 percent of all elementary-age children were enrolled in schools, by 1978, 75 percent of all Iranian children were attending such schools. Even so, the goal of creating a nationwide educational system was not realized until after the Pahlavi era. However, during this period of time, the government made an attempt to meet the needs of children with special skills and talents. The shah relied on the expertise of the American National/State Leadership Institute for the Gifted and the Talented, an organization directed by Irving Sato through the leadership of Dr. James Cowan, Superintendent of the Ventura County of Schools in the United States. Through Sato's leadership, a national system of gifted/talented education programs was established in the Iranian educational system.

Also during the same period of time, the country instituted a program of educational television in order to meet the needs of children in the more remote parts of the country. An attempt was made to create instructional educational programs in several languages other than Persian, since more than one-third of the population had a difficult time speaking and writing the country's major language.

MULTICULTURAL EDUCATION EFFORTS

Iran did not respond to the authors' multicultural education survey. However, an examination of the literature seems to show a decided gender bias throughout the country's history in favor of an educational system which tends to the needs of boys and the elite as opposed to girls and the lower-income groups. However, during the academic year 1986–1987, the Minister of Education stated that 11.5 million students were registered in the country's elementary and secondary schools. While accurate statistics have been rare since the 1979 revolution, it has been estimated that this number includes approximately 78 percent of the eligible elementary-age children and about half of the secondary-age children.

The nation's largest university is the University of Tehran. However, the school enrollment dropped dramatically in 1980 when the government dismissed a large number of instructors who were not considered to be of the true Islamic faith. There has been a perception that the European universities were of superior quality, and in 1983 only about 10 percent of the institution's student body consisted of females.

Moreover, with the exception of the Reza Shah's reforms, the Iranian schools have been heavily influenced by the Islamic religions, unlike many other countries which historically have fought to separate the church and state, particularly in the educational systems. Indeed, the history books of the Pahlavi period often emphasized Iran's pre-Islamic past and the role of some of the country's most influential kings. Consequently, after the revolution, the nation's textbooks made the knowledge of Islamic rules a prerequisite for being accepted into the university. Indeed, the universities themselves have suffered due to the loss of many intellectuals and experts who left the profession or moved to other countries. In short, the country is said to have succumbed to revolutionary zeal rather than to academic excellence.

SUMMARY

It can be safely said that today's Iranian schools do not seem to be particularly concerned about multicultural education issues. Probably the greatest concern is the lack of educational opportunities for tribes persons in the rural areas. Because of some of the basic Islamic tenets, there still seems to be a lingering perception that education for girls is not of the greatest importance. However, there is still a strong interest in literacy in order for young people to become knowledgeable of the basic philosophical principles of the Islamic religion.

REFERENCES

Conversations with Dr. James Cowan, Ventura County (California). Spokane, WA, 1994.

Ehteshami, Soraya. "The Role of Radio and Television in the Improvement of Education in Iran." Master's Thesis, Eastern Washington University, Spokane, WA, 1977.

Frye, Richard N. *The Heritage of Persia.* London: Weidenfeld and Nicholson, 1961.

Ghirshman, R. *Iran: From the Earliest Times to the Islamic Conquest.* London: Pelican Press, 1954.

Gonen, Amiram. *The Encyclopedia of the Peoples of the World.* New York: Henry Holt Publishing Co., 1993.

Hunter, Shireen T. *Iran After Khomeini.* New York: Praeger, 1992.

Metz, Helen Chapin. *Iran: A Country Study.* Washington, DC: U.S. Government Printing Office, 1989.

Rezun, Miron. *Iran at the Crossroads.* Boulder, CO: Westview Press, 1990.

Sabzalian, Ali. *Iran.* Berne, Switzerland: Embassy of the Islamic Republic of Iran, 1987.

Wilber, Donald N. *Iran.* Princeton, NJ: Princeton University Press, 1976.

21

Ireland

HISTORY OF THE SYSTEM

During the late eighteenth and early nineteenth centuries, several European countries were in the process of making a number of major changes in their educational systems. Nations such as Greece, Denmark, Italy, France, and Spain were reacting to the Industrial Revolution, an increase in urban dwelling, and changing political and social values which had a profound influence on European societies. The country of Ireland was used as a testing ground for various policies which were perceived to be questionable in England. Moreover, an emerging new issue was centered around the functioning of the educational system itself. The argument centered on the state's involvement in various sorts of educational provisions. A privy council on education in 1839 and the Education Act of 1870 provided Ireland with the capacity to shape its system of education more readily.

The Catholic Church believed it was being treated unfairly since it was not provided with funds to treat the Catholic populace; and the Presbyterians had been seeking state support for their own schools. Thus, it can be seen that the history of education in Ireland cannot be analyzed without investigating the religious history of the nation.

One of the motivating factors for the early beginnings of Irish education was the notion that the country needed to become literate in order to establish a significant role in the attempts at industrialization during the nineteenth century. The Irish state wished to operate a nondenominational system of primary education in which children of all religious faiths would be educated together. While this would be the procedure for secular subjects, it was thought that separate procedures would be created for religious instruction. The distinction between religious and secular education would become a major point of controversy throughout the years.

The history of Irish education during the early 1800s reflected a series of social policies, which also saw the creation of an organized police force and improved health services in the decade of the 1830s. During the earlier years of modern Irish education, the issue of school finance presented a continual argument. The upper socio-economic classes were generally against the support of the country's educational system.

But Ireland's interest in education dates back to the monarchic schools during the "Dark Ages" of Europe, and the bardic schools which were instrumental in preserving a great deal of Ireland's cultural heritage. The nation had enjoyed a long tradition of concern for education in the English tongue. Through various types of legislation, a number of schools were created, such as parish, diocesan, royal, and charter schools. However, because the efforts were fragmented, their influences never really affected the mass of Irish people.

Prior to 1922, Irish education tended to be rather haphazard and uncoordinated. However, the Department of Education in the Republic of Ireland was established during 1924. It was made responsible for intermediate education (secondary schools) and for technical instruction and reformatory and industrial schools.

The Department of Education has been responsible for the establishment of a highly centralized system of education, and exercises control of nearly all of it. Following independence, many of the bitter conflicts between church and state during British control tended to disappear.

World War I created many new problems for the Irish system of education. Teachers were beginning to suffer because of inadequate salaries, but also during the war the notion of a more egalitarian society appeared. This had an impact on the Irish educational system. In 1918, the Killanin Committee on primary education proposed the idea of levying a local tax for education. Many of the proposals of the two committees were incorporated into the Irish system of education. In addition, key proposals included the promotion of local committees which would be responsible for school maintenance and operation, the organization of school medical and dental services, the provision of school meals, and a school books plan. In addition, raises in teacher salaries were recommended, along with restrictions on the employment of school-age children, compulsory attendance laws, and the amalgamation of small schools.

Toward the late 1800s, the country experienced a resurgence of interest in the Irish language, dance, mythology, literature, history, games, and music. This new interest among the Irish people led to a new demand that these ethnic activities become a part of the school curriculum. This phenomenon helped promote the concept of the nation and a national culture which became even more pronounced with the establishment of the Irish Free State.

A national educational policy devised in 1934 remained intact for nearly four decades. A change in 1948 allowed school managers to arrange English instruction for 30 minutes a day in the infant schools. However, the general school program tended to focus on a rather narrow range of subjects which centered around the perpetuation of the Gaelic tradition. All of the nation's schools, both urban and rural, followed a common curriculum, and mastery of the Irish language became the primary goal of Irish education.

During 1929, an optional primary certificate examination was introduced to the nation's educational system. It included sections which measured the student's competence in Irish, English, mathematics, history, geography, and needlework for the girls. The exam was rather unique in that it included written, oral, and practical segments. Since it was optional, only about 25 percent of all students took it, and they were mostly from the urban areas. However, by 1940 there was talk of making the exam compulsory. Emon de Valera, Minister of Education, argued that making all students complete the exam would inject a new level of accountability into the teaching profession. He felt that the public had a right to know how its education tax dollars were being spent. He also, believed that the results achieved by the nation's teachers were more important than the methods they employed.

By 1943, the Primary Certificate examination did become compulsory but it only included three written papers in Irish, English, and arithmetic. This resulted in a national curriculum which emphasized written Irish rather than spoken Irish. While the nation's teachers tended to oppose this policy, it remained intact until 1967. The success rate was between 70 and 80 percent.

After independence, the preparation of teachers was carried out in boarding colleges which were supported by the Irish government. Six residential colleges were established, with the first four of these residential schools becoming operational by 1926. They were heavily involved in teaching the Gaelic language and traditions.

During the years of World War II, the inflated costs of living resulted in rather high levels of dissatisfaction among the nation's teachers. Eventually, a strike was called in 1946 which resulted in a seven-month dispute between the Teachers' Organization and the government. It was only settled at the request of the Archbishop of Dublin who persuaded the nation's teachers to return to duty. Even with a more sympathetic administration as a result of the 1948 election, few major changes in teachers' salaries occurred.

The Free State government made major changes in its secondary schools. While the state formerly funded the schools on the basis of their test scores, the new funding formulas were derived according to the number of students who took approved courses. However, all schools had to adhere to a curriculum which was geared toward the certificate examinations. Individual students could still win monetary awards by scoring high on the state examination.

Prescribed textbooks for all subjects were abolished in 1924 by the Free State Department of Education. General course guidelines were still in existence but teachers were allowed to create their own methods and strategies for dealing with the content in the schoolroom. However, Irish teachers had been used to preparing their students for the national exams, and many of them were uncomfortable with these new freedoms. Also, the results of the examinations were

published each year, which put a high degree of pressure on the nation's teachers. Hence, these new freedoms and the national examinations caused a great
deal of professional discomfort for many teachers. So, by 1940, required texts
were designated for English, Latin, Greek, and the modern continental languages. By 1941, a required text for Irish was utilized.

The policies at that time required students to ''fit in'' to the prescribed curriculum. One prominent Irish educator took issue with this policy since it was
based on the old British system which was based on the notion that the child
must fit the system.

By the beginning of the twentieth century, many nations had concluded that
funds expended on their children's education created a sound economic investment in the nation's future. This phenomenon did not occur in Ireland until the
1960s. In fact, the level of per capita expenditure on education was extremely
low compared to other western nations, averaging 3.2 percent of the gross national product (G.N.P). By way of comparison, England and Wales spent 3.9%,
Northern Ireland 5.4%, Scotland 6.5%, Japan 4.3%, and the United States 5.5%.

Since Ireland tended to lag somewhat behind other European countries in
industrial development, the nation was rather slow in creating a well-coordinated
system of technical/vocational education. By 1924, technical instruction had
become a branch of the Department of Education. During the early years of an
independent Ireland, it could be seen that improvements were needed in the
existing technical instruction programs. In a 1937 report by a commission which
studied the problem, it was concluded that the work of the schools was not
related closely enough to the needs of commerce and industry. The commission
then concluded that major changes were necessary in order to meet the basic
needs of the country's industrial complex. A total of 90 recommendations were
made. One major recommendation was that all sixth standard primary students
should have a school-leaving certificate.

The Commission on Technical Education formulated the primary concepts for
the Vocational Education Act of 1930. The act addressed both continuation
education and technical education. The administration of both continuation and
technical education was left to the local statutory committees, similar to the Act
of 1899. The technical instructor committees were eventually replaced by vocational education committees (VECs) which were designed to be smaller and
more efficient.

Under the Vocational Education Act, continuing education was seen to continue and supplement education provided in the elementary schools, and also to
incorporate into the curriculum appropriate instructional sequences designed to
provide practical training in the preparation of young persons for employment
in trades, and practical training for improving young people during the very
beginning stages of their employment. The program was designed for students
between the ages of fourteen and sixteen but was never designated as a compulsory act of education. In 1931, the Department of Education issued guidelines

for the nation's vocational education program, but it also allowed local education agencies latitude in the various educational plans which they prepared.

Technical education in Ireland refers to the Vocational Education Act of 1930, which addressed educational endeavors concerned with the trades, manufacturing, commerce, and other industrial activities. The act was also concerned with education in science and art and physical training. The two main purposes of technical education were to prepare young people for entry into a profession and to upgrade the work skills of employed persons.

The Commission on Technical Instruction had been concerned about a lack of effective strategies for apprenticeship training. Eventually, an apprenticeship act was passed in 1931 which enabled the Minister for Industry and Commerce to make an order involving trade. These orders would result in apprenticeship committees which were empowered to make rules and regulations. The committees consisted of employer and employee representatives. Finally, in 1960, a National Apprenticeship Board was created with the capacity to require employers to send their apprentices to the appropriate training courses.

During 1927, the Commission of Technical Education decided that Ireland did not have adequate provisions for the training of technical teachers. As a solution to the problem, a number of short special courses and summer refresher courses were established. Also, many teachers of rural science, math, commerce, English, and Irish were not required to participate in teacher preparation programs. From 1944 on, teaching candidates for teaching Irish had to pass the Teastas Timthire Gaelige, which was an advanced qualification for Irish.

As the 1950s came to an end, many Irish people criticized the general condition of vocational education. Many of these vocational education schools were rather small, which often made it difficult to hire specialized instructors. Due to these and other problems, technical and vocational education became major educational issues which would be addressed throughout the country in subsequent years.

During the past four decades, Irish education has experienced a number of major changes. It was subjected to major revisions which reflected the changes occurring in Irish society in general. In fact, there were a number of policy initiatives which dramatically altered the shape of the country's educational system.

Changes in the national attitude were occurring because of the country's increased involvement with major international organizations such as UNESCO and The Council of Europe. Irish teachers were making more trips to the United States and Europe, and the Irish section of the European Association of Teachers was started in 1962. Many countries adopted a slogan of ''equal education opportunities.'' This philosophy stimulated a number of major changes in the country's system of education. Indeed, the expansion of research in the behavioral sciences of psychology and sociology helped to focus the attention of educators on the problems involved in removing various types of education equality. This also has tended to lead toward an enrichment of educational and pedagogical studies.

In recent years, educational groups such as Tuairim, the Federation of Irish Secondary Schools, the Teachers Study Group, and a number of teacher organizations provided forums where dialogues, debate, criticisms, and educational proposals took place. Political parties finally became more concerned about education because of election factors. It became politically useful to address educational needs.

During the mid-1960s, the country experienced a decline in the school population. This resulted in a rather large number of underpopulated rural schools. The country's educational system found that it was increasingly difficult to staff schools properly because of accompanying financial constraints. Moreover, a large number of schools were quite old, thus causing rather severe maintenance problems. So Ireland began closing down some of them and amalgamating others.

Also, between 1960 and 1980, a number of curricular changes occurred in Ireland's schools. Technical and applied subjects began receiving more support as a result of the country's move toward a greater level of industrialization. During the 1970s, they adopted a more child-centered approach to education, with a greater emphasis on a "discovery approach" to learning. However, many of these changes were viewed as being incompatible with the country's public examination policies. These policies were all based on the country's Constitution of 1937 which granted all citizens of the Irish Free State the right to free elementary education. And, for the first time, in the 1960s, special educational programs were established for persons who were deemed to be handicapped or disadvantaged. The educational system acquired a more positive attitude about people who were partially sighted, hard of hearing, or who had other sorts of communication problems.

During the decades of the 1970s and 1980s, the state also commenced to examine third level education levels. As a result of this interest, an increase in the number of regional colleges and national institutions of higher education were added to the colleges of technology.

The teaching profession enjoyed an increased level of unification with the establishment of a single salary schedule for teachers in 1969. The teacher education efforts also underwent a number of major changes, particularly with the establishment of the single salary schedule. The teacher unions had become more harmonious, and the profession moved in the direction of a graduate-level preparation program. A final characteristic of Irish education during the 1960s and 1970s was a decline in the Church's control of schooling. Some suburban communities called for multidenominational national schools.

STRUCTURE OF THE SYSTEM

Although Ireland is a small island nation with only about four million people, the country presently has a quite well-developed educational system. It is a system which has been shaped by religious traditions, its colonial history, and its economic difficulties. Throughout its history, the Catholic Church has played a major role in the country's system of education. However, the educational system is primarily state controlled, with the state (through the Department of Education) playing the major role in the determination of the country's educational policies. While the schools used to be segregated by gender, they currently are mostly coeducational in nature. Attendance is compulsory between the ages of six and fifteen. However, there are some provisions for parents to "home school" their children.

The country's educational system has a three-level organizational structure. The first level is known as the national school. These schools are mostly controlled by the Catholic Church. However, the state does provide about two-thirds of the building costs of these schools, the salaries of teachers, and most of the basic expenditures. In addition, there are a small number of private primary schools for Ireland's first-level students.

Secondary schools are mostly denominational in nature and many were built by religious groups. While they received no funds for construction, the state now supplies about 80 percent of such costs. The state also pays most of the teaching salaries and operational expenses. Vocational schools are the other second-level educational facilities in Ireland. They are controlled locally and maintained by both local education agencies (LEAs) and the central government. Another type of second-level school is the comprehensive and community school which blends both applied and academic subjects. They are built by the state which also provides all of the funding for their maintenance and operation.

The University of Dublin and the National University of Ireland have been the primary providers of third-level education programs until recent years when the nation has experienced a major growth in the number of universities and the students are more pluralistic. Other changes in third-level education have occurred in the teacher preparation institutions which have tended to become more closely associated with the universities. They reflect the Irish model of funding which often sees the state paying for capital and current expenditures through the Department of Education while the school maintains its private ownership.

Ireland's educational system is still highly centralized. The Department of Education maintains either direct or indirect control over most phases of its operation. Many of the ugly battles over church/state issues disappeared after the country achieved its independence. In fact, during recent years, the Irish system of education has attempted to make a number of changes in order to meet the educational needs of students more effectively. For example, the Department of Education designated some eleven million pounds for the computerization of the various support services in nearly 250 Irish schools. Just under 200 secondary (third-level) schools are now participating in a Computerized Local Administrative System for Schools (CLASS) program. Through a well-coordinated partnership between the schools and industry, user-friendly software has been created. These new computerized programs have the capacity to handle students' attendance and school progress factors, along with curriculum assessment data and even factors pertaining to financial planning. An assessment module developed in 1993 even made it possible to assist teachers in preparing individual education plans which would meet the unique educational needs of students.

Recent efforts in meeting the needs of Irish students who are gifted and talented generally have occurred outside the formal system of education. The Irish Association for the Gifted Children has been involved with a number of efforts which provide support for able learners in the country. Among its many activities, this organization has conducted seminars for teachers, health nurses, social workers, and parents. It has also sponsored a number of residential holidays for bright children, and sponsors Explorer Clubs similar to those in England. One of the primary functions of the Explorer Clubs is to sponsor Saturday enrichment classes. The funding for the Saturday classes comes primarily from local grants.

Several years ago, the association successfully persuaded the Inspector of Schools for Special Education to assume the responsibility for gifted/talented education. Consequently, the state has provided some support for able learners during the past decade, even though no ''per pupil'' funding has been available. Ireland has five level-two (secondary) schools which are referred to as ''secondary tops'' which cater to advanced students. Our Lady of Mercy College also operates a special preparation program for teachers interested in receiving special work in teaching able learners.

The major curriculum topics addressed in Irish programs for gifted and talented students are concerned with the development of higher level thinking skills and creative problem solving. These topics are addressed in some of the privately sponsored programs such as the Bray Vocational Education Committee, the City of Dublin, and the Limerick Explorers Club in St. Edna's Community School.

One current problem in Ireland is the increased demand for education at a time when funding has become increasingly difficult. Like educational systems around the world, computer technology has created financial needs which have been difficult to meet. But not only the explosion in computer technology has caused financial difficulties; various forms of distance learning, video recorders, recorder instruments, and television have further strained educational budgets at all levels.

The many changes in Irish education during recent years have caused Irish educators and politicians to reexamine constitutional issues affecting Irish education. In 1922, the constitution of the new Irish Free State simply stated that ''All citizens of the Irish Free State have a Right to free elementary education.'' However, the 1937 constitution contained more information about the rights of parents, churches, the state, and the child.

MULTICULTURAL EDUCATION EFFORTS

Compared to many other countries, the Irish macroculture is extremely homogeneous, with only a small number of minority microcultures in the country. Even compared to England, the number of Asian, African, and West Indian inhabitants is quite small. Some sociologists refer to the 4 percent Protestant population as a cultural minority. Also, about 1 percent of the population professes to be Jewish. However, this small number of Jewish persons have actually been in the country for a long period of time. But it is still important to remember that these two groups have their own schools which are primarily subsidized by the state. These schools follow the curriculum of all other Irish schools apart from their own religious instruction and, in the case of one Jewish secondary school, the provision of Hebrew studies. Hebrew studies received full recognition from Ireland's universities as the equivalent of a matriculation subject.

In spite of the dearth of ethnic minorities, the curriculum guidelines are quite multicultural in nature. While there is no office or specific person charged with the responsibility of nurturing and maintaining a cogent multicultural education program in the nation's school system, the educational guidelines seem broad enough to allow for such efforts. As reported in the country's response to the authors' multicultural education survey, there are no funds specifically designated for multicultural education. It was further reported that the question of the need for such programs has not arisen because of the absence of cultural minorities. However, the curriculum of the schools does seem to encompass considerable treatment of cultures in Ireland and elsewhere. For example, both history and geography are required subjects until students are fifteen years of age; and in these programs, a variety of multicultural issues are addressed, specifically in world history and geography. Since Ireland has had a history of colonialization, there is a heightened interest in cultural minorities. This interest has also been intensified by the experience of many Irish missionaries.

As mentioned before, the culture of Ireland is primarily homogeneous, but the Gaelic (Celtic) culture has been a prominent part of the nation's curriculum. Moreover, the Irish language has been a compulsory subject for all students. Recently, the country has expressed grave concerns over the maintenance of the Irish language. It has been argued that Ireland has only about 20,000 native speakers of Gaelic, and less than 50 percent live and work in Irish-speaking locales. Moreover, some Irish educators have argued that rural poverty and isolation have sustained the language in the rural enclaves in the western portion of the land but not elsewhere in Ireland.

While mention has been made of the Protestant and Jewish cultures, they vary quite a bit from the mainstream Catholic population's way of life. In spite of the small population of both groups, they have contributed substantially to the Irish macroculture.

While the country has been viewed as having a conservative posture regarding social issues, the schools do not seem to reflect this conservatism, and tolerance and understanding seem to drive much of the school curriculum which is utilized in the schools. In spite of the interest in the Irish language, English is the official language of instruction in the schools, and there seem to be only minimal efforts to include native language instruction in the normal school curriculum.

SUMMARY

Based on the responses to the multicultural survey and the other research, it can be seen that, in general, Ireland has not seemed to place a great deal of importance on multicultural education. Since the country is primarily culturally homogeneous, the perceived need for such programs has not materialized. However, in light of the problems the country has experienced with its religious microcultures, it seems that such programs might be forthcoming in the future.

REFERENCES

Akenson, Donald H. *A Mirror to Kathleen's Face. Education in Independent Ireland, 1922–1960.* Montreal: McGill-Tweens, University Press, 1975.

Coolahan, John. *Irish Education: Its History and Structure.* Dublin: Institute of Public Administration, 1990.

Currie, Annie. "A Class of Their Own." *Times Educational Supplement* (November 6, 1992).

Gonen, Amiram. *The Encyclopedia of the Peoples of the World.* New York: Henry Holt Publishing Co., 1993.

Hindley, Reg. *The Death of the Irish Language.* London: Routledge Publishing Company, 1990.

Hogan, John. "Education in the Republic of Ireland." In Robert Bell et al., *Education in Great Britain and Ireland.* London: Open University Press, 1973.

Ireland. Department of Education. *Dail Eireann Proceedings.* Dublin: Department of Education, May 1941.

Ireland. Department of Education. *Report of the Commission on Technical Education.* Dublin: Department of Education, 1927.

Ireland. Department of Education. *Report of the Department of Education.* Dublin: Department of Education, 1924.

Ireland. Department of Education. *Vocational Continuation Schools and Classes, Memorandum for the Information of Committees.* Dublin: Department of Education, 1931.

Ireland. Department of Education. *Vocational Education Act of 1930.* Dublin: Public Statutes of the Direchtas, 1930.

Lovett, T., Gunn, D., and Robson, T. "Education, Conflict, and Community Development in Northern Ireland." *Community Development Journal,* Vol. 29, No. 2 (1994), pp. 177–186.

Mitchell, Bruce and Salsbury, Robert. *A National Survey of Multicultural Education.* Cheney, WA: Western States Consulting and Evaluation Services, 1988.

O'Donnell, Michael. "Irish Education Today." *Iris Hibernia,* Vol. 1, No. 1 (1962), p. 20.

Pearse, Patrick. "The Murder Machine." In *Political Writings and Speeches*. Dublin: Talbot Press, 1966.

Williams, W.G. and Mitchell, B. *From Afghanistan to Zimbabwe: Gifted Education Efforts in the World Community*. New York: Peter Lang Inc., 1989.

22

Israel

HISTORY OF THE SYSTEM

Israel is unique in that it is one of the world's newer nations, with a strong influence of Jewish history dating back to biblical times in addition to the Zionist movement in nineteenth and twentieth century Europe. Historians argue that some Hebrews migrated to present-day Israel approximately 4,000 years ago. It has been said that they arrived from a city named Ur which was located in present-day Iraq. After the end of World War II, land for the new nation was acquired through a United Nations resolution which created both an Arab and a Jewish state out of Palestine.

David Ben-Gurion declared the establishment of the State of Israel in Tel Aviv in 1948. After their long exile, the Jewish people were reunited in their ancient homeland with the issuance of a proclamation based on a Biblical passage (Lev. 25:10) which read in part: "Proclaim liberty throughout the land and to all the inhabitants thereof."

Prior to the time when Napoleon emancipated Jewish populations in much of Europe, Jews had been forced to live in ghettos which were segregated from other ethnic groups. After that time (1791), many Jews became assimilated into other communities. However, due to an increased degree of ethnic nationalism, Jews were sometimes unable to participate in the political systems. Some historians have argued that this lack of a Jewish nation state has been an advantage because they were able to escape the kinds of political problems that have plagued other nations. Indeed, this ethnic group was bound together by their strong religious ties.

During World War II, the Holocaust intensified the spirit of Zionism. The Nazi annihilation of six million Jews made the world's Jewish populations more determined than ever to create the new State of Israel. In addition to the spirit of Zionism, many Jews tended to feel that their very survival depended on the creation of a homeland in which they could be safe.

The State of Israel was formally established on May 14, 1948. But on the very next day, Arab forces started to invade the new nation; but by the following January (1949), Israel had captured new territories. During the first half of 1949, the Israelis held peace talks with the Arabs. A peace settlement was agreed upon, but no formal peace treaties were enacted, and the threat of hostilities from the surrounding Arab countries was constant.

After statehood was achieved, the new nation was plagued with other problems as well. Jews inhabited Israel from Persia, Turkey, Libya, Egypt, Poland, Romania, Bulgaria, and Yugoslavia. A few years later, other Jews arrived from Algeria, Morocco, Tunis, Hungary, and other European nations. The arrival of the new residents caused major logistics problems of housing, education, health and welfare, and employment. Indeed, the new government's infrastructure was greatly strained.

The newly partitioned state was a victory for David Ben-Gurion who was viewed as a pragmatic Zionist. In the 1949 elections, his opponent, Hurot, only received between 10 and 12 percent of the vote as a member of the new country's labor party.

The hostile feelings between the Israelis and Arabs persisted after the elections, and finally culminated in several conflicts, starting in the Suez Canal area in 1956. By this time, Israel had established a well-equipped sophisticated military defense which was necessitated by their close proximity to hostile Arab lands. The Israeli air force was well trained and well supplied with some of the latest equipment. Much of the funding for the creation of their military units came from the United States.

Prior to the Suez conflict, the Suez Canal had been nationalized by the Egyptian leader, Gamal Abdel Nasser, and Israeli shipping was prohibited from using the canal. Thus, when Israeli forces rolled through the Sinai and Gaza on October 29, 1956, they had a narrow focus of aims which were to recapture the Suez and create an international regime for its management. In air battles, the French-made Mysteres out-dueled the Russian-made MIGs and the Israeli Navy captured an Egyptian destroyer. By November 5, the Egyptian portion of the Suez conflict was terminated and enormous losses had been inflicted on the Egyptians. One thousand Egyptians were killed, compared to less than 200 Israelis. Huge amounts of equipment and armaments were captured. These actions took about 100 hours.

In the beginning, France and Great Britain were in collusion with Israel. However, after witnessing the enormous and quick Israeli victory over the Egyptians, they backed away from the conflict. Eventually, the United States, the Soviet Union, and the United Nations persuaded Israel to withdraw by promising freedom of Suez navigation, relief from threatened economic boycotts, and the termination of Arab raids into Israeli territory.

For the next ten years, Egypt attempted to mobilize the other Arab states into an anti-Israeli movement to eliminate Israel altogether. The number of border raids by Syria and Jordan increased, and Israel declared that it would retaliate severely for such incursions. The United Nations' peacekeeping efforts were not working, and demands by Egypt (who was backed by the Soviet Union by this time) further exacerbated the situation. On June 5, 1967, the Israelis attacked Egypt, Syria, and Jordan. The Egyptian air force was destroyed and the air forces of Syria and Jordan were badly damaged. During this war, which lasted just six days, the Israelis occupied the Gaza Strip, the Sinai, the west bank of Jordan (including the old city of Jerusalem), and the Golan Heights which overlooked the Sea of Galilee and served as a base for the staging of terrorist activities.

The victory by the Israelis was devastating to the Arabs. The Israelis were then located on the east bank of the Suez Canal which was closed to shipping. Nasser responded to his defeat by maintaining a "War of Attrition." Due to the small population of Israel, compared to Egypt, Israel could not survive a war of equal casualties in the various raids. So the Israeli government initiated a policy of severe retaliation for any Egyptian raids in order to inflict the highest level of casualties possible.

After the Six-Day War of 1967, the Palestine Liberation Organization (PLO) established a base in Jordan in order to achieve its goal, which at that time was total annihilation of Israel. Also after the loss of Israel, Nasser went to the Soviet Union in hopes of acquiring aid in the form of surface-to-air missiles. The Soviet response was an agreement to help re-train the Egyptian military units. But in 1970 the Israeli Air Force shot down four Egyptian planes which were being flown by Russian pilots. At that time, the Israelis did not know if they could rely on American support, and so in 1970 they agreed to sign a cease-fire with the Egyptians.

Just three years later, a surprise attack was initiated by the Syrians and the Egyptians against the Israelis. The attack occurred on Yom Kippur, October 6, 1973. After some initial Arab victories which inflicted heavy casualties on both sides, the Arabs were once again repulsed. But as the Israelis were about to initiate enormous measures of retaliation, the United States, the Soviet Union, and the United Nations intervened and a cease-fire was imposed on the antagonists. By this time, Anwar Sadat had assumed the leadership role of Egypt.

In 1976, Jimmy Carter became the President of the United States, and he extended invitations to Anwar Sadat and Manachem Begin to come to Camp David in hopes of negotiating a peace settlement between Egypt and Israel. By this time, a major breakthrough had occurred in the relationship between the two countries when Sadat had addressed the Israeli Knesset in Jerusalem. Finally, on March 26, a peace treaty was signed between the two countries.

But during this period of time, the PLO had stepped up its actions against the Israelis, causing major unrest. The PLO base of operation had been moved to southern Lebanon. In July 1981, Israel reacted to PLO rocket attacks in northern Israel by bombing the PLO in southern Lebanon. One of the reasons that Israel took the retaliatory action was that in the early 1980s, the Arab world was in a general state of disarray. The unity that the Arab world generated in denouncing an Israeli–Egyptian peace settlement dissipated in a little over a year. In 1982, Israel initiated an assault on Lebanon (called Operation Peace) in an attempt to dismantle the PLO. A sports stadium used for storing PLO ammunition was bombed by the Israelis, but the PLO retaliated by shelling Israeli towns in Galilee. Israeli troops were involved in an invasion of southern Lebanon in order to free northern Israel from PLO rocket attacks through the creation of a 40-kilometer-wide security zone in southern Lebanon. By 1985 the Israeli people had grown weary of it. Finally, in 1985, when Shimon Peres was prime minister and Rabin was defense minister, the Israeli cabinet voted to withdraw their forces from Lebanon. It had turned out to be as unsuccessful as the United States' Vietnam, the Soviet Union's Afghanistan, or the French's Indochina.

STRUCTURE OF THE SYSTEM

Today's Israel has a number of primary socio-political sources, but most of them come from Judaism and Zionism, a modern political movement. The notion of Zionism called for a return of exiled Jews to their biblical homeland. It was also a reaction to the oppression of Jews in eastern Europe. The country consists of four general areas, including the coastal plain which is fertile, humid, and thickly populated, stretching along the Mediterranean Sea; the central highlands, including the Hills of Galilee in the north; the arid Judean Hills in the south; and the Jordan Rift Valley and the Negev Desert, which includes about half of Israel's area.

The population of Israel presently is estimated at 4.5 million persons, including about 82 percent Jews. The literacy of the Jewish people is about 90 percent. The average life expectancy rate is approximately 74 for Jewish males and approximately 77.5 for females. Israel's government is a parliamentary democracy headed by a president who is the titular head of the state. The executive power rests in a prime minister and cabinet ministers who represent the dominant political blocs in Knesset. The Knesset is a unicameral parliament consisting of 120 members who are elected at-large every four years by secret ballot under a system of proportional representation. Israel's system of government is not based on a comprehensive constitution, but on nine basic laws enacted by Knesset.

Politically, the country has a multiparty system which is divided into four categories including left-of center parties; right-of center parties; right-wing religious parties, and Arab parties. There are six administrative districts and fourteen subdistricts under the jurisdiction of the Ministry of the Interior. The occupied territories of the West Bank, the Gaza Strip, and the annexed Golan Heights are all administered by the Israel Defense forces.

Hebrew became the primary language of the country, and the acceptance of this ancient language provided Israel with a unifying cultural bond. But the language issue also impacts religious considerations, and has resulted in a great deal of controversy. In fact, the secular versus religious arguments impact *all* segments of Israeli society. For example, there is a constant argument in Israel over the religious practices which influence the educational system.

Generally, it can be said that the political system is patterned after those of western Europe. There are democratic procedures, multiple parties, higher voter participation, a free press, and an independent judicial system which is the primary custodian of the country's civil liberties. Questions of human rights have been considered to be extremely important issues throughout the country's history. The Declaration of the Establishment of the State of Israel states that the country should develop itself for the benefit of all its inhabitants. Moreover, the State of Israel will be based on freedom, justice, and peace as envisioned by the prophets of Israel. Also, it will ensure complete equality of social and political rights to all persons regardless of religion, race, or gender. In addition, all inhabitants are guaranteed freedom of religion, conscience, language, education, and culture.

Education in Israel is deeply rooted in the Jewish culture which has always placed an extremely high value on the acquisition of knowledge. In 1969, Israel passed a compulsory education law which mandated school attendance between the ages of five and fourteen for all children regardless of race, creed, or gender. This was perceived to be a major step for a country in the midst of Islamic fundamentalism which had limited their educational systems to boys only. It also created controversy among parents who had previously sent their sons to work at the age of eleven or twelve. But the effects of the law were amazing, in that the attendance rate for Jewish children was 97 percent.

Israeli children are required to attend school for at least ten years in addition to preschool. The system consists of four levels, including preschool from ages three to six; primary education from grades one to six; intermediate school from grades seven to nine; and secondary school from grades ten through twelve. The secondary school includes three types: vocational, agricultural, and the general academic high school which prepares students to take the national matriculation examination.

The Ministry of Education and Culture makes the major decisions about budgets, curriculum, and the hiring, training, and licensing of teachers. One rather unique facet of the Israeli system of education exists because of the country's historical need for a strong military force. It is obligatory for most secondary students to spend fifteen days yearly, one hour per week, during the ninth grade. This amount increases to about forty days a year during the senior year of high school. While the training emphasis originally focused on weapons familiarity and drilling, it presently emphasizes physical fitness, sports, and camping.

The major universities in Israel include the Israel Institute for Technology, the Hebrew University, Tel Aviv University, Bar-Ilan University, Haifa University, Ben-Gurion University of the Negev, and the postgraduate Weizmann Institute of Technology. Since the 1948–1949 academic year, the higher education enrollment has grown from approximately 1,635 students attending degree-granting institutions to over 68,000. The nation's largest higher education institution is Tel Aviv University.

MULTICULTURAL EDUCATION EFFORTS

Israel's two main minority groups are the Arabs and Oriental Jews, and the Jewish majority represents about 83 percent of the country's population. In the authors' multicultural education study, the respondent stated that both the Jewish and non-Jewish factions in the land favored segregated schools. It was felt that the Arabs perceived integration as threatening to their identity and to their way of life. Responses also revealed that Israel utilized a pluralistic philosophy in regard to various educational issues. Although not sponsored by the Office of the Minister of Education and Culture, a formal program of multicultural education was in operation through the Oriental Jewish Heritage Center. The Ministry of Education offers in-service training for providing leadership in multicultural education. However, in spite of these efforts, the country has no formal multicultural preparation requirements for teacher certification.

Approximately 50 percent of the nation's schools are culturally integrated while the other 50 percent are segregated. The history of indigenous persons is part of the curriculum, and the Israeli Ministry of Education and Culture has a special procedure for the evaluation of curriculum materials, library holdings, and textbooks for racist/sexist content. The same survey also revealed that more in-service training and multicultural curriculum development was needed in the country, along with better dissemination of existing projects.

Throughout the history of Israel's educational system, the nation has been known for exemplifying a positive attitude toward immigrants. Indeed, Israel has utilized the "law of return," the first constitutional law, which places an extreme value on integration. Immigrant children are viewed as important citizens of the future, ranking high on the national priority list. Immigration programs are well funded and there are ample opportunities for children to become adjusted to the Israeli experience. The Israeli schools are viewed as having a primary responsibility to assist immigrant children in becoming assimilated into Israeli society.

In discussing the issue of pluralism and assimilation, it should be pointed out that a distinction has been made between multicultural and monistic assimilation. Proponents of monistic assimilation have tended to regard cultural heterogeneity as a negative concept and argue that cultures are socially healthy proportionately to their cultural homogeneity. Pluralistic cultural traditions are thought to constitute a great deal of strife unless they are dealt with from an assimilationist philosophy.

A further analysis of multicultural education issues in Israel reveals that these waves of immigration created enormous changes in the Israeli macroculture. Before 1948, approximately 90 percent of the immigrants to the country arrived from Europe. But after that time, nearly half of the immigrants came from underdeveloped, semifeudal, traditional societies in the Middle East and the Saharan regions of Africa. Consequently, the Israeli schools were presented with the problem of attempting to rapidly modernize and westernize these new immigrants and their linguistic, cultural, ideological, political, and socioeconomic integration into a Western-style technological and scientific civilization with a democratic way of life. Moreover, the families from the Middle-Eastern and North-African countries were poorer and larger than their European counterparts which put them ''at risk'' in the Israeli schools.

Thus, the Ministry of Education and Culture made a concerted effort to provide school programs that addressed these problems in order to minimize existing educational inequalities, and to close the socio-economic gaps which have done such a disservice to many school children in the country. Some of the measures were deemed to be quite harsh, and the Ministry has been under heavy criticism at times. However, by and large, the measures have proven to be quite effective in closing the gap.

Yet another problem relating to multicultural issues has centered around the religious pluralism of the country. Religious Jews make up about 30 percent of Israel's Jewish population. They tend to be identifiable by their dress and their way of life which is dictated according to religious dogma. Some of them have formed their own schools and have also developed their political parties. As a nation, Israel has had a long-standing commitment to Zionism which tended to provide a tolerant view toward both its religious and nonreligious followers. For example, the country has attempted to provide adequate education programs for its Iraqi and Romanian immigrants.

Further evidence of the country's attempts to meet the needs of its ethnically different students has occurred in the Center for the Integration of Oriental Jewish Heritage through the offices of the Ministry of Education and Culture. It was found that many teachers had inaccurate information about the children representing the new ethnic groups coming to the nation's schools. Consequently, new in-service programs were crafted and presented to teachers in an attempt to make them more sensitive to the children's cultures in order to communicate more accurately and effectively. The research on such programs has proven them to be extremely successful and capable of effecting positive attitude changes about the microcultures represented by these new immigrants.

SUMMARY

Perhaps no country in the world has been forced to deal with the kinds of problems which have faced Israel during the past four and one-half decades. Located in the midst of hostile Islamic neighbors, Israel has been involved in almost constant conflicts. Moreover, the goal of much of the Arab world has been to drive the Israelis out of the area.

The country has met this threat with military action and education. Its education has been strong and well funded. It has believed strongly in the axiom of survival through education. While the country has stressed an assimilationist philosophy, it has done so out of survival reasons, believing that too much pluralism might mean too much internal strife.

Evidence of the country's strong educational system can be seen in its large numbers of professional and technical people who have been necessary for the country's survival. The fact that education has been highly valued throughout the history of the Jewish people has further added to the strength of the educational system.

REFERENCES

Abba Eban, Solomon. *Personal Witness: Israel Through My Eyes.* New York: G.P. Putnam's Sons, 1992.

Cohen, Mitchell. *Zion and State: Nation, Class, and the Shaping of Modern Israel.* New York: Basil Blackwell, 1987.

Dayan, Moshe. *Breakthrough: A Personal Account of the Egypt-Israel Peace Negotiations.* New York: Knopf, 1981.

Eisikovits, Rivka and Beck, Robert H. "Models Governing the Education of New Immigrant Children in Israel." *Comparative Education Review* (May 1990), pp. 177–178.

Kovacs, M.L. and Cropley, A.J. *Immigrants and Society.* New York: McGraw-Hill, 1975.

Leslav, A., Krausz, E., and Nussbaum, S. "The Education of Iraqi and Romanian Immigrants in Israel." *Comparative Education Review,* Vol. 33, No. 2 (1995), pp. 178–194.

Metz, Israel and Metz, Helen Chapin. *Israel: A Country Study.* Washington, DC: Library of Congress, 1990.

Mitchell, Bruce and Salsbury, Robert. *An International Survey of Multicultural Education.* Cheney, WA: Western States Consulting and Evaluation Services, 1991. (See Appendix.)

Naamani, Israel T. *The State of Israel.* New York: Praeger, 1980.

Perlmutter, Amos. *Israel: The Partitioned State.* New York: Charles Scribner's Sons, 1985.

Stahl, Abraham. "Introducing Ethnic Materials to the Classroom." *Urban Education* (October 1985), pp. 257–271.

Yaacov, Inam. "Israel." *Education and Urban Society* (August 1986).

Zureik, E. "Education and Social Change Among the Arabs in Israel." *Journal of Palestine Studies,* Vol. 23, No. 4 (1993), pp. 73–93.

23

Italy

HISTORY OF THE SYSTEM

Central Italy, between Rome and Florence, was inhabited by the Etruscans long before the birth of Christ. Providing the region with some of its first cultural heritage, the Etruscans were sea wanderers who came at different periods of time from their original homeland, which historians believe was in the eastern Mediterranean regions. They seem to have intermingled with the natives, apparently having had no interest in colonizing the area.

The Etruscan civilization was strong at about the same time that the Greek colonists arrived in southern Italy about 750 B.C. But, unlike the Romans, the Etruscans did not seem to exhibit the organizational spirit for nation building. The cultural contributions of the Etruscans are well known. For example, their tomb murals are considered to represent the joy, sensual pleasure, frenzy, and life of the times. Some of their murals contain sensual scenes which emphasize the music and merriment which apparently were a significant part of their culture. Many of these murals contained a great deal of nudity. While they sometimes copied Greek statues, they preferred not to carve out of marble, but more often used clay, porous volcanic stone, and bronze.

The Etruscans contributed many of the elements which would later comprise the Roman Empire. It is thought that the Roman numerals were most likely Etruscan in their origin, as was the "Roman" toga. The Romans liked to play the Etruscan trumpets in their ceremonies, and the name of the most famous Italian city (Rome) seems to have been taken from an Etruscan word which means "River Town."

However, the Etruscans were never noted for their discipline and organization. Even though they seem to have been fierce fighters, they were overrun by the Romans, and after about 200 years of intermittent fighting, the Romans finally created a colony in 396 B.C. The Etruscans were essentially assimilated into the Roman culture.

The Greeks, who profoundly influenced both the Etruscans and the Romans, first arrived in Italy during the eighth century B.C., establishing a colony on the Bay of Naples. Because of this influence, the Etruscans and Romans acquired many of their ideas and began worshipping Greek gods and learning the alphabet. The Greeks have also been given credit for bringing the olive and grape to Italy. In fact, it has been generally believed that Italy became part of western civilization because of the influence of the Greeks.

However, it was actually Rome which provided the area with a process for preserving this civilization up to modern times. It has been argued that the Greeks were the creators of antiquity and time, but the Romans made their mark as organizers and administrators. Their history has been traced back as far as 1000 B.C., probably arriving in the area of the Danube basin, crossing the Alps in the process.

Roman law also became known as one of the most important contributions, not only to Italy, but to the western world as well. The creation of the Twelve Tables was probably made possible because of the Roman's phobia for organization and administration. The Twelve Tables codified the legal structure and took the administration of law away from the religious factions, making it the responsibility of government magistrates. Roman law also became part of the school curriculum for several hundred years.

Another important contribution of the Romans was the notion of citizenship. Indeed, citizens enjoyed immunity from torture or threats, and they had the right of appeal to the assembly and eventually to the emperor. Citizens had to be males who were over fifteen years of age, and freed slaves could become citizens along with some aliens.

The Roman government was established with a very advanced system of checks and balances. Two magistrates were elected to serve for one year. They could veto each other's proposals. In order to become a candidate for a magistrate position, a man had to pass through the lower offices. The Senate consisted of 300 members who were elected by the people. Even though it was an advisory body, it enjoyed such great prestige that its recommendations were almost always accepted.

During the Punic Wars, Rome eventually mastered the western Mediterranean. It occupied Spain, Sicily, Sardinia, Corsica, and the North African shores. By the first century A.D., Rome had also taken over the remainder of Greece, Macedonia, and Egypt. But the acquisition of all these territories created a major change in Roman society. The growth of Rome resulted in an enormous increase in the wealth of the country. Thus, Rome became transformed from a rather austere, conservative, and quite religious country to one in which inflation and corruption became the norm. The newly acquired provinces were governed by the Senate, and farmers were pushed off the lands to live in poverty in the cities. Some of them were forced into slavery.

Under the leadership of Caesar Augustus, the administrative organization of the Roman Empire was restructured, and a 200-year period of relative peace ensued. This era, referred to as the Pax Romana, saw the development of a sophisticated transportation network, the creation of the legal system, art, culture, and the creation of a language system which would influence European countries throughout the future. However, many of the emperors who followed Augustus were less talented. Roman society became corrupt and a series of severe plagues, coupled with the overextension, would eventually lead to the downfall of the Roman Empire.

Constantine I moved the center of the empire to Byzantine, renamed it Constantinople, and adapted Christianity as the official state religion in A.D. 315. Rome was overrun by the Visigoths in 410, and was vulnerable to attack from that time on. By 476, the last Roman emperor, Augustulus, was forced out of office, and from that time until 1860 there was a lack of any appreciable political unity in Italy. The only unifying body was actually the Catholic Church during all those years.

During the Dark Ages, Gregory I, who was pope from 590 to 604, was influential in the increasing political influence of the papacy in the government of Italy. Gregory reorganized Rome's administrative structure and was responsible for repairing a badly damaged infrastructure. He was also referred to as Gregory the Great. He was successful in reorganizing the city's administration, and repairing aqueducts, feeding the poor from the papal stores, heading the militia, and keeping the Lombard king away from Rome. Interestingly enough, he also has received credit for reorganizing the liturgical music of the church in the form of the Gregorian chant which is still used in modern worship services all over the world. But the Lombards eventually prevailed. They managed to hold their power until 774 when Charlemagne was crowned emperor of the Franks and the Lombards. This served to reunite the lands of the Roman Empire, which became known as the Holy Roman Empire. The Holy Roman Empire thrived during the Dark Ages and the Renaissance.

The fourteenth century was a time of social unrest, famine, war, and plague. This was a major change from the previous 100 years. The population was estimated at between seven and nine million people who were concentrated quite heavily in the cities and towns of the northern and central areas. This heavy concentration of people tended to create a great strain on the agricultural infrastructure. At that time in history, the agricultural techniques tended to be rather primitive.

The Renaissance has been divided into two sections by some historians. The pre-Renaissance occurred in a time period of some 125 years, ending about 1375. During this time, there was a general reexamination of Roman thought, political philosophy, literature, art, and architecture. The next 150 years have been generally described as the Renaissance period. Perhaps at no other time in history had such a great number of scholars been congregated in such a small area. Besides the scholars, there were many brilliant painters, such as Leonardo da Vinci and Michelangelo, and many great writers and architects. Italy became known as a major cultural center, and the ideas developed there quickly traveled to other parts of Europe.

The Renaissance has generally been thought to be primarily a cultural movement rather than a political phenomenon. Even though a number of independent communes continued to exist, the political history of the Italian Renaissance was dominated by the five major Italian city states: Venice (sometimes referred to as the Venetial Republic), Milan, Florence, the papal states, and Naples.

The dominant intellectual force during this period of time was humanism. Universities were created and their influence spread throughout Europe. The invention of the printing press made printed materials available for the masses, and suddenly reading became the most important topic of the school curriculum. Moreover, the expansion of the cultural audience coupled with a liberalization of the artistic environment helped foster the notion of nationhood more fully. The Church became the most visible Italian institution.

Also of great importance during this period was the keen interest in discoveries and explorations. More sophisticated sailing ships were constructed, and existing maps were changing constantly as a result of the identification of new territories which were previously unknown in Europe.

But along with Martin Luther in northern Europe, the Catholic Church was criticized by Niccolo Machiavelli who wrote *The Prince,* which was an attempt to portray people, particularly men, as naturally selfish, greedy, cowardly, stupid, and treacherous. Anyone who wished to rule others must be half lion and half fox. In short, it was necessary for them to become more efficient despots.

During the seventeenth century, Italy was again plagued by warfare. The Thirty Years War, which involved much of Europe, erupted in Italy. By this time, Italy had been challenged commercially by the growing power of the Dutch and English. The country was again decimated by another plague, and it would not recover commercially for nearly 100 years. The last half of the eighteenth century had witnessed the restoration of peace, and a number of reforms were instituted in most of the Italian states, including the southern portion which no longer was ruled by the Spanish.

As the nineteenth century began, a new nationalistic sentiment was emerging. In 1803, the sculptor Antonio Canova created an allegorical figure which depicted Italy. It was the very first time that Italy appeared in the visual arts. It marked the beginning of Italy's Romantic Age, an era which was characterized by artistic and intellectual enterprises stressing emotionalism and a rejection of classical forms. It was a time when the operas of Rossini and Verdi were gaining worldwide attention.

By 1806, Napoleon had annexed large parts of Italy, including Rome. However, his defeat in 1815 reestablished the national equilibrium and the old boundaries were restored. The nationalist wave, referred to as "Risorgimento" (rebirth), intensified, but by 1860 only a small percentage of the people were able to speak the national language. However, the interest in unification was strong among the middle class. With the acquisition of Venetia after a third war with Austria, the Kingdom of Italy was established as a centralized unitary state with a powerful monarchy and a parliamentary government. The king was still the dominant figure, with the power to dissolve parliament whenever it was expedient.

The country eventually developed a parliamentary government, electoral law, and voting based on the basis of tax payments. Consequently, by 1870, only about 2 percent of the population were able to vote. From the very early beginnings as a nation, Italy was actually governed by a small political class, primarily from the north, and it consisted of the aristocracy and the wealthy industrial middle class.

By the 1880s, a huge growth spurt, led by heavy industry and a rapidly growing military–industrial complex, allowed northern Italy to become economically competitive with the rest of Europe. However, the southern part of the country was not nearly as prosperous because of a relative lack of industrial clout, and by 1885 the situation had become so acute that the south was besieged with rural strikes, riots, and tax rebellions.

In spite of the dissatisfactions, the labor movement in Italy did not really materialize until the early 1890s. During this period of time, many intellectuals became enamored of socialism which dwelled on the evils of industrialization and pressed for a number of social reforms. Much of this socialist activity was centered in Milan where Filippo Turati organized the Milanese Socialist League in 1889. By 1900, the elections seemed to strengthen the state. Even though public dissatisfaction seemed to crest at that time, the infrastructure of the social institutions was solidified. Giovanni Giolitti was the prime minister, a position he held until 1914. He initiated a labor reform program which limited the working day of women to eleven hours, prohibited the employment of children under the age of twelve, and provided for a holiday each week. He was replaced by Antonio Salandra, a conservative. After the assassination of Austrian Archduke Francis Ferdinand in 1914, World War I began between the Triple Entente (Britain, France, and Russia) against the Central Powers (Austria-Hungary and Germany). Italy remained neutral at the outset, but finally signed the Treaty of London, entering the conflict on the side of the victorious Triple Entente in 1915. The war absolutely decimated the country's economy, and an estimated 600,000 troops were killed. By 1920, inflation had risen 200 percent over wartime inflation and the lira dropped by over 300 percent. Strikes broke out everywhere and many people were attracted by the socialist revolution in Russia.

By 1921, the Fascist party, under the leadership of Benito Mussolini, wrested away the leadership of the liberals. Gradually, Mussolini was able to dismantle the basic elements of the liberal regime, and by the end of 1925 his new government had control of the press. In 1935, Italy invaded Ethiopia, claiming it needed new territories for the overcrowded south. Mussolini participated in the dismantling of Czechoslovakia in 1938, winning a great deal of prestige through playing the peacemaker between Hitler and the West. But during World War II, Hitler never seemed to take the Italians seriously, and the Allies were greeted as liberators when they invaded Sicily in 1943. The Allied advance was actually slowed as the Germans sent troops to the area and put up a stiff defense which delayed their invasion of Russia.

At the end of World War II, Italy was treated as a defeated power and was forced to pay reparations to Greece, Yugoslavia, and the Soviet Union. In December 1945, a tripartite coalition government joined the Christian Democratic Party under the leadership of De Gasperi, the first Catholic Prime Minister of Italy. By 1955, Italian politics had taken a major swing to the right. But by the late 1950s, Antonio Segni formed a minority caretaker government with center-right support which provided a short-lived but badly needed period of stability for the country.

After two decades of economic growth during the 1950s and 1960s, a number of student strikes broke out during the late 1960s, precipitating work strikes and some plant occupations. Consequently, the elections of 1972 sought to restore law and order to the country. However, they did not solve the problem, and by 1976, the country experienced an economic recession. In 1979, elections were called and the big winner was the Radical Party. It also seemed to signal major limits to communist growth.

STRUCTURE OF THE SYSTEM

In recent years, Italy has had one of the more complicated political systems among the major western democracies. It has been characterized as a politically divided country, with a plethora of political parties which makes any sort of significant policy making quite difficult. It has shifted from a period of dominance by the Christian Democratic Party from 1948 to about 1960, to a period of collaboration between the Christian Democrats and the Socialists in the center-left alliance of the mid- to late 1970s when the Italian Communist party openly supported the government. This was followed by a revived five-party center-left coalition during the 1980s.

Following the termination of World War II, a constitution was framed in 1948. A parliamentary system was created in which the president had only limited powers. The president is elected for a period of seven years as a result of negotiations between the Senate and the Chamber of Deputies. The president may resign at any time for any reason. There is an executive, legislative, and judicial section. The legislative body includes the Senate and the Chamber of Deputies. In addition to the president, the executive branch includes a prime minister who is responsible for twenty different ministries including agriculture and forestry, budget and economic planning, cultural assets, defense, education, environment, finance, foreign affairs, foreign trade, government holdings, health, industry, commerce and crafts, interior, labor and social security, merchant marine, pardons and justice, posts and telecommunications, public works, tourism, transport and civil aviation, and treasury. The judicial branch includes a constitutional court, court of cessation, council of state, and a court of accounts. Under the Court of Cessation are the appeal courts, assize courts, tribunals, praetors, and justices of the peace.

In addition to Italy's significant contributions to the world's art are the many gifts of music. Two contributing factors affecting the evolution of Italian music in the early twentieth century were the romantic opera of the nineteenth century, and the nationalist movement. The work of Rossini, Verdi, and Puccini are well known, as are the contributions of such singers as Enrique Caruso.

The country's educational system has enjoyed remarkable progress from 1930 to the present. The literacy rate, which was about 80 percent in 1930, improved to 97 percent over the next five decades. During the 1950s and 1960s, the eight years of compulsory education were made available to more children because of an improvement in the country's level of financing for public education. Until that time, the educational system divided the country's school children into two groups: one being elitist, and the other a similiterate mass.

The compulsory years of education occur between the ages of six and fourteen. About 80 percent of the country's children attend public and private preschools. The primary schools serve the needs of children between the ages of six and ten. They are self-contained, with one teacher being responsible for the instruction in all subjects. Oral and written examinations are used for determining admission to middle school level which includes children from age eleven to thirteen. The subjects taught at this level include Italian, foreign languages, mathematics, social studies, technical and artistic skills, music, and physical education. Students with academic difficulties receive special help. Again, examination scores are used to determine admission to the next level, the upper secondary schools.

At this level, students are able to choose between classical, scientific, linguistic, and artistic lyceums, technical or vocational schools, specialized schools for music and the arts, or normal schools for elementary school teacher training.

Two types of degrees may be obtained in Italian universities: the *laurea* and the doctorate. *Laurea* is a term used in ancient times which referred to the crown of laurels bestowed on scholars. Some of Italy's more than 65 universities have long histories. The University of Bologna was founded in 1088, the University of Padua in 1222, and the University of Naples in 1224. In 1981, Italy's University Act was an attempt to initiate certain reforms in the country's university system which would make it easier for higher education institutions to make needed changes.

MULTICULTURAL EDUCATION EFFORTS

Cultures represented in Italy include native Italians, Jews, Islamics from North Africa and the Middle East, Central Africans, Filipinos, Chinese, and Sri Lankans. The country does not have any formal multicultural education programs for the schools. There are no multicultural components required in the process of teacher certification. The country's official language is Italian, and there are special school programs which attempt to teach students in their mother tongue.

Public schools in Italy, from elementary to university levels, are racially and culturally integrated. However, there is no formal procedure for evaluating textbook and curriculum materials for racist and sexist content; this is done at the local level. There is an office in the Ministry of Education which is called the Cultural Affairs Office, but formal multicultural education programs in Italy seem to be restricted to the university level.

Italy has had its share of influential educators who have made an impact on educational programs around the world. Serving as a useful role model for female educators was Maria Montessori who was the first female medical school graduate from the University of Rome. Working with children in the slums of Rome, she became interested in the education of such poverty youth, and her early methods became part of a popular educational movement.

However, the education of the underclass is a problem for Italy as it is elsewhere in the world. For example, in a poor section of Rome, teacher Simona Manganozzi has been operating a class for immigrant and disabled children. Other schools are relatively well funded, but this one is unable to buy toilet paper, let alone pencils or paper.

The Italians and other European countries have been wrestling with the issue of interactive integration of European peoples. But Italian youths migrating to German schools have described a number of difficulties. Perhaps the most perplexing problem for migrating Italian youth has been the necessity of choosing between their German friends and their Italian culture and family. Problems such as these have sometimes caused Italian students to acquire a variety of physical and psychological problems.

SUMMARY

At first glance, it appears that relatively little is happening in the way of multicultural education programs in the Italian schools. But the country did participate in the 1991 international survey, and an office for such enterprises does exist in the Ministry of Education.

However, the programs which occur in the schools appear to be quite minimal and fragmented. For example, the Ministry of Education takes no leadership for the screening of educational books and materials for the exclusion of racist and sexist content. Moreover, there do not seem to be any national multicultural requirements for teacher certification.

In spite of the absence of such programs on an extensive basis, the literature continuously suggests that the European schools must create program changes which would help children acquire more positive attitudes about microcultures from other common market nations. European countries are close together, and

Europe must learn to interact successfully with persons from different racial and ethnic groups if the common market concept is to grow and flourish.

REFERENCES

Cochrane, Eric. "Disaster and Recovery: 1527–1750." In John Julius Norwich (Ed.), *The Italians: History, Art, and the Genius of a People.* New York: Abrams, 1983.

Crow, John A. *Italy: A Journey Through Time.* New York: Harper & Row, 1965.

Hale, J.R. "Humanism and Renaissance: 1350–1527." In John Julius Norwich (Ed.), *The Italians: History, Art, and the Genius of a People.* New York: Abrams, 1983.

Hinkle, Pia. "A School Must Rest on the Idea that Children Are Different." *Newsweek* (December 2, 1992).

Lovett, Clara. *The Democratic Movement in Italy, 1830–1876.* Cambridge, MA: Harvard University Press, 1982.

Mitchell, Bruce and Salsbury, Robert. *An International Survey of Multicultural Education.* Cheney, WA: Western States Consulting and Evaluation Services, 1991. (See Appendix.)

Portera, Agostino. "Is an Interactive Integration of the European Peoples Possible? An Example of Italian Youth in the West German Republic." *Journal of Multilingual and Multicultural Development,* Vol. 12, No. 4 (1991), pp. 271–276.

Procacci, Giuliano. *History of the Italian People.* New York: Harper and Row, 1968.

Shinn, Rinn-Sup. *Italy: A Country Study.* Washington, DC: U.S. Government Printing Office, 1985.

Tannenbaum, Edward R. and Noether, Emiliana P. *Modern Italy: A Topical History Since 1861.* New York: NYU Press, 1974.

24

Japan

HISTORY OF THE SYSTEM

Perhaps no other nation in the world has attracted so much international attention because of its amazing educational success as Japan. The incredible economic advances during the past three decades are well documented. The nation is among the top five in educational math/science test scores, low infant mortality rates, per capita income level, low incidence of handgun murders (and crime, in general); and the list goes on and on. Indeed, educators and social scientists the world over are hard pressed to explain the amazing success story in this island nation.

One partial explanation for the success of Japanese schooling is the nation's high regard for its children. Indeed, the care of children is perhaps the single most important concern of the entire country. Child care is a national obsession, and the full resources of Japan are available for the education and nurturing of young people. Also, this narrow island country often has felt itself the victim of meager natural resources, and has been vulnerable to earthquakes, fires, and enemies. The nation has been viewed by many as a country which created a strong educational system because of its high level of vulnerability.

At the time of the Meiji restoration, more than 100 years ago, about 80 percent of the Japanese people lived on farms. The lack of available land, and major concerns about a climate which could devastate crops in a very short time, created a high level of anxiety for Japanese farmers. This tended to create a situation which allowed only the most industrious to survive economically. Also, education was not deemed as a universal resource at this time in history. Children who grew up in rural areas often attended school for only a few years because the needs of the farm were perceived as being more important than school attendance.

Arguably another part of the reason for the country's educational excellence may be its historical roots in the country's religious dogma. One virtue of Japan's religious traditions has been high educational achievement. Now, the possibility for excellent achievement is open to all Japanese children, regardless of economic or social circumstances.

STRUCTURE OF THE SYSTEM

In 1946, General Douglas MacArthur and his advisers helped the Japanese create a new constitution following the country's surrender to the United States at the end of World War II. In effect, the new constitution transferred all political power from the emperor to the Japanese people. Moreover, the country's army and navy were abolished, and the country agreed to give up the use of war as a political weapon.

Among the economic changes were the land reforms which made it possible for Japanese farmers to own their own land. Also, the zaibatsu firms were broken up, and labor unions were formed for the country's different working groups. By 1951, Japan signed a peace treaty with 48 different countries. At the same time, Japan signed a security treaty with the United States, allowing the U.S. to have military bases in Japan. However, it was not until 1956 that Japan and the Soviet Union finally signed a treaty which formally ended World War II hostilities between the two nations. At this time, Japan was able to join the United Nations when the USSR terminated their veto against the admission of Japan.

Economically, Japan has been forced to rely on imported raw materials to make its manufacturing economy function properly. Since the end of World War II, the country has enjoyed the fastest rate of economic growth of all the industrialized countries of the world. For many years, Japan was learning from the western nations—adopting its ideas and technology. (Ironically, during the 1980s, the western countries were looking at Japan in order to improve their own production technology.)

In 1955, members of Japan's political groups united in order to form the Liberal-Democratic Party (LDP). This conservative political party controlled Japan's politics and government from the time it was formed until 1993. But the party lost its power during the early 1990s, and in the 1993 elections Morohiro Hosokawa, the leader of the New Party, was elected prime minister. It was the first time that someone other than a member of the LDP led the country. However, his time in office was short-lived, and in 1994 Tsutomu Hata of the Japan Renewal Party succeeded Hosokawa as prime minister. However, Hata resigned just two months later, and the LDP and Japan's leftist Social Democratic Party combined to form a new government. Tomiichi Jurayama became prime minister of the country.

Mothers historically have played an extremely viable role in the education of Japanese children. Their major goal in life is to see that their children are raised successfully. A great deal of the success factor relates to school performance, and the mothers spend much of their time helping their children pursue academic excellence. Moreover, the Japanese mother tends to explore the desires and needs of the child's inner self. She responds to the signals given by the children in such a way that many Japanese seem to avoid situations in which the child causes trouble or discomfort to others (Meiwaku o Kakero). This, in turn, seems to help children acquire a kind of sensitivity and interest in responding to the subtle mood swings of other people.

During the pre-school years, mothers also spend a great deal of time working with their children on the various readiness functions so that their offspring will be ''ready to learn'' as soon as they reach school age. Many mothers (particularly in the more urban areas) teach their young children the phonetic alphabet as well as basic concepts in math, such as counting to 100 and performing simple computational problems. Mothers also spend time in various types of cooperative games and other activities such as drawing, reading, and playing writing and counting games. Indeed, Japanese mothers seem to function as surrogate pre-school teachers.

In general, there seems to be an attitude that ''kindergarten is too late.'' In fact, a book by Masaru Ibuka, the CEO of the Sony Corporation, argues that the pre-school years are the most important times in a child's life for learning. This work has been instrumental in rekindling an interest in pre-school education for Japanese youth.

Recent writings have tended to characterize Japan's educational system as a model for the rest of the world because of its intellectual rigor and scholarship. Arguably, it is somewhat responsible for much of the nation's tremendous success during the past two decades. Since the end of World War II, the country has adapted a number of western practices, making it an interesting combination of traditional Japanese and Western influences. This amalgamation makes it one of the more unique countries of the world.

Like many other nations, education in Japan has had an elitist history. Its feudalistic society, complete with a hierarchical system of social relationships, was its primary trademark well until the middle of the nineteenth century. Children were taught from an early age to honor and respect differences in gender, rank, class, and (most importantly) age. Many of these practices changed when Japan altered its isolationist posture and instituted many of its modernization policies. These changing factors led to the creation of its universal education system.

Through the influence of such countries as Germany and the United States, the Japanese commenced to provide a universal comprehensive education program for six years. In the early part of the reform period, secondary education was still elitist, however, being reserved primarily for male students from the upper echelon. Gradually, a two-track system emerged. One system addressed the curriculum of the lower classes which stressed obedience, national morals and patriotism. The system for the elite stressed the academics and preparation for elitist positions.

Things changed drastically for the nation after 1943, and the end of World

War II. The egalitarian spirit of the United States and European countries had a profound influence on Japan. The nation made major changes in its system of secondary education so that it too became comprehensive in nature. The Ministry of Education decided to adopt the 6-3-3 system which was popular in many western countries, and by the end of the 1970s, 90 percent of all Japanese children were completing high school—a statistic that was the envy of educators from all over the world. This blessed the nation with one of the world's highest literacy rates, and Japanese students were leading the world in comparative examinations.

The Japanese educational system is highly competitive in nature. After attending the comprehensive elementary school for six years, students are promoted to the middle school (junior high). While most middle schools have no entry tests, some private and even national schools, which are considered to be more prestigious, do require entry exams. For most students, the middle schools are a preparatory stage for determining what sort of high school they shall attend. After the ninth year, students are tracked into an academic route leading to high school, or a vocational track which prepares them for the world of work. The reputation of the junior high school rests on the success rate of its students in getting into the "good" senior high schools. Fierce competition in the form of test scores determines which students are able to matriculate to the best high schools.

Most comprehensive high schools provide two tracks for students. One track is an academic one which leads to a university education and the other is more terminal in nature and leads to employment after graduation. The universities are extremely selective, with only about 20 percent of the students being able to pass their entry exams.

The schools are rather plain compared to those found in some other western countries. Often, they are constructed in concrete L- or U-shaped formations. While they are rather plain from an architectural point of view, they are comfortable and pleasant. Typically, one can see many displays of the children's work, and the rooms are brightly lighted and conducive to good teaching and learning.

Responsibility for the education of Japanese children tends to be a function shared equally by the home and school. Parents are expected to assist their children with homework on a daily basis. The country begins giving homework to children in the first grade, and 65 percent of the students in Japan spend over five hours a week doing homework.

The school success of Japanese children is well documented. However, Japanese education is not without its critics. Some educators tend to be concerned about the rigid system of examinations which extracts a great deal of energy and creates an intense level of competition. As students near the completion of junior high school, they have a diminishing amount of free time, and the pressures for exceptional academic performance seems to increase, reaching a peak during the high school years. Indeed, successful school performance becomes a springboard to the better-paying jobs.

Two companion features to the Japanese educational system are the *juku* (supplementary help) and the *okeikogoto* (enrichment lessons). *Okeikogoto* begins quite early in a child's life and consists of a number of classes, such as music lessons, knitting, cooking, tennis, and the like. These classes are available for Japanese people throughout their lives. Even retired persons pursue a number of different class offerings.

On the other hand, *juku* occurs during the elementary and secondary school years. Some of these classes may be conducted with only a few students in the home of the teacher (sensei), while others are held in large schools with much larger groups of students. These extracurricular offerings cover a variety of subject areas and meet the needs of remedial students and able learners alike.

Japanese senseis are held in high esteem. Starting each day, the students bow and show their respect for their teacher. They ask them to do the students the honor of instructing them. Japanese teachers earn a good living, and their salaries increase according to the length of their tenure. Since the profession is highly valued, teacher preparation institutions accept only about one-fourth of the applicants. Teachers are expected to make home visits since the belief is that they can provide better instruction if they know the families of their students.

The first teaching years are perceived to be a kind of apprenticeship. During this time, the senseis' performance is carefully monitored, and they have regular meetings to discuss their teaching strategies in order to improve their performance. Since parents are unable to select their teachers, the school tends to feel strongly that the children and parents deserve excellent instruction.

Japanese teachers belong to a powerful teachers' union which has tended to resist any attempts to revise the strong egalitarian principles which that body espouses. They particularly reject any kind of attempts to turn teachers into "drill instructors." Controversies sometimes ensue between the Ministry of Education and the Japanese teachers' union. The union tends to view the ministry as the "educational establishment."

MULTICULTURAL EDUCATION EFFORTS

Direct responses to the initial survey from Japan stipulated that no multicultural education programs existed in the nation's curriculum. However, cultural pluralism is stressed in the curriculum and instruction. The official language of instruction is Japanese, and the biggest problem facing multicultural education programs is the lack of willingness of the Ministry of Education to implement them. It was stated that the biggest improvement would be curriculum components which would lead to a better understanding of the origins of majority and minority cultures which comprise the Japanese society.

Minority groups do exist in Japan, although statistically their numbers are rather small. There are about two to three million *barukumins,* one million Okinawans, and about 500,000 other, including Koreans and Ainus. The *barukumins* are one of the most persecuted minority groups in the country. Their origin extends back about 1,000 years. This group was considered to have certain "impurities" which were hereditary and communicable. *Barukumins* were forced into occupations deemed less desirable, such as skinners, butchers, leather workers, cremators, and tomb watchers. Most important for the issue of multi-cultural education in Japan was that they did not participate equally in the Japanese educational system.

In order to improve the educational lot of the *barukumins,* an organization called the Kaiho Domei has been the leading champion of educational reform for *barukumin* school children. There have also been demands to change the criteria for placement and hiring of teachers in order to establish the same quality of education which other Japanese children receive. Other demands have included free textbooks and financial help for the support of study in regular and private schools.

The Ainu are the original inhabitants of the islands, and have sometimes been compared to the Native American Indians of the United States. In general, they have been pushed to less desirable parts of the island throughout the country's history. Discriminated against in a variety of ways, they have been viewed paternalistically and are considered as primitives. Their educational lot has not been good and there seems to be no sign of this group becoming assimilated into general Japanese society.

Koreans in Japan attempted to provide educational alternatives because of their perceived discrimination by the Japanese. Only about half of all Korean children finish high school, and Korean students have a difficult time acquiring entry to Japanese universities. The North Koreans have provided rather extensive education opportunities at both the pre-college and collegiate levels. Chosen University is accredited in Tokyo. The instruction is entirely in Korean, and there is an emphasis on Korean identity. However, in the main, it appears that most Korean families are becoming assimilated into Japanese society. It has been estimated that about 80 percent of Korean children use a Japanese surname, speak only Japanese, and seem to adopt Japanese values.

The primary Japanese educational reforms affecting multicultural education began after World War II. It was hoped that new egalitarian measures would contribute to the democratization of the country. However, a conservative regime attempted to overturn these reforms, leading to a major clash with the Japanese teacher's union (Nikkyoso). Gradually, through the actions of the teacher's union and a few sympathetic government figures, the egalitarian concepts spread to other elements of Japanese society, particularly the workplace.

This egalitarian sentiment has become a major part of the Japanese educational system through the utilization of values education. This "egalitarian sentiment" consists of three components. The first part relates to an egalitarian orientation to jobs. The emphasis is on the manner in which all jobs contribute to the greater good, and consequently are of equal importance. Jobs are not graded in order of their importance and all are deserving of respect. A second element stresses individualism. The emphasis is on the development of personal goals as opposed to "fitting in" the accepted way. In the workplace, striving for intrinsic rewards is stressed as opposed to lusting after status and income. The third element focuses on group participation and its importance. There is also an emphasis on challenging traditional patterns of hierarchical authority in the family, the workplace, community, and the political theater.

SUMMARY

Japan's educational system is unique. Because of its monocultural society and its long tradition of respect for learning, the country has emerged as one of the world's educational leaders. Indeed, the nation has an extraordinary literacy rate, and Japanese students excel internationally on test-score comparisons. Some scholars of international education have argued that one reason for the great success of the Japanese educational system is the monolinguistic population. Very few non-Japanese speaking students have populated the schools in recent times, which has meant that the country's educators have not been forced to deal with the bilingual education problems which have hampered countries such as the United States.

But Japan has been blessed with a reverence for education which few other countries have been able to enjoy. For example, the school teacher (gakosensei) has a status that few other education professionals have attained elsewhere in the world. A final reason for the success of the Japanese educational system has been the country's high regard for its youth. Children are viewed as the country's most important natural resource, and the people are anxious to ensure their success.

Interestingly, school reform movements in Japan and other countries such as the United States have been moving in opposite directions during recent years. Under the Office of Education leadership during the Reagan and Bush administrations, the United States has sought a higher level of national uniformity in curriculum, student performance, teacher certification, and the like. On the other hand, Japanese reformers have been investigating ways to terminate some of the rigid uniformity that has characterized the Japanese Ministry of Education policies during recent times.

Since formal education became so solidly established during 1886, Japan's educational system has been highly centralized and formally controlled. The country's National Council on Educational Reform has proposed to replace the present system with a structure which would be characterized by flexible diversity. A more international approach to education, and a higher regard for individuality, are two of the predominant characteristics of this group's new proposals.

REFERENCES

Cummings, William K. *Education and Equality in Japan.* Princeton, NJ: Princeton University Press, 1980.

Gonen, Amiram. *The Encyclopedia of the Peoples of the World.* New York: Henry Holt Publishing Co., 1993.

Hawkins, John N. "Japan." *Education and Urban Society* (August 1986), pp. 412–422.

Iwao, Sumiko. "Skills and Life Strategies of Japanese Businesswomen." In Merry White and Susan Pollak (Eds.), *The Cultural Transition: Human Experience and Social Transformation in the Third World and Japan.* London: Routledge & Kegan Paul, 1986.

Shigaki, Irene. "Child Care Practices in Japan and the U.S." *Young Children,* No. 29 (1993), p. 38.

U.S. Department of Health, Education, and Welfare, Office of Education. *Education in Japan: A Century of Modern Development,* by Ronald S. Anderson, No. 74-19110. Washington, DC: U.S. Government Printing Office, 1979.

Vogel, Ezra F. *Japan as Number One: Lessons for America.* Cambridge, MA: Harvard University Press, 1979.

White, Merry. *The Japanese Educational Challenge.* New York: The Free Press, 1987.

25

Kenya

HISTORY OF THE SYSTEM

While some anthropologists have posited that modern Kenya may have been the setting for some of the earliest developments of the human species, the ancestors of the country's current residents probably migrated to that part of Africa about 1,000 years ago. Different microcultural groups of nomads settled in the country's interior. While some 40 different microcultures originally inhabited the region, the Kikuyu emerged as the dominant group in the country's fertile interior. However, on the coast, Kenya came under Islamic influence some 1,000 years ago when Arab and Persian merchants began founding towns which became links to the middle-eastern trade ports. Eventually, the Swahili culture developed, which was actually a combination of the Islamic influence of the Arabs and the African Bantu cultures.

Eventually, the area was part of the British sphere of influence. In fact, the country derived its present name from the British, who called it "Kenya" after a 5,200-meter mountain peak which the Kikuyu called "kere nyaga," meaning the mountain of whiteness.

Britain's interest in the area was the region's economic potential. However, when Britain discovered the fertility of the Kenyan highlands, the white minority colonized the country. It was not until after World War II when political movements would eventually lead to independence in 1963. Jomo Kenyatta was one of the prime movers of the quest for more control for the black majority.

During 1920, Kenya became a British Crown Colony instead of a territorial segment of the British East African Protectorate. At this time, the country had its own education board, and this body reflected the multiracial composition of the area. The first half of the twentieth century saw Kenya going through three phases of educational development. First, during the 1920s there was an increase in the catechetical or "bush" schools which were later to become the village elementary schools. Phase two began with the Kikuyu Independent Schools Movement motivated by the Kikuyus' dissatisfaction with the existing mission schools. The Kikuyus wished to establish schools which would raise the standards of African education. Nationalists such as Jomo Kenyatta argued for compulsory education for all African children up to level six. However, the effects of the worldwide depression by about 1934 curtailed many of the reform efforts.

Due to Hitler's occupation of the Rhineland in 1936, the British implemented a number of improvements to the African colonies' educational systems. Ushering in this third phase, the colonial administration in Kenya improved the quality of the eight-year primary schools. Secondary and higher education programs were also greatly improved.

During World War II, primary education expanded because the war stimulated a higher income level for Kenyans. During the war years, two Colonial Development and Welfare Acts were passed by the British Parliament. These pieces of legislation provided for funds to be expended for social and economic development in Kenya and the other dependencies.

After World War II, a partnership concept was implemented between the Europeans and the African nations. Although a few Africans were appointed to the Ministerial Council, it was still dominated by the Europeans. But after achieving independence in 1963, the Kenyan educational system continued to reflect the British system which had influenced the colonial model.

A system of examinations was in effect, and students were unable to progress from one level to the next unless they passed the tests. Consequently, only a few students were able to progress to secondary school and the secondary education level. Another reason for this enrollment decline during the later years was that, until 1974, school attendance required fee payments which made it difficult for poorer students to participate in school at all.

After Kenya first became independent in 1963, it was a constitutional monarchy until 1964 when the country formally achieved its new status as a republic within the Commonwealth of Nations. Led by a president, Kenya had a one-house parliament known as the National Assembly. The one legal party became the Kenya African National Union. The new Kenyan government strongly supported education, and most children attended primary schools which were entirely supported by the government. However, following primary school, advanced education became quite competitive, and only a few of the students who went on to secondary school were able to attend the University of Nairobi or any of Kenya's smaller colleges.

STRUCTURE OF THE SYSTEM

Kenya became an independent member of the Commonwealth of Nations in 1963, and a republican constitution was developed in 1964. It combined the Senate and the House of Representatives in the unicameral National Assembly. During 1969, a revised constitution consisting of 128 sections was adopted. The

Kenyan African National Union (KANU) is the only political party, and parliamentary candidates must be members and nominated by KANU.

A bill of rights includes thirteen sections of the Kenyan constitution. Among other guarantees are personal liberty and protection from inhuman or degrading punishment. Also part of the bill of rights are freedom of religion and freedom of assembly. Other guarantees include freedom of color and politics.

The legislative power rests with the parliament which includes the president and the National Assembly. However, the ultimate power rests with the president who can always rely on the support of the National Assembly to enact his programs. As far as the organizational structure of the country is concerned, there are 7 provinces and 40 districts. Each district commissioner is aided by district officers who are in charge of divisions.

The highest court in the land is the Court of Appeal which has the ultimate jurisdiction in both criminal and civil matters. The civil rights of Kenyans are held in the highest esteem along with constitutional and legal safeguards. The Kenyan bill of rights provides citizens with a wide range of protections from arbitrary actions.

At the time of Kenya's independence, less than one million children attended the country's primary schools. However, by the second decade of independence in 1983, the enrollment for primary schools had jumped to more than four million. Much of the increase occurred after 1974 when the tuition fees were terminated. During 1985, the primary cycle was lengthened to eight grades. This required the construction of more than 13,000 new classrooms.

However, most of these new classrooms were built in the urban portions of the country, and not many rural areas of the country had the appropriate educational resources necessary for the new reforms. In fact, the new syllabi were not even available in the rural sectors when the new changes were implemented.

One primary reason for lengthening the primary cycle was to help students acquire the necessary skills for self-employment. Consequently, agriculture and crafts subjects became a crucial part of the school curriculum. During the first six years, there was a major emphasis on literacy and math skills, while the final two years of the primary level stressed the acquisition of practical skills which might improve rural life. One reason for this strategy was due to the fact that many children would not have any access to the secondary schools.

However, in spite of these reforms in the primary education program, there has been a prevailing perception that access to the "good life" rests in an education which extends through the secondary level. This is the gateway to the more lucrative government-dominated workforce, as well as other better paying occupations which are alternatives to the agrarian pursuits.

Since the 1985 reforms, a new curricular emphasis stressed the teaching of pre-vocational skills outside the field of agriculture. One of these new curriculum topics is in business studies. The curriculum includes simple accounting, use of credit, and other subjects related to establishing and operating small businesses.

Enrollment in secondary schools grew by about 130 percent during the seven-year time period between 1973 and 1980. In spite of this encouraging increase, secondary school enrollment has continued to lag well behind the number of students at the primary level. Qualified primary students are then able to matriculate in secondary-level government-supported schools, the Harambee schools, and unaided private schools. Even though some of the private schools are considered to be quite good, many Kenyans prefer to attend the maintained schools. The Harambee school students in 1980 made up 23 percent of the total. These schools, in general, were constructed by local communities and tended to limit their enrollment to the students who resided in the local community.

The University of Nairobi has been Kenya's main source of higher education. The school offers a diversified set of programs leading to the baccalaureate degree. These programs include liberal arts, science, agriculture, medicine, and law. About 25 percent of the students have been involved in the liberal arts program, and about 17 percent in science. Also, some 14 percent have participated in the medical school. Other programs, such as food science, technology, forestry, veterinary science, and law, were also fairly popular. Programs in architecture, economics, design, fine arts, dentistry, and pharmacy attracted small numbers of students.

During the final stages of the colonial period and the first few years of independence, large numbers of young African students were sent to North America and Europe for higher-education programs in order to acquire a cadre of educated people. This practice declined during the 1970s, and during the 1980s the Kenyan government terminated its financial support for overseas involvement in higher education. Kenyatta University College became the teacher-education school for Kenya during the 1970s. There were also a few graduate-level education students at the school. Two of the other main schools for teacher education were Siriba and Hagumo colleges.

As in most countries, there has been a great deal of disagreement over the preparation of Kenyan teachers. A 1983 World Bank report argued that: ''There appears to be a minimum level of basic education needed if training for primary school teachers is to have any effect on student achievement. Beyond this threshold there appears to be diminishing returns on the degree to which teacher training can be expected to be effective.''

However, in spite of the criticisms, the country has made large investments in teacher training. While the 1985 reforms necessitated the hiring of significant numbers of underprepared teachers, serious attempts were undertaken to improve their pedagogical skills through the implementation of in-service programs. These have been sponsored by teacher advisory centers which are allied with district education offices.

The country has also been concerned with teacher absenteeism and lateness. This has been a problem in some of the rural areas of the country. In fact, a study of three Kenyan private schools revealed that about 33 percent of the teachers were absent on a given day, and between 45 and 70 percent arrived to their jobs late. One reason for this was thought to be the great distances which

Table 25.1
Number of Periods per Week in Primary School by Subject

Subject	Standard			
	1	**2**	**3**	**4–7**
Arts and Crafts				
Needlework and Domestic Science	4	4	4	4
English	4	4	7	10
Geography	–	–	3	3
History and Civics	–	–	2	3
Mathematics	6	6	7	8
Mother Tongues	10	9	5	–
Physical Education and Games	5	5	4	3
Music and Singing	1	1	1	1
Religious Education	4	3	3	3
General Science	1	3	4	6
Kiswahili	–	–	–	4
Total	35	35	40	45

many teachers had to travel in order to reach their schools. To compound this problem, very few schools have adequate numbers of substitute teachers to meet the needs.

One characteristic of the present Kenyan educational system is the national examination system. Since the new reforms in primary education, the country has relied more heavily on multiple choice tests. However, during the early 1970s, an attempt was made to include more higher-level thinking questions, requiring the inclusion of more essay questions.

The primary school program in Kenya is seven years in length. At the end of this time, all students take the Certificate of Primary Education examination. This is the testing instrument for selecting students for secondary school. The test includes sections in English, mathematics, history, geography, and science.

Table 25.1 shows the number of periods per week in the country's primary schools.

MULTICULTURAL EDUCATION EFFORTS

Speaking from a multicultural perspective, one of the interesting changes during post-colonial Africa was the creation of multiracial communities as a result of new labor forces which were needed in various parts of the continent. As a result, like many of the other newly formed countries, Kenya's population became more pluralistic.

After the colonial period, Kenya's minister of education created a commission to review the country's system of education. During 1964, this Commission identified seven basic educational principles for guiding the nation's new post-colonial educational system, which were to:

1. express the aspirations and cultural values of an independent African country;
2. take account of the need for trained manpower to facilitate economic development;
3. take advantage of the initiative and service of regional and local authorities and volunteer bodies;
4. contribute to the unity of Kenya;
5. respect the educational needs and capacities of children;
6. have due regard for the resources, both in money and personnel, likely to become available for educational services; and
7. provide for the principle educational requirements of adults.

These seven basic principles seem to perpetuate the educational focus on nation building. The commission seemed anxious to help children acquire a better understanding of their nation's history and cultural values. Moreover, the report went on to recommend that English be the primary language of instruction, and that instruction in Kiswahili should be compulsory in primary school as a means of helping the country become more nationally unified.

Questionnaire responses to the International Study of Multicultural Education indicated that Kenya actually had no formal multicultural education program. The country's primary microcultures were reported to be ''African,'' ''Asian,'' and ''Western.'' The curriculum stresses assimilation into the dominant culture, and English is still the official language of instruction throughout the school system. However, for the first three years, instruction is provided in the child's mother tongue. All Kenyan schools are culturally and racially integrated. The history of indigenous peoples is part of the curriculum, and the Ministry of Education evaluates all library holdings, textbooks, and curriculum materials for racist and/or sexist comments.

An interesting gender issue in Kenya pertains to the number of males and females enrolled in the primary schools compared to the secondary level. In the first two forms, slightly more than 40 percent of the students were female in 1980. However, this proportion declined to just 30 percent during forms V and VI.

Regarding the issue of church verses state control in Kenyan schools, a 1964 report by the Kenyan Education Commission stipulated that churches should not be involved in the administration of maintained schools. On the other hand, the same Commission argued that should parents, in general, wish for a school to be under a particular religious influence, then their wishes should be respected. However, the report fell short of specifying how this could be carried out in actual practice, resulting in a great deal of confusion.

SUMMARY

Since becoming an independent nation, Kenya has experienced many interesting changes in its educational system. The arguments over agrarian reforms and new technological issues have impacted the nation's school system and created interesting controversies regarding needed curriculum changes. Moreover, the country has struggled to maintain an adequate standard of education in the rural sectors of the land.

As a developing nation experiencing the usual financial difficulties, Kenya has not been able to implement all of the educational programs which would improve the system. Nevertheless, the country has taken a number of important steps as far as multicultural issues are concerned. Perhaps most interesting is the use of the child's mother tongue during the first part of the schooling process, followed by the eventual transition to English in order to compete more successfully in business and commerce.

Of further interest has been the post-colonial attempts to educate girls as well as boys. Even though the percentage of girls drops in the later forms, the improvements since 1964 have been most impressive as the country has striven to become a more competitive participant internationally.

REFERENCES

Chang, M.C. "Teacher Training." Paper presented to the World Bank Conference on School Quality. Harper's Ferry, WV, 1983.

Eisemon, T.O. *Benefitting from Basic Education, School Quality and Functional Literacy in Kenya.* Oxford: Pergamon Press, 1988.

Fafunwa, A. Babs and Aisiku, J.V. (Eds.). *Education in Africa.* London: George Allen & Unwin, 1982.

Foster, P. *Education and Social Change in Ghana.* Chicago: University of Chicago Press, 1965.

Gonen, Amiram. *The Encyclopedia of the Peoples of the World.* New York: Henry Holt Publishing Co., 1993.

Indire, Filomina. "Education in Kenya." Cited in A. Babs Fafunwa and J.V. Aisiku (Eds.), *Education in Africa.* London: George Allen & Unwin, 1982.

Mitchell, Bruce and Salsbury, Robert. *An International Survey of Multicultural Education.* Cheney, WA: Western States Consulting and Evaluation Services, 1991. (See Appendix.)

Nelson, Harold D. *Kenya: A Country Study.* Washington, DC: The American University, 1984.

Republic of Kenya. *Report of the Presidential Working Party on Education and Manpower Training for the Next Decade and Beyond.* Nairobi: Government Printer, 1988.

Shindu, J. "Self Employment Efforts Among Primary School Leavers in Kenya." Unpublished Doctoral Dissertation, University of Nairobi, Kenya, 1977.

Sifuna, D.N. *Revolution in Primary Education: The New Approach in Kenya.* Nairobi: East African Literary Bureau, 1986.

Somerset, A. ''Examinations Are an Instrument to Improve Pedagogy.'' Cited in S.P. Heyneman and I. Fagerlind (Eds.), *University Examinations and Standardized Testing.* Washington, DC: World Bank, 1988.

26

Korea

HISTORY OF THE SYSTEM

Korea's history, like that of many other nations, has partially been shaped by its geography. The country is surrounded by water on three sides, while the north is next to the southeastern part of the Asian continent. Throughout history, Korea has been heavily affected by the various civilizations located in the contiguous areas of the Asian continent.

Korean society experienced the rise and fall of three dynasties. The unified Silla Dynasty existed from 668 to 935. It was characterized by the development of new legal, political, and education institutions. Domestic and foreign trade flourished, and scholarship in Confucian learning, mathematics, astronomy, and medicine also developed to unprecedented levels. Toward the end of this period of Korea's history, a number of rebellions led to the beginning of the Koryo Dynasty which started in 918 and existed until 1392. Wang Kon, the founder of this era, along with his heirs, strengthened and solidified the political and economic foundations of the Korean peninsula. It was a period during which the bureaucratic and land-grant systems of the Chinese were copied rather closely in the country. During this time, the Koreans were enlisted by Kublai Khan of the Mongol Empire in two unsuccessful expeditions against the Japanese. The Mongol influence deeply affected the Koreans, and the two ill-fated attempts against the Japanese in 1274 and 1281 were at least partially responsible for the development of ill feelings between the Japanese and Koreans which has persisted throughout history.

However, the Koryo Dynasty was finally terminated because of a number of internal problems. The land had been owned by the government, but some of the more powerful clans and the Buddhist Church had managed to acquire a significant percentage of the country's farmlands. These farms were excluded from the tax rolls which caused major constraints on the national treasury. The dominant religious forces in the new Choson Dynasty consisted of devout Confucianists who believed that Buddhism was not a true religion. Indeed, many of the Buddhist monks had been economically corrupted, which greatly strengthened the intensity of this perception.

During the Choson Dynasty, great strides were made in the fields of arts, science, and technology. Also, during this time period, scholars developed a Korean script (han 'gul) which was used commonly in the nation during the twentieth century. But during the latter part of the fifteenth century, the country began to decline as a result of poorer leadership than Korea enjoyed during the first phase of the Choson Dynasty. Corruption became a problem, farmers were suffering because of a very difficult tax burden, and the Japanese attacked in 1592 and 1597. Moreover, there were Manchu assaults in 1627 and 1636.

After the resulting economic and social depression of the seventeenth and eighteenth centuries, a new intellectual movement transpired in Korea, motivated and pioneered by a Confucian scholar named Yi Su-kwang, which means "the new thought" in the Korean language. His ideas were developed as a result of his visits to Beijing, China. Western thought began to reach the country during this dynasty. Much of it was motivated by Roman Catholic missionaries. However, since the new Christianity rejected ancestor worship, Western learning became gradually banned.

During its modern history, the Japanese became the first foreign power to make any impact on Korea's isolationist policies. The Japanese negotiated a treaty with the Koreans in 1876 after a warlike act of hostility occurred one year earlier. Three Korean ports were opened up for trade with the Japanese, and Japanese nationals were given extraterritorial rights. Before the turn of the century, Korea had signed treaties with the United States, Great Britain, Italy, Russia, and several other countries.

At the end of the World War II, Korea was divided by the United States and the Soviet Union. From that time forward, the country consisted of two parts: the North (known as the Democratic People's Republic of Korea) and the South (Republic of Korea). From 1949 to 1953, the two nations were involved in a bloody and costly civil war. North Korea remained a staunch Communist nation under the leadership of Kim Il Sung, who ruled the nation for more than four decades. South Korea became a liberal democracy which entered the world of "high technology" through the production of the Hyundai automobile and a variety of other industrial goods. In fact, the Republic of Korea has experienced one of the highest rates of economic growth of any country around the world during the past two decades.

As a country deprived of rich national resources, Korea's incredible economic growth has been truly astounding. Much of its success can be traced to its highly developed educational system which has been designed to meet the needs of the entire population. Since the end of World War II, there has been a close relationship between the growth of the country's economy and the development of Korea's system of public education.

STRUCTURE OF THE SYSTEM

When the United States took control in 1945 under the military government, Korea went to a 6-6-4 educational plan. Under this format, the primary grades consisted of six years, and there were also six years of secondary school. But the Education Law of 1949 declared primary education to be compulsory, and divided secondary education into a four-year middle school and a high school period of two or three years. The Korean Ministry of Education then went to a 6-3-3 plan which was enacted after the Korean War. A system of junior vocational schools was initiated at the high school level along with higher trade schools, and a number of three-year miscellaneous secondary schools. In addition to four-year colleges, Korea has many two-year junior technical colleges, the College of Air and Correspondence, and two-year schools of nursing. Three-year graduate schools are also part of the nation's educational system.

Since 1968, entrance to Korean colleges and universities has been decided through examinations, and the students are then assigned to the schools of their choice by virtue of the test scores. There is a tendency for high scorers to attend several key universities, while lower scorers often matriculate at the provincial universities.

As is the case in other Asian countries with a Confucian heritage, South Korea has long believed in the great importance of a formal education. In fact, the literacy rate during the late 1980s has been estimated at about 93 percent. The percentages of South Korean children who attend school are equally impressive. During 1985, more than 99 percent of all primary-age children went on to optional middle school, and about 34 percent of all secondary-school graduates went on to college. This rate was one of the highest in the world.

The recent expenditures on education by the South Korean government have been substantial. By 1986, the government expenditures reached 4.5 percent of the gross national product.

The nation's educational goals have been in existence during the past five decades. They were designed to support a democracy similar to that of the United States and to perpetuate a capitalistic economic structure. The educational goals are to develop: the knowledge and habits needed to maintain good health and to develop an indomitable spirit; the patriotic interest in preserving national independence and advancing the cause of world peace; Korean culture as an aspect in the development of world culture; scholarship and scientific ways of thinking to promote creative activities and a national way of life; harmonious social lives with possession of such virtues as love of freedom, sense of responsibility, sincerity, and cooperative spirit; aesthetic feelings and skills for creation and appreciation of the fine arts; and an improvement in economic behaviors which will help make Korea a good producer and a wise consumer.

While primary schools in Korea are coeducational, many of the nation's middle schools and secondary schools are not. During the decade of the 1980s, expansion in the Korean kindergartens or pre-schools was quite pronounced.

The actual increase in the enrollment at the kindergarten/pre-school programs was approximately 700 percent during that time. About 92 percent of the teachers of Korea's young children are women. However, at the secondary level, approximately 70 percent of the teachers are males, while about 54 percent of the primary-level teachers are men. Teachers in Korea have enjoyed a high status, but they tend to be overworked and somewhat underpaid. This situation helped lead to the creation of a National Teachers' Union in 1989. The primary goals of the organization were to improve working conditions and reform the nation's school system. Korean educators believed that the nation's schools suffered from excessive control by the national Ministry of Education. However, the union members did not have the right to strike, since they were civil servants. Also, the government tended to view teachers as role models for Korean children, and striking teachers could undermine the positive image the government wanted teachers to exemplify. Moreover, the government accused the teachers' union of spreading propaganda which tended to be supportive of the leftist government of North Korea.

Korea's Ministry of Education is responsible for the operation of all schools, establishing enrollment guidelines, certification of teachers and schools, curriculum development, and the allocation of resources. The programs and policies of the Ministry of Education are designed to help the country in its quest to challenge the Japanese in various high-tech production enterprises.

The college degree is deemed to be of utmost importance in Korean society. For example, it is a prerequisite to middle-class status along with some careers in the military. In fact, people without degrees are sometimes treated as second-class citizens by white-collar college-educated managers, in spite of any valuable and unique skills which were acquired in the absence of a college degree. This value on the degree has precipitated the enormous competition for placements in the more prestigious colleges and universities. So, in this regard, Korea is much like Japan. Like the old Confucian model, this situation has tended to create an educational system which relies heavily on the use of rote memorization in the nation's schoolrooms.

MULTICULTURAL EDUCATION EFFORTS

Responses to the authors' study of multicultural education indicated that there were no multicultural education programs in Korea. So the official position of the Korean Ministry seems to be similar to that of many other monocultural societies around the world. The Korean response stipulated that only one cultural group existed in Korea, making such educational themes irrelevant. The respondent stated that many of the small number of Chinese students reside in their own enclaves and attend segregated schools in which Chinese is the language of instruction. Due to the monocultural society, the curriculum topics stress cultural similarity rather than subcultural diversity. And while curriculum materials are systematically screened for racist and sexist statements, library materials are not.

According to the survey response, there are only about 25,000 Chinese-Koreans, and most of them still have Chinese citizenship. The South Koreans tend to view themselves as a tightly knit, cohesive national community with a common identity, and one of the main problems of cultural identity pertains to the division of the country into North and South. For example, many young South Koreans who were born after the division of the country believe that South Korea's dependence on the United States has been responsible for the inability to reunify the two countries which are culturally alike, but opposed politically.

Belief in the spirit-inhabited world is probably the oldest form of Korean spiritual worship. Female shamans conduct services called "kut" which are supposed to secure good fortune, cure illness, exorcise evil spirits, or guide the spirit of a deceased person to heaven. Also, in some of the fishing villages, people hold on to animistic beliefs.

Buddhism and Taoism became part of the country's religious options between the fourth and seventh centuries. Confucianism held a relatively minor role until the establishment of the Choson Dynasty. Roman Catholic missionaries arrived during the latter 1700s. However, some of the converted Roman Catholics refused to participate in the ceremonial rites, and so the Korean government prohibited the proselytization of Christianity. In fact, some Catholics were actually executed during the early 1800s.

Protestant missionaries reached the country during the mid-1880s, and they were successful in converting quite a large number of people to Christianity. These social reformers created schools, universities, hospitals, and orphanages. Many of the newly converted Protestants lived in the north, because it tended to be farther away from the southern influences of the Confucians.

One of Korea's relatively new religions is Ch'ondogyo. It is a synthesis of Confucianist, Taoist, Buddhist, Shamanistic, and Catholic philosophies. It grew out of the Tonghok learning movement which was established by Choe Che-u, who professed to have had an encounter with God which resulted in a belief that God instructed him to preach to the world. He was deemed a heretic by the government and executed in 1894. However, by that time, he had recruited a substantial number of followers who would help promote the nationalistic movement.

At the present time, about 43% of South Korea's populace professes to being members of the country's organized Christian sects. The Buddhists comprise 20%, while there are about 16% Protestants, about 5% Roman Catholics, and some 1% Confucians. In 1954, the Unification Church was founded by the Reverend Sun Myong Moon, who claimed to be a messiah from God. Moon believed he was supposed to unify all the world's people into one religious body.

Gender issues in Korea tend to stress the concepts of males working and women managing all of the household functions. While these stereotypical roles have been changing in some Western nations, they seem to be intact in Korean society. In the elementary schools, girls are taught to be dutiful while boys are taught to be leaders. Even the revised textbooks of 1989 seemed to carry this message. According to Paek Young-ok of Sung Shin Women's University, these new books identified 45 future occupations for boys in such areas as the mass media, government, and farming, while the 26 jobs which were considered to be good for girls included nurse, factory worker, and teacher. Girls in college tend to be directed toward literature or education rather than law, medicine, or engineering. While a high percentage of Korean women attend college, only about 30 percent of them find work.

In modern day Korean society, both men and women have the right to obtain a divorce. Historically, women were not empowered to gain a divorce. But economic factors often make it difficult for divorced women to support themselves.

Throughout Korean history, women were expected to be totally submissive to their husbands. However, in contemporary times, this attitude only persists in a few of the country's smallest and most remote rural areas. Also, until recent times, a great deal of gender segregation existed both inside and outside the house. In fact, it has been argued that the pasttime of "noltwiggi," a game of jumping up and down on a device resembling a seesaw, was created by bored women who wished to find out what the real world was like outside of the high walls of their family compounds.

Korean factories still tend to hire huge numbers of very young women in the construction of electronic equipment, shoes, clothes, and textiles. In fact, much of Korea's recent financial success can be traced to the utilization of cheap labor sources. However, the majority of these women only work until they get married.

SUMMARY

Due to its monocultural society, Korea has not seen fit to develop multicultural education programs. The Ministry of Education has put no one in charge of such efforts, and the attitude seems to be that it is not necessary. However, there are some concerns about the gender issues pertaining to equity considerations.

Moreover, religious issues have played a role in all of this. For example, Neo-Confucian orthodoxy has dictated that once a woman was separated from her parents, it was her responsibility to provide a male heir for her husband's family; and once a woman married, she left her parents' household and occupied the lowest position in her husband's family. Often, this would result in a certain amount of mistreatment by both her mother-in-law and sisters-in-law.

But these conditions appear to be changing. In fact, during the confrontations between police and students during the late 1980s, both male and female students participated. However, it appears there is very little possibility that the Ministry of Education will initiate multicultural education programs such as those in the more pluralistic countries in the near future.

REFERENCES

Chung, J.S. "Women's Unequal Access to Education in South Korea." *Comparative Education Review,* Vol. 38, No. 4 (November 1994), pp. 487–505.

Jeong, I. and Amer, J.M. "State, Class & Expansion of Education in South Korea: A Comparative Review." *Comparative Education Review,* Vol. 38, No. 4 (1994), pp. 531–545.

McGinn, Noel et al. *Education and Development in Korea.* Cambridge, MA: Harvard University Press, 1980.

Mitchell, Bruce and Salsbury, Robert. *An International Survey of Multicultural Education.* Cheney, WA: Western States Consulting and Evaluation Services, 1991. (See Appendix.)

Paek, Young-ok. "A Woman's Place." *News Review* (December 1992), p. 30.

Savada, Andrea and Shaw, William. *South Korea: A Country Study.* Washington, DC: Department of the Army, 1992.

Seoul Ministry of Education. *Statistical Yearbooks of Education.* Seoul: Ministry of Education, 1953.

UNESCO. *Republic of Korea: Educational Services in a Rapidly Growing Economy.* Paris: UNESCO, 1974.

UNESCO. *UNESCO Korean Survey.* Washington, DC: UNESCO, 1960.

27

Liberia

HISTORY OF THE SYSTEM

Modern Liberian history is sometimes characterized as beginning in the 1820s, when the American Colony for Colonizing the Free People of Color of the United States of America helped African-Americans return to Africa. The ethnic groups they encountered in Africa had come from the Sudanic region more than 200 years earlier. These indigenous groups belonged to three main linguistic categories: tribal clusters of Kwa-, Mada-, and West Atlantic-speaking peoples. The interaction of these groups led to the present-day nation of Liberia.

These early migrants to Liberia developed schools which have been referred to as PORO and SANDE, which were manifestations of an organized system of secret societies. These "bush" schools were found among the sixteen major ethnic groups in the area, and were even known to have existed in Sierra Leone and Guinea. These systems existed until about 1820, when settlers from Europe arrived and instituted Western education programs. After that, the two systems coexisted, competing for the education of children.

Starting in the early 1820s, the only schools which existed in the area were elementary schools, which were run by settlers who were members of various Christian churches. From the early 1930s onward, a number of church missions functioned in Liberia and played a major role in the education of children from this part of Africa.

However, these schools tended to meet the needs of a rather small group of people. Their students often came from the children of European settlers, recaptured Africans, and native residents who may have happened to dwell in the new settlement areas. Forty years after the European intervention, there were approximately 600 students in some 30 schools.

The American Colonization Society, which sponsored a number of the settlements, tended to be indifferent to the establishment of educational enterprises.

Also, due to the illiteracy requirements among African slaves imposed in the United States, many of the migrants from that country had attained only low levels of education. Also, many of these persons who migrated to Liberia were poor.

However, by the late 1880s, this new and struggling government began an education effort which led to the enrollment of some 10,000 students in the country's elementary schools. By 1951, there were nearly 25,000 students enrolled in Liberia's elementary schools. Education at the secondary level commenced with the Protestant Church missions during the early 1800s. One of the first such schools was begun by the Methodists in 1839 at Monrovia. This mission school functioned from 1839 to about the middle of the nineteenth century. A number of other mission schools were active from the late 1840s to the early 1860s. One of the more noteworthy efforts was a Presbyterian mission which began in 1849. The primary goal of these mission schools was to train ministers, teachers, and other persons for the various missions.

The first college in the country opened its doors in 1862. At the time, there were just two secondary schools in operation, and only a total of 50 students were enrolled in the two institutions. Consequently, it was necessary for the college to start a preparatory school in order to guarantee an adequate number of students.

It would not be until the 1900s that the concept of high school education would be renewed. However, the growth of these schools was slow. Many of the country's rural areas were without high schools and, even by 1951, there were only 874 high school students enrolled in nine high schools. However, the decade of the 1950s would see an amazing increase in the number of high school students due to the government's increased interest in this particular educational pursuit. Also, this time period saw major changes in the structure of the nation in general. The number of elementary years was changed to six, while six years were also required at the high school level.

Technical education in Liberia has been a problem for many years. The missionary schools during the 1870s were primarily occupied with religious goals and, consequently, very little was offered in the area of vocational education. Also, many settlers from the "New World" tended to frown on this type of education, since they tended to come from backgrounds which shunned the acquisition of vocational skills in high school. These changes would not come until the twentieth century, and even then on a very limited basis. However, one successful venture was the Booker T. Washington Agricultural and Industrial Institute, which was established about 45 miles from Monrovia in Kakata. The school was made possible through funds from Mrs. Olivia Phelps-Stokes who wished to establish the name of Booker T. Washington in Liberia.

The school had a foreign board of trustees which consisted of representatives from a number of funding agencies. It continued to function until 1953, when it was taken over by the Liberian government. The school emphasized industrial/technology programs rather than the more traditional academic offerings of most other schools. In spite of this school and others like it, development in the technological/vocational areas has lagged throughout the country.

The growth of teacher education has been sporadic and inconsistent in Liberia. It wasn't until the mid-nineteenth century that previously organized institutes were offered on a regular basis in Monrovia, and then later in other parts of the country. During 1947, the William V. S. Tubman School of Teacher Training was established as a joint effort of the government, the Methodist Church, and the Episcopal Church. This effort merged with Liberia College in 1951 and several other schools in order to form the University of Liberia.

The first higher education institution to operate in the country was Liberia College which opened its doors in 1862. The school suffered from a lack of students and inadequate funding. While it originally relied on foreign financing, the country took over its funding in 1900 when it struggled for survival for many years. However, due to the economic growth during the middle of the twentieth century, the University of Liberia was established along with Liberia College, and the William Tubman School of Education. A law school was added in 1954, and in 1957 a college of forestry was established.

STRUCTURE OF THE SYSTEM

Liberia's governmental system prides itself on holding free elections which are based upon the principle of universal suffrage for all citizens over 18 years of age. The country enjoys a balance of power between executive, legislative, and judicial entities. While Liberia has no legal restrictions against a multiparty system, the government has generally been successful in thwarting any sort of organized opposition to the country's True Whig Party.

The major power in the country rests in the hands of the executive branch. Over the years, the length of office for the presidency has been extended from two years to eight. Currently, the presidency is limited to one term. Candidates must be at least 35 years of age and citizenship by birth is required. Naturalized citizens of at least 25 years in the country are also eligible for the presidency.

The branches of government include the People's Supreme Court and the People's Special Court on Theft and Related Offences; the People's Redemption Council; and the Cabinet, headed by a Minister of State for Presidential Affairs. Seventeen ministers report to that person, including the Minister of Education.

Liberia's judicial system has a Supreme Court of five members, which consists of a chief justice and four associate justices which are all appointed by the Liberian president. This five-member body hears final appeals from other court agencies and rules on the validity of laws which might not be consistent with constitutional tenets. The country's criminal code is based on an adoption of the New York State criminal code in the United States.

The microcultures of Liberia consist of about 95 percent indigenous populations, including such groups as the Kpelle, Bassa, Gio, Kru, Grebo, Mano, and several others. About 5 percent of the population includes repatriated descendants of American slaves who are referred to as Americo-Liberians. Most Liberians practice traditional religions, but about 20 percent are Muslims and another 10 percent are Christians.

At the present time, there are actually two school systems in Liberia. The indigenous school system seems to have been losing ground in recent years. The government schools have become more popular and are organized into three levels including elementary, high school, and college. There have been recent efforts to integrate the indigenous school system and the government schools.

The nation's school system is highly centralized, with all schools falling under the direction of the Ministry of Education. Because of this, the curriculum is fairly consistent around the country. This curriculum content includes topics related to farming, hunting, fishing, and artistic skills such as singing, dancing, drumming, handicrafts, history, law, and religion. At the lower elementary level, the emphasis is on reading, writing, spelling, grammar, arithmetic, and geography. Latin and Greek are present in the high schools, along with music and the science of teaching in some high schools.

Financing educational efforts in Liberia is also centralized. The funding for all educational ventures is part of the general revenues. As is typical in most countries, about 65 percent of the educational budget is spent on teachers' salaries (the largest expenditure is for elementary education).

During the early 1980s, primary education in the country was far from being universal, and secondary education programs served only a small percentage of the eligible students. Consequently, the literacy rate for Liberians over the age of five was just 24 percent, according to the best available estimates.

MULTICULTURAL EDUCATION EFFORTS

The country has no formal program of multicultural education according to the responses received in the Mitchell/Salsbury survey. Liberian microcultures include the Kru, Vai, Memde, Gola, Kpelle, Gio, Dahns, Mandingo, Lorma, Bassa, Belle, and several others. While the language of instruction is English and there are no bilingual instruction programs, the curriculum content stresses cultural pluralism, but the history of the indigenous populations is not included in the basic instructional components. For the most part, children attend racially and ethnically integrated schools, even though some indigenous students attend the traditional "SANDE and PORO schools."

While there is no office for multicultural education within the Ministry of Education, and no special funding for such programs, the ministry does evaluate curriculum and textbook materials for racist/sexist statements. The survey respondent for Liberia stated that better cultural awareness programs needed to be included in the curricular offerings.

Traditionally, female enrollment in Liberian schools has been much less than the enrollment of males. This has been due to both economic and sociocultural reasons. While there is a small, rather elite group of well-educated women in the country, the education of females has lagged behind the education of males. To a great extent, this has been due to the heavy workload demanded of Liberian women both in the home and sometimes in the field. These demands have resulted in 88 percent of the female population not completing even one grade in school.

SUMMARY

Liberia exhibits many of the problems of developing countries the world over. Beset with the usual issues of survival, the country's Ministry of Education has yet to address the issue of multicultural education in the country. Indeed, the respondent to the Mitchell/Salsbury survey indicated that education components dealing with the issue of cultural awareness needs to be implemented in the schools. But it is unlikely that such programs will be incorporated into the educational system in the near future.

REFERENCES

Brown, M.A.G. "Education and National Development in Liberia." Unpublished Doctoral Dissertation, Ithaca, NY, 1967.

Carter, Jeanette. "Liberian Women: Their Role in Food Production and Their Educational and Legal Status." Unpublished Paper, University of Idaho, Moscow, 1982.

Fafunwa, A. Babs and Aisiku, J.V. (Eds.). *Education in Africa.* London: George Allen & Unwin, 1982.

Gonen, Amiram. *The Encyclopedia of the Peoples of the World.* New York: Henry Holt Publishing Co., 1993.

Liberia. *Annual Report of the Minister of Education to the National Legislature.* Monrovia: Ministry of Education, 1988.

Mitchell, Bruce and Salsbury, Robert. *An International Survey of Multicultural Education.* Cheney, WA: Western States Consulting and Evaluation Services, 1991. (See Appendix.)

Nelson, Harold D., Ed. *Liberia: A Country Study.* Washington, DC: Department of the Army (Foreign Area Studies), 1985.

28

Malaysia

HISTORY OF THE SYSTEM

Valid historical references pertaining to the Malay Peninsula are rather rare. Some of the Chinese references are felt to be the most reliable since they include official histories of the imperial dynasties, as well as the Buddhist journals of Buddhist pilgrims who lived in the fifth century A.D. From these and other reliable documents, it has been rather clearly established that the Malay Peninsula and Borneo were integrated into a consolidated economic and cultural system as early as a few centuries after the birth of Christ.

The ocean provided a transportation system for the exchange of goods, ideas, and peoples of differing ethnic backgrounds. Fifteen hundred years before the Industrial Revolution, a modest international economic system was functioning. Between the fourth and sixth centuries A.D., a trade network linked the Middle East, India, the Malay Peninsula, and the islands of the Western Indonesian Archipelago.

Some historians have argued that the Malay history actually began with the development of Malacca. Located on the west coast of the peninsula, at the start of the fifteenth century it became a trade center and a successor to Srivijaya, and it provided a common unit for the Malay people in the region. It became a blend of the Hindu-Buddhist heritage and also the newer Islamic sects.

Malacca developed a reputation as a favorite port, which was particularly attractive to the Chinese merchants throughout the coastal Asian regions. However, by the fifteenth century, the Portuguese had taken a prominent role in the European Age of Discovery. Motivated by commercial and religious interest, they spread Christianity throughout the world and carried out a crusade against Islamic factions, hoping to wrest control of some major sea lanes from Muslim ships which were involved in the spice trade.

However, the Dutch eventually were able to construct speedier and more efficient ships, and they were able to acquire some of the control from the Portuguese interests. The Dutch encroachments in the area eventually led to their capture of Malacca in 1641. Many of their economic interests on the peninsula were concerned with tin. But, eventually, the British became the dominant European power in the region as a result of activities by the British East India Company, which established a naval base at the eastern rim of the Indian Ocean. During the early parts of the nineteenth century, Thomas Stamford Raffles, a British East India Company executive, helped to solidify the British colonial rule of the area. Finally, after World War II, the 1948 Federation of Malaya Agreement contained a British promise to grant independence. This finally took place in 1957.

Prior to the period of British involvement, a number of educational efforts existed in the Malay areas. Perhaps the earliest educational programs attempted to train artisans and shamans. The two main types of artisan training were in metal-working and weaving. Learning from books was introduced by Buddhist missionaries. This was also a practice of Muslim missionaries who helped the concept become well established in the Malay culture. Young students were required to recite the Koran in Arabic.

After Britain prevailed in its life-and-death struggle with Napoleon, there was no other nation which was able to challenge its international influence. Throughout the nineteenth century, the country established its industrial might. Malaysia (then known as Malaya) was heavily influenced by the involvement of Britain's East India Company, which would eventually be known as the India Office. By 1867, the political conditions in the Malay states of Selangor, Perak, Pahang, and Negri Sembilan attracted the British who intervened in those internal affairs. Soon after the Pangkor Treaty of 1874, the states of Perak, Selangor, Negri Sembilan, and Pahang became known as the Federated Malay States.

In 1963 an agreement was negotiated between the United Kingdom and the new country of Malaysia, which was granted sovereignty. Malaysia had a population of approximately 10,000,000 people, including a heterogeneous population of Malays, Chinese, Indians, Ibans, Land Dyaks, Malanaus, Dusuns, Kadazans, Muruts, and Bajaus. Two years later Singapore became an independent nation in 1965.

The British control of the Malay peninsula and north Borneo helped them to profit from their colonial holdings. During this period of time, the British exploited the region's mining and rubber resources. When the British reached the area, it was rather sparsely populated. The largest ethnic group was the Malays, who were mostly Muslims. They spoke the Malay language and were primarily involved in fishing and farming. Because the native Malays chose to work their lands, the British imported Chinese and Indian laborers to work their mines and plantations. Additionally, other Chinese people migrated to the area and settled in the cities to become involved in a number of trading activities.

The educational status of Malaysian ethnic groups goes back to the middle of the nineteenth century. In 1850, elementary education in the regional language was provided, under the direction of the governor of the Malay Straits Settlements. By 1892, 7,200 of these primary schools had been established.

Geographically, Malaysia consists of the Malay Peninsula and the coastal portion of Borneo, a large island. These two regions are separated by some 400 miles of the South China Sea. The Malay Peninsula is located at the sea routes between East and West, and between China and India. Due to being the center of several waves of emigration, many problems of ethnic pluralism have affected the development of the region.

During the British period of the country's history, there were two types of schools. Vernacular schools were commonly found in the rural areas. They utilized the Malay and Tamil tongue. English schools were found in the more urban regions of Penang, Malacca, and Singapore. These educational efforts were dominated by trade and business.

An English-language school (the Malay College) was established for Malay boys of good families. Also, a few trade and vocational schools, a vocational school, and an agricultural college were operating in the country by the start of World War II.

During the British colonization period, the central thrust of the school system was to provide children with an education in the reading and writing of English, as well as a strong background in arithmetic. It was believed that the acquisition of such skills would provide young students with marketable employment skills.

Following World War I, English schools in the region were divided into several departments, consisting of primary, middle, and secondary. After World War II, a major effort was undertaken to reunite the country by unifying its three main ethnic groups: the Malays, Chinese, and Indians. Eventually, the National School was established. It consisted of just one school which was administered and financed locally.

When Malaysia became a nation, the Malays lagged behind the Chinese and Indians in educational attainment, particularly in the crucial curriculum areas of science, business, and technology. These curricular areas were the very ones which were so necessary for competing in the post-World War II community.

Governmental policies have been particularly concerned with creating a national system of education which would help facilitate the nation's goals for achieving national unity and upgrading economic growth and modernization. However, the system has had difficulty in meeting the basic manpower needs in industrial, technical, and industrial areas.

Another key educational problem in the country has been the disparity of educational programs between rural and urban areas of the nation. The Ministry of Education attempted to improve the quality of teacher education, and by 1975 established a long-term goal of universal lower-secondary education. It was felt that this would help to resolve the problem of unequal access to employment opportunities by the ethnic groups throughout the country.

STRUCTURE OF THE SYSTEM

Malaysia's highest public official is the paramount ruler (king), but his role is primarily symbolic. The actual operation of the government is carried out by the prime minister who is the country's political leader. The parliament consists of a senate and a house of representatives. The prime minister's cabinet includes the deputy prime minister and ministers. The Supreme Court is the highest court in the country.

Under the Malaysian constitution, Islam is the nation's official religion, but other religious faiths may be practiced without government interference. The constitution guarantees fundamental freedoms for peaceable assembly, speech, and press; political participation; and privacy of home.

Malaysia views education as a top government priority. While there was very little formal education before the British colonial period, the limited efforts that did exist had a strong Islamic influence. The greatest expansion of education occurred during the 1960s and 1970s. The system has expanded to provide universal education for all children at the primary level, and significant increases in the numbers of students enrolled in secondary schools have been impressive in recent years. The Ministry of Education determines the educational content, and instruction in Malaysian schools follows national syllabi. Common values taught in the schools include belief in God, loyalty to the king and the country, the rule of law, good behavior and morality, and upholding the constitution.

During modern times, Malays have become increasingly concerned about the quality of professionals and the ethics of business persons. It has been argued that many young students who have become educated abroad have returned home with the attitude that the government owed them a living. Consequently, some Malaysians have become concerned that a rift has occurred between the English-educated urban-born and -bred and the Malay-educated young persons who have tended to be the more recent arrivals to the towns. This has exacerbated a rural–urban split.

As in other countries around the world, the modern definition of success is wealth. Thus, the rallying cry among the ethnic groups in the country has been to acquire economic status in order to achieve success. Consequently, Malaysia has seen a number of problems resulting from the competition between ethnic groups for economic power.

MULTICULTURAL EDUCATION EFFORTS

During the authors' international survey of multicultural education, Malaysia responded that there was a multicultural education program which was integrated into the curriculum of the schools, especially in civics and moral education. There was no office which was responsible for multicultural programs. However, civics and moral education were integrated into the total school curriculum. Hence, its teaching was funded by the federal government but there was no special or specific fiscal allocation. No leadership for the creation or maintenance of multicultural programs was offered from the Ministry of Education.

As was previously mentioned, and as reported by Malaysia's respondent to the international survey, the primary cultures in the country were Malay, Chinese, Indian, and several cultures of other indigenous people. No special multicultural education certification requirements for teachers exist. The curriculum and instruction stresses integration with the Islamic/Malay culture as the dominant culture rather than cultural pluralism or assimilation. The official language of instruction is Bahasa Malaysia after the primary level. There are two special programs to teach immigrant or indigenous children in their ethnic language. One is the provision of primary school education in the ethnic languages of the main social groups. The other is the provision of "pupils ethnic language" classes at the secondary education levels.

Some of the Malaysian children attend racially integrated schools, while others do not because of distance or cultural and religious preference. The history of the indigenous peoples is taught through subjects like history, civics, and moral education.

The Ministry of Education evaluates curriculum materials, library materials, and textbooks for racist and sexist statements. The two biggest problems facing multicultural programs in Malaysia result from sociocultural and political factors.

According to the respondents, the biggest improvements would be to have one uniform integrated multicultural program and to minimize the aforementioned problems.

The writers of the constitution for the Federation of Malay defined a Malay as "a person who professes the Muslim religion, habitually speaks the Malay language, and conforms to Malay customs." However, many modern Malays are Muslims of Malay stock, but sometimes of a different ethnic origin. Some of them speak other languages and harbor diverse cultural characteristics, including non-Islamic religious beliefs. Defining diverse ethnic groups such as the Malays has occurred because the government has been providing special school programs for people designated as Malays. Such educational offerings have not been available to Chinese and Indian students.

During 1980, the country became concerned because the Dewan Bahasa dan Pustaka argued that over half of the country's population could not speak the national Malay language properly. Given the complex pluralistic composition of the country, a great deal of controversy has existed over the role of language. Fluency in English has been viewed as a measure of affluence and status. However, since Malay is the national language, it is felt that it can become a unifying factor for the country's pluralism.

Life for women in the country can be difficult, particularly on the plantations. The women must prepare the day's lunch and start by five o'clock to tap the trees. By the time a typical country woman returns home and cooks the evening meal, it is normally about 9:00 P.M. Older girls do not usually attend schools because they are needed at home to care for the younger children and meet a number of other household responsibilities.

SUMMARY

Malaysia presently does not have a formal multicultural education program as defined in this book. However, the country is addressing many of the issues in spite of the fact that no formal program is in place. The issue of gender equity in the educational system appears to be one of the country's major need areas.

REFERENCES

Andaya, Barbara Watson and Andaya, Leonard V. *A History of Malaysia.* Kuala Lumpur: Oxford University Press, 1975.

Aznam, Suhairi. "The Women's Burden." *Far Eastern Economic Review* (June 1990), p. 18.

Constitution of the Federation of Malaya, Article 160–2.

Gonen, Amiram. *Encyclopedia of the Peoples of the World.* New York: Henry Holt Publishing Co., 1993.

Kee, Francis Wong Hoy and Hong, Ee Tiang. *Education in Malaysia.* Hong Kong: Heineman Educational Books (Asia) Ltd., 1975.

Thomas, Murray. "Malaysia." *Education and Urban Society* (August 1986), pp. 399–400.

Vatikiotis, Michael. "Purity and Perception." *Far Eastern Economic Review* (December 1991), p. 30.

Vreeland, Nena et al. *Area Handbook for Malaysia.* Washington, DC: United States Government Printing Office, 1980.

Wolters, O.W. *Early Indonesian Commerce: A Study of the Origins of Srivijaya.* Ithaca, NY: Cornell University Press, 1967.

29

Mexico

HISTORY OF THE SYSTEM

The first Mexicans may have been descendants of Asian nomads who took part in a number of migrations across the Bering Strait land bridge. This probably occurred during the Pleistocene era. By the end of this era, a melting of the ice cap raised the ocean levels, resulting in a termination of the migrations to North America.

Mexico's formative period was characterized by the effective cultivation of plants which had already been domesticated. Toward the end of this era, the temple/pyramids emerged and these pyramids became the building blocks of many villages and towns. Tlotihuacan began to create itself between 200 B.C. and A.D. 900. Mexo-America was the site of several high civilizations, and this period has been referred to as the Golden Age of Mexico. This was a period of time in which the arts and sciences thrived and a high degree of literacy occurred. A mathematical system was developed which made it possible to make accurate recordings of time. Between A.D. 300 and 900, the Mayan culture was developing and the Mayan calendars were created. Mayan art displayed more human forms in various decorations and carvings than those in other nearby regions. In mathematics, the Mayans are generally credited with the creation of a number system and the discovery of the zero. Religious ideology was polytheistic, and the forces of nature were held in high esteem through the gods of rain, water, the sun, and the moon. Quetzalcoatl, the feathered serpent, was the most important deity of all. Metals made their appearance during the end of this period; and during this same era, the architectural structures in Teotihuacan, the Temple of the Sun at Palenque, and the Pyramid of the Niches at El Tajin in the state of Veracruz were all built. They still are standing.

Mexico's three most important ancient history sites were Teotihuacan, Monte Alban, and the Maya complexes (in the states of Chiapas, Tabasco, Compeche,

Yucatan, and Quintanna Roo, plus the nearby nations of Honduras, Guatemala, and Belize). By the end of the Classic era, scientific achievements had peaked. Due to long-distance trade enterprises, metallurgy reached Mexico from South America during the post-Classic era. The Mexicans also became accomplished craftsmen in gold, silver, and copper.

North of present-day Mexico City was the city of Tula. During the tenth century, it was the largest militaristic site of the post-Classic period. The city was built by the Toltecs, but it actually had a life span of only about 200 years. Its legends and consciousness proved to have a dramatic effect on the Aztecs about 500 years later. A great deal of the panegyric was concerned with the ruler Tolpitzen-Quetzalcoatl, who was the source of all good. But eventually the fall of Tolpitzen-Quetzalcoatl prompted the Toltecs into a new phase which can be characterized by an emphasis on the warrior code and a greatly expanded emphasis on human sacrifice. But the Toltec culture was devastated by drought and famine. In addition, the country was plagued by warfare. Tula was eventually abandoned and various microcultures fought for the control of the Valley of Anahuac.

By the tenth century, an important influence of Toltec culture was brought into Yucatan. The influence of the Toltecs was highly evident in the art and religion and also led to a glorification of warfare. Internal dissension led to the demise of Chichen Itzas hegemony and the rise of Mayapan. After the collapse of the Tula during the twelfth century, refugees from that city settled into the area south of the valley of Mexico, eventually founding the cities of Colhuacan and Xico which would become the centers for the dispersion of the Toltec culture to the tribes of the north.

Most historians believe the Aztecs were the last nomadic Chichimecs to arrive in the Valley of Mexico. The most popular theory about their original residence is that they migrated to that region from a mythical island called Aztlan which was located off the Pacific coast. This probably happened about A.D. 1111. Then after a number of skirmishes with the existing residents, they arrived at the Lago de Texcoco, on the east side of Mexico City. According to the legends, they saw an eagle perched in a tree with a snake in its beak. Supposedly, this was a sign that marked the site on which their city should be constructed. In fact, the Mexican flag has a picture of the eagle and snake which has come to commemorate the event.

Aztec power was finally consolidated under Itzcoatl, the ruler who appointed Tlacelel as his adviser in 1427. Tlacelel implemented a number of reforms which were successful in establishing the ultimate power of the Aztecs in the area. He destroyed all existing records which did not glorify Aztec victories. But between 1450 and 1451, unseasonable rains, snow, and heavy flooding created a major famine.

It has been argued that Aztec society was a curious combination of beauty and brutality. Indeed, the Aztecs were known for their ability to create splendid murals, stone sculpture, and pyramids. Yet their religious ceremonies included human sacrifices to the gods.

Another crucial segment of Aztec society was the *pochteca* (merchants), who were responsible for local and long-distance trade which sometimes extended into Central America. But the greatest proportion of the population consisted of farmers, servants, vendors, and lower civil servants who lived in *calpullis* (neighborhoods or barrios). The lowest segments of society were the mayeques and slaves. The slaves had some rights, and their period of bondage could actually be a temporary arrangement for a specific purpose.

The Aztecs were committed to education, and two kinds of schools were available. Wealthy, upper-class children were trained for high posts in the government and for the priesthood in schools known as *calmecacs*. Children from the lower classes attended schools which were designed for practical training, learning a trade, or a career in the military. These schools were mostly for boys. Girls stayed home and acquired homemaking skills.

But during the late 1400s, the fall of Granada, Spain (in 1492) would ultimately lead to a permanent change in the country of Mexico. The end of Moorish occupation in Spain unleashed a period of discovery and exploration which began as a result of Columbus and his voyage to Hispaniola. By this time, the Aztecs had developed a highly sophisticated society with a moralistic social organization, and people were punished according to the nature of the offense and the social status of the offender. The Aztec craftsmen excelled in their work with jewelry and feather mosaics, and architects created beautiful stone-carved buildings. In spite of the sophisticated Aztec society, it fell apart when the Spanish Conquistadors arrived in 1519, led by Hernan Cortes.

Along with his armada of 11 ships containing over 500 soldiers, 100 seamen, 16 horses, guns, and ammunition, the armada sailed for the Yucatan peninsula. At Potachan, in the present state of Tabasco, the Spanish were victorious over Native Mexicans; and after reaching San Juan de Ulua, an inland march was begun by Cortes and his forces. Another victory by the Spaniards occurred at Cholulu. News of this victory reached Moctezuma who was despondent over the news of Cortes' arrival. The Spaniards marched from Itztapalopa, crossing a drawbridge to enter the city, and were greeted by Moctezuma who was waiting to greet them.

Cortes and his army were treated royally even though the Spaniards were concerned about possibly walking into a trap. Eventually, Cortes decided to place Moctezuma under house arrest. Meanwhile, Cortes had learned of the arrival of a Spanish fleet which landed at San Juan de Ulua with orders to arrest Cortes. He decided to meet Panfilo de Narvaez, the leader of the newly arrived fleet. Leaving the command of his men to Pedro de Alvarado, he met Narvaez, was successful in establishing his authority, and returned to Tenochtitlan.

Before he arrived, Aztecs had attacked the forces of Alvarado who had made a number of critical errors in his dealings with them. Heavy Aztec attacks resulted in the death of about 860 Spaniards in La Noche Triste (the Sad Night).

However, Cortes eventually led a successful attack with a force of thirteen launches, fifteen cannons, three heavy guns, and 900 armed Spanish soldiers. Finally, Tenochtitlan fell and the victory marked the end of the great Aztec empire for all practical purposes. But the Aztec leader, Cuauhtemoc, who was captured as he tried to flee after the Aztec loss, is still considered to be Mexico's first national hero.

After Tenochtitlan, the Spanish were determined to expand the new territories under their control. These new Spanish lands in Central America and Mexico were called New Spain. Cortes sent emissaries to the king of Spain in order to secure these new territories. However, he had a number of influential enemies in Spain who were attempting to build a case against his involvement in New Spain. Finally, by 1522, Cortes became governor and captain general of New Spain. And six years later, Cortes returned to New Spain and convinced the king to confirm his newly acquired positions of leadership in New Spain. He was also given the title of Marquise del Valle de Oaxaca.

Entrepreneurship was the primary motivation for the new acquisitions of the European countries. In an attempt to enrich and strengthen the mother countries, new colonies such as Mexico supplied raw materials to Spain who would produce the goods and sell them back for a tidy profit. From the mid-1500s, land grants were made available for persons who were interested in raising livestock and farming the land. Many intermarriages occurred between the Spaniards and Native Mexicans who became employed as peons, laborers, servants, and artisans. Mestizos who would later shape the country's future can trace their heritage back to these unions which occurred frequently during this period of Mexican history.

Also, colonial society was stratified by race and wealth. The three main groups were Europeans, *Costas* (mixed blood), and Native Mexicans (the indigenous population). Also during this time, historians have described the development of a dual economy in New Spain. In the Valley of Mexico, the hacienda economy was taking form, while the mining economy was materializing in the north. The unifying force in the Spanish colony was the Catholic Church.

During the 1500s, Mexico was devastated by disease and the decline of the silver mines. Millions of Native Mexicans fell victim to the ravaging illness because of a lack of immunity to European diseases, and the terrible problems pertaining to the plague did not really decline until the mid-seventeenth century.

Also contributing to the suffering of the Native Mexicans was the ruthless treatment by Spain. The Spaniards really went to Mexico to become rich, and if the wealth could not be realized in the mines, the people themselves could become a main target. So cheap labor became critically important for this group of Europeans.

In addition to the diseases and the cruelty of the Conquistadors, the Native Mexicans also suffered at the hands of some of the friars who defended them. Determined to erect shrines and perpetuate the Catholic tradition, a great deal of the traditional cultural values of Mexico's indigenous groups would be lost forever.

By the beginning of the eighteenth century, Spain had encountered a number of major setbacks due to conflicts at home and to a number of wars abroad. Consequently, some attempts were made to modernize the colonies. As a result, a number of economic reforms occurred in Mexico. Most of the reforms occurred in the mining and trade sectors. Miners were able to organize themselves into guilds. Free trade arrangements came into existence and many of the Spanish ports were finally able to trade with the colonies. As a result, the monopoly held by merchants at the port of Cadiz disappeared, and the same thing occurred at Veracruz and Acapulco. So, to a certain extent, both miners and merchants were able to acquire financial independence.

During the 1700s, Mexico was affected by a number of reforms under the Bourbon king of Spain, Charles III. In 1765, a royal inspector was sent to New Spain to conduct a survey of the economic, political, and defense conditions in the colony. Because of the sparse population in the northern part of the colony, Spain was worried about possible encroachments by competing nations. In order to solidify its colony in New Spain, the structure of New Spain was reorganized into twelve intendencias under a single commandant general in Mexico City who reported directly to the king. Two regiments of Spanish soldiers arrived for duty in the region.

Miguel Hidalgo y Castillo was a parish priest of Dolores in the present state of Hidalgo. In his house he led discussion groups which were composed of poor Native Mexicans, mestizos, and criollos. In these discussions, the topics related to his concerns about social and economic issues and the eventual uprising against the Spanish government. On September 16, 1810, Hidalgo started his independence movement against the Spanish. The people were alerted by the ringing of church bells which was the signal to join him against the Spanish government. Grito de Dolores (Cry of Dolores) became the famous rallying cry: "Long Live Our Lady of Guadalupe. Death to bad government. Death to the gachupines." Independence forces went to Gunajuato where they were joined by miners and the revolution was underway. The battles lasted until 1821. The revolutionary forces consisted of mostly guerrilla groups. Finally, in 1821, the Treaty of Cordoba was signed which granted Mexico its independence. A provisional government was established with a brand new independent congress.

The 1824 constitution created a nineteen-state federal republic which consisted of four territories. The power was divided into the standard legislative, executive, and judicial divisions. A president and vice president were elected for four years. By 1829, under the leadership of Santa Anna, the last Spanish troops were leaving Mexico. But an agreement between Santa Anna and the new Texas government led to the emergence of the Lone Star Republic, which became independent from Mexico. After the war between the United States and Mexico, the United States and Mexico signed the Treaty of Guadalupe Hidalgo which resulted in Mexico losing about one-third of its original territory.

By 1861, President Benito Juarez was plagued with an empty treasury after his election, and foreign creditors were demanding payment. After declaring a moratorium on all foreign debt repayment, Spain, Britain, and France occupied the Mexican coastal areas in an attempt to force repayment. But on May 5, 1862, General Ignacio Zaragosa won a major victory over the French at Puebla. However, the French regrouped, captured Puebla, and eventually occupied Mexico City. Ferdinand Maximilian Joseph became the Mexican ruler under the approval of Napoleon III. However, the remaining French troops were defeated in 1867 after Napoleon withdrew his troops from Mexico. Maximilian was tried and executed in 1867 and Mexico became independent once again.

Toward the end of the nineteenth century, Mexico was still rural and in poor economic health in spite of the efforts of Juarez and others to initiate a number of major reforms. The country had a huge poverty population, an elite element, and virtually no middle class at all.

By 1910, Francisco Madero had created a revolutionary plan which convinced the people that President Porfirio Diaz was responsible for their suffering. By 1911, the revolutionary forces had achieved victories in the state of Chihuahua, and the revolution spread throughout other parts of Mexico until Diaz finally resigned in 1911 and Madero made a triumphant return to Mexico City. Emiliano Zapata and Pancho Villa were key figures in the revolution and became Mexican folk heroes.

By 1920, the country was changing because of new roads, buses, and automobiles. Electric power was making its way to the rural areas, and rural schools began to replace the church as a center of community activity. Medical care was becoming a bit more readily available, and the new motion picture and radio industries were starting to create changes in the culture. Artistic works by gifted painters such as Diego Rivera were beginning to attract attention throughout the Western hemisphere and in the rest of the world as well.

During World War II, Mexico declared war on the Axis powers after a number of ships were sunk off the Mexican coast. During 1942, President Avila Camacho and President Franklin Roosevelt of the United States signed an agreement initiating the Bracero program, which allowed Mexican laborers to work in the United States. By 1958, another revolutionary period materialized for the next several years. During that time, a number of social welfare programs were initiated along with a national railroad strike and a student uprising against the ousting of leftist teachers from the Mexico City teachers' union.

Conditions in Mexico became somewhat stabilized from the mid-1960s to the early 1980s. Business interests received priority, and student and labor unrest was kept at a minimum in order to maximize economic growth. One of the highlights of the era was Mexico's hosting of the Olympic Games, which allowed the country to interact with other nations in a new and friendly manner. A population explosion was dealt with by the Mexican government, which took steps to participate in family planning and health programs. Also, during this era equal rights were granted to women under the constitution.

STRUCTURE OF THE SYSTEM

The federal government of Mexico includes the legislative, executive, and judicial branches. The president is able to formally proclaim a law and sign it into action. Mexican presidents are also able to veto all or parts of legislation passed by the legislature. However, presidential vetoes may be overridden. Pieces of legislation sponsored by the president take precedence over everything else. The constitution allows the president to issue basic rules which have the same legal effect as a statute.

The Mexican constitution has specific requirements for addressing matters of public policy. It forbids foreigners and churches from owning property, and assigns original ownership of fuel, power sources, seas, waters, and natural resources to the nation. Religious groups are excluded from any kind of political activity and they are not allowed to participate in public education. The government is also allowed to redistribute land as long as it is in the public interest.

The executive branch includes the president of the Mexican republic, the administrative structures of the country, about 376 government-owned businesses, and some semiautonomous corporations. The president is elected by popular vote for a six-year term of office. Presidents are not allowed to be reelected. The federal legislature consists of a senate and chamber of deputies. Senatorial terms run for six years, while chamber members serve for a period of three years. Mexico's judicial system consists of federal and state court systems. The state courts have jurisdiction over cases involving minor sums of money and divorce cases. The federal courts have jurisdiction over kidnappings, bank robberies, and most major felonies except for murders which are heard by state courts.

Federal courts have three levels including the Supreme Court which includes 26 justices. The middle level court is the circuit court system. There are sixteen of these. The third level is the state supreme court. These exist in each of Mexico's 31 states. Decisions rendered at this level can be overturned by the federal courts. The judiciary does not normally hear cases which are deemed to be political in nature. Consequently, the judiciary is more independent from the president than the legislature.

Political parties first must be legally registered by the Federal Electoral Commission prior to running candidates in elections. During recent years, the Party of National Action has been the major party representing the political right. Centrist positions are generally represented by the Popular Socialist Party, the Authentic Party of the Mexican Revolution, and the Socialist Workers' Party. Views of the political left are reflected in the United Socialist Party of Mexico, the Revolutionary Workers' Party, the Movement of Socialist Action and Unity Party, and the Political Action Movement.

The Mexican educational system consists of the elementary, secondary, and higher education levels. Kindergartens are available for children from the ages of 4 to 6 on an optional basis. The primary school level is structured for children from age 6 to 14. High schools for Mexican students consist of three years of education and include day schools for adolescents, night schools for working adults, and technical schools which provide commercial and industrial training. After completing the basic cycle, a number of upper secondary schools are available. Most have been controlled in some way by the universities.

Probably the biggest problem for Mexican educators has been the provision of education in the large rural sections of the country. Rural areas having populations of less than 1,000 have often been neglected, which sometimes meant that children had little or no access to a formal education. Rural schools for Native Mexicans usually had Native Mexican teachers, and the classes have been sometimes conducted bilingually in Spanish and the local mother tongue.

The Secretariat of Public Education is responsible for all levels of the Mexican educational system in the Mexican states. This office also sets the academic calendar, determines the curriculum content, distributes free textbooks, and also establishes grading scales and graduation requirements. But even though public education in Mexico is free, its inaccessibility to some students, as well as the relatively poor economy of the country throughout the years, has made it difficult for the country to provide suitable educational opportunities for all of the country's children. As a result, the literacy rate of the country is only about 18 percent.

MULTICULTURAL EDUCATION EFFORTS

While Mexico does not formally have a multicultural education program, the country has been forced to address many of the multicultural education issues which have concerned other countries. For example, there has been a constant criticism that the textbooks used in the schools have a strong bias toward the urban populations. Their focus on the middle-class populations has meant that poor Mexican students have had a difficult time relating to their content.

Another problem has been the provision of suitable educational offerings for the ''bi-national'' student. The term refers to young people who spend substantial amounts of time out of the country, necessitating their absence in Mexican schools in order to help earn a living for their families. The fact that funding for school is extremely limited in Mexico has meant that many Mexican children only have access to a sixth-grade education.

Anthropologists have usually divided the Mexican population into two primary groups: the Native Mexican (or ''Indian'') and the Mestizo. However, as in most countries, it is rather difficult to use these two classification systems because of the microcultural differences of the Toltecs, Zapotecs, Mayas, Olmecs, and Aztecs, which are five of the larger groups. Intermarriage and the infusion of African blood from the slaves which the Spaniards brought have resulted in a plethora of racial and ethnic groups which almost defies classification.

The language of instruction is Spanish; but while some Mexican school children speak Castillian Spanish, others, particularly those close to the United States border, speak an idiom which includes many English phrases and is sometimes referred to as "Tex Mex." Some bilingual programs for Native Mexicans are found in the rural schools.

Since 1936, Mexico has had a Department of Indian Affairs which has been responsible for improving the education of Native Mexicans. Moreover, it had the responsibility of addressing the wrongs suffered by Mexico's indigenous populations throughout the country's history. The Department attempted to improve living conditions in Native Mexican communities. Cooperatives were organized to help teach Spanish to Native Mexican people, and provided special schools which were primarily vocational schools designed to teach agricultural skills to boys and homemaking skills to girls.

While more women have been attending school in recent years, very few of them have sixteen years of education compared to their male counterparts. However, the great majority of primary teachers are women, contrasted with only about 13 percent of the faculty at the National University.

SUMMARY

Mexico has been afflicted with problems which are quite similar to other developing countries. The long period of occupation by Spain kept the nation from making the same kinds of advances experienced by some other countries. Indeed, the people were exploited for cheap labor, and when Mexico gained its independence from Spain the economic system was in a shambles.

That set of circumstances impacted the educational system, as can be expected. So instead of developing an educational system which offered a comprehensive education to all young people regardless of their racial or socioeconomic circumstances, the country was forced to struggle in order to provide even the most basic educational program.

Obviously, such restrictions force a country to prioritize its capabilities when constructing a comprehensive plan of education. Consequently, it was simply impossible to pay attention to educational issues like multicultural education programs. On a positive note, however, Mexico has been relatively free of many problems involving racial issues which have afflicted other countries. Unlike its neighbor to the north, the deep racial hostilities resulting in slavery have not occurred quite as much in Mexico. Moreover, since Mexico never did have a strong industrial base, there was never a need for cheap labor from different racial groups which later could have resulted in severe racial hostilities.

REFERENCES

Chevalier, Francois. *Land and Society in Colonial Mexico: The Great Hacienda.* Berkeley: University of California Press, 1963.

Contreras, Maxmilliano. "The Binational Student." *Equity and Excellence,* Vol. 23, Nos. 1 & 2 (1986), pp. 77–80.

Marks, Richard. *Cortes.* New York: Alfred A. Knopf, 1993.

Meyer, Michael C. and Sherman, William. *The Course of Mexican History,* 2nd ed. New York: Oxford University Press, 1983.

Rudolph, James. *Mexico, A Country Study.* Washington, DC: Department of the Army, 1985.

Ruiz, Ramon Eduardo. *Triumphs and Tragedy.* New York: W.W. Norton & Company, 1992.

Sierro, Justo. *The Political Evolution of the Mexican People.* Austin: University of Texas Press, 1988.

30

New Zealand

HISTORY OF THE SYSTEM

Located about 1,000 miles southeast of the Australian mainland, two small is-lands—about the size of the state of Colorado (or five-sixths the size of Great Britain)—make up the country of New Zealand, a self-governing Common-wealth of the British Empire. New Zealand was first discovered and colonized by Polynesians around the year A.D. 800, and developed as a civilization in relative isolation from other Polynesian cultures. The present-day Maoris are descendants of the early east Polynesian settlers and comprise New Zealand's indigenous microculture.

The first significant European contact took place in 1769, when Captain James Cook and his associates arrived in New Zealand. Abel Tasman had visited the country briefly in 1642 on behalf of the Dutch East India Company, and had given New Zealand its present name. Cook's arrival resulted in mapping the country's coastline, observation of the Maori civilization, and the beginning of a relationship with the Maoris which was based on eighteenth century views of the "noble savage," a much more accepting and benign attitude than that dem-onstrated during the brief period of the Tasman contact.

During the period from first English contact in 1769 until the signing of the Treaty of Waitangi in 1840, which annexed New Zealand to the United King-dom, the country changed in many ways. Flax production and exportation, seal-ing, whaling, and timber products became the dominant economic enterprises and brought many more people to the country. Through all of this period, how-ever, the culture and civilization was more Maori than British, with the Euro-peans interacting with their hosts in a socio-political environment that might be described as a positive sort of pluralism.

With the signing of the treaty providing for annexation of New Zealand and its subsequent designation as a Crown Colony in 1841, settlement of the country began in earnest. After several false starts, the government and private companies, such as the New Zealand Company, worked together to encourage settlement. This included the buying, selling, and trading of land with the Maoris, along with the tensions and violence of the wars of the 1860s which accompanied such rapid and monumental change in the Maori society. The differences between the old and the new were made even more clear when one considers that the aim of the New Zealand Company was to further the development of a new and essentially English colony, replete with customs and traditions—in short, to create a new culture in a foreign land.

For many years, the Maoris and settlers of English stock have coexisted in New Zealand. Sometimes referred to as the Maori and the Pakeha, the two cultures have maintained a pluralistic society. Even though the government and economy appear more British or international than Maori, the latter have managed to maintain their own identity far better than most indigenous people who have been the subjects of colonization and settlement. Like other countries, such as Australia, which have become culturally influenced, if not dominated, by Europeans, the English newcomers and their descendants have also gone through a period of ethnocentricity and racial/ethnic consciousness in which the indigenous microculture as well as successive waves and groups of immigrants are compared against the ''whiteness'' of the dominant settlers.

This was particularly true in Australia and New Zealand where both countries, at times, have been concerned about the potential impact of significant waves of Asian immigration, primarily from Japan and/or China, and, more generally, by other groups of non-English settlers. Although New Zealand did not adopt a ''White New Zealand'' policy as did Australia, similar concerns have been raised and expressed throughout the nation's history.

As New Zealand has moved into more modern times, it may be characterized by efforts in democratic government, labor reform, and societal improvement. Some examples have included women's suffrage (1893), land reform and redistribution, and labor laws emphasizing mediation and arbitration.

For many years, New Zealand has been dependent on the United Kingdom as a sole market for her exports, primarily farm products like meat and wool. Since 1984, the government has attempted to move toward a more globally oriented free market economy with a larger number of trading partners. Initial results, though modest, have been encouraging.

STRUCTURE OF THE SYSTEM

New Zealand's government is a constitutional monarchy. The British queen is the monarch of the country. She appoints a governor to represent her, but the governor has only limited power. The New Zealand legislature, prime minister, and cabinet comprise the national government.

New Zealand was given a constitution by the British in 1852 when the country was a British colony. However, throughout the years, many of the original elements of the country's constitution have been altered by the legislature, and some New Zealanders have argued that for all practical purposes the country has no working constitution.

The house of representatives consists of 97 members, and this body is also referred to as the parliament. People in the voting districts elect one member of the parliament, and four seats are set aside for Maori candidates. Parliamentary elections are normally held every three years, and the voting age is eighteen for all New Zealand citizens. The party leader of the political unit which wins the most seats becomes the prime minister. The prime minister then appoints cabinet heads to run the various departments. These department heads are called ministers, and the prime minister and the cabinet are called the government.

The main political parties in the country are the Labour Party and the National Party. Traditionally, the Labour Party has tended to favor governmental control and public regulation of industry, while the National Party has tended to favor free enterprise. However, it has been argued by political scientists in the country that there is little difference between the two parties. In fact, in the mid-1980s, the Labour Party adopted a free-market policy.

New Zealand's legislature elects an ombudsman who is in charge of investigating complaints against the government by New Zealand citizens. After researching the complaints, the ombudsman sends an opinion to the department involved. If the ombudsman is not satisfied with the action taken by the department, the findings may be submitted to the parliament for further action.

The highest court in the land is the Privy Council, followed by the Court of Appeals. These two courts only hear cases that have been appealed from a lower court. The High Court is the third highest court. It handles cases involving serious offenses and most of the appeals from the district courts which are the lowest, hearing only minor cases.

New Zealanders have a commitment to the principle of equal rights for all of its citizens. The Maoris and Pakehas live in an atmosphere of common trust, and prominent Maori leaders play major roles in the life of the country. Nonetheless, Maori leaders continue to argue for better housing and employment opportunities, and better access to education.

Education in New Zealand has grown rather spasmodically, and the random nature of the country's school administrative structure seems to reflect this. Throughout the nineteenth century, primary schools were the major form of education and were the responsibility of the provincial governments. However, the provinces were abolished in 1875, and from that time on, education was thought to be a national responsibility. In fact, the primary schools were joined together because of the Education Act of 1877.

For 100 years, the decisions for hiring, firing, capital projects, and so on have been carried out by boards of education. However, these decisions only affected primary schools, since the secondary schools were largely independent and had their own established administration systems and a keen desire to maintain their own control.

These secondary education enterprises became more common during the first quarter of this century due to a "baby boom" during the 1950s and 1960s. These new secondary schools adapted the administrative structure of the earlier schools. A board of governors dealt directly with the Department of Education for finance, construction projects, and the maintenance of school structures.

After World War II, the New Zealand educational system was undergoing major change during the 1950s and 1960s. Intermediate schools had been established during the 1920s. These junior high schools were designed to provide an education for students who were unlikely to pursue a secondary education. They also met the needs of a rapidly expanding student population between the ages of 11 and 13. They took the enrollment pressure off the primary schools and provided a wider range of school programs for students.

Also during this period of time, early childhood education programs increased. Much of the growth was initially motivated by private efforts, but eventually they acquired their own national organizations. Pre-school programs provide noncompulsory education and care to children up to the age of 5. Kindergartens were started in 1989. Play centers are organized through local associations which are affiliated with the New Zealand Playcentre Association. They are actually parent cooperatives; parents are trained through the Association and are paid modest fees for their work as supervisors.

Kohanga Reo are pre-school centers for Maori children. Starting in 1982, these centers are based on Maori values and are conducted entirely in the native Maori tongue. Each Kohanga Reo is administered by a local group which is part of the Kohanga Reo Trust, a national group.

Finally, child care centers, run by community and church groups, volunteer agencies, and licensed commercial operators, provide educational and custodial services for children under the age of seven years. The compulsory attendance age was raised to fifteen in 1944, and free education was available to all students through the age of nineteen.

New Zealand's compulsory education laws require children to attend school by the age of six. However, in reality, most actually start at the age of five. The schools for young children are primary schools for students up to the age of ten or twelve, or intermediate schools. Over 2,000 of these are public but there are also 76 private schools. Responsibility for the normal administrative functions of each school rests with school committees which consist of householders in each area. These elected members are responsible for the purchasing of textbooks, library books, and the maintenance of their school. Moreover, they are responsible for such issues as religious instruction and after-hours use of school buildings. While they assist in the selection of principals, that task is carried out by local boards.

Secondary schools in New Zealand consist of 212 state schools which are run by boards of governors, 20 private schools, and 49 integrated schools which are part private and partly run by the state.

An extensive review of New Zealand's educational system began in 1987.

For the next four years, a government-appointed task force came to the conclusion that the administrative structure for education was overly centralized, too complex, and in need of a number of major reforms. The task force recommended that the administrative structure should be based on choice, providing a wide range of options for students and parents. It should also be based on cultural sensitivity, equity, and sound management.

As a means of instituting the needed reforms, a number of education agencies were established or reorganized. The Ministry of Education is responsible for establishing policy advice to the Minister of Education for the country's educational functions. This advice pertains to issues of funding, legislation, national curriculum objectives, and the compilation of educational statistics.

These new reforms dealt with a number of practical schooling issues. One issue was the compulsory schooling age. It remained unchanged, meaning that children are required to attend from age 6 to 15. While the country has national curriculum objectives, optional elements can be determined through a process of collaboration between institutions and communities.

The New Zealand learning institutions are agencies which control educational resources throughout the land. They are actually partnerships between the professionals and the community. Their board of trustees sees to it that the overall objectives of the state are carried out. Charters are drawn up which are actual contracts between the community, institution, and the State.

MULTICULTURAL EDUCATION EFFORTS

As New Zealand goes through a restructuring of tomorrow's schools, the issue of educational equity has been a central planning theme. The major equity objectives are to:

1. ensure that a new program of education administration promotes and progressively achieves greater equity for women, Maoris, Pacific Islanders, minority groups, and for the working class, rural and disabled students, teachers, and communities;

2. ensure that equity issues are integrated into all aspects of changes in education administration and not treated as optional;

3. acknowledge that the present system of education administration includes some features which promote equity and which should not be lost as a result of change;

4. recognize that equity is best achieved through systems which combine enabling legislation with awareness and education; and

5. ensure that the systems which are put in place enable the monitoring of progress toward equity control.

Another major interest in multicultural education has centered around the needs of New Zealand's indigenous peoples, the Maoris. Opportunities are made available to parents who wish to have their children learn or be educated in the

Maori language. The whanau (extended family structure) will be able to participate in the New Zealand educational system. Persons within the whanau will
be eligible for participation in board of trustees elections, and enjoy close participation between the committees and the institutions. Finally, Maori parents,
along with all other New Zealand parents, will be able to home-school their
children or establish their own institutions if the existing schools do not meet
the needs of their children.

As described previously, there exists a positive and pluralistic relationship
among the indigenous Maoris and the predominantly English-descended New
Zealanders. This may be demonstrated by current efforts to revitalize the use of
the Maori language in everyday life in New Zealand. A study by Nicholson and
Garland concluded that there was at least a ''passive tolerance'' to the presence
and use of the Maori language in contemporary society, and that this might
serve as a base for a language revitalization program. The researchers also
pointed out that a language revitalization effort would need to extend beyond
the schools, although the educational system would play an important role in
the overall effort, i.e., as basically a marketing program which might include
such things as bilingual signage in public places and additional emphasis through
the print and broadcast media. Such an effort seems to be a positive initiative
and a continuing recognition of and respect for the Maori culture as an important
component of a modern-day forward-looking New Zealand.

Another current issue in New Zealand education is the new emphasis on
''gender inclusive curriculum.'' In developing such a program, one researcher
has suggested four school-level programs:

1. establishment of a gender equity committee;

2. staff discussions of gender equity, perhaps with an outside resource person;

3. attendance of staff members at any local course on gender equity; and

4. in-school teacher development on gender equity.

SUMMARY

Multicultural education in New Zealand is presently embroiled in debates
between education groups which seem to espouse an approach to education
which emphasizes a more pluralistic, multicultural approach to the education of
New Zealand children and the more Euro-Centric philosophy of right-wing
groups. Some educators have argued that the very ethnic integrities of the Maoris
have been directly undermined by the new right, resulting in an attempt to
dismiss the viability and legitimacy of the Maori language, knowledge, and
culture because new-right theory has no interest in dealing with ethnic issues.
Many educators have advocated the inclusion of bilingual/bicultural education
programs in the curriculum.

The argument over multicultural education continues. People involved in teacher/student groups have argued that the bias toward European heritage in artistic areas especially needs to be corrected, and multiculturalism should be required, along with more emphasis on other cultures and their needs. However, one husband and wife argued that "This entire series is attempting to foist on parents your preconceptions of what you want to include; our opinions will of course be totally ignored. Most of us don't want your multicultural garbage—we want our children to be taught basics."

Even though the new reforms are somewhat controversial, it would appear that New Zealand's new educational blueprints have been crafted in such a manner as to ensure the maintenance and development of strong multicultural education efforts.

REFERENCES

Capper, Phillip (Ed.). *Proceedings of the Post Primary Teachers Association Curriculum Conference.* Christchurch: Post Primary Teachers Association, 1991.

Chapman, Ruth. *Social Engineering in the Curriculum.* Workshop conducted at the Post Primary Teachers Association Curriculum Conference, Christchurch, 1991.

Gordon, L. "Controlling Education: Agency Theory and the Reformation of New Zealand Schools." *Educational Policy,* Vol. 9, No. 1 (March 1995), pp. 54–74.

Lange, David. *Tomorrow's Schools.* Auckland: Ministry of Education, 1990.

"New Zealand." In *The Cambridge History of the British Empire.* London: Cambridge University Press, 1933.

New Zealand. Ministry of Education. *Education in New Zealand.* Wellington: Ministry of Education, 1992.

Nicholson, Rangi and Garland, Ron. "New Zealanders' Attitudes to the Revitalization of the Maori Language." *Journal of Multilingual and Multicultural Development,* Vol. 12, No. 5 (1991).

Oliver, W.H. and Williams, B.R. (Eds.). *The Oxford History of New Zealand.* Wellington: Oxford University Press, 1981.

Smith, Graham H. *Reform and Maori Educational Crisis: A Grand Illusion.* Keynote Speech at the Post Primary Teachers Association Curriculum Conference, Christchurch, 1991.

Taskforce to Review Education Administration. *Administering for Excellence.* Wellington: Taskforce to Review Education Administration, 1988.

Taskforce to Review Education Administration. *Administering for Excellence.* Wellington: Taskforce to Review Education Administration, 1990.

U.S. Department of Education. *The Educational System of New Zealand,* Education Around the World, No. 80-14016. Washington, DC: U.S. Government Printing Office, 1980.

31

Norway

HISTORY OF THE SYSTEM

In examining the history of Norway, it is evident that the sea has affected the people and the country as much as, if not more than, it has any other nation. The ocean teems with fish, providing the people with their way of life; and the protected waters of the fjords and other coastal areas encouraged settlement. The Vikings were among the world's important navigators.

The country experienced a long period of decline at the time of the Black Death, reaching its peak during the Protestant Reformation. At that time, Norway was more like a Danish province. But thanks to the sea, the country recovered due to the shipping of lumber to Amsterdam and to the British Isles for rebuilding London after the great fire. During the 1700s, timber, fishing, shipping, and metal exports were responsible for creating a vibrant economy. By 1661, Denmark and Norway had become twin kingdoms, in which each person was an equal subject of an all-powerful sovereign. The capital of both countries was Copenhagen.

Norway was one of the few European states in which the 1789 French Revolution failed to create much excitement. Actually, during this volatile time in European history, Norway was undergoing some rather dramatic changes in the Norwegian Church, as a result of the preaching tours of a lay evangelist, Hans Nielsen Hauge. Hauge was eventually jailed for his efforts, but his influence had lasting effects on the Norwegian Church.

The Treaty of Kiel in 1814 resulted in Norway being ceded to the Swedish king. However, this created a great deal of irritation among Norway's more vocal factions. Norway had been independent from Denmark for several years and a spirit of nationalism had grown. Also, the well-educated Norwegians argued that the doctrine of popular sovereignty justified the unwillingness to be transferred to a new owner. But eventually, at the Convention of Moss, a treaty was signed after brief skirmishes between Norway and Sweden. On November 4, 1818, Charles XIII of Sweden was elected as the king of Norway. The two countries remained united kingdoms until 1905, when Norway and Sweden became independent nations as a result of the deliberations of the Karlstad conventions.

A nine-year period leading up to the beginning of World War I was a significant period of time for the Norwegian people, who finally were totally in charge of their political destinies. Haakon VII was coronated at Trondheim Cathedral in 1906. The new king adhered to the basic principles of the constitution, and because of the Norwegian constitution, it was illegal to use the veto in constitutional matters.

Politically, during this nine-year era, the nation's politics were influenced by the 1906 adoption of single-member constituencies with a second election among the candidates when nobody received a majority during the first election. The second factor was the franchising of women in 1907. A lobbying organization collected about 250,000 signatures for universal suffrage. This helped Norwegian women gain the right to vote.

Norway's party system was dominated at the outset by Christian Michelson. He had wanted to preserve the bourgoise coalition based on the United Party which he had started in 1903. But the election of 1906 produced unclear results since the leftist party had a clear victory even though many of its members had supported the United Party.

During 1906, the first public grants were made available for unemployment insurance. During 1908 and 1911, accident insurance was made available to about 90,000 fishermen and seamen. Fishermen paid half of the expense themselves, while the ship owners paid half of the fees for the seamen. The state paid the other half. The funds for health insurance programs came from increases in taxes.

The nation's agricultural industry also experienced substantial growth. By 1912, improved tillage and the utilization of better seed corn from Sweden caused a great increase in corn production. By 1907, milk production had doubled since the previous 50 years. Tractors were introduced to the country in 1908. The conversion from sail to steam-driven ocean craft was hard for Norway because of the lack of coal and iron in the country. But between 1908 and 1911, the output of whale oil quadrupled. During the same period of time, Norway's labor movement had begun because of the new industrial development and also due to the examples set by its Scandinavian neighbors.

One of the country's most noteworthy accomplishments has been its polar explorations. Roald Amundsen navigated during the summer of 1918 from Oslo in an attempt to sail over the North Pole in a specially designed ocean-going craft called the *Maud*. Amundsen finally was able to fly over the Pole with Lincoln Ellsworth shortly after Byrd had done the same in an airplane.

The 100-year anniversary of the free Norwegian Constitution was celebrated in 1914. But even with 100 years of independence and relative calm, compared to many other European countries, the country was encountering many problems. The labor conflicts and increasing criticisms of social injustices were causing major debates throughout the land, and the Norwegian farmers complained bitterly about foreign tariffs which had been creating big problems for the production of Norwegian grain. The result was a number of abandoned Norwegian farms.

King Haakon VII opened up a national exhibition in May of 1914. Located in Christiania, the king and queen were the first to tour the exhibits, featuring sections which displayed Norway's successful pursuits in agriculture, handicrafts, fisheries, and various Norwegian industries.

Shortly after, World War I presented major problems for the country due to the neutral path it attempted to follow. The Allies exerted pressure to utilize the Norwegian exports of raw materials and fish. German submarines took a toll on neutral Norwegian shipping which cost the lives of some 2,000 Norwegian seamen. King Haakon VII was a supporter of the British from the very beginning of the hostilities. The declaration of neutrality was published by the Norwegian government soon after the outbreak of the war. The Norwegian position tended to be more in favor of Britain, while neutral Sweden tended to side with the Germans due to the Swedish economy which relied heavily on German exports.

The previously mentioned German attacks on Norwegian shipping greatly upset the people, and King Haakon ordered a royal decree which closed the territorial waters to all foreign submarines. Of course, this was a thinly veiled mandate against the Germans. As expected, the Germans initiated a heated response, and the Norwegians were worried about being drawn into the conflict. The Norwegian's response to the German rejoinder was carefully worded and denied that British pressure had led to the ban on submarine activity which was announced by the Norwegian king.

When the United States entered the war in 1917, the Norwegians negotiated with the Americans for the exportation of essential supplies. But during the same year, the Russians participated in the Bolshevik Revolution, causing still more difficulties for Norway. King Haakon was concerned about the fate of the tsar and his family. He was also afraid that the Russian revolution might possibly lead to separate peace negotiations with the Germans which ultimately might result in a German victory.

Because of the effects of the war, Norway was experiencing demonstrations over the high cost of living and a number of extravagances among the small number of Norwegians who benefited financially because of the war. However, during the conflict, the royal family cut back its own expenditures quite dramatically. They seldom went to the theater and concerts. The king even plowed up parts of the palace park in order to plant potatoes, giving the surplus crops to the poor.

The loss of cargoes and military personnel constituted only a portion of the losses suffered by Norway during World War I. The lack of raw materials had caused the country's fledgling industries to be vastly curtailed in some instances and completely terminated in others. Farming had also suffered because of a shortage of seeds and fertilizers. And the lower standard of living was caused by the disappearance of many imports. Rationing and price control took their toll as well, and Norway had a war economy even though the country was not directly involved in the actual fighting.

Due to Norway's neutrality during the war, it was unable to participate in the peace talks when the victors imposed a peace settlement on the defeated powers. In spite of its enormous losses, Norway received no compensation or any portion of the confiscated German shipping. After about ten years, the families of drowned and injured Norwegian seamen received 6.6 million gold marks as a voluntary compensation from the republican German government.

As far back as 1848, Norwegian towns had been required to provide public elementary schools, and adequately paid teachers for the instruction of all children from the age of 7 until they were confirmed. This did not apply to children who attended private schools. However, it was considered too expensive to provide the same kind of educational opportunities for children in the more rural sectors. But in 1860, after studying the Scottish system, a new law was passed requiring the construction of a new school building wherever at least 30 children needed to be educated. The reading material in the primary schools included geography, nature, and science. Secondary education was primarily an urban phenomenon at the time, and the middle schools were instituted toward the end of the 1800s in order to provide students with a springboard for matriculation at the gymnasium. These schools were based on the German model.

A public school law was passed in 1889. It ended the control of the parish clergy and bishops on the schools. Also, the influence of folk high schools helped to create changes in the curriculum so that the public elementary school (folkskole) commenced to become available for Norwegians from every socio-economic background. These schools became closely allied with the secondary schools which provided Norway with a very highly integrated school system for that time in history.

The 1918 election marked the beginning of a period of increasing influence of the Norwegian Labour Party in the Storting. In an 18-year period of time, that party went from 18 seats to 70 seats in 1936. On the other hand, the Conservatives dropped from 50 to 36, and the Leftists from 54 to 23. The Labour Party actually maintained its strength in the Storting until 1972.

Also, during the late 1930s, King Haakon VII became concerned that the resignation of Britain's Anthony Eden in 1938 was a signal that the situation in Europe was about to unravel completely. He was particularly upset that Neville Chamberlain had attempted a reconciliation with Benito Mussolini of Italy. The Chamberlain cabinet had been hoping that Italy could be separated from Germany which possibly could have prevented the incorporation of Austria into the greater Germany. This resulted in an aborted effort to create a pro-British attitude among the Italian power structure. This would have required the recognition of Benito Mussolini's conquest of Ethiopia. However, King Haakon did not believe in any sort of recognition of rights obtained by force, which was what happened in Ethiopia.

The Germans occupied Norway between 1940 and 1945 because of Norway's close ties with Britain. One of the primary reasons for the German occupation was the refusal of the Norwegian people to repudiate the British government. However, Norway was able to resist the German invasions for two months, which was enough time for the Norwegian king to sail to London on a British warship along with the cabinet. Also, the gold reserve of the Banks of Norway was saved and sent to Britain.

After they failed to capture Norway's legal government, the Germans made use of Nazi turncoats. During the war, the Norwegian resistance movement became quite strong and proved to be a significant deterrent to the German occupation army. The Norwegian people withstood concentration camps, torture, execution, and terror. When liberation occurred in 1945, King Haakon VII and the exiled cabinet returned to Norway.

After the post-World War II elections of 1943, the Labor Party of Norway came into power, maintaining its leadership. The party stayed in power for a period of twenty years. Only one minister lost his post because of actions by the Norwegian Storting. One result of the war was that it helped to strengthen Norway's spirit of unity and solidarity. This national attitude helped to speed Norway's recovery. In fact, the post-war recovery was so fast that by 1947 the gross national product was the same as it was before the war. Also, the standard of living reached the same pre-war levels by 1947.

While Norway had been somewhat reluctant to enter the League of Nations after World War I, the nation was a full participant in the 1946 San Francisco Conference which led to the formation of the United Nations. In fact, the Norwegian, Trygve Lie, became the first secretary general in the country. Norway also became a member of the North Atlantic Treaty Organization (NATO). In the full membership of fifteen states, Norway ranked twelfth in population but fifth in territorial size. Moreover, except for Turkey, it was the only NATO member which was contiguous to the USSR. Even though the defense interests of the Norwegian people were represented through NATO, they also believed that the United Nations was the type of institution which should be given the country's full support.

The economic policies of the Norwegian Labor Government have subjected private enterprise to public control. But economic recovery occurred rapidly during the first two years after World War II. By the late 1950s, the annual volume of industrial production had increased to a level which was nearly three times greater than it had been in the late 1930s. Labor's largest employers were in iron, metal, and food processing. Then enterprises were closely followed by chemical plants, pulp, paper, and textiles. By this time, the country's exports were flourishing because of the abundant supplies of timber, winter power resources, and minerals. These three resources historically have accounted for about 20 percent of Norway's industrial jobs and 25 percent of all industrial production.

Fishing, whaling, and shipping are still some of the main sources of Norway's vibrant economy. About 70,000 people are employed in the fishing industry. The annual average tonnage of fish caught doubled by the late 1950s. However, Norway's whaling industry declined in the next four decades, largely because of pressure from the United Nations due to the world's diminishing whale population. But the Japanese still failed to heed the whale-catch limitation mandates of the U.N. along with Russia. The processing of whale oil, once a main Norwegian industry, practically disappeared during that time.

By the end of 1962, only 0.03 percent of the Norwegian people were without electricity, making them the world's largest consumers of electricity on a per-capita basis. One major reason for the stable Norwegian economy from the late 1940s to the present has been the availability of cheap energy. This phenomenon has also made it possible for even the simplest Norwegian home to have access to cheap electricity.

After World War II, the Norwegian system of education experienced a number of major changes. By 1959, the maximum hours of instruction for the rural schools became equal to the number of hours required in the urban sectors. Moreover, the Norwegian school system, under the direction of the Ministry of Education, became coordinated so that the various stages of schooling from the elementary level to the highest level of instruction followed a national progression in all types of education. The compulsory ages of attendance were from 7 to 16 years. Also during this time, increasing numbers of Norwegian students commenced attending the ''gymnasier,'' whose courses qualified them for admission to the university.

Because of the burgeoning interest in higher education, the Norwegian Storting approved funding for a second university at Bergen, which quickly acquired a student body of 2,000 by 1965, and has been growing steadily ever since. The Technical High School in Trondheim doubled the number of students from 1946–1947 to 1965. A third university was then constructed at Trondheim along with a university at Tromso to meet the needs of students in the far-north regions.

Interest-free loans have been available from the Norwegian government for students who wished to attend college. Many of these loans were sought for the acquisition of vocational degrees, thus making it easier to repay the loans. But a substantial number of young Norwegians also took degrees in sociology, psychology, and political science, which seems to verify that an egalitarian spirit is still prevalent in the country.

The work of local education leaders has been augmented by five-member school management committees which helped to make educational decisions at the local level. Three of the five members were elected by the parents of students, and the students were able to participate in various sorts of decision making themselves. At the university level, the students now have the right to make certain decisions about the curricula and various sorts of discipline issues.

STRUCTURE OF THE SYSTEM

Presently, Norway has one of the world's most vigorous economies. Compared to other countries, their Storting has not had to grapple with many economic problems. Indeed, the stable economy has made it possible for Norway to fund its educational institutions so that all Norwegian children are entitled to an excellent free public education.

The country is able to provide this exemplary level of education to all children because of its high level of taxation. But in addition to the excellent educational system, the country also enjoys one of the world's leading health care institutions. The high level of health care is also attributable to the taxation levels which are much higher than the levels found in other countries, such as the United States. But the positive byproduct of the high tax base which funds these and other important social programs is that Norway has a powerful middle class and almost no poverty or extreme wealth. The ultimate payoff is that Norwegian students are among the world's top achievers in school, and the country enjoys one of the lowest infant mortality rate of all countries. This compares favorably to such countries as Mexico and the United States, which have been either unable or unwilling to create an adequate tax base to provide the kinds of social programs which would vastly reduce poverty and inadequate health care as well as restricting excessive wealth.

The Norwegian educational system is handled by the Ministry of Church and Education. The nation's teachers are highly respected by both students and parents, and there appears to be a high level of respect for students by the nation's teachers. There is a prevailing philosophy in the country that teachers have a responsibility to teach and not to discipline students. This appears to have created a kind of "self-fulfilling prophecy" because discipline problems in Norwegian schools are practically nonexistent. Indeed, there are no rude comments to teachers, no trash thrown on the floor, nor are there any fights among the students.

Norwegian schools also try to have a bare minimum of school rules. There is very little restriction of movement. If students have no class, they can go where they wish to study. They may even go home. If they are late for class, they are not punished but they are responsible for the material they may have missed.

The Norwegian high schools are generally constructed to house about 450 students. Of course, this is more expensive to operate compared to the large high schools, such as those in places like the urban areas of the United States where some high schools house 3,000 students or more. Norwegian high schools have ten minutes between classes, which gives students a chance to relax and be ready for the next class. Also, teachers tend not to have their own rooms, which usually means that the classrooms lack any sort of stimulating room environment.

In Norway, students take the same courses in given areas of instruction. This is partly because of the rigid examination system in the country. In all Norwegian schools, students and teachers eat lunch at the same time. Teachers eat in a "teachers' room" which is of ample size to accommodate the entire staff. During the lunch period, announcements are made, brief meetings are sometimes held, and ideas can be shared.

Norwegian students also spend a great deal of time in writing activities, and the students are highly fluent in the reading and writing of Norwegian, as well as English. Interestingly, no multiple-choice tests are given in Norway in the social sciences and humanities; only essay tests are used.

In general, the elementary schools adhere to the same educational philosophy of the high schools. The school day and the school year are about the same length. There seems to be a prevailing philosophy among educators that students do not learn how to live in a democratic society if the school system in which they were educated is autocratic in nature. Therefore, the schools try to emulate the democratic way of life enjoyed by Norwegians.

While the Ministry of Church and Education establishes the educational system's basic educational guidelines, many of the key decisions are made at the local level. But the local education leaders are able to make many major decisions which have a profound effect on the quality of education which is provided in the local community.

MULTICULTURAL EDUCATION EFFORTS

The multicultural education efforts in Norway are primarily integrated in the general school program with some specialized courses for migrant students. While the Ministry of Church and Education has no specific unit which is responsible for multicultural education, advisors are responsible for migrant education at various levels. In 1991, there was funding equivalent to $52.5 million for the teaching of migrants.

A recent phenomenon for Norway's schools has been the new influx of immigrants from different parts of the globe. Now, the Norwegian microcultures consist of Pakistani/Hindu, Vietnamese, Latin-American, Iranian, African (Ethiopian and others), and North American/European. In order to meet the needs of such students, a number of special programs have been put in place. One study done at the University of Oslo attempted to examine linguistic minority (LM) children's understanding of the language used by a teacher who was responsible for the schooling of LM and Norwegian children. The results of this study showed that LM children had major comprehension problems even though they were born in Norway and received their education in Norwegian schools. This study serves to verify a number of other conclusions, e.g., that it takes several generations before a second language can be woven into an existing culture to the extent that a level of fluency in the second language reaches the same level of competence as the original mother tongue.

Efforts to provide a more effective education for immigrant children who arrived in Norway during the 1960s, 1970s, and 1980s have been described by several educators. A cooperative project among the Scandinavian countries of Sweden, Finland, Denmark, and Norway stressed the creation of definitive education policies for refugees and immigrants. The specific program elements related to minority language, culture, and group development. It is expected that the minority populations in Norway will increase substantially in the coming years. One nagging issue concerning the education of migrant children has related to the type of special preparation their teachers need. Of particular concern has been the issue of preparing Norwegian teachers for working with Muslim children. In general, it has been found that Norwegian teachers have sometimes had a lack of sensitivity to the problem, a lack of materials and support structure, and, most importantly, a lack of information and an understanding of the nation's new microcultures.

These and other multicultural problems related to the Norwegian school system have become major topics of conversation throughout Norway. Of major concern has been the issue of instruction in the mother tongue with comparison instructional sequences in Norwegian as a second language (NSL). Similar problems have been argued in countries such as Brazil, Australia, and the United States, but the problem has surfaced more recently in Norway and it has become a major topic of concern in recent times. One faction tends to believe in "total immersion" (sink or swim in Norwegian), while the other group worries that if bilingual education programs are not present, some children may be "at risk."

No special course work in multicultural education is required in Norway. However, special studies and extra training for mother-tongue teachers were deemed to be desirable according to the Senior Executive Officer in the Ministry of Church and Education. Cultural pluralism is stressed in the curriculum of Norwegian schools, and Norwegian is the primary language of instruction. All children attend racially integrated schools and racial segregation is not allowed. The history of indigenous people is stressed throughout the curriculum. Curriculum materials and textbooks are evaluated for racist and sexist content by the Ministry of Church and Education along with the Ministry of Cultural and Scientific Affairs.

SUMMARY

Perhaps the most fascinating issue regarding Norway's multicultural education efforts has related to the recent influx of immigrants. Throughout the history of the nation, Norway has been primarily a monocultural society—until recently. While the educational system has done an excellent job of meeting the needs of the nation's school children, a new controversy seems to center around the issue of language and how it relates to an adequate education. Given the increase in the number of microcultures in Norway, it would appear that strong multi-cultural education programs need to be put in place.

But Norway's trump card may be the country's willingness to tax itself in order to provide an effective level of social services, particularly in the area of education. This basic concept, coupled with the country's egalitarian spirit, seems to have helped Norway to create successful social programs which can be envied the world over.

REFERENCES

Brown, Larry. "Hunger in the U.S." *Scientific American* (February 1987).

Busskohl, Tordis. This information is based on conversations with Busskohl, a prominent educator of pre-school children in Norway and the United States. Spokane, WA, 1994.

Derry, T.K. *A History of Modern Norway.* Oxford: Clarendon Press, 1973.

Derry, T.K. *A History of Scandinavia.* Minneapolis: University of Minnesota Press, 1919.

Furre, B. "Norske Historie." In T.K. Derry, *A History of Modern Norway.* Oxford: Clarendon Press, 1973.

Grert, Tim. *Haakon VII of Norway.* New York: Hippocrene Books, 1983.

Johnson, Kristi-Planck. *The Nordic Council and Immigrant Education Policy.* Oslo: EDRS Price, 1989.

Koht, H. "In Place of Almueskole; School for the Common Person." In T.K. Derry, *A History of Modern Norway.* Oxford: Clarendon Press, 1973.

Larsen, Karen. *A History of Norway.* Princeton, NJ: Princeton University Press, 1948.

Lie, Suzanna. "Linguistic Minority Children's Comprehension of Language in the Class-room and Teachers' Adjustment to Their Pupils' Performance: A Norwegian Case Study." *Journal of Multilingual and Multicultural Development,* Vol 12, No. 5 (1991).

Mitchell, Bruce and Salsbury, Robert. *An International Survey of Multicultural Education.* Cheney, WA: Western States Consulting and Evaluation Services, 1991. (See Appendix.)

Neilsen, Jorgen S. "The Training of Teachers of the Children of Migrant Workers: Cultural Values and Education in a Multicultural Society." Report of the European Teachers 13th Seminar, Federal Republic of Germany, 1981.

Nelson, Murray. "Learning from and in Norwegian High Schools." *Social Education,* Vol. 55, No. 5 (September 1991), p. 294.

Schluter, Ragnhild. "The Immigrant Project, 1980–1981." *European Journal of Teacher Education,* Vol. 9, No. 2 (1986), pp. 153–168.

Wuorinen, John H. *Scandinavia.* Englewood Cliffs, NJ: Prentice-Hall, 1965.

32

The Philippines

HISTORY OF THE SYSTEM

The Philippines have very little recorded history prior to the arrival of foreigners. When Magellan made his global voyage in 1521, there was no central government and no sense of national identity. The country's history of foreign involvement created a polycultural set of influences due to the interaction of the Chinese, Muslims, Malays, Arab traders, and the Spanish.

The Spaniards were interested in the Philippines because the country served as a stopping point on the way to China and the New World. Chinese silk was transported by Spanish galleons to Madrid for about two and a half centuries. In many ways, the Philippines were considered to be a subcolony of the Spanish empire in Mexico, since most of the connections between the Philippines and Spain were via Mexico.

The Philippines' governor was also the captain-general of the country, as well as vice patron of the Roman Catholic Church. In addition, he was the king's own representative. But the tenure of the governor tended to be rather insecure, and the longevity of the term of office depended on the whims of the monarch. The governor was also dependent upon the friars. Actually, governors tended to think their tenure in office would be brief; but they also expected to return home to Spain as rich men. As a result, they rarely attempted to reform the colony in any way. The governorship was a patronage position for the king, and the expectations were that the governor should receive a substantial profit. In general, this practice seems to have been quite readily accepted as long as he did not plunder too badly.

During 1762, the British occupied Manila. This act occurred as a result of Spain's alliance with France against the English. But while Manila was captured in short order, Don Simon de Anda escaped to the interior of the country. He renounced the surrender and organized an effective resistance which limited the presence of the British to the Manila bay area. Even though they returned the land to the Spanish two years later, the British sacked Manila, seized the Santisma Trinidad (a galleon carrying about three million pesos), seized the ships in the harbor, and left with all the bullion they could get.

The lucrative galleon trade finally ended with the collapse of Spanish rule in Latin America. Many South American Spaniards made their way to Manila. In that country, they encountered an area which was becoming quite pluralistic because of the interaction of Chinese and Spanish mestizos, Caucasian Creoles born in Mexico or Peru, Spanish Filipinos, and native Filipinos. Some of the earliest ethnic residents were the Negritos, a group of aboriginal people. Next came the Malays, who gradually created the lowland peasant culture. Filipinos who resided in the mountains tended to be migrant slash-and-burn farmers. Lowland dwellers often were rice farmers or fishermen.

During the nineteenth century, the Philippines developed an agricultural export colony. Many non-Spanish merchants came from the large banking and trading countries of the United States, China, and Europe. But Spanish control of the Philippines tended to be repressive and there were 50 governors-general between 1835 and 1898.

On the morning of May 1, 1898, Commodore George Dewey sailed into Manila Bay and destroyed the Spanish fleet. During August of the same year, American land forces captured Manila, thus ending the reign of the Spaniards which had existed for more than 300 years. Finally, by formal treaty, the Philippine Archipelago became a domestic territory of the United States. In the Diamond Rings Case (183 U.S. 176), the United States Supreme Court rendered the following decision.

By the 3rd Article of the treaty Spain ceded to the United States "The archipelago known as the Philippine Islands," and the United States agreed to pay Spain the sum of $20,000,000 within three months. The treaty was ratified; Congress appropriated the money; and the ratification was proclaimed. The treaty-making power, the executive power, the legislative power, concurred in the completion of the transaction.

The Philippines thereby ceased, in the language of the treaty, "to be Spanish." Ceasing to be Spanish, they ceased to be foreign country. They came under the complete and absolute sovereignty and dominion of the United States, and so became a territory of the United States over which civil government could be established. The result was the same, although there was no stipulation that the native inhabitants should be incorporated into the body politic, and none securing to them the right to choose their nationality. Their allegiance became due to the United States, and they became entitled to its protection.

As viewed by the Filipinos, their relationship with the United States tended to be that of two allies joined in a common struggle with Spain. The Filipinos supplied crucial intelligence, informing the Americans that there were no mines or torpedoes which could damage Dewey's fleet. Aguinaldo's 12,000-man force engaged the Spanish forces, keeping them at bay until the U.S. forces arrived.

Following Dewey's victory, Manila's bay was filled with warships from Germany, Japan, France, and Britain. In fact, the Germans, with a fleet of eight ships, were interested in possible colonial acquisitions themselves, ultimately coming close to a confrontation with the United States.

On June 12, 1898, a declaration of independence was announced. It was modeled after the U.S. Declaration of Independence. A revolutionary congress was convened at Malalos on January 23, 1899.

The Treaty of Paris granted control of the Philippines to the United States and gave Guam and Puerto Rico to the United States along with the Philippines. Cuba was granted its independence. However, during February 1899, hostilities between the United States and the Philippines broke out when two United States privates on a patrol killed three Filipino soldiers near Manila. The event precipitated a war which lasted for two years.

In 1899, President McKinley appointed the first Philippine commission to study the situation on the islands and to make recommendations. The gist of the report findings stipulated that while the Filipinos were interested in acquiring their independence, they were not ready for it to happen. A second Philippine commission, headed by William Howard Taft, helped draw up a judicial system, establish a Supreme Court, and organize a civil service. The 1901 municipal code provided for presidents to be elected by the populace and, from the outset, the primary consideration was when the Philippines would be ready for self rule.

Led by a new group of nonradical politicians, the Nationalistic Party dominated the country's political scene until after World War II. By 1916, the Nationalistic Party won all but 1 senate seat and 83 out of 90 seats in the House. During this period of time, the Filipinos established a system of public education. The Spanish had exhibited relatively little interest in spending much money on education. The Americans were instrumental in developing a system of education which would help the country establish a better sense of democracy. The instruction was in English because the Americans believed that utilizing the language of the United States would help to spread American ideals.

This period of American control lasted until the Japanese attack in 1941. General Douglas MacArthur evacuated Manila and declared it an open city. With the Japanese takeover in January 1946, many of the pre-war politicians collaborated with the Japanese forces which occupied the area. However, the Filipinos viewed the Japanese as marauders and Filipine guerrillas had the sympathy of most of the population. By the time the Japanese were defeated in 1945, many of the people were homeless and many were starving. The transportation system was nearly inoperable, and the medical and sanitation facilities were practically destroyed.

By July 4, 1976, Manuel Roxas had become the president of a newly independent republic of the Philippines. For about 25 years, the nation was in a rebuilding process. However, during the election of 1965, Nacionalista Party candidate Ferdinand Marcos won the presidency, and after being reelected in 1969, declared martial law in 1972. He argued that martial law was necessary for creating a "New Society." But Marcos ruled by dividing his enemies. He cleverly played one clan against the other and managed to keep his opposition from establishing a united front. His strategy was successful until 1986 when Corazon Aquino won a chaotic election which was sullied by fraud, intimidation, ballot box stuffing, and improper tabulating. The new government was actually a coalition because it tended to draw support from all parts of the political spectrum. The Philippine middle class supported her quite well and viewed her as a democratic alternative to Marcos. Many leftists hoped that she would be able to reform the country's political system.

But while Marcos rode a wave of popularity, like most politicians, Aquino was unable to deliver on many of her campaign promises. The same problems that had baffled Marcos quickly resurfaced and Aquino's popularity reached an all-time low in 1991. Protesters accused her of failing to keep her promise to ease poverty, eliminate corruption, and increase the level of democracy. However, she was able to start the healing process, in spite of having to address the problems of corruption and inefficiency. Ironically, the Commission on Good Government, which Aquino established in order to recover the assets stolen by the Marcos family, has also been accused of corruption.

STRUCTURE OF THE SYSTEM

The nation's governmental structure is divided into three parts: the judicial, executive, and legislative branches. The judicial branch includes the Supreme Court and the Sandiganbayan and Court of Tax Appeals which are beneath the Philippine Supreme Court. The Sandiganbayan tries all government employees and officers charged with violating the country's Anti-Graft and Corrupt Practices Act. The Supreme Court includes the chief justice and fourteen associate justices. They are appointed by the president from a list of three, provided by the country's bar association. Supreme Court justices must be at least 40 years old when they are appointed, and they must retire by age 70.

Under Article Six of the 1987 constitution, the presidential system was restored with several changes. Elected by a vote of the people, a president serves for six years with no reelection options. In order to run for office, a candidate must be at least 40, a natural-born citizen, and have lived in the Philippines for the ten years immediately preceding the election. The president controls all executive bureaus and offices, and sees to it that all laws are executed faithfully. The Philippine constitution contains a number of key clauses which are in place to ensure that there will be no abuses like those experienced during the Marcos years.

The Philippine constitution established a 24-seat senate and a house of representatives which consists of 200 elected representatives, and 50 which can be appointed by the president. Senators serve for six years and can be reelected once. They must be at least 35 years of age. They must be native-born Filipinos. The representatives serve three-year terms and cannot be in office for more than three consecutive terms. They must be at least 25 years old in order to run for office.

All education in the country is governed by the Department of Education, Culture, and Sports, which has direct supervision over public schools, and sets mandatory policies for the country's private schools as well. The educational system offers six years of elementary education and four years of secondary schooling. Children start school at the age of seven. By 1991, a free public school elementary education was being provided for about 96 percent of that age group. The high school enrollment rate was about 56 percent.

Filipinos look upon education with great regard. The people tend to view schooling as a necessary vehicle for upward mobility. The influences of the United States has tended to contribute to a belief in the validity of a free public education for the masses as a vehicle which is a prerequisite for maintaining a workable and viable democratic society. However, the country has had many difficult educational problems to address. For example, during the 1960s and 1990s, the country worried about the large number of students who finished college and then were unable to find a suitable job.

The Philippine interest in schools escalated after World War II. By 1965, the country had over 168,000 teachers and a teacher-pupil ratio of about 34:1. In 1962, there were over 28,000 secondary teachers with a teacher-pupil ratio of about 30:1.

Within the Philippine Department of Education, Culture, and Sports is a branch of the Education Ministry which has attempted to promote special programs for gifted/talented education. National funding has been made available for such special programs around the world. However, most of them have existed in the urban sectors of the country, and the Philippines has been forced to deal with the problem of securing the services of teachers with special expertise in the schooling of gifted/talented students. Nonetheless, the country has been viewed as a world leader among developing countries which have attempted to craft special programs for bright youngsters.

It can be said that in the Philippines, the emphasis in the public sector education program has been at the primary level. Only 5 percent of all the elementary schools in the country are private compared to 79 percent of the secondary schools and 83 percent of the colleges and universities. Thus, it can be seen that the Philippines, like other developing countries, have tended to provide solid public school programs for young children, but have been unable to craft suitable programs in the public sector due to severe financial limitations.

Research data have shown statistically significant correlations between per-capita income and the intellectual performance of young students. There is also a correlation between the per-capita income of students and their school performance. After reviewing the literature on private education, it can be seen that, similarly to other countries around the world, developing nations quite often are hard pressed to provide educational opportunities beyond the primary level.

During recent years, vocational education programs have received greater attention than ever before. Such programs have proven to be quite popular in the Philippines and other third world countries because they sometimes are viewed as a means of breaking away from the primary school mentality of many public school teachers in the Philippines.

MULTICULTURAL EDUCATION EFFORTS

The Philippines have multicultural education programs in both the schools and nonschool activities. The Office of the Deputy Minister for Higher Education is responsible for multicultural education, but there has been no national funding for such enterprises.

Ethnic groups in the country include Catholics, Muslims, Buddhists, Protestants, Animists, Chinese, Mestizos, and native Filipinos. Perhaps the most significant social group in the Philippines is the racially mixed community of Mestizos. In the Philippines, the term refers primarily to mixed-blood Filipinos and Spanish Filipinos. Roman Catholicism has been a key factor in this issue and other multicultural issues around the country. Mestizos helped in the development of the sugar industry and were important in developing indigo for export. Moreover, they moved into rice production, when they vacated the urban areas and moved into the Island of the Negro.

Chinese-Filipinos have always represented a rather small percentage of the country's population. As in other countries such as the United States, the Chinese have been seen as a source of cheap labor. In the beginning, most of the Chinese immigrants were men. However, by the 1990s, the gender ratios were about even. In some cases, the Chinese-Filipino Mestizos tended to adapt the cultural values of the Filipinos, giving up their Chinese heritage in many cases. However, the Chinese tended to view their culture as superior and they attempted to maintain it by establishing a separate school system which relied on a separate language of instruction. Much of the curriculum focused on Chinese literature and history.

This attitude of many Chinese-Filipinos possibly can be traced to thousands of years of Confucian teaching which stresses that education exists for the improvement of society through the process of helping people to become better citizens. A second purpose of education is to create peace and prosperity as well as moral training.

Christian Malays (also known as the Lowland Christians) make up about 91 percent of the nation's population. This large group can be divided into a number of regional subpopulations. The Tagalogs tend to be the most visible native Filipino group because of their location in metropolitan Manila and adjacent provinces which surround the immediate area. In addition to the indigent Tagalogs are the Cebuanos, whose language is dominant in the Visayan Island area; the Ilocanos, who had a reputation for being willing migrants; the Ilongos; the Bicolanos; the Waray-Warays from eastern Leyte; and the Pampangans of the central Luzon Plain and the Pampanga Province. When these groups immigrated to the city, they tended to band together in enclaves which housed people who were primarily Lowland Christians.

While differing from most Filipinos, the Muslims were one of the key minority microcultures in the Philippines. After independence, the Philippine government decided that a specialized agency was needed for dealing with the Muslim minority and an Office of Muslim Affairs and Cultural Communities was created. Filipino nationalists envisioned a country in which Muslims would be assimilated into the dominant culture.

The two official languages of instruction in the schools are Filipino and English, but the primary mode of instruction in the schools is English. However, as previously stated, Chinese schools tend to use the native Mandarin language, although children also are taught English. In the country's public schools, there are some supplemental language programs, particularly those which are crafted for indigenous children who have difficulty with the language of instruction. An international school has special programs for teaching English to the children of foreigners, and a Summer Institute of Linguistics helps the tribal schools' student populations to become more fluent in their native languages. It is feared that if such children lose their native language, they may lose their culture also.

Schools in the Philippines are racially and culturally integrated for the most part. Curriculum guides include information which helps teachers create lesson plans which assist students in learning to understand and value the nation's microcultures. Curriculum materials, library holdings, and textbooks are evaluated by the Ministry of Education in order to verify that all teaching materials are free of racist and sexual content.

The authors' study of worldwide multicultural education efforts concluded that Filipino educators were concerned about negative influences from Western "cultures." Some of these influences were deemed to be sexual permissiveness and a less than adequate appreciation of cultural heritage. Responses to the question of what improvements should be made to the nation's multicultural education efforts indicated that the schools should be more Filipino oriented.

One major educational argument in the Philippines addresses the issue of the language of instruction in the schools. When the Americans became involved in the Philippines, they brought the English language along with them. But presently, the country is in the midst of an argument over language usage. Bienvenido Lumbara is one of the prime movers of a national effort to make English a second language. Since 1974, the country has had a bilingual education law operating. (Of special interest is that this law was passed during the same year as the famous *Lau v. Nichols* Supreme Court Decision in the United States.) But since 1974, studies in the country have tended to show that the English skills of Filipino students have suffered except in the elite private schools. Some college instructors have conducted their classes in a hybrid form of "Taglish." While only 1% of the population uses English at home, 37% speak Talagog, 51% understand English, and 41% said they understand Cebuano.

SUMMARY

The Filipino educational system has addressed many of the multicultural problems which have plagued many other countries the world over. Perhaps the most interesting controversy centers around the issue of language usage. Similar to the situation in other countries such as Ghana, the people speak languages other than their national language (English) when they are home or in other informal settings.

Being a pluralistic society, it would seem that more effort might be given to multicultural education programs which helped young students learn to appreciate and understand all of the country's microcultures. But the country is not financially able to provide such programs, and the current effort tends to focus most heavily on the provision of basic education programs for all students.

REFERENCES

Dolan, Ronald E. (Ed.). *Philippines: A Country Study.* Washington, DC: Department of the Army, 1993.

Kee, Francis Wong Hoy. *Comparative Studies in Southeastern Asian Education.* Singapore: Heinemann Educational Books, 1973.

Mitchell, Bruce and Salsbury, Robert. *An International Survey of Multicultural Education.* Cheney, WA: Western States Consulting and Evaluation Services, 1991. (See Appendix.)

Porter, Ed. "Foreign Involvement in China's Colleges and Universities." *International Journal of Intercultural Relations,* Vol. 11, No. 4 (1987), pp. 369–370.

Scott, Margaret. "Confusion of Tongues." *Far Eastern Economic Review* (July 6, 1989), pp. 44–46.

Steinberg, Joseph. *The Philippines: A Singular and a Plural Place.* Boulder, CO: Westview Press, 1990.

UNESCO. *Bulletin of the UNESCO Regional Office for Education in the Asian Region,* Vols. 1, 2, 1965.

Williams, B.R. *The United States and the Philippines.* Garden City, NY: Doubleday & Co., 1925.

Williams, W.G. and Mitchell, B. *From Afghanistan to Zimbabwe: Gifted Education Efforts in the World Community.* New York: Peter Lang Inc., 1989.

33

Poland

HISTORY OF THE SYSTEM

Well over a thousand years ago, the Polish tribes of the Vistula and Oder basins between the Carpathians and the Baltic were united by Mieszko, one of the first major rulers of the Piast dynasty, into one nation. Mieszko made Poland a Catholic nation after he was baptized in A.D. 966. He found his country squeezed by two new powers, and ended up siding with the Latin west under the protection of the Papacy.

By 1569, a Polish-Lithuanian union was consummated which resulted in common rulers who were jointly elected. Their diets were combined into one legislative body which had supreme authority. This resulted in approximately one-tenth of the population of this Commonwealth enjoying certain freedoms at a time when the rest of Europe tended to be ruled by absolute governments.

During 1684, under the influence of John Sobieski, a Polish–Austria alliance was expanded to include the Papal states and Venice. But the strength of this alliance gradually waned with the death of Sobieski in 1696. Just one year later, hard times would befall the country due to interference by Germany and Russia, the country's next-door neighbors.

After a period of turmoil and partitioning, Poland was partially restored as a nation in 1807 as a result of the Napoleonic Wars. However, it was not until the end of World War I that Poland became reunited into a country, with its boundaries becoming more or less stabilized after the end of World War II. The Yalta Conference in 1945 resulted in a new provisional government of national unity. However, a number of Polish leaders were in exile, and many of them did not believe the Yalta agreement was in the country's best interests. Later, a new coalition government was formed July 5, 1945, with both Britain and the United States agreeing to the new settlement.

After the long period of warfare ended, Poland moved into a transformation era which saw the country become a Soviet satellite, with the Church being the last center of independence for the country. Wladyslaw Gomulka assumed leadership of the Polish Party in 1956 when he became the First Secretary. Nikita Khrushchev of the USSR allowed Gomulka to maintain his leadership after extracting promises from him that Poland would remain communist and back the Soviet alliance with other Eastern Bloc nations.

The Polish government at that time was modeled after that of the Soviets. The Russians introduced a form of government to Poland which was primarily Soviet in form, but Polish in practice. It was highly centralized, with all the power extending from the central administration which included the Council of State and the Council of Ministers. Control of the country emanated from Warsaw. The strongest guiding force was the Politburo of Poland's United Workers' Party.

Poland's close ties with the USSR left a lasting impression on the Polish People's Republic, and many of the Stalinist innovations had a strong effect on the country for many years. In 1952, the Constitution of the People's Republic was inaugurated. It guaranteed civil liberties, universal suffrage, parliamentary government, and a Council of Ministries which answered to the Assembly. However, the government was still dominated by the Soviets. Due to the Cold War and the arms race with the United States, the Polish army expanded to a force of 400,000 men.

The period of *DARNOSC* (the *Solidarity* movement) would see the involvement of worker activists, intellectual advisers, students, Catholics, peasants, and old-age pensioners. Beginning in 1980, solidarity was involved with a number of disputes, conflicts, and various reform projects. This new self-governing trade union was headed by Lech Walesa. A First National Congress for Solidarity was convened in Gdansk during 1981. At this time, the movement's statutes and resolutions were adapted. With nearly ten million members, most of the families in Poland were involved in the movement. As a nonviolent movement, it had no weapons for its defense against an attack by communist security forces which were armed with tanks and guns.

The successes of the Solidarity movement helped to lay the groundwork for the breakup of the communist bloc, and by the mid-1980s, it was clear that the days of socialism were numbered as a new social order commenced to take form.

Like other former communist bloc countries, Poland has had to make major economic changes in a move from the Soviet model of state control of the country's means of production. Unlike many of the former members, Poland has served as a flagship (or model) for successful transition to a market economy. Having gone through a gradual breakup of the old Soviet-backed regime, again, under the heroic leadership of the Solidarity movement, Poland entered this dramatic period of change with both a positive attitude expressed by the people, and with a positive image in the eyes of the democratic nations of the world. As a result, Poland has received both monetary and consultant aid from the major industrial powers and appears to be making a successful transition.

STRUCTURE OF THE SYSTEM

Since its very beginnings as a nation, Poland has been forced to deal with an extremely difficult education problem, for there were five different educational traditions—the result of former partitioning. First, there was a strong tradition of independent Poland prior to the days of partitioning. Second, there were the educational systems found in the countries which were responsible for the partitioning (Austria, Prussia, and Russia); this occurred between 1795 and 1918. The final educational tradition was the private, and even clandestine, education which many Polish people received following 1795. The educational system was reformed during the second half of the eighteenth century. In fact, the National Commission of Education which was developed in 1773 resulted in the creation of the first National Commission of Education in the world. At that time, the country's educational system created a seven-year primary school which was free. Also, the Austrian system of eight-year gymnasia made it possible for young people to have access to a college education. Entrance examinations were required, along with at least four years of elementary education.

Education during World War II can best be described as tenuous. Underground elementary schools met the needs of approximately 1.5 million students during that period of time. Certain subjects such as geography and history were formally forbidden but provided in a clandestine fashion. Presses were illegal, but they still managed to print forbidden textbooks. Nazi plans to lower the intellectual performance of Polish children were at least partially thwarted by the creation of a Department of Education and Culture by the Polish Secret Administration.

Faced with a shortage of technical workers during the war, particularly during the latter stages, the Nazis were forced to allow technical schools to function. Consequently, there were actually more technical schools in operation during the war than at any other time in the country's history. The technical schools sometimes became centers for underground instruction, and proved to be a valuable training resource for young Polish people whose skills were in great demand after the termination of the war. During this period of time, there were terrible reprisals by the Nazis against the Polish intelligentsia. Polish teacher organizations have claimed that between 20 and 40 percent of their profession were killed during the war. Also, it has been reported that approximately 6,000 medical doctors were murdered during that time.

Perestroika had an enormous effect on the country's educational system, and the changes are still occurring rapidly. Prior to the major changes in the political system, the nation's school system could perhaps be best characterized by its uniformity. All students were required to master the same knowledge, and the schools were heavily influenced by the Marxist-Leninist philosophy. The schools were driven to produce students who would exemplify the values of a classless, egalitarian, and collective society.

Much criticism of the Polish school system has centered around the issue of "overloading." This refers to the practice of requiring teachers to teach an unrealistic amount of information during an inadequate time frame. Moreover, teachers were forced to teach a number of ideological principles. The new changes mandated that teachers must have at least 30 percent of their professional teaching set aside in order to allow for the individualization of instruction and the pursuit of learnings which were not pre-ordained or pre-planned. Meeting the needs of exceptional children (i.e., the talented and gifted students) is the general responsibility of the classroom teacher.

After the collapse of the nation's old political and economic system in 1989, a number of changes occurred in the nation's educational system. Teachers were granted much more autonomy in determining what their course content should be, and they were granted free planning time. This allowed teachers to become more inventive and innovative, but it created problems for history teachers since the existing textbooks were obsolete, making it necessary for them to create their own materials until revised texts could be published.

Poland's relationship between the church and state as it pertained to education became a problem after the dramatic changes of 1989. The role of the Catholic Church in Poland had been suppressed by the Soviets until that time. However, it began to play a more influential role, which has resulted in conflicts regarding the issue of church and state in the country's educational system.

During the 1990–1991 school year, a directive was issued by the Minister of Education which allowed religious instruction to become part of the schools' curriculum if parental approval could be secured. This applied to younger children, but approval of the students themselves had to be secured for older students.

The new educational reforms had a great effect on the literature curriculum in the nation's schools as well. For example, the first year of high school literature utilizes the old and new testaments of the Bible, the Apocalypse of Saint John, the poems of Francois Villon, the "Little Flowers" of Saint Francis, Saint Augustine, Johan Huizinga, Francois Rabelais, Giovanni Boccaccio, Rene Descartes, and Blaise Pascal.

Poland has approximately one-half million teachers, and about one-third belonging to Teachers' Solidarity. The rest of the country's teachers belong to the Polish Teachers' Association. However, a majority of the nation's teachers have not participated in Solidarity, which means that unlike other sectors such as industry, transportation, or communication, there has not been a natural base for the evolutionary changes. In the light of this lack of transitional activity prior to the breakup, changes in the educational system have been even more significant and dramatic.

In the old regimes in countries like Poland, Czechoslovakia, and Hungary, educational programs were totally in line with the Soviet-dictated goal of using the schools to create the model future communist. With the major change in government and guiding philosophy of education brought about by the disintegration of the Communist Bloc, schools have moved from total compliance with the ''party line'' to a form of ideological pluralism. Procedurally, this has included a change in emphasis from Marxist to Christian philosophy, particularly in the ideological/moral dimensions; freedom in the selection of both curriculum and materials; and efforts to restructure both the form and governance of schooling.

MULTICULTURAL EDUCATION EFFORTS

The Polish Ministry of Education is responsible for the education of Polish children. Responses to the authors' questionnaire survey revealed that the country does not have any formal office for multicultural education. The language of instruction in the schools is Polish, but in the schools for ethnic minorities, several mother-tongue languages of instruction are used.

Of interest to the discussion of multicultural education in Polish schools is a Polish policy which mandates that: ''political directives—formulated in laws, acts, and regulations—provide for a stable percentage of students from manual workers' and peasant families in institutions of higher education.'' From the early grades on, the country attempts to identify students with college potential. Current percentages for the different groups enrolled in college are as follows: 31.9% from workers' families; 10.4% from peasant families; 54.5% from the intelligentsia; and 3.2% from other classes.

Poland also has a number of private institutions of higher education with religious affiliations, which are non-Catholic. One example is Warsaw's English Language School (Osrodek Jezyka Angielskiego), sponsored by the Methodist Church and headed by a Methodist minister. Founded in 1921 by American Methodists, it had been operating continuously until the German occupation during World War II. Although it was backed by Methodists, the school was secular in nature and accepted students at the age of fifteen.

SUMMARY

As can be seen, Poland does not seem to have made a concerted effort in multicultural education in the nation's schools. However, one reason may be due to the tremendous turbulence in the country during this century. Because of the breakup of the USSR and the recent problems in eastern Europe, the country has been concentrating its efforts on basic educational reforms.

However, there are some encouraging signs. The nation has rewritten its history books in order to present a less biased picture of Poland's traditions. Also, the educational system has seen fit to provide instruction in the native language of certain minority students. Even though traditional bilingual education programs are not common in the schools, this constitutes an effort to ensure the best education possible for its minority populations.

REFERENCES

Barnett, Clifford R. *Poland: Its People, Its Society, Its Culture.* New Haven, CT: HRAF Press, 1958

Bartnicka, K. "Education in Poland: Past, Present, and Future." *History of Education Quarterly,* Vol. 34, No. 3 (1994), pp. 370–372. (Book Review.)

Committee of Experts. *Edukacja—narodowym autorytetem (Education—A National Priority).* Warszawa: Panstwowe Wydawnictwo Naukowe (Scientific Publishing House of State), 1989.

Davies, Norman. *Heart of Europe: A Short History of Poland.* Oxford: Clarendon Press, 1984.

Eurich, Nell P. *Systems of Higher Education in Twelve Countries.* New York: Praeger, 1981.

Halecki, Oscar (Ed.). *Poland.* New York: Praeger, 1957.

Kozakiewicz, Mikola. "Educational Transformation Initiated by the Polish Perestroika." *Comparative Education Review,* Vol. 36, No. 1 (1992), pp. 91–101.

Program Nauczania: Historia Dla Szkoly Sredniej (Program for Teaching History in High Schools). Warszawa: Ministerstwo Edukacji Narodowej (Ministry of National Education), 1990.

Rust, Val D. "Reforms in East Germany, Czechoslovakia, and Poland." *Phi Delta Kappan,* Vol. 73, No. 5 (1992), p. 389.

Siemaktylikowska, A. "Curriculum Development in Secondary Schools in Poland." *Journal of Curriculum Studies,* Vol. 25, No. 1 (1993), pp. 89–93.

Swick, Thomas. *Unquiet Days: At Home in Poland.* New York: Ticknor & Fields Publishers, 1991.

Szebenyi, Peter. "Change in the Systems of Public Education in East Central Europe." *Comparative Education,* Vol. 28, No. 1 (1992), pp. 19–31.

34

Russia

HISTORY OF THE SYSTEM

Recent Russian history can be traced back to 1812, when Moscow was in flames. The incident which precipitated this was one of the major events occurring during the conflict between the French and Russian-tsarist empires. Five years earlier, Tsar Alexander I had made peace with Napoleon after a number of losses which caused major defeats for Russia. The treaty resulted in a separation of Russia and Prussia, and also contained a promise to abide by Napoleon's Continental System. This treaty (referred to as the Treaty of Tilset) helped give the Russians a free hand in Finland, and Tsar Alexander I overthrew the Swedish occupation forces. Russia then ruled the country for a period of 100 years. So, Finland was part of the Russian Empire until 1917.

However, Tsar Alexander I eventually appointed himself commander-in-chief of the Russian Armies and was finally persuaded by Russia's military leaders to rally the country against its enemies, which included the Turks, Swedes, and ultimately the French. But gradually his popularity waned as he became perceived as a person who betrayed the Russian people when he agreed to the treaty with Napoleon. Many people argued that the treaty disgraced the Russian people.

When Napoleon invaded Asian Russia in 1912, the Russian forces consisted of about 120,000 men, and the French forces had shrunk from about 500,000 to only 130,000. The Russians had a well-developed artillery for that time, and even though historians have not described the first major battle at Borodins as a Russian victory, Napoleon failed to win it. The Russians viewed this as a testament to their courage and the "esprit de corps" of the total country.

When the French left in 1912, Alexander had a major decision to make. Should he pursue the French forces or terminate the hostilities? He was unable to resist the opportunity to capitalize on his victory and attempt to liberate

Europe. Eventually, he negotiated a treaty with the French in which Napoleon was able to maintain his sovereign stature in Elba, and France was able to maintain its 1792 borders. A constitution was created which granted French subjects a number of basic rights.

At the time of the Napoleonic incursions with Russia, the population was about 41 million. At the same time, the population of Great Britain was about 18 million. Thus, Russia had enormous manpower advantages which enhanced its spheres of influence in Europe. Muscovites made up about half of the total population, and the next largest group consisted of the Ukrainians. In addition to the Belorussians ("White Russians") were the Cossacks ("free warriors") who became tough, fierce people descending from Russian ancestors who decided to go to Muscovy or Poland to evade serfdom. Gradually, many of the Cossack empires were converted to military units which became famous for pursuing defeated enemies and for looting.

Russia also had a fairly sizeable group of people who were non-Slavic. This body consisted of the Germanic, Jewish, and Finnish peoples. The Finns included indigent people from Finland and the remainder of some Finnish tribes which originally lived in Muscovy. Also residing in Russia by this time was a substantial number of Mongols who were mostly the remnants of the Tartars who had invaded some of the early Russian settlements. The great proportion of Russians during this time did not live in towns. The population of St. Petersburg was 308,000 and Moscow had about 270,000. Less than 2 percent of the population belonged to the nobility.

Following the death of Alexander in 1825, a great deal of confusion existed in regard to his successor. However, Tsar Nicholas became the country's leader for a period of 30 years, until 1855. Sergei Uvarov, the Minister of Education, initiated a program of "autocracy, orthodoxy, and nationality." In this approach to national leadership, the people were asked to be loyal to the tsar, who had unlimited authority. However, many of these principles were not supported by the population in general, and this led to a great deal of general repression and a suppression of non-Russian groups. The Russian Orthodoxy was the states' main religious body, and the Uniste Church in Ukraine and Belorussia was suppressed during 1839.

The death of Nicholas I led to the leadership of his son, Alexander II, who had a difficult term because of the highly autocratic rule of his father; and while his reforms created a few liberal changes, the leadership style he exhibited was still autocratic. During his tenure, the judiciary became independent in 1864, the serfs were freed in 1861, and the universities received a higher level of autonomy in 1863.

Late in the 1800s, the backward agricultural policies of the country were at least partially responsible for a major famine which resulted in the loss of about one-half million lives in 1891. But the decade of the 1890s eventually was generally profitable for the country due to the efforts of Sergie Witte, the country's finance minister under the regime of Czar Nicholas II. In spite of a depression at the end of the century, Russia's production of iron, steel, coal, and oil tripled during the decade. The rail mileage doubled, making the country second in the world in the number of rail miles; only the United States had a more extensive rail system. One reason for this proliferation of rail mileage was the completion of the trans-Siberian railroad.

Relations between Russia and Japan had reached a new low, but Nicholas was determined to avoid conflict at all possible costs. When it did begin, he dismissed it as a rather insignificant spat. The ''insignificant spat'' was actually a surprise attack by the Japanese at Port Arthur which gave them control of the ocean and provided safe passage of their troops. Finally, after one and one-third years of war, the numerical superiority of the Russian forces eventually resulted in the Treaty of Portsmouth which terminated the hostilities between the two nations.

The 1914 war saw Rasputin installed as a family confidant to Nicholas. Because of his relationship with the wife of Nicholas, Rasputin was able to become installed as an advisor to the empress. Russia was able to turn back an Austrian offensive and eventually they managed to push into eastern Galicia. In general, it was a war during which the Russians, with larger armies, were able to defeat the Austro-Hungarians but experienced terrifying losses against the Germans and/or the combined forces of German-Austrian military units. Near the end of 1916, Russia saved Romania, which had recently entered the conflict. By that time, Russia was thought to have had between four and five million casualties during the various phases of World War I. During 1916, high food prices and very little fuel resulted in a number of strikes in some cities. Even the rural parts of Russia were becoming unsettled. Soldiers became insubordinate. Finally, in an attempt to turn around the situation, Rasputin was murdered by several nobles in December 1916. However, his assassination resulted in virtually no changes. Shortages of food and fuel resulted because of deteriorating rail transport and troops were brought in to terminate these disorders. Eventually, three centuries of Romanov rule were terminated as a result of a virtual disappearance of support for the tsarist regimes.

Russia's involvement in World War I devastated the country. Millions of lives were lost, and the economy was seriously disrupted by the events of the war. Angered by food shortages, hungry citizens, many of whom were on strike, became involved in a number of demonstrations and riots. Workers commenced to take control of their factories, and peasants took their lands away from the state and the church. The Bolsheviks, headed by Vladimir I. Lenin, acquired the country's leadership by capturing the provisional government's cabinet at the Winter Palace headquarters.

After the 1917 Bolshevik revolution, and the victory of the Vladimir Elich Ulyyanov (Lenin) faction, the eventual new economic policy motivated a number of changes in the country's educational system, which always had Marxist-Leninist foundations. Some new concepts included futurism, modernism, and constructivism, all part of cultural experimentation and avant-garde movements.

But the underlying principle of Soviet education was to help perpetuate the welfare of the state. Blomsky, a prominent educational psychologist, argued that education needed to be both social and political. It was also Blomsky's idea to create a labor school which eventually became the Soviet general secondary labor polytechnic.

A nine-year curriculum began in the 1920s. It consisted of elementary and lower secondary school for seven years; a secondary school for nine years; a seven-year factory school; a school for rural youth with variable lengths of time; and a trade school or a four-year vocational/technical school. Curriculum changes occurred in the sciences, arts, and physical education. This emphasis on physical education would eventually help the country to excel in Olympic Games competition following World War II.

In 1929, a ten-year secondary school plan was initiated. It became a national model for Soviet secondary schools until the early 1960s. Also established at this time were more of the young people's organizations, known as Pioneer organizations, which attempted to provide young children with the proper values for communist society.

Joseph Stalin assumed power in 1934, and Marxist-Leninist ideology became the overriding dogmas for Soviet education. During the Stalin era, a number of major changes occurred in Soviet education. Examinations were reintroduced after being abolished in the 1920s during the country's progressive movement. Standardized textbooks were required in the schools. A standardized curriculum was mandated in the nation's elementary and secondary schools. Students were required to wear uniforms to school. Finally new strict levels of classroom discipline were maintained.

After an interruption of educational reforms during the war years, compulsory education was reestablished at the mandated ten-year level as a result of actions taken at the Nineteenth Communist Party Congress in 1952. The ten-year requirement constituted a three-year increase in the previous seven-year stipulation. During the Brezhnev era, beginning in the mid-1960s, the nation decided that students had too many classes and too much homework. The argument was that the curriculum should contain more political indoctrination and a greater emphasis on physical education. During 1968, all boys were required to register for compulsory military service. During the same year, a shortage of skilled and semi-skilled people in the rural areas necessitated a new emphasis on the importance of vocational education programs.

By the 1970s, a new Russian education problem commenced to surface. Many Russian educators became convinced that there was too much rigidity in the system. While Soviet educators were still convinced of the importance of the math/science, a large number of interesting changes occurred during the decade, including creativity development rather than an overreliance on rote memorization; a reexamination of teaching methods and textbooks; and a number of changes in the math curriculum, including the addition of mathematical induction, linear equations, logarithmic and trigonometric functions. The study of physics was revised to include molecular, kinetic, and algebraic analysis. Also, the physics curriculum was revised and included in the grade 6–8 science curriculum.

It is important to note that throughout the history of the Soviet Union, education has been free and available for students of both genders. The country derived many of its philosophical precedents from the work of the famous American educator, John Dewey. One of Dewey's beliefs was that education was a social process; therefore, the school's primary function was to help transform the society through the promotion of socially minded individualism. In fact, Russia's most progressive educator, S.T. Shatsky (1878–1934), harbored many ideas which had their roots in Deweyan philosophy, and these ideas became part of the educational reforms he championed. However, Shatsky was also influenced by Tolstoy who believed that education should exemplify freedom and joy. But he still believed that the Soviet system of education should ensure that Soviet children would grow up to be good Soviet citizens.

The year 1984 saw major changes occur in the Soviet educational system on the "eve of perestroika." Among the major changes in the country's educational system was the lowering of the compulsory starting age to 6, the merger of general and vocational education, making available better provision for working mothers, and reducing class size.

In all aspects of Soviet life, perestroika has created a questioning of all traditional values, including educational practices. In fact, it has involved a great deal of questioning the old values and deciding how they should be altered or replaced. The teachers' newspaper *Uchitel' Skayagazeta* had provided a kind of forum for the country's educators to air their views. During the start of the 1986/1987 school year, a small group of the most famous liberals were invited by the newspaper to a two-day conference to exchange their ideas. The results of the meeting were published in the form of an 18-point education manifesto which was titled *Pedagogy of Cooperation.* It constituted a major challenge to the accepted practice as recommended by the USSR Academy of Pedagogical Sciences. It was considered to be a quite revolutionary document.

Eventually, by the year 1990, the concept of the "Soviet Union" was falling apart. The educational program was becoming more decentralized, and much of the underlying philosophy was being challenged. It was felt by many that Soviet education needed new methods and new relationships which were based on cooperation and trust between teachers, pupils, and parents. This philosophy would in effect replace the old notions of compulsion and a fear of failure. But it should also be noted that since the publication of the 1986 manifesto, Russia's educational community has been in a state of turmoil.

STRUCTURE OF THE SYSTEM

On Christmas Day, 1991, Mikhail Gorbachev, president of the Soviet Union, made a short speech in which he announced the breaking up of the Soviet Union.

It was one of the most significant incidents of the twentieth century because this expression of Marx's utopian notions had lasted for 75 years. But the events which occurred from the late 1980s through the early 1990s were equally dramatic. The Berlin Wall was taken down and the two Germanys became one. An election was held in Poland and the communists were soundly beaten, with the Solidarity Union winning an amazing victory. The Hungarians cut down all the barbed wire on their Austrian border. The balance of power shifted from Gorbachev to Boris Yeltsin, who created an alternative government in Russia. He had been elected in 1991 after a failed coup. Yeltsin had a degree in civil engineering. A very intense man, he went about anything he did with enormous energy and enthusiasm.

By 1993, the delegates who were involved in the Kremlin for a Constitutional Conference were on shaky ground. They were extremely divided over the sort of political system that Russia should have. One group represented Yeltsin and his advisors; a second group represented the Russian legislator; while the third group consisted of the leaders of the 21 "autonomous republics and districts." These bodies comprise about 15 percent of the population of the Russian Federation. A final major group at the meetings consisted of leaders from the provinces and territories. Due to the deep divisions in the agendas of the four groups, a rather incoherent constitution was crafted. It actually created two sovereign entities: the president *and* the parliament. But Yeltsin dissolved the Supreme Soviet and parent Congress of People's Deputies. While admitting that his action was unconstitutional, he was successful in his effort because he had carefully cultivated the military and police garrisons.

With perestroika, a need arose for major changes in Russia's educational system. However, the country was reeling with its economic problems which consumed much of the country's financial and human resources. But the teaching ranks were experiencing a major change through the development of the Creative Union of Teachers, which had been founded in 1988. It was intended to include teachers, parents, and all types of educators. It had its first full conference during 1989 in Sachi. The union's goal was to solve the main problems of educational policy on which the renewal of Russia's society relied. The union members believed quite strongly that the country's educational system needed to assume a strong leadership role in creating a new Russia, based on the brand new notion of Western capitalism and the other basic tenets of the perestroika movement. In order to do this, the union argued for acquiring a higher level of prestige for teachers, increasing the scope of pedagogical creativity, and soliciting community support for educational perestroika.

The Eureka Movement in Russia began in the 1950s. The basic issues related to the development of personality and creativity, humor, and sincerity. The organization has argued that teachers should act like an older friend who can listen well and provide cooperation and friendship.

During the perestroika era, several new types of schools appeared in Russia. While the Eureka Movement attempted to change the entire educational system, the new schools tended to merely provide alternatives for Russian students. For example, School No. 734 in Moscow became the first Author School. Here, the goal was for students to discover ways of learning for themselves. In part, this school utilized some of A.S. Neil's ideas in his English school, Summerhill. The lycee and gymnasium were also developed by 1989. Both schools were interested in establishing a more liberal curriculum which would include the history of local culture and art, world culture, and a study of cinema and theatre.

Other model schools included Gymnasium Number 13 in Moscow, which offered instruction in German, English, Latin, Philosophy, elementary economics, sociology, logic, psychology, and world artistic culture. There was also a degree for boys with special talents which became available in 1990. Specifically, it was established as a school in which students would specialize in the humanities, receiving instruction in Russian language and culture, history and literature of the Middle Ages, world religions, ethnography, and so on.

One of the nagging problems of Russian education has related to school finance. There has been a major lack of funds for needed programs. Many new schools were needed in the early 1990s because of the great number of schools which had deteriorated. Many were no longer usable. Because of the lack of classroom space, only about half of the eligible kindergarteners were able to attend school in 1990. Prominent educators spoke of a crisis in Russian education due to problems of underfunding. The number of criminal offenses by minors had risen dramatically by 1988, when some 80,000 children between the ages of fourteen and seventeen were sent to penal colonies. In 1960, UNESCO statistics ranked the USSR second in the world in the education of its children. But by 1990 it was lower than fiftieth.

A prominent film director also has criticized the amount of money spent on Russian education. Rolan Bykov, speaking at the Congress of People's Deputies in 1989, compared the 80,000 dollars spent in capitalist countries to provide the education for a higher education specialist to the 12,000 rubles which were expended in Russia.

Soviet educators have also expressed concerns about the educational picture in rural Russia. A lack of funds has created major difficulties for teachers in such areas. A study of rural areas revealed that teachers cited a lack of cooperation with school councils, promises of new schools which were never completed, outside toilets which students were forced to use in −15°C weather, no clothes to buy, only horsemeat and sausage to purchase, and no milk. Some teachers were expected to work in classrooms with temperatures below zero. In fact, statistics on village schools in 1989 showed that 90,000 of them had no piped water, 1,353 had no sewer systems, 68,000 had no heating, and 6,000 were without electricity.

The government has operated all Russian schools with the exception of a very small number of seminaries which were operated by religious bodies. Two Russian words have tended to frame the philosophical parameters of the Russian system of education: *vospitomie* (upbringing or rearing) and *obrazovanie* (formal education). Historically, the schools have relied heavily on the Marxist-Leninist doctrine. But with the advent of perestroika, some Russians have been worried that the country has lost its moral rudder and there is not much of anything to take its place.

During 1988, the Politburo of the Communist Party created the State Committee for Public Education, which attempted to combine the Ministry of Education, the Ministry of Higher and Specialized Education, and the USSR State Committees for Vocational and Technical Training. The Chair of the State Committee for Public Education has Ministerial rank. This body is responsible for establishing educational policy and standards.

Regardless of the recent declarations of sovereignty among most of the fifteen Soviet republics, education still tends to be housed in Moscow. For example, the Ukrainian parliament passed legislation which declared it had full autonomy in all matters of education, and the Ukrainian language was designated as the official language of the republic.

Due to this state of flux which has occurred within the Soviet Union, the regulations and rules have been directly affected. For example, admission requirements for the schools tend to emanate from Moscow. Admission forms are printed in Russian. However, the republic parliaments have granted official status to the various native languages.

Russian children generally enter school at the age of 6 where they receive functional skills in reading, writing, arithmetic, hygiene, and social behavior. The middle school grades are subject based and, upon completion, the students receive a Testament to the Completion of Incomplete Secondary Education. About half of the ninth grade graduates then become involved in a general secondary school. Actually, the secondary schools are of two types. The first type is the obshchaia srednaia shkola, which is the most direct entry way into a university, polytechnic, or institute. The second type is referred to as a lycee or gymnasia. Entry into such schools is extremely competitive because the students usually come from the home of urban professionals and provide better opportunities for students to secure admission to the most prestigious universities and institutes. Table 34.1 shows the curriculum of the General Secondary School for the Russian Republic.

Teachers in Soviet society have long been regarded with very high esteem. Ironically, salaries have not really been commensurate with this high regard. Some have argued that the low pay was a result of the large percentage of women in the field, which is a problem in many other countries. Preparation sequences normally consisted of a study of the major discipline or disciplines to be taught and courses in teaching methodology. Prior to perestroika, the preparation programs also included courses in Marxism/Leninism.

MULTICULTURAL EDUCATION EFFORTS

Attempting to understand the extent of multicultural education efforts is difficult because of the rapid changes occurring in the Russian republic. But the country is highly pluralistic and many of the basic problems will need to be

Table 34.1
Curriculum Plan for the General Secondary School in the Russian Republic,
1989–1990

Subject	I	II	III	IV	V	VI	VII	VIII	IX	X	XI
					Hours per Week by Grade						
Russian Language	9	10	12	11	7	6	4	3	2		
Literature					4	3	2	2	3	4	3
Mathematics	4	5	5	6	6	6	6	6	6	4/5	4
Computer Science										1	2
History					2	2	2	2	3	4	3
Soviet Law									1		
Family Life									1		
Soviet Society											1
Environment	1	1									
Nature			1	1	1						
Geography						2	3	2	2	2/1	
Biology						2	2	2	2	1	1/2
Physics							2	2	3	4	4
Astronomy											1
Chemistry								3	3/2	2	2
Drawing							1	1	1		
Foreign Language					4	3	2	2	1	1	1
Graphic Art	1	1	1	1	1	1	1				
Music 1	1	1	1	1	1	1	1				
Physical Education	2	2	2	2	2	2	2	2	2	2	2
Military Training										2	2
Labor/Vocational Study	2	2	2	2	2	2	2	3	3	4	4
Total	20	22	24	24	30	30	30	30	32/31	32	30/31

addressed shortly. In reviewing the pluralistic issues in the old USSR, it represents a fascinating mosaic of twelve ethnic groups which have accounted for about 90% of the population: 51% of the people are Russian; 15% Ukrainians; 6% Uzbeks; 4% Belorussians; 3% Kazakhs; 2% Azerbaijanis; 2% Tartars; 2% Armenians; and 1% Tadzhiks, Georgians, Moldavians, and Lithuanians. Problems of anti-semitism still exist.

The language of instruction in Russian schools is Russian. Apparently, little attempt has been made to provide bilingual/bicultural programs similar to those found in such countries as Australia, Brazil, and the United States. However, even though the primary language of instruction is Russian, the Russian schools are attempting to provide language instruction in accordance with the student's ethnic background. Moreover, the Russian educational system is also attempting to provide students with English instruction—the international language of business and commerce.

One of the continual arguments in the Russian republic has related to the issue of assimilation versus pluralistic maintenance. One interesting case in point relates to the Korean-Russians. Approximately five million Koreans live outside of their country—approximately 500,000 residing in the Soviet Union, many of them in the Russian republic. Initially, Koreans migrated to Russia for economic reasons. Then, after Korea was annexed by Japan in 1910, many of them fled to Russia for political reasons.

Russian-Koreans refer to themselves as either Koryo Sarons (people from Koryo, the name of the Koryo Dynasty, 932–1392) or Chosun Saron (People from Chosun, taken from the ancient name for Korea, which actually means "Land of the Morning Calm." Because of the Koreans' interest in the importance of education, they tended to become upwardly mobile after mastering the Russian language. In fact, during 1985, more than 100 Soviet-Koreans in Central Asia were academicians, journalists, scientists, administrators, researchers, or artists.

Among non-Russian ethnic groups, there have been concerns over the Soviet language policy. However, the Korean language has not been taken seriously as a language of instruction in Russia. But under Gorbachev, new programs in Korean education were put in place; and a new bibliography, including a collection of Korean literary works which have been translated into 22 different Russian ethnic languages, has become available for the first time. While this is encouraging for Korean-Russians, other ethnic languages seem to have not assumed such a prominent role.

Armenian-Russians have tended to resist any efforts to become assimilated into the Russian macroculture. One possible reason for this extends to the very unique nature of the Armenian language itself. Consequently, the Armenians have managed to maintain the primary elements of their microculture because of their language. Legally, all citizens of the USSR have been able to choose their mother tongue or any other Soviet language for the schooling of their children. This was guaranteed in the USSR Constitution, Article 121. Many of these other ethnic groups use Russian as a second language. But among all Russian ethnic groups, the Jews and Georgians do the best in educational attainment. In Russia, Jews are considered to be a nationality.

Turning to the issue of religious instruction in Russia, it must be remembered that Lenin chastised organized religions with his famous statement that "Religion is the opiate of the people." Thus, ever since the 1917 revolution, religious instruction has been banned from the Soviet/Russian curriculum, and the Russian law makes it illegal for the educational enterprise to espouse a specific religious dogma. This principle is similar to the "separation of church and state" concept in the United States.

SUMMARY

Perhaps no other nation in the entire world provides the scholar of multicultural education with so many critical issues to investigate. The original Marxist doctrine emphasized the issues pertaining to wealth (or the lack of it), yet was relatively silent on such issues as race, ethnicity, and gender. Now, with the phenomenon of perestroika and glasnost, the Soviet Republic will be forced to deal with various educational issues related to educational equity.

However, even more basic will be the need to articulate new philosophies of multicultural equity. Under the Marxist/Leninist years, many of these concepts were clearly articulated. For example, the schools were required to emulate the basic Marxist principle of egalitarianism. While the Marxist writings tended to define these principles in economic terms, it will now be necessary to address the nagging issues of race, gender, and ethnicity.

REFERENCES

Bykov, R. *Slova i tribuny-ekonomika nashego detstva.* Moscow: Current Digest of the Soviet Press, 1989.

Conversations with Francis Kazemek and William Williams, Professors of International Education, University of Eastern Washington, August 1994.

Dunstan, John. *Soviet Education Under Perestroika.* London: Routledge Publishing Co., 1992.

Frish, G. *Kogda, Partii Postuchatsya v Shkoly.* Moscow: Current Digest of the Soviet Press, 1990.

Hart, Gary. *Russia Shakes the World.* New York: Harper Collins Publishers, 1991.

Parkhurst, H. *Education on the Dalton Plan.* London: Bell Publishing Co., 1922.

Popovych, Erika and Levin-Stankevich, Brian. *The Soviet System of Education.* Washington, DC: American Association of Collegiate Registrars and Admission Officers and NAFSA, Association of International Educators, 1992.

Roger, Hans. *Russia in the Age of Modernization and Revolution.* Burat Mill, England: Longman Co., 1980.

Tomiak, J.J. (Ed.). *Soviet Education in the 1980s.* New York: St. Martin's Press, 1987.

Urusov, S.D. *Memoirs of a Russian Governor.* London: Oxford University Press, 1908.

Westwood, J.N. *Endurance and Endeavor.* Suffolk, England: Bungay, 1973.

Yergin, D. and Gustafson, T. *Russia, 2010.* New York: Random House, 1993.

Zickel, Raymond E. (Ed.). *Soviet Union, A Country Study.* Washington, DC: Department of the Army, 1991.

35

Singapore

HISTORY OF THE SYSTEM

The island of Singapore has been known by mariners since the third century A.D. By the seventh century A.D., the Srivijaya Empire linked many ports and cities along the coast of Sumatra, Java, and the Malay Peninsula. Singapore could have been one of the several outposts of Srivijaya and a supply point for Arab, Javanese, Malay, Thai, and Indian traders.

By 1819, a local chieftain, the Temenggond of Jahor, signed a preliminary treaty with Sir Stamford Raffles which allowed for creating a British trading post. By this time, Singapore had approximately 1,000 people. The ethnic composition included about 500 Orang Kallang, 200 Orang Seletar, 150 Orang Gel, and a few Malays.

The first recorded evidence of a true "Malay" political unit is that of Langkasuka. Most historians believe that it occupied the area which is referred to as the Thai Malay province of Patoni, centered around Songkhla in southern Thailand. In the fourteenth century, Srivijaya was overrun by Majapahit, the last of the powerful Javanese Hindu states, and the Malay Peninsula became heavily influenced by the Majapahit for many years.

The development of Malacca at the start of the fifteenth century marked the beginning of a Malay system of values and politics which has endured to modern times. It became a vital force when it was adopted and nurtured by the first Sultan of Malacca who was converted from Hinduism to Islam. This section of southwestern Indonesia grew rapidly due to its location, which made it a natural trade center between East and West. The products of China and the Far East were exchanged for products from the European markets. Along with Malacca's success as a trade center was its role in the spread of Islam. Many nearby areas became Islamic, and consequently the cultural/religious values of the region had a dramatic influence on further developments.

Nonetheless, the nature of the Islamic ideology that reached Malacca was a combination of the orthodox and the mystic. Thus, present-day Islam in Malaysia does not contain the degree of orthodoxy which tends to be found in some of the more rigid Islamic countries.

Similar to what happened during the history of several countries such as Ghana, the Portuguese made an appearance as one of the first European groups to reach the area. However, the Portuguese presence seemed to have had few long-lasting effects. But Malacca was an easy target, and after just five days, it fell to the Portuguese in 1511. When the Dutch repeated the hostile action of the Portuguese in 1606, their seizure of Malacca seemed to be motivated primarily by commercial interests, and the Dutch were fairly tolerant of local rules and customs. However, the British influence became significant after 1785 when Captain Francis Light acquired the island of Panang. Eventually, the British sought to turn Penang and Singapore into cosmopolitan trade centers.

Sir Stamford Raffles was an official of England's East India Company which had centers in West Sumatra and also at Penang. During a series of military conflicts with France, lasting until 1815, the East India Company took temporary possession of Dutch colonies in the East Indies, including Malacca and Java. Eventually, Britain gave Java and Malacca to the Dutch, and later they opened negotiations to hand over Bencoolen for the remaining Dutch territories in India. Private British merchants resisted this withdrawal because they had expanded their trade routes.

Raffles is a historical figure who has a somewhat confusing life history. While he had enormous ambitions and exceptional physical stamina, he had no formal education which somehow instilled in him a great appetite for learning. Having come from a rather genteel poverty background, he loved being around the upper classes. Moreover, Raffles was a poor administrator who became an embarrassment to his employers and also to the British government. He attempted to thwart Dutch expansion in South Sumatra but the governor-general of India permitted him to visit Calcutta in 1818 and share his ideas. He was authorized to help protect Britain's trade routes through the Straits of Malacca. He also was able to create a post at Riau, provided that he didn't bring the West Indies Company into a conflict with the Dutch.

When Singapore was finally granted statehood in 1819, Raffles believed he was improving the character of the area. He also was convinced that the action terminated the Dutch domination of the eastern seas. He described Singapore as a new country which he personally loved and cherished. One of his favorite projects was his plan for higher education. He wished to revive the cultural heritage of the region which he felt had been degraded due to the exploits of Chinese, Dutch, and Arab entrepreneurs.

There were mixed reactions to the new British-dominated country under Raffle's leadership. In London, officials of the British East India Company were afraid that their negotiations with the Dutch would be upset by Raffle's actions. As a matter of fact, the Dutch were furious over Britain's actions since they believed that the area was part of their sphere of influence. But Raffles left, leaving William Farquhar in charge of the small English military unit. Being a free trade port, the commercial interests grew rapidly. In fact, when Raffles returned a few months later, he found that the new settlement had grown to almost 5,000 people, including Malays, Chinese, Bugis, Arabs, Indians, and Europeans. Thus, the pluralistic nature of Singapore's population was beginning and would be a factor throughout the country's history.

This new free-port trading post saw the arrival of the first Siamese junk in 1819 and the first Chinese junk appeared in 1821. Chinese traders from South China were attracted to Singapore by the ease of doing business compared with the port of Malacca on the Malay Peninsula. And along with the Indian traders came Indian indentured servants and convicts who would provide a badly needed source of cheap labor for Singapore.

Because of the economic potential, Singapore was quite enticing to Chinese entrepreneurs. In fact, by 1836, the Chinese population exceeded that of the Malays. The continued growth of the Chinese microculture finally reached the point when it included 74 percent by 1976. The proportion of Malays has steadily declined while the percentage of Indians has tended to remain constant. But even though the Chinese had the largest group, the small European community was the most influential. This European population consisted of British merchants, lawyers, and newspaper editors.

Regular steamship services to China, India, and Britain came to the area in the 1840s, but most of the cargoes continued to be carried by sailing ships until the 1870s. Also, between 1846 and 1864, three banks and a major drydock company were developed and the first telegraph was laid between Singapore and Batavia.

One major problem affecting the port of Singapore was piracy. In the early 1830s, piracy nearly stopped any kind of trade in the area. Due to actions by patrol boats which were operated by Chinese merchants, the piracy was somewhat curtailed for a short period of time. But eventually the pirates were openly using Singapore to arm their ships and sell their captured goods. By 1854, the attacks were so frequent that only about half of the trading ships from Asia actually reached Singapore. However, treaties signed by China and the Western powers in 1860 finally caused an ultimate decrease in piracy, so that by 1867, Singapore had become one of the most prosperous ports in the British empire.

Later in the nineteenth century, trade continued to be prosperous, and the opening of the Suez Canal along with the increased use of steamships allowed Singapore to continue its success as a free trade port. Also, the processing of tin and rubber produced in the Malay Peninsula became a major part of Singapore's economy. In addition, Singapore became the world center for the distribution of tin and rubber.

During the last three decades of the nineteenth century, the nature of Singapore changed dramatically. In 1867, the straits settlements became a Crown

Colony. But even though the Singapore businessmen had acquired major economic interests in the resources of the Malay peninsula, the general conditions in the area were extremely unstable due to fighting between the new groups of immigrants and the traditional Malay authorities and because of rivalries between a number of Chinese secret societies. This was a major growth period for Chinese immigrants, and in 1877 the colonial government created the Chinese Protectorate in an attempt to address a number of major abuses of the labor trade.

The first Chinese Protector was William Pickering, the first British official in Singapore who was able to speak and read Chinese. He had the authority to board incoming ships in order to better protect the incoming immigrants. By the early 1880s, he also offered protection to Chinese women who had entered the country and were forced into prostitution. During this time, Chinese secret societies were no longer able to engage in illegal immigration practices, but they continued to create problems because of their involvement in illegal gambling. However, a law passed in 1889 banned the secret societies in Singapore. Even though they went underground and participated in extortion, gang fights, gambling, and robbery, their power was broken and they would never be a significant a problem in the future.

By the start of the twentieth century, most of the Chinese population still planned on returning home to China. Interestingly, a Chinese microculture known as the Straits Chinese had emerged. This group's ethnicity was primarily Malay or English. Some of these families traced their roots to forebears who had resided in Malacca. They tended to be more loyal to England than China, possibly due to the fact that many had English as the mother tongue. By 1900, there was a Straits British Chinese Association, and just one year later a Straits Chinese volunteer infantry had been formed. When Singapore's status as a Crown Colony was terminated after World War II, the first leaders who became politically active were primarily English-educated Straits Chinese people.

As might be expected, a wide gulf existed between the more recent Chinese immigrants and the Straits Chinese factions. Because of this split between the two groups, the elite element was unable to create a large popular political structure until the formation of the People's Action Party (PAP) in 1954. Consequently, political control over the Chinese Singaporeans was in the hands of the communists for much of the time. The influence began about 1911 after the Chinese revolution. It was also strong when the communists opposed the Japanese invasion of Manchuria in the 1930s, and during the Japanese invasion of Malaya during the 1940s. It was also quite active in 1950 when the communists were successful in the Chinese revolution.

World War I did not affect Singapore to any great extent. However, the British were forced to concentrate their fleet in other areas. This allowed Japan to gain control of the Chinese Seas. Eventually, the British decided to build a major naval base in Singapore for their eastern fleet. After the 1931 Japanese invasion of Manchuria, work on the British military facility accelerated and by February of 1938 it became operational. However, with the sinking of two unprotected British battleships in the area, Singapore suddenly found that it completely lacked any sea defense. The Japanese advanced down the Malay Peninsula and occupied the city of Singapore until the war was over in 1945. During the occupation, many Chinese people were rounded up and victimized by the Japanese people. Some were put to death.

Shortly after the war, the British created a plan to unite the peninsula states while Singapore would remain separate. Thus the Federation of Malaya was the new political unit as of 1948. The British controlled both the new Federation and the Crown Colony of Singapore. However, as the 1950s arrived, Singapore was on the verge of becoming independent. Elections were held for legislative councils, and in 1953 the British appointed a commission to make recommendations for developing a new constitution for Singapore. The merger of the Federation of Malaya and Singapore finally occurred in 1963 but only lasted until 1965 when Singapore no longer was part of the union. It became an independent republic.

By 1964, serious race riots between the Malays and Chinese occurred over a political argument. But gradually the government became successful in developing Singapore's industrial and commercial potential. There had been an infusion of foreign capital, and many foreign-owned factories were lured to the country because of profitable tax breaks. The result has been that Singapore's economy became a healthy mixture of both public and private entrepreneurs.

During the 1960s, Singapore was forced to deal with the problems of ethnicity. But the People's Action Party (PAP) enjoyed an enviable level of success in dealing with a number of quite difficult social issues such as this. For example, this major Singapore political party encouraged the construction of physically integrated residences and prohibited culturally isolated ethnic enclaves. The party hoped that such a strategy would serve as building blocks to racial and ethnic integration.

STRUCTURE OF THE SYSTEM

Modern Singapore would be difficult for Sir Thomas Stamford Raffles to recognize. During the 175 years since he became a prominent figure in Singapore's development, the country has reached the point where it has become one of the world's busiest ports. In fact, it was the busiest port in the world in 1988. With five port terminals, each specializing in a different type of cargo, it has the capacity to accommodate more than 36,000 ships each year. The country has been involved in major efforts to improve other types of transportation. There are two major airports. Singapore Changi Airport is used for international flights, while Seletar is used for charter and training flights. There are also several smaller fields.

Five freeways totaling 95 kilometers and more than 2,800 kilometers of other roads meet the needs of the motorists, and Malayan railroads provide services in Singapore. There is also a mass rapid transit system which provides trans-portation services for more than 800,000 people each day.

Located off the southern tip of the Malay Peninsula, Singapore is connected to Malaysia by a causeway. The total land area is about 636 square kilometers, which includes the one main island and some 58 islets. The main island is about 52 kilometers long and 23 kilometers wide. The country's coastline is about 138 kilometers in length. Originally covered in tropical rain forests, Singapore's hills have been leveled and swamps have been drained to the extent that only about 2.5 percent of the country is still forested.

Since it became fully independent in 1865, this city-state has acquired an international reputation as a country with political stability and an efficient, honest government. In general, the government has a reputation for its rather authoritarian style, with limited tolerance for dissent or criticism. It was felt that this was important if Singapore was to survive in a rather hostile world.

Singapore's governing structure is patterned on the British parliamentary sys-tem. The legislative process consists of a unicameral parliament. Eighty-one members are elected for five-year terms. Members of parliament are elected from 42 single-member constituencies. The group-representation constituencies were intended to ensure multiracial representation in the parliament. Also, if members change political parties during their term of office, they are forced to resign. The government is headed by a prime minister, a first deputy prime minister, and a second deputy prime minister. The thirteen ministers are in charge of defense, education, environment, finances, foreign affairs, home affairs, law, labor, community development, communication and information, health, na-tional development, and trade and industry.

Singapore's constitution can be amended by a two-thirds vote of parliament. The constitution allows for a four-year presidential term, and the president ap-points a personal staff from a list of candidates provided by the Public Service Commission. Members of the legislature must be at least 21 years of age and able to communicate in either English, Malay, Mandarin, or Tamil. They also must be of sound mind.

The judicial system of Singapore is vested in the Supreme Court which consists of a chief justice and a number of other judges which are appointed by the presi-dent who acts on the advice of the prime minister. As is the case in many other countries, the primary responsibility of the judiciary is to guard the constitution.

Modern times have caused a change in religious factors in the country. While wealthy citizens have contributed significant funds in recent years for the re-newal of the city's churches, Chinese temples, mosques, Buddhist monasteries, and Hindu temples, many immigrant groups have modified or even dropped many of the traditional ceremonies and rites which were part of their ethnic traditions at one time. During the 1980s, the government of Singapore viewed religion as a positive social force which could be used as a shield against west-ernization. In fact, religion became part of the country's secondary school cur-riculum during the 1980s. But the Singapore government also had concerns over the effects of some religious enterprises. For example, Islamic fundamentalism was a topic which was seldom discussed. The activities of some religious groups, such as the Jehovah's Witnesses, who were actively opposed to military service, were greatly restricted.

The primary goal of Singapore's educational system is to develop the talents of all persons so that everyone would be able to contribute to the general welfare of the country. A secondary goal, which is extremely critical to the country, is to utilize these talents in a way that would help Singapore become productive and competitive in the world's marketplace. About 4 percent of the country's gross domestic product (GDP) has been devoted to the educational system, and the percentage has gradually increased since 1989.

Tuition at the National University of Singapore has ranged from about 2,600 U.S. dollars (for students involved in programs for the arts, social sciences, business administrations, and law courses) up to over 7,000 U.S. dollars (for the medical program). While the university-level tuitions were expected to force the rich to bear a greater proportion of the country's educational expenses, a system of loans, need-based awards and scholarships for academically talented students resulted in a situation where no gifted students were disallowed access to higher education due to a lack of funds.

The government of Singapore has developed both government and government-aided primary schools which enroll more than 270,000 students each year. The "government-aided schools" are mostly private and they teach the standard curriculum as prescribed by the Ministry of Education. In return, they receive government subsidies and agree to employ teachers who are approved by the Ministry of Education. The organizational structure consists of a six-year primary school, a four-year secondary school, and a two-year junior college for students wishing to enter college. The Ministry has created a flexible advancement concept so that students who require more time to complete certain grades are allowed to do so. This strategy was designed to help cut down on the country's dropout rate.

Singapore utilizes a rather sophisticated tracking system which was designed to lower the country's dropout rate and provide all students with marketable skills. This was in part a reaction to the practice of "warehousing" students during the 1960s, and 1970s, which had the effect of graduating fairly large numbers who had failed to acquire the skills necessary for the available occupational areas. A major effort was made to match up the school graduates with the various occupational needs of the business community. An emphasis was made to create a testing program which would provide educators with better data regarding the school success of the nation's youth.

MULTICULTURAL EDUCATION EFFORTS

Presently, Singapore does not have a formal multicultural program in the country's schools. However, a number of multicultural education issues are addressed in some social studies classes in the primary and secondary grades. Multicultural education concepts are also used in the country's moral education programs.

As previously stated, Singapore has a population of about 75 percent Chinese-Singaporeans. In addition to such a sizable microculture, other ethnic groups of people moved to the country and attended the nation's schools. The Malays (6 percent) and Indians (6 percent) were the other two major microcultures.

English is the primary language of instruction in the schools, and there are no programs which attempt to provide instruction in the mother tongue of immigrant children. In fact, it has been argued that one unique thing about the Singaporean educational system has been the willingness of the Chinese population to accept English as the primary language. While the country does have four official languages (English, Malay, Tamil, and Chinese), all the street signs in Singapore are in English only. This is not true in some countries such as Hong Kong where the street signs are printed in both Chinese and English.

However, even though the Singapore schools use English as the primary language of instruction, Mandarin is taught as a main second language. This is also atypical compared to Hong Kong where only one international school, the Chinese International School, teaches Mandarin as a second language.

The Office of Education provides no leadership in multicultural education, and teachers receive no special instruction in multicultural education as part of the teacher certification process. Nonetheless, Singapore's school system has been affected by the multiethnic composition. This phenomenon sometimes resulted in schools which were segregated on a de facto basis.

Recent programs of modernization and heightened levels of education attainment have resulted in a number of changes in religious practices. During the 1980s, Singapore experienced a surge of efforts in remodeling the city's churches, mosques, Chinese temples, and Buddhist monasteries. Many immigrants have modified their traditional religious practices, and the schools have tended to maintain a level of separation between religious issues and the school curriculum.

The country's schools are racially and culturally integrated, and very few segregated classrooms have existed throughout the country's educational history. The nation's children represent nearly all racial groups found around the globe. Because of Singapore's diverse populations, history and social studies classes are taught from a pluralistic perspective.

Singapore's educational enterprise has articulated a vision of the country's leadership more clearly than many other Singaporean social institutions. There has been a concerted attempt to reject special privileges for any group, and the integrated school environment has helped to create a unique attitude about racial and ethnic groups which differ from each other. During the 1980s, a number of key multicultural education issues were settled, such as the use of English as the primary language of instruction and the conversion of Malay and Chinese, and Anglican missionary schools to standard government schools. But in the final analysis, it was through the schools more than any other Singaporean institution that the abstract values of Singaporean identity and multiculturalism were verified.

SUMMARY

An examination of Singapore's history reveals some rather atypical occurrences, as compared to many other nations. Perhaps the most unique phenomenon relates to the issue of language. Despite the majority of Chinese-speaking Singaporeans, English became the official language of the schools and the entire country as well. Language has long been a sensitive and often volatile issue among many people. In fact, Canada has quarreled about the French/English issue for decades and it appears that one or more of the French-speaking provinces may actually secede.

However, all Singaporeans who study English are expected to learn a second language. A recent debate in Singapore has suggested that the second languages are not equal, however. While it is mandatory for all Chinese people to learn Mandarin, they cannot study Malay even though other ethnic groups, such as the Indians and Malays, cannot study Mandarin. In real life, it seems that most students study the language of their ancestors.

Another problem for the Chinese majority in Singapore has been the difficulty that urban and rural Chinese residents have experienced in communicating with each other. There has been a tendency for the more rural Chinese residents to maintain more of their Chinese ethnicity than their urban counterparts, particularly in the area of language. So the recent emphasis has been for Chinese people and students in the schools to learn Mandarin as a second language. Indeed, some far-eastern economists have argued that such a strategy could help Singapore compete more successfully with Hong Kong since Cantonese is the main language there and Peking prefers to deal with Mandarin-speaking Singaporeans.

Some observers have speculated that this emphasis on the Mandarin language might propel the Chinese community into the role of the dominant community in Singapore, and the usual arguments over the attempt to produce bilingual people have prevailed among educators and other factions as well. The chief concern is that many people end up being strong in one language and weak in the other or, even worse, just mediocre in both.

But the key factor relates to economic issues, and many observers say that English will probably still be the primary language because of its international importance as a commercial language. In spite of the debate, it is interesting to note that even with the lack of a formal multicultural education program sponsored by the government, the country of Singapore—with its interesting pluralistic society—has historically been free of many of the problems encountered by other pluralistic communities.

REFERENCES

Balakrishnan, N. "A Broad Education." *Far Eastern Economic Review* (January 1991), p. 18.

Balakrishnan, N. "Speak Singaporean." *Arts and Society* (February 1989), pp. 40–41.

Emerson, Rupert. *Malaysia: A Study in Direct and Indirect Rule.* New York: Macmillan, 1937.

Fletcher, Nancy. "The Separation of Singapore from Malaysia." Ithaca, NY: Cornell University Southeast Asia Program, Data Paper No. 37, 1969.

Gonen, Amiram. *The Encyclopedia of the Peoples of the World.* New York: Henry Holt Publishing Co., 1993.

Hall, D.G.E. *A History of South East Asia,* 3rd ed. London: Macmillan & Co., 1968.

Leitch-LePoer, Barbara (Ed.). *Singapore: A Country tudy.* Washington, DC: Department of the Army (DA Pam 550-184), 1991, pp. xiii–xvii.

Mitchell, Bruce and Salsbury, Robert. *An International Survey of Multicultural Education.* Cheney, WA: Western States Consulting and Evaluation Services, 1991. (See Appendix.)

Pridmore, F. *Memoirs of the Raffles Museum.* Singapore, 1955.

Singapore. Ministry of Communication and Information, Information Division. *Governmental Structure.* Singapore: Ministry of Communication and Information, 1989.

Tan, E.T. "Language, Society, and Education in Singapore: Issues and Trends." *International Journal of Educational Development,* Vol. 15, No. 1 (1995), pp. 95–96.

Turnbull, C.M. *A History of Singapore.* London: Oxford University Press, 1977.

Vreeland, Nena. *Area Handbook for Singapore.* Washington, DC: American University Foreign Area Studies, 1977.

Wellington, Stanley. *Balaysia and Singapore: The Building of New States.* Ithaca, NY: Cornell University Press, 1978.

Wheatley, Paul. *The Golden Khersonese.* Kuala Lumpur: University of Malaya Press, 1961.

Winstedt, Richard O. *The Malays: A Cultural History* (rev. ed.). London: Routledge & Kegan Paul, 1950.

Wong, Soon Teck. *Singapore's New Education System: Education Reform for National Development.* Singapore: Institute of Southeast Asian Studies, 1988.

36

South Africa

HISTORY OF THE SYSTEM

Archaeological discoveries in South Africa have revealed that groups of persons who have inhabited South Africa for several thousand years resemble the present-day Khoi and San. The evidence seems to suggest that they had goats and sheep by about the first century A.D. During the beginning of the Christian era, the ancestors of the Bantu moved south from the Congo region, and migrated to the area in the vicinity of the Zambezi River. This group of people had an understanding of agriculture and iron-making. Eventually they crossed the Limpopo River which is the northern boundary of present-day South Africa. By that time (shortly before A.D. 500), many of them had also acquired cattle.

Some anthropologists believe that black Africans, referred to as Nguni, Zulu, Xhosa, and Swazi, crossed the Limpopo about 1300 and forced out some of the earlier inhabitants, while absorbing some of the others. The Nguni inhabited the regions between south of the Limpopo to the Great Kei River and between the Drakensberg Mountains and the Indian Ocean.

The first known contacts between South Africans and Europeans occurred about 1488, when a Portuguese expedition sailed around Africa's southern tip for the first time. This expedition was led by Bartholomew Diaz, and on the return to Europe, they sailed around the Cape of Good Hope, becoming the first Europeans to accomplish this. Because of the spice trade between the East and Europe, the route became quite popular with the Portuguese who began to make an impact on this part of the African continent.

However, by the end of the sixteenth century, Portugal's influence in the area began to wane and the Dutch and English competed to replace them on the lucrative spice trade route. Dutch interests were intensified when a ship was wrecked there and the crew reported on its favorable assets after they finally were able to return from Europe.

In 1651, an expedition set out for the South African cape in an attempt to establish a station which would supply ships of the Dutch East India Company at the midpoint of their voyage to the East. This party, led by Jan van Riebeeck, gathered together a group of 100 men and 4 women who landed at Table Bay during April of 1652. This entourage would provide the impetus for further Dutch involvement in the area.

Van Riebeeck was able to establish friendly relations with the Khoi tribe, whose chief had acquired a very rudimentary understanding of English because of his involvement with a number of passing trading ships. At that time, the total population of the Khois (Hottentots) and Sans (Bushmen) who populated that part of Africa was estimated at about 255,000. The European settlers started farms and traded food for sheep and cattle with the passing ships.

However, a problem soon arose when the Khoi noticed that the Europeans seemed to have designs on becoming permanent residents in the area. Moreover, the Khoi considered the sheep and cattle to be wild game, and they procured a number of the animals for their own personal use. A clash of cultures occurred over the definition of animal "ownership" and the disappearance of Khoi and San grazing lands which were increasingly becoming part of the agricultural enterprises of the Europeans. Consequently, the Dutch declared war on the Khoi and San in 1659. Eventually, plots of land were actually given to individual Europeans who became entrepreneurs, farming for profit as private landowners.

By 1713, a smallpox epidemic obliterated a large number of the Khoi and several tribes disappeared completely. While many of them left the area, many remained, becoming absorbed into the Dutch population and eventually comprising a substantial portion of the "coloured" microculture. During this time, the Sans retaliated against the encroachment into their grazing lands and attacked the Dutch with poisoned arrows, inflicting considerable casualties.

As the herds grew and the population increased, more grazing land was needed by the Dutch. This motivated them to wander around the land in search of new locations. This group became known as Trekboers (wandering farmers). Their extended families tended to include the man's wife, his sons and daughters, and his sons' children if they had married. But also closely associated with the extended family were the Khoi servants and the black African slaves who had been acquired.

The first Bantu-Africans encountered by the Dutch were the Xhosa. By 1778, the first treaty was negotiated between the Dutch Cape Colony governor and two of the minor Xhosa chiefs. However, arguments over territorial boundaries eventually erupted into a serious conflict which became known as the First Kaffir War. By 1812, the Dutch government used its military forces in wars with the Khosas and permanent military outposts were established. Also, during this period of time, the British assumed an active role in the area, and by 1815 a major rift between the Dutch and British occurred after a brief period of friendship. After the British abolished slavery in 1833, many of the area farmers experienced severe financial hardships. Reacting to a situation which they deemed to be intolerable, the Boers decided to leave Cape Colony and find a land of their own which would be free of British interference.

They finally wound up on the Transvaal Plateau which had been depopulated due to continual tribal warfare in previous years. Three combined groups formed a loosely confederated government. However, the three factions disagreed on leadership, where to settle, and also on religious issues. Finally, the Boers proclaimed the Republic of Natalia, having its government at Pietermaritzburg. It consisted of an elected council of 24 members with supreme legislative, executive, and judicial functions. However, by 1847, the British had annexed the territory and Natal became a separate British colony.

By 1882, the Boer leaders were guaranteed freedom from British interference, and a unified constitution was adapted which provided for a president, and executive council, a legislature (Volksraad), and a high court which ruled the new republic from Pretoria. The first president of the Transvaal (Pretorius) was finally replaced in 1872 by T.F. Burgers, a reformed Dutch minister who was a religious liberal.

During the same year, gold was discovered in the Transvaal at Lydenburg. Influenced by the potential mining interests, the British created a scheme to annex the Transvaal. Finally, by 1880, the Boers, led by Paul Kruger, were successful in defeating the British in the first Anglo-Boer War of 1880–1881. The British were also fighting against three separate groups of black Africans, and accepted an armistice after being defeated in the Battle of Mujuba Hill. In 1884, the Boers claimed a large section of the Zulu lands. A few years later, the term "Afrikaner" began to be used as the term of identification for the Boers.

The mining industry enjoyed a great surge during the last quarter of the nineteenth century. In addition to the gold discoveries of 1872, diamonds were found five years earlier and the mining industries became more lucrative as time went by. The development of the mines attracted Cecil Rhodes, who made a fortune in diamonds by the time he was just 21 years old. He was elected prime minister of the Cape Colony. But a number of conflicts between the British and Afrikaners eventually led to the Anglo-Boer War of 1899, when the Transvaal declared war against Britain. After three years of hostilities, the Boers decided to accept the settlement terms offered by the British. As a result, the Boer forces surrendered and were forced to accept the sovereignty of the British king. The British promised to grant self-government at an early date.

The constitutions of the Boer republic forbade any equality between races, even in the churches. The constitution of Cape Colony granted equality in the courts and the polls as well. Afrikaners, Coloureds (mixed-race persons), British, and Blacks were all allowed to vote as long as they had appropriate property qualifications. However, these qualifications were restrictive enough to prevent most Blacks from voting.

An election bill was passed in parliament by the Boer and British parties. About 30,000 Blacks were stricken from the voting rolls, neutralizing their rapid increase in numbers between 1872 and 1887. The election focused on financial rather than educational restrictions because it was feared that paying attention to education and restricting the votes of Blacks because of inadequate levels of educational attainment might motivate them to attend school and receive an education.

At about the same time, Blacks also began to create separate Christian churches, and this phenomenon became known as the Ethiopian Movement which was first led by Nemiah Tile, a black African who had been a Methodist minister. By the early 1890s, the Ethiopian Movement had attained rapid growth from the African Methodist Church in the United States, and a number of African members were actually trained in the U.S. African Methodist Church.

By 1896, Mohandas K. Ghandi took up residence in South Africa and he became the leader of the growing Indian population in the area. It was in South Africa that he developed his philosophy of nonviolent resistance which he would later utilize when he returned to India in his attempt to gain independence from Britain. His first campaign occurred in 1906 when the Transvaal government began requiring all Indians to carry passes.

By the time the Union of South Africa was formed in 1910, diamond and gold mining had replaced agriculture as the principle industry. The Union of South Africa consisted of four states, including the Cape, Natal, the South African Republic, and the Orange Free State. From this time until the major changes in the 1990s, racism became institutionalized and this ultimately led to the formation of the African National Congress.

South Africa was affected by the great inflationary cycles of post–World War I land due to rising costs in 1921, so an organization of mine owners, called the Chamber of Mines, decided to reduce the wages of white miners and use Blacks for the semi-skilled jobs which had previously been held by Whites. As could be expected, this move incurred the wrath of the Mine Workers' Union, launching strikes and riots which persisted for ten weeks and resulted in the loss of 230 lives. Even though the plan to use Blacks in semi-skilled jobs was reversed, the salaries of white mine workers was cut by 25 percent.

By 1931, the worldwide depression affected South Africa, resulting in job cutbacks and creating enormous fiscal problems for the country's agricultural industry. Due to the increasing levels of separatism between Blacks and Whites in South Africa, the 1935 convention of the African National Congress (ANC) reached a heightened level of intensity and a new interest in the involvement with Coloureds and Indians was initiated.

At the beginning of World War II, there was an attempt to keep the country neutral, but the parliament eventually voted to enter the war on the side of the British. But war-time elections in 1943 saw a strong political victory by the Reunited National party, now referred to as the National Party. The economic development of the cities during the war caused great increases in the urban black population, and the National Party argued for the maintenance of apartheid as a means of preserving and nurturing the white labor market.

Also during World War II, the African National Congress (ANC) attempted to ameliorate the grievances of black citizens by approaching the central government directly. At this time, Nelson Mandela was just getting involved in the struggle for recognition of black African rights. In time he would become a true African folk hero.

But substantial changes in race relations would be slow in developing. In 1948, the white electorate voted the National Party into power with a mandate to introduce apartheid. Also, at the midpoint of the century, a number of laws were passed which were designed to prevent further miscegenation. The first piece of legislation was the Prohibition of Mixed-Marriages Act of 1949. A companion measure was called the Immorality Amendment Act of 1950 which extended a prohibition of carnal intercourse of Whites and Bantu to relations between Whites and Coloureds. The Population Registration Act of 1950 required every person to be registered as either White, Coloured, or Bantu. Indians were classified as "Coloured."

By 1958, an ANC subgroup called the African National Congress Youth League (ANCYL) had been formed and a subgroup of the ANCYL left the ANC and formed the Pan-African Congress (PAC). The group was greatly affected by Kwame Nkrumah, the first elected president of Ghana, after that country had just achieved its independence from Britain. The group was composed of younger African leaders who espoused a more militant stance. In 1962, Nelson Mandela was arrested and convicted of sabotage. He would spend the next 27 years as a political prisoner.

During the 1960s and 1970s, negative sentiment toward South Africa intensified because of its hard-line positions on apartheid and its refusal to relinquish control over Namibia. The other African states applied more and more pressure on the country to reform its positions, and were effective in driving South Africa out of a number of key international agencies. Finally, in 1974, the credentials of the South African representative were rejected in the U.N. General Assembly. In spite of the country's attempts to adapt a more conciliatory approach toward its African neighbors, the system of apartheid constituted an insurmountable barrier.

For the next ten years, South Africa experienced major civil unrest and extensive violations of human rights. During 1974, serious disturbances occurred in the industrial areas near Johannesburg because of rent increases and the arrests of a number of black community leaders who were unwilling to support several constitutional changes. When P.W. Botha became prime minister in 1978, the stage was set for serious disagreements between the white government and the black African groups. On March 25, 1985, police opened fire, killing 20 people in a funeral procession. In fact, during the period of time between September 1984 and November 1985, a total of more than 800 civilians were killed by the police because of the unrest.

Mandela in jail was an immense problem for Botha because if he died there, the rage in the black townships would be unmanageable even by the well-equipped national army. Mandela had a prostate operation in 1985, and there was a new concern about his health as he grew older and much more popular. In 1986, Bishop Desmond Tutu appealed for a worldwide effort to apply punitive sanctions against the Botha government so that a nonracial government could be established in South Africa.

STRUCTURE OF THE SYSTEM

Eventually Botha was unseated and replaced by F.W. de Klerk, who was successful in securing the country's first national election which finally established a new nonracial government. Apartheid in the formal sense was terminated in 1990 when Pretoria's ban on the African National Congress ended and Nelson Mandela was released from prison after a 27-year period of incarceration. Tutu closed his inauguration remarks with the following quote: "Bless this beautiful land with its wonderful people of different races, cultures, and languages so that it will be a land of laughter and joy, of justice and reconciliation, of peace and unity, of compassion, caring and sharing. We pray this prayer for a true patriotism in the powerful name of Jesus who died and rose again and now reigns with you, O Father, and the Holy Spirit, one God, forever and ever, Amen."

The United Nations was an active participant in the dramatic changes which occurred in South Africa. Between 1960 and 1988, the United Nations Security Council adapted 25 resolutions relating to the struggle of the South African people to terminate apartheid and establish a democratic society. During 1993, the secretary-general of the United Nations met with President de Klerk, congratulating him on the South African parliament's decision to establish a Transitional Executive Council. He also promised that the United Nations Observer Mission to South Africa (UNOMSA) would be strengthened before the 1994 elections. The U.N. also helped frame the legal parameters for the 1994 elections and assisted in their supervision.

The South African parliament is voted on by the people in free elections. One major change following the election was the nonpolitical appointment of Supreme Court members who consist of women, black, coloured, and white justices in order to reflect the racial and ethnic diversity of the country. Under the leadership of Nelson Mandela, the nation's schools became desegregated. In classes with great amounts of racial diversity, English is usually the language of instruction. Due to limited classroom space and an increased number of students, the class size in South Africa now averages about 40 students, and a major effort is underway to prepare black teachers.

South Africa has a Ministry of Education which is responsible for perpetuating the national interest in education. However, education is the responsibility of the provinces which have a superintendent of education. Education is compulsory for the first seven grades (primary) and optional in grades 7–12. The old racist funding formulas have been changed and the government spends the same amount of money for all students regardless of their race or ethnicity. The curriculum is in the process of being totally revised in order to reflect the dramatic new changes in the country.

April 1994 was a turning point in the history of South Africa, because it marked the country's first nonracial elections based on one person one vote. Voters elected a national assembly that debated and drafted a constitution for a nonracial democratic republic. During April 1994, Nelson Mandela was elected as the president of South Africa, representing the African National Congress. He was inaugurated at the Union Buildings in Pretoria. The inauguration was witnessed by an enormous throng that reportedly was the largest gathering of heads of state since the funeral of John F. Kennedy.

MULTICULTURAL EDUCATION EFFORTS

No discussion of the country's multicultural education efforts in the schools would be complete without paying tribute to Nelson Mandela, who was imprisoned by Whites and became one of the main architects for a multicultural, democratic government which was based on the representation and participation of all of the country's microcultures. Not only was he viewed as a national folk hero in South Africa, but the spirit of his extraordinary qualities of leadership touch the souls of Africa's other sub-Saharan countries as well.

It can be seen that, historically, the country's educational system has greatly stressed the education of Whites. In fact, during the long years of apartheid, the country's education budget has reflected the disparity between minority (white) education and majority (black and "coloured") education in the expenditure of funds. Only 6 percent of the amount of money spent for each white student has been spent on the education of black children; for the education of "coloured" children, the rate has been about 22 percent of the amount spent on each white child; and for Asians, the amount has been about 31 percent. Of course, since the election of Mandela, all that has changed.

In the past, South Africa had four separate educational systems: the Department of Bantu Education for Blacks; the "Coloured" People's Representative Council, for those of mixed racial background; the Department of Indian Affairs for Asians; and the main system of education, which managed the schools for "Whites only." South Africa has enjoyed a literacy rate of over 50 percent for persons past the age of fifteen, which makes it one of the highest rates on the African continent.

Until the new changes of 1994, South Africa had no programs in multicultural education. However, as stated earlier in this chapter, the country is now in the process of completely revising its curriculum, and it is expected that this topic will be one of the major issues to be addressed, along with other concerns, such as how the history of indigenous populations will be addressed in the curriculum structure.

SUMMARY

The rapid changes in South Africa have been astonishing, to say the least. The apartheid system lasted for 46 years and, suddenly, one election created some of the most dramatic changes that any nation has ever experienced in such a short time. The sanctions by the United Nations are largely responsible for the new climate, but one cannot overlook the amazing efforts of Desmond Tutu and Nelson Mandela. Indeed, it is hard to visualize these changes having occurred in the absence of their leadership.

However, in examining this swift social revolution, much credit must be given to F.W. de Klerk, the last South African president under the apartheid system. He must be considered to be one of the nation's true patriots because of all he did to prepare the white minority for the new changes. Indeed, it has been surmised that had other more militant white leaders been in power, the country might have become embroiled in an ugly civil war with dire consequences.

Finally, the rest of Africa can and will learn from the events which have occurred there. Mandela's commitment to interracial cooperation and harmony is remarkable. Others who were political prisoners for such a lengthy period of time have become bitter and consumed by the need for revenge. Indeed, Mandela's postincarceration behavior provides great inspiration for us all. Hopefully, his actions will provide the same message for the entire world.

REFERENCES

Anzovin, Steven. *South Africa: Apartheid and Divestiture.* New York: H.W. Wilson, 1987.

Clark, Steve (Ed.). *Nelson Mandela Speaks.* New York: Pathfinder Press, 1993.

Conversations with Dr. J.T. Nelson, a professor of Education at Gonzaga University, and an expert on South African Education. Spokane, WA, 1994.

Moodie, T. Dunbar. *The Rise of Afrikanerdom: Power, Apartheid, and the Afrikaner Civil Religion.* Berkeley: University of California Press, 1975.

Nelson, Harold. *South Africa: A Country Study.* Washington, DC: U.S. Government Printing Office, 1981.

Omer-Cooper, J.D. *The Cambridge History of Africa.* Cambridge, England: Cambridge University Press, 1976.

Robertson, Neville L. and Barbara, L. *Education in South Africa.* Bloomington, IN: PDK Fastback Series, #90, Phi Delta Kappa, 1977.

Sampson, Anthony. *Black and Gold.* New York: Pantheon Books, 1987.

Tutu, Desmond. *The Rainbow People of God.* New York: Doubleday, 1994.

United Nations. "South Africa." *U.N. Chronicle,* Vol. XXXI, No. 2 (September 1994).

Voslou, W.B. "The Coloured Policy of the National Party." In N.J. Rhoudie, *South African Dialogue.* Philadelphia: Westminister Press, 1972, pp. 265–366.

Wilson, Monica. "The Hunters and the Herders." *Oxford History of South Africa.* New York: Oxford University Press, 1969.

37

Spain

HISTORY OF THE SYSTEM

Spain's national history has been traced back to the fifth century A.D., when a Germanic state was established in the Roman diocese of Hispania by the Visgoths. Following a period of turbulence during the Middle Ages, the present boundaries were established late in the fifteenth century, making it one of the oldest nation-states in Europe.

However, the country is unique in that it is closer to the African continent than any other European nation. The Straits of Gibraltar are only about 15 kilometers from Africa; and interactions with the rest of Europe have been difficult because of the Pyrenees range which make communication with central and northern Europe difficult (except by sea).

The Mediterranean portions of Spain and the central regions have been in opposition since the south was Iberian and the north Celtic. The Iberians migrated to Spain in the third millennium B.C. They were named by the Greeks because they resided along the banks of the Rio Ebro. Although there is disagreement as to their original homelands, they are generally believed to have migrated to the area from the eastern shores of the Mediterranean seas.

After being defeated by the Romans in the First Punic War (264–41 B.C.), Carthage compensated for its loss of Sicily by rebuilding a commercial empire in Spain which became a staging ground for Hannibal's famous invasion of Italy during the Second Punic War (218–201 B.C.). The country was invaded by Roman armies and the name Hispania was provided by the Romans. Hispania was divided up into three provinces which were separately governed. By the fourth century A.D., the number of provinces had increased to nine.

The Iberian Peninsula has historically been one of the more pluralistic parts of Europe. In addition to the different ethnic groups such as the Iberians and Celts, Spain has also seen the involvement of violently opposed religious fac-

tions, particularly the Islamics and the Christians. However, other conflicts ensued between the Castillians and Catalans. Both of these ethnic microcultures
exhibited immense pride, but the language of the Castillians prevailed and this
eventually became the ''mother tongue'' of the country.

During the early portions of the eighth century, North African armies began
to invade the country, and eventually Spain was under the influence of the
Moors. In 711, Tariq ibn Ziyad entered Spain with an army of some 12,000
men, and just one year later Musa ibn Nusair did the same. In three years he
was successful in subduing all of Spain except for the northern mountainous
regions. Islamic Spain was referred to as Al Andalus, and the Islamic domination
of the country lasted for several centuries. Resistance to the Muslim invasion
had been limited to small groups of Visigoth warriors who eventually retreated
to the Asturias Mountains.

In 981, Castille became an independent country and Spain recaptured its territories from the Moors. Valencia was seized from its Muslim emir and became
federated with Catalonia and Aragon in 1238. This new union became known
as Aragon, and eventually the tripartite federation rivaled Genoa and Venice for
control of Mediterranean trade.

Gradually, the Muslim leaders became weakened through disunity and began
to fall to the Castillians. After the fall of Toledo in 1085, the Almoravids, a
party of strict Muslims, tried to initiate a religious revival which was not too
effective. They were then replaced by the Almohads who became a major threat
to the Christian states. However, they were defeated in the battle of Las Navas
de Tolosa in 1212, and the Muslim strength in Spain continued to erode until
the golden age of Ferdinand and Isabella.

The year 1469 was an important one in Spain's history because Ferdinand
and Isabella were married. Ferdinand was from Aragon, while his cousin, Isabella, was from Castille. This marital union helped bring a level of stability to
both of these kingdoms. But even with the union of the Castillian and the
Aragonese crowns, Castille, Aragon, Catalonia, and Valencia remained constitutionally distinct political entities, and they retained separate parliaments and
councils of state. They resumed the re-conquest which had been dormant for a
long period of time. In 1492, they were able to capture Granada and became
referred to as Catholic Kings. After Islamic Spain did not exist, they were able
to pay full attention to the threat of hundreds of thousands of Muslims living
in the recently incorporated Granada. At that time, Spain seemed to be intent
on becoming involved in a quest for an unattainable purification.

In other parts of Europe, it was thought that religious unity was necessary for
political unity, but Spain is said to have led the way for religious conformity.
Spain's population was much more heterogeneous than the other European
nations, and it contained a significant number of non-Christian microcultures.
In some of those communities, Muslims were given the choice of converting to
Christianity or becoming voluntarily exiled. Many Jews converted to Christi-

anity and went on to fill important governmental positions. Others purchased their way into various positions of nobility.

By 1525, all residents of Spain were officially Christian, but not all Christians were able to become integrated into Spanish society unless they had "purity of blood" (limpieze de sangre). So many families began reconstructing their family trees.

It was a period of great colonization enterprises, led by the first of a long line of famous seamen, Christopher Columbus. Motivated by a rivalry with Portugal, Ferdinand and Isabella agreed to fund his voyage to India using a western route.

The rest of Spain's exploits into the "New World" proceeded rapidly. Vasco Nunez de Balboa reached the Pacific in 1513, and the survivors of Ferdinand Magellan's expedition completed the circumnavigation of the earth in 1522. Hernando Cortes subdued the Mexican Aztecs in 1519; and between 1531 and 1533, Francisco Pizarro overran the empire of the Incas and established the Spanish domination of Peru.

Vast sums of money had been expended for shipbuilding ventures and for the various explorations into the Americas and Africa. During the middle of the sixteenth century, there was no other nation which could rival Spain's military strength. Due to its ownership of the Low Countries and some of the provinces which constituted present-day France, it had great power. At that time in history, England had not yet acquired the enormous power which it would soon possess.

In the Mediterranean, Spain controlled the north coast of Africa but was not able to fend off the power of the Muslims. In Mexico and Peru, it had access to mines which provided great wealth to the countries. It established a series of forts along the coastal regions of the eastern parts of North and South America to protect its heavily laden galleons which took advantage of the trade winds on their way back to Europe. Through its control of northern Africa, it was able to fend off the Muslim power of Turkey. Spain was able to pressure the Papacy in order to get favorable decisions during the periods of time when it was not engaged in out-and-out hostilities with the Pope.

The Spanish Armada was the best in the world, and the Spanish Army was the pride of Europe. It was during this period of time that the Spanish universities began to acquire their well-known prestige. The country also produced some of the world's finest painters. It was a period of intense pride and extraordinary accomplishments for the country.

However, sixteenth-century Spain actually suffered a demise because of its great riches. Due to the great militaristic expenditures for the Spanish fleet and the armies of Cortes, Pizarro, and the other military leaders, domestic production was not properly stimulated. The precious metals from America which were spent on the Spanish military establishment hastened inflation throughout Europe and put the Spaniards in a position where they were unable to pay their debts, causing the Spanish goods to become so overpriced that they could not compete in international markets.

The economic problems led to a period of great decline in the seventeenth century. During the reign of Charles II, the last of the Spanish Habsburgs, the country's treasury was ravaged, and famine, floods, drought, warfare with France, and the Plague devastated the country. After France and Spain signed the Treaty of the Pyrenees, the French seized the Spanish Netherlands as partial payment for a dowry debt owed to Louis XIV for his Spanish wife, Maria Teresa.

A period of economic recovery finally occurred during the Enlightenment era under the reign of Charles III. As in the rest of Europe, attempts were made to reform society in order to solve the nagging social, political, and economic problems. Anticlericalism was an integral part of the Enlightenment ideology. Monasteries were suppressed by the state, and the Jesuits, who were antiregalism, were expelled.

Up to this time in Spain's history, education had been carried out in the private sector, particularly by the Catholic Church. The Court of Alfonso X of Castile advocated that the clergy have instruction in science and legal matters, but theology was taught in the convents of Dominican and Franciscan friars. The Spanish universities were practically nonexistent until the latter part of the fourteenth century.

Spain suffered a number of military setbacks which led to a popular uprising in 1808, ultimately resulting in a new constitution which was written in 1812. The primary goal of this document was to prevent the arbitrary and corrupt rule of monarchs and provide for a limited monarchy. It was a liberal constitution which established a centralized administration and favored the commercial class in the new parliament. However, it was a revolutionary document, and when Ferdinand VII was restored to power, he refused to recognize it.

This chaotic period caused Spain's American colonies to exploit this new problem, and by 1825, all of them except for Cuba, the Philippines, and Puerto Rico proclaimed their independence. Efforts to reestablish Spanish control were unsuccessful, and by 1898, Spain had granted independence to their last three colonies as a result of treaties signed in Paris at the termination of the Spanish-American War.

From 1909 to 1926, the Spanish army had been allied with France in expeditions against Abd al Krim's Riff Berbers in Morocco. It was not a popular war and casualties were exceptionally high. Consequently, Spain was beleaguered with citizen opposition to the conscription process which was being used to recruit troops. During the World War I period, Spain remained neutral. However, its involvement in the African conflict continued to take a heavy toll and there was an increase in communist activity in Spain. Miguel Primo de Rivera, a general officer, assumed power in 1923, dissolved the Italian parliament, and crafted a ruling military government until 1930. His authoritarian rule was popular both with the people and the Crown.

During the 1931 elections, the antimonarchist parties won a substantial majority of the vote. A constitutional convention consisting of multiparties met at San Sebastian to usher in the Second Republic of Spain. As a result of the San

Sebastian meeting, the army was reformed, regional autonomy was granted, there was a separation between church and state, and the role of the Church in the country's educational system was terminated. The first general election resulted in a coalition party win for the Republican Left, a middle-class party which was radical in nature, and a labor party.

By 1936, the country was embroiled in a civil war between the Republicans and Nationalist forces, with Franco assuming the leadership of the Nationalist forces. Franco was known as a highly professional, career-oriented combat soldier who had become a skilled officer. He was commissioned at the age of eighteen and volunteered for service in Morocco where he became known as a highly effective, courageous leader, even though he was also known as a humorless, studious, and withdrawn man. Finally, Barcelona fell to the Nationalist forces in 1938, and Franco assumed the authoritarian regime that came into office after the civil war. He would rule until 1975.

After the termination of World War II, Franco attempted to impress the victorious democracies by issuing a Spanish Bill of Rights which guaranteed Spaniards the right to express their opinions but still made it illegal to attack the basic principles of the Spanish state. There were also a number of pardons and reduced prison terms for civil war crimes prisoners. It was also possible for issues to be submitted by means of popular referendum, as long as Franco agreed to have the idea submitted to the people for a vote.

Franco's European loyalties were toward the Axis powers during World War II, even though he declared Spain to be neutral during the beginning of the international conflict. This was altered in 1940 after a number of major German victories. When the United States entered the war and landed on Casablanca in 1942, Spain reversed itself and reestablished its neutrality. But after the end of the war, the United Nations would not allow Spain to become a member because of Franco. However, the United States was interested in establishing strategic contacts with Spain because of the fall of Czechoslovakia, the Berlin Wall, and the outbreak of the Korean War. Eventually, relations between the U.S. and Spain were normalized and Spain became a United Nations member in 1950.

But with the selection of Juan Carlos, Franco's chosen heir, an amazing transition occurred in the country. Even though Juan Carlos was chosen to be the new king of spain, in the late 1970s, a number of major events occurred which led to Spain's ultimate democratization, and free elections were held in 1977. Political parties were legalized and the first election was won by moderate political parties. A new constitution was drawn up proclaiming Spain to be a parliamentary monarchy. Citizens were guaranteed equality before the law, and a full assortment of individual liberties, including religious freedom, was mandated. Submitted to a referendum, it was approved by 89 percent of the population in 1978. At this time, the school system was under the control of the government which was then able to inspect and license schools, and provide some funds for private education. Children in the state schools could be provided religious instruction as long as their parents approved.

STRUCTURE OF THE SYSTEM

The most powerful governmental institution of the Spanish state is the Cortes, which consists of a lower house, the congress of deputies, and the senate, which is the upper chamber. In defining the state as a parliamentary monarchy, the Spanish constitution stipulates that the king is not sovereign and that sovereignty resides with the Spanish people through their democratically elected parliament. However, the king is a hereditary monarch who is the "head of state." This concept is actually a sort of compromise which came about when the constitution was being crafted.

In addition to the constitution and the hereditary king, the Spanish governmental structure includes the usual three branches (legislative, executive, and judicial). The Cortes is made up of the lower house (congress of deputies) and the upper house (senate). In addition to the king, the executive branch consists of the council of ministers, the prime minister, deputy, and the cabinet ministers. The judicial branch functions under the constitutional premise that justice emanates from the people and that the system operates in the name of the king through independent judges and magistrates who cannot be removed from office. The justice system is headed by the supreme court which is the highest judicial body in the land.

During the 1980s, Spain spent about 8 percent of its national budget on education. However, during the late 1970s, the country admitted that even though the Spanish constitution guaranteed a free education to all of its citizens, the nation was unable to hire teachers or build schools quickly enough to meet the educational needs of Spanish children. One solution was to involve more students in the private schools and provide some of the public funds for serving that purpose. The compulsory attendance ages are from six to fourteen. Secondary school attendance has been optional, but if students choose to attend secondary schools, they are forced to participate in vocational education programs when they are fifteen and sixteen.

By 1987, about 80 percent of Spain's children between the ages of four and six went to nursery schools. However, most of the public nursery schools were actually day care centers with little instruction being provided. Only one-third of the nursery-age children went to public schools where the pre-school programs were stronger. It has been posited that this situation has led to a rather high failure rate in the country's schools. But another source of school problems for Spain has been the low teacher salaries. During 1989, approximately 200,000 of Spain's public school teachers went on strike for a 14 percent pay raise. It was finally put down by the government after a number of violent demonstrations.

Spain's universities also have suffered from funding problems which have resulted in a per-pupil spending level which is only about one-third of the expenditures in western European countries. Still another problem has been the overpreparation of students in overcrowded fields and the failure to entice university students into badly needed new programs such as the computer sciences. Finally, since very few scholarships have been available for low-income students, the Spanish universities have largely been accessible only to the middle-class and wealthy students.

MULTICULTURAL EDUCATION EFFORTS

The Assistant Director General of Compensatory Education is in charge of multicultural education programs in Spain. Approximately 500,000,000 pesetas are budgeted annually for such educational enterprises. Multicultural education programs of various types are necessitated by the country's relatively pluralistic population. The indigenous microcultures are primarily composed of Castillians, Catalans, and Basques. Immigrant microcultures consist of Asians and black Africans, while the religious groups are composed of Jews, Muslims, Christians, Catholics, agnostics, and atheists.

While the official language of Spain is Spanish, each of the Spanish states is allowed to use the instructional language of their choice. Normally, bilingual instructional programs are not part of the regular curriculum, nor are curriculum sequences which address the historical involvement of indigenous populations. However, in certain situations, Portuguese is used in the education of some students in order to ensure better success in the schools.

Parents register their students in the school which is closest to their home, so racially segregated schools have not been part of the Spanish school system. While there are no nationally mandated requirements for the screening of textbooks and curriculum materials for racist and sexist content, they do monitor such materials in order to make sure that they do not violate the Spanish constitution.

The Spanish respondent to the authors' multicultural education study also mentioned that one of Spain's biggest problems in education occurs in some of the remote parts of the country. Many of these isolated communities maintain their own identity and have a difficult time in learning to appreciate the pluralistic microcultures in the rest of the country. The same respondent also felt that bilingual education programs were badly needed in order to meet the educational needs of children from the various microcultures.

For many years, Spain placed many restrictions on women, and very few on men. For example, divorce was not legalized until 1981 and the society followed a strict moral code. Prostitution was accepted. However, with the democratization of the country, the role of women began to change. For example, by 1984, about one-third of all Spanish women had entered the job market. During the Franco regime, women were prohibited from traveling away from home, owning property, or even securing employment without their husband's approval.

Finally, it is important to note that the new changes which stress equity in the social milieus occurred as a result of Jose Maria Maravall Herrero, the Minister of Education and Science during most of the 1980s. His writings have stipulated that the country's educational system must "promote the cohesion of the nation" (cultural integration); "contribute to the integration of society" (social integration); "foster equality of opportunity" (economic integration); and "socialize citizens to hold democratic values" (political integration).

SUMMARY

Few countries have encountered such dramatic philosophical changes in such a short period of time. In just a few years, Spain went from a long history of governance by monarchs to a system of democracy, complete with national elections. Of course, the educational system reflected this dramatic turnaround. From a system of rather spasmodic education efforts, mostly for children from upper income families, Spain adapted a comprehensive system of public education which attempted to provide educational services to all Spanish children regardless of their socio-economic status.

Of course, one of the biggest problems in meeting such goals always seems to relate to finances, and Spain is no exception. While the country has mandated compulsory education for all school-age students, a lack of adequate funding has made this difficult. The pre-school programs do not always offer instructional sequences which are crafted by certificated teachers. Some of them have been little more than typical day care operations.

This situation has resulted in some children who seem to be unprepared for the regular school years. Moreover, inadequate funding has led to poor salaries, resulting in work stoppages and teacher strikes which resulted in violence at times. In spite of these difficulties, the country has made enormous strides, and it is quite likely that Spain will continue to improve its educational institution in the future.

REFERENCES

Hillgarth, J.N. *The Spanish Kingdoms.* Oxford: Clarendon Press, 1976.

Hooper, John. *The Spaniards: A Portrait of New Spain.* New York: Penguin Books, 1987.

Mackay, Angus. *Spain in the Middle Ages: From Frontier to Empire, 1000–1500.* New York: St. Martin's Press, 1977.

Michener, William. *Iberia.* New York: Random House, 1968.

Mitchell, Bruce and Salsbury, Robert E. *An International Survey of Multicultural Education.* Cheney, WA: Western States Consulting and Evaluation Services, 1991. (See Appendix.)

Ramsey, John F. *Spain: The Rise of World Power.* Birmingham: The University of Alabama Press, 1980.

Rix, R. "Education for the New Spain." *Bulletin of Hispanic Studies,* Vol. 71, No. 2 (1994), pp. 291–292. (Book Review.)

Solsten, Eric D. *Spain: A Country Study.* Washington, DC: Department of the Army, 1990.

Tura, Jordi Sole. ''The Spanish Transition to Democracy.'' In Robert P. Clark and Michael H. Haltzel (Eds.), *Spain in the 1980s.* Cambridge, MA: Ballinger Publishers, 1987, pp. 25–34.

38

Sweden

HISTORY OF THE SYSTEM

In order to understand Sweden, it is necessary to examine the geographical history of the country when that part of the world saw the massive inland ice cap start to disappear. By A.D. 800, the prehistory period of Sweden ended and the Viking era started. This period of time has been viewed as a buffer between prehistory and the Middle Ages which reached present-day Sweden about 1050.

Sweden has been described as a land of contrasts. The southern tip stretches south as far as the Baltic, and the north goes all the way to the Arctic Circle. Consequently, there is an enormous range in the climatic conditions from the northern tip to the southern climes. In fact, the average temperature is 17 degrees warmer in southern Skane than it is in the north.

There is some evidence that human beings first appeared in present-day Sweden about 8000 B.C., particularly on the Arctic shores. Most of Sweden was populated with persons moving to that part of the world from southern Europe. A larger number of these adventures actually came from southern Europe. Over the years, many of the country's immigrants had German roots.

The Iron Age created a number of positive advantages for Scandinavia, particularly Sweden which still enjoys rich deposits of iron ore. Historians also believe that during the Iron Age, European Celts were coming to the region, bringing with them another kind of knowledge which was prominent in that part of Europe. However, accurate information is difficult to acquire because cremation seems to have been preferred to burial. The Iron Age is said to have occurred during the five centuries before the birth of Christ.

However, the Scandinavians were also attracted by bronze products being made in countries as far away as Hungary. Consequently, a network was established in which local Swedish products were being traded for items which came from Hungary, Spain, and France. Swedish people traveled in horse-drawn carts and oar-driven ships. As trade barriers developed, the Swedes and other Scandinavian groups conducted various types of sea raids. This led to the term "Vikings" which was used to characterize the Scandinavian raiders who would sometimes hide in a creek or bay and swoop out and attack passing vessels. The term *vik* means "creek" in the languages of Scandinavia.

The age of the vikings finally began to draw to a close during A.D. 1000. By that time, three distinct kingdoms had emerged. In addition to Sweden, Norway and Denmark were considered to be the main part of Scandanavia. At that time in history, the traditional religions of the country were still in force. Christianity had not yet gained a solid foothold and the country was greatly divided between pagans and Christians. During the first 200 years after A.D. 1000, Sweden went through a period of solid trade expansion. Eric XI (Eric the Lame) succeeded the last king of the Sverker dynasty. He was only 6 years old when he became the king of Sweden. However, the king's brother-in-law, Birger Magnusson, became the jarl, or earl of the realm. When he took over the country's leadership, he brought in German craftspersons and miners who were instrumental in laying the groundwork for the development of the country's industrial foundations.

Up until the time Magnusson came to the throne, cases were judged on a "trial by ordeal" basis. Sometimes an accused person would be thrown into deep water and the guilt or innocence was decided on the basis of whether the accused person sank or floated. Or the person could hold a red-hot iron, and guilt or innocence was based on the extent of damage to the person holding the iron. However, Magnusson abolished this system of assessing guilt or innocence and established a system of courts which were more similar to the ones used during modern times.

It has been argued by some that Sweden has been able to enjoy more security than many nations in the world because of its isolation which has allowed it to escape much of the conflict and warfare which plagued the rest of the world throughout history. When the industrial revolution occurred in the country, Sweden was rather quickly transformed from a rural nation to a highly industrialized one which has enjoyed one of the highest standards of living in Europe. Moreover, the country has been almost totally free of the ravages of poverty.

By the time King Magnus Ericsson came of age in 1332, Sweden had peaked as far as its power and prestige were concerned. But the new king had many major problems to address. The kingdom of Sweden was fairly large but sparsely populated, making it rather difficult to manage. German traders had arrived in the kingdom and decided to settle there.

However, by the time of the Thirty Years War, Sweden became considered as a new world power. By this time, the city of Goteburg had been rebuilt and Louis DeGeer had begun large-scale mining and the processing of the country's immense deposits of iron ore. DeGeer was actually a Dutch industrialist and he brought to Sweden a number of French-speaking Belgians (Calvinist Walloons) who settled down in the country with a growing number of Lutherans who were typical of the Christian sects which had arrived in northern Europe by that time.

During the sixteenth century, Sweden still tended to maintain a medieval posture. During that time, Finland, which was a part of the kingdom of Sweden and Denmark, and considered to be one of the country's primary enemies, controlled the routes to western Europe. This motivated Sweden to adapt a policy of expansion which attempted to gain control of the routes to western Europe. When the House of Hapsburg became interested in establishing a Catholic empire and advanced toward the Baltic regions, crushing a number of Protestant princes on the way, Gustavus Adolphus, the grandson of Gustaf Vasa, decided to become involved in a military campaign which would become known as the Thirty Years War. With the help of Dutch and other military experts, he created a peasant army which became one of the most sophisticated military units of that time.

His victorious military units were noted for their firm discipline and courage. During 1631 and 1632, he reached Frankfort and marched through Bavaria shortly after. But during the battle, Gustavus Adolphus was killed and the expansionist policies were terminated. The Peace of Westphalia Treaty was signed in 1648 and Sweden managed to maintain some of its important possessions on the southern shores of the Baltic. This ended the Thirty Years War.

After Sweden's newly acquired status as a world power, the country was still forced to face enemies on two fronts—namely, the Danes in the south and west, and Russia in the east. However, a new threat loomed in the form of its German possessions. Under Charles X Gustavus, wars on all three fronts were going on at the same time, creating an enormous hardship for the country. By the end of the eighteenth century, the standing army had grown to nearly 57,000 men and there were also more than 32,000 mercenaries.

Charles XII (known as Charles the Strong) embarked on a number of military ventures during the early 1800s. After Peter the Great of Russia attacked Swedish forces at Narva, on the Gulf of Finland, Charles won a major victory, taking a large number of Russian prisoners. He also attacked Poland, capturing Cracow and defeating an army of Poles and Saxons at Kliszow. By the winter of 1707–1708, he had invaded Russia, and was advancing toward Moscow. However, that winter happened to be one of the worst Russian winters on record. Bitter cold, coupled with spring floods, led to a major Swedish defeat resulting in the surrender of about 14,000 Swedish forces.

After traveling to Turkey in an attempt to persuade them to attack the Russian tsar, Charles returned home to Sweden in order to defend the country against a coalition of European forces (the Northern League) which were preparing an attack on the country. By 1715, Sweden had lost all of its Baltic possessions. By 1720, the Swedish conflicts with Denmark, Hannover, and Prussia had ended but the hostilities with Russia continued on.

When the American Revolution began in 1775, Swedish sympathies were with the Americans. A number of Swedish officers joined forces with the French and other Swedish men volunteered for the French navy. After the termination of hostilities between England and the United States, Sweden became one of the first countries to sign a treaty of commerce with the United States.

By 1792, Gustav III had assumed a great deal of power in Sweden but was assassinated by a group of noblemen. Gustav IV, his son, then ascended to the throne and decided to side with England in the confrontation with Napoleon. Alexander I of Russia had become an ally of Napoleon who urged Russia to enter into warfare against Sweden. As a result of the ensuing actions, Sweden became reduced to its present boundaries.

During the nineteenth century, Sweden became transformed from an isolated agricultural nation to a greatly industrialized one. An "open-field" system had developed during the Middle Ages. The fields of entire hamlets were managed as units, and their houses along the village streets were surrounded by the arable land. During the first part of the nineteenth century, the peasant population of Sweden wished to maintain this type of life style. However, there were increasing number of demands for change, mostly coming from the enlightened nobles who eyed the financial gains which could be acquired by trading with England and the low countries.

The country then moved to the "enclosure system" which involved the uprooting of peasants who were given large plots of land on which they resided and tilled the soil. This ended the earlier practice of peasants residing together in towns and farming narrow plots of land. It tended to create a situation where the uprooted peasants were isolated, self-centered, and lonely. Some became suspicious of their neighbors.

However, this new practice also created a new awakening in the country and the issue of education became greatly discussed. By 1841, the parliament decided to pass legislation which led to the country's first compulsory education laws. Each parish was required to have an elementary school and a teacher.

By 1848, Europe became involved in the "Year of Revolutions" which provided the motivation for many people to emigrate to other countries. Crop failures also contributed to the exodus. Many of them went to the United States where they tended to settle in the Great Lakes region of the country. They were able to acquire land through the country's Homestead Act. During this period of time, Sweden lost nearly 25 percent of its population. By 1855, Britain and France signed the November Treaty which guaranteed the sovereignty of Sweden.

The industrial growth of the country during the last half of the nineteenth century continued, and by 1899 a number of cooperative societies had sprung up throughout the country. During that year, these societies met at Stockholm and formed a coalition which was called the Kooperativa Forbundet (KF). By the start of World War II, most of the co-op members came from the working classes. However, the membership gradually expanded so that more lower-middle and middle-middle class participation occurred. However, there was fierce opposition to the cooperatives by the upper classes until the Great Depression. Throughout the history of Sweden's labor movement, there has been a constant argument as to the involvement of socialist ideology within the capitalistic economic system. The Social Democratic Party has attempted to separate political convictions from their cooperative activities.

While only one-tenth of Sweden's population lived in urban areas in 1870, by the beginning of World War II about one-fourth of the people resided in cities. While the country had built up its merchant fleet so that international trade had expanded dramatically, the nation's inland transportation system was not adequate. Consequently, Nils Ericson embarked on a project to create a national rail system which would link the entire nation and stimulate economic growth. Parliament approved the plan and eventually the entire country would become connected by rail.

Sweden was devastated by the Great Depression of the late 1920s and early 1930s. Unemployment rose and wages dropped. The bad economic conditions led to a number of ugly incidents which peaked in northern Sweden when five citizens were killed by troops who were called upon to stop a violent labor demonstration in May 1931.

During World War II Sweden managed to remain neutral. The country was the wealthiest of the Scandinavian nations and, unlike Denmark and Norway, it was not invaded. Sweden managed to escape invasion because of a number of concessions it made to Germany. However, one of these concessions irritated the Norwegians because the Swedes allowed the Germans to use the country's rail system for the transportation of troops, arms, and supplies to Norway. Because of the Swedish neutrality during World War II, the country was much stronger economically than some of its neighbors, such as Denmark and Norway.

STRUCTURE OF THE SYSTEM

Sweden is a constitutional monarchy, with the king serving as a mostly ceremonial head of state. The country's political power is divided into the executive and legislative branches by virtue of their constitution. While a multiparty system exists, the nation has been reasonably stable since the early 1930s. The latest constitution went into effect in 1975, replacing what had been Europe's oldest constitution, established in 1809. The new constitution maintained the concept of the king being the head of state, but without any appreciable power. No longer does the king preside over the cabinet meetings and assume the leadership of the country's armed forces network. Moreover, he lost his power to declare meetings of the Riksdag and became forced to pay taxes and customs. Also, no longer would he be immune from being prosecuted in a court of law. If there were no male heirs, the Riksdag would name a regent. But only males are allowed to ascend to the throne. There is a bill of rights which outlines the broad civil rights of the Swedish citizenry.

The prime minister is the actual head of state in Sweden. He presides over the cabinet which is composed of some twenty ministers. The ministers are not in charge of the routine administration of the routine administrative work. That type of work is performed by central boards, leaving the ministers to spend their time formulating appropriate procedural policies.

During 1871 the Riksdag became unicameral. Candidates for office are nominated by their parties. The functions of the Riksdag are to accept, reject, or revise governmental proposals for new laws, pass budgets, impose taxes, and to control the administration. On any issue it is possible to solicit the views of the electorate through consultative referendums.

Sweden's concern to educate all of its citizens actually started in the nineteenth century. Because of the country's excellent educational system, the illiteracy rate in the country is only about 1 percent. The primary goal of the system is to allow each child to rise as far educationally as possible. A nationwide, nine-year comprehensive school system is one of Sweden's proudest institutions. The schooling which follows the first nine years consists of the gymnasiums, the continuation schools, and the vocational institutes. After completing their compulsory education, about half of the students continue to receive their instruction in one of the three schools. The final scores during the ninth-grade year are used to determine entrance to the gymnasiums which offer three years of study in liberal arts, social sciences, economics, natural sciences, and technical arts. Everyone except for students in the technical arts programs must study three foreign languages for one year each.

The University of Uppsala was the country's first institution of higher education. In addition, four other universities include Lund, Goteberg, Stockholm, and Umea. Degrees are available in humanities, social sciences, and natural sciences. All tuition is free, and no attempts are made to monitor the behavior of university students outside the school. Swedish students have nearly complete freedom of behavior.

MULTICULTURAL EDUCATION PROGRAMS

Approximately 10 percent of the Swedish population consists of aliens, and just half of these students continue with upper-secondary schooling. These ethnic minorities consist of Lapps, Finns, Estonians, Poles, Russians, Czechs, Germans, Ugandans, Indians, Greeks, Danes, and Norwegians. There are eight state-operated nomad schools, and the Lapp languages and culture are taught as part of the regular school program.

A 1975 law stressed that all of these ethnic groups have access to the same educational opportunities, rights, and responsibilities as the population at large. The general aim of immigrant child education is to promote active bilingualism. Students should be taught in the mother tongue if parents so desire, but Swedish as a second language should also be part of the school program in order that all Swedish children can master the country's primary language in order to become productive participants in Swedish society. Also, adults are given the opportunity to learn Swedish. Instruction in English is widely provided in the schools since it is the primary language of international trade and commerce.

Some have argued that the host countries should keep and develop their mother tongues, and that both integration into the mainstream and cultural identity should be fostered by educating both the migrants and host peoples in order to promote a mutual understanding and appreciation of all the country's microcultural contributions. Such an approach would lead to a more functional view of culture and language.

The argument has addressed the issue of using a multicultural approach to solve educational problems. The argument has also been that the use of linguistic principles coupled with the basic tenets of humanistic sociology will provide a meaningful framework for conducting future research and crafting successful multicultural education programs.

Among other unique intercultural programs in Sweden is an exchange project between university students from Sweden (University of Lund) and India (Orissa). The goal of the program is to provide opportunities for developing and developed countries to learn from each other. Primary aims are to improve teacher training and support of educational research. Program components include Visiting India; Visiting Sweden; The School Practice Program; Sister School; The Preschool Development Center; The Teacher Training Center; The Student Circle; The Seminar Program; The Information Program; The Sponsor Program; The Program for Organization Cooperation; and The Research Program.

SUMMARY

Sweden, like most of the other Scandinavian countries, has a deep commitment to many of the basic notions of multicultural education due to their deep belief in egalitarian principles. When compared with England in the examination of educational policies for minority students, one interesting fact prevails. While both countries strongly emphasize the acquisition of the language by the majority culture, the role of the mother tongue in Sweden has been heavily emphasized.

Among the other important characteristics of Sweden's view of multicultural education is the notion that all children in the country are entitled to equal educational opportunities. Moreover, education in the country is free, and children are all entitled to free lunches if they so desire.

One of the reasons for Sweden's commitment to many basic principles of multicultural education has been the number of foreign nationals who have become a part of Sweden's labor force in recent years. As the country became more industrialized, the need for a greater labor force made it possible for Sweden to recruit persons from the rest of the world. Because of the egalitarian philosophy which prevailed, the children of these new immigrants were entitled to equal educational opportunities.

REFERENCES

Bronwojciechowska, A. "Education and Gender in Sweden: Is There Any Equality?" *Women's Studies International Forum,* Vol. 18, No. 1 (1995), pp. 51–60.

Butler, Ewan. *The Concise History of Scandinavia.* New York: American Heritage Publishing Company, 1973.

Carlgren, W.M. *Swedish Foreign Policy During the Second World War.* New York: St. Martin's Press, 1971.

Ekstrand, Lars. *Children in India and Sweden.* Lund, Sweden: University Center for Multicultural Studies, 1990.

Fleisher, Frederic. *The New Sweden.* New York: David McKay Inc., 1967.

Fris, Ann-Margaret. "Policies for Minority Education. A Comparative Study of Britain and Sweden." Unpublished Doctoral Dissertation, University of Stockholm, 1982.

Lindblad, S. and Wallin, E. "On Transitions of Power, Democracy, and Education in Sweden." *Journal of Curriculum Studies,* Vol. 25, No. 1 (1993), pp. 77–78.

Lundquist, Sven. "Experience of an Empire: Sweden as a Great Power." In Michael Roberts, (Ed.), *Sweden's Age of Greatness.* New York: St. Martin's Press, 1973.

Oskaar, Elis. *Language—Integration—Identity: Socio-Cultural Problems of New Minorities.* ERIC No. ED 269485, 1982.

Stenberger, Marten. *Sweden.* New York: Praeger, 1962.

39

Taiwan

HISTORY OF THE SYSTEM

The recorded history of the island of Taiwan can be traced back to the sixteenth century, when it became a base of operations for Chinese and Japanese pirates during the early part of that century. During much of the seventeenth century, a struggle for control of the island existed between Spain and Holland. Finally, in 1662, the Europeans were ousted by Cheng Ch'eng-kung, a pirate chief of both Japanese and Chinese ancestry.

After a short period of control by the Chinese during the latter portion of the Ming Dynasty (1368–1644), China assumed full control of the island until 1895. China then ceded the island to Japan when it was defeated by that country, forcing them to also give up Korea. This action occurred as a result of the Treaty of Shimonoseki which stated that Taiwan and the Pescadores (Penghu) were to become part of the Japanese empire.

However, shortly after the treaty was signed, local Chinese officials declared the island to be an independent republic. When the Japanese arrived to assume control, they were met by an armed force of approximately 50,000 Taiwanese. Even though the Japanese prevailed and occupied the island, resistance continued for about five months. After that time, the skirmishes decreased substantially and things remained relatively calm despite a pair of minor uprisings against the Japanese during 1907 and 1928.

The Japanese posture regarding Taiwan was based on the country's interest in gaining a world reputation as a colonial power. The governmental functions were carried out by a governor general who was personally appointed by the Japanese emperor. He was usually an army general or an admiral who was given absolute power. Even though there were some token local officials, Japanese officials dominated all levels of administration and the authority was highly centralized.

A civilian police force of about 12,000 persons was maintained and supplemented by special forces who were responsible for overseeing the aboriginal areas. The police were quite efficient in maintaining control, and a great deal of the efficiency was due to a system of using informers. The Taiwanese people were divided up into groups of about 100 families who were headed by a senior member who was selected by each unit as long as that elected person was acceptable to the Japanese leaders. Punishment for any sort of infractions was extremely severe.

The Japanese occupation forces continued to be harassed by aboriginal tribesmen until 1930 when they were finally severely defeated. The Japanese confiscated their weapons, forced them to give up hunting and live solely on the basis of their agricultural production. In order to survive, they were forced to move to valleys where cultivation was simpler and it was easier for the dominant Japanese to control them. However, a program was initiated which provided 200 elementary schools and a number of vocational schools for the aboriginal inhabitants of the country.

The Mukden Incident, in 1931, had the effect of plunging Japan into war against China. In January of 1932, the Japanese navy attacked Shanghai, the heart of China's commercial and industrial efforts. On March 9, the Japanese government created the puppet state of Manchuko, with Chiang Kai-shek signing the Tangku Truce which placed Japan in a position of dominance along China's south coast.

This turn of events placed the Taiwanese inhabitants in an awkward position. Due to the years of colonialization, the Taiwanese had acquired many of the ethnic characteristics of the Japanese colonialists. This irritated the Chinese who resented the fact that they had given up many of the traditional Chinese ethnic characteristics. Moreover, the Taiwanese had become increasingly prosperous, causing a rift between the country of China and Taiwan. During the 1930s, China was also plagued by the Nationalist government of China being harassed by local military governments and also by the Chinese Communists who were becoming stronger.

Chiang Kai-shek decided that it was necessary for him to defeat the Communist faction in order to acquire enough strength to defeat the Japanese. By 1934, he had succeeded in expelling the Japanese from Kiangsi province. However, the bulk of the Communist army was able to escape to Shensi province. Two years later, Chiang Kai-shek was actually kidnapped and held prisoner for several days in a failed attempt to force him to collaborate with the Communists in a joint military effort against the Japanese.

Finally, in 1937, a battle occurred at Marco Polo Bridge near Peiping, and the military struggle between the Chinese Nationalists and the Japanese had begun. By 1940, the Yangtze Valley, the coastal regions, North China, and Manchuria were all controlled by the Japanese, and Chiang Kai-shek had been forced to withdraw his government to Chungking. When China became a partner of the Allies during the beginning of World War II, the country was hopelessly isolated and extremely vulnerable.

During the 1930s, Japan had spent a great deal of money on the development of Taiwanese schools. Japanese had become the language of instruction and students were forced to view themselves as Japanese subjects. Enrollment in the nation's schools increased rapidly and dormitories were constructed for students who lived great distances away. Students had access to free rail and bus passes, so the schools were readily available to everyone. However, education in the rural areas was a major problem because many families needed to have their children help out in agricultural pursuits. Compulsory education laws were not in effect at the time.

Critics of the educational system imposed by the Japanese argued that the primary goals of the schools were to teach children how to read and obey orders. By 1937, there were about 1,000 elementary schools, but while about a half million children were in primary schools, only about 4,000 Taiwanese students were enrolled in secondary schools. Taiwanese students compared well to students from other countries in foreign language courses. Most of them had been bilingual for many years.

During World War II, the United States supported the Nationalist Government of Chiang Kai-shek but, in actuality, the Chinese Communists fought the Chinese Nationalists with about the same vigor as they exhibited in their battles against the Japanese. By the end of the war in 1945, the distrust between the two Chinese groups was too deep to be reconciled. The Taiwanese were quickly disillusioned when the country was placed under the military rule of the Chinese government. Moreover, most of the homes and industries owned by the Japanese were taken over by the new Chinese arrivals from the mainland. The situation deteriorated rapidly, and by 1947 an uprising occurred which was precipitated by the death of a woman who supposedly had been selling black-market cigarettes. An estimated 10,000 Taiwanese people were killed in the ensuing attempts to quell the riots.

By 1949, Chiang Kai-shek's position on the mainland was untenable. His forces had become overrun by the Chinese Communists so he repositioned his navy and air force on the island and transported his army to the island of Taiwan. The Republic of China was then established and Taipei became the capital. President Chiang Kai-shek then instituted a number of economic reforms, and a large-scale land redistribution program was instituted in 1953. Technical and financial aid was also provided in forestry, commerce, manufacturing, and fishing.

In 1954, the People's Republic of China announced an all-out effort to capture Taiwan and a number of other islands under control of the Taiwanese government (Republic of China). Hostilities escalated with the shelling of offshore islands owned by the Republic of China, culminating in a week-long attack on Quemoy during which an estimated 50,000 shells were launched. The Chinese Communists also captured the Tachen and Nanchi Island groups after the United

States assisted in the evacuation of the island's defenders. Finally, the United States declared its loyalty to the Republic of China and promised to defend it if it were attacked by the People's Republic of China.

STRUCTURE OF THE SYSTEM

Taiwan continues to function under its constitution, which includes fourteen chapters. It specifies that the country shall be a democratic republic of the people which shall be governed by the people and for the people. The people of Taiwan are guaranteed equal rights and duties regardless of political and/or religious beliefs. The basic freedoms of speech, beliefs, residence, publication, privacy of correspondence, assembly, and association are guaranteed in the document.

The constitution also established provincial governments and sets forth the four political powers of the people: suffrage, recall of officials, and initiative and referendum under the law. The National Assembly elects the president and vice president, can recall the president or vice president, amends the constitution when necessary, and votes on proposed constitutional amendments submitted by the legislative Yuan.

As chief of state, the president represents the country in foreign affairs and at state functions. All actions of the state are conducted in the name of the country's president. The five branches of government include the executive Yuan which has a president (premier) and a vice president (vice premier). In addition, there are a number of ministers and chairmen. The executive Yuan has a total of eight ministries including interior, foreign affairs, national defense, finance, education, justice, economic affairs, and communication. The Ministry of Education supervises and promotes the country's system of education programs which include higher education, technology and vocational education, secondary education, elementary education, social education, physical education, and general affairs.

The second branch of government is the legislative Yuan which carries out all legislative actions on behalf of the Taiwanese people. Its members are elected to represent provinces and Mongolian leagues and banners. The judicial Yuan has the responsibility of safeguarding Taiwanese citizen rights, maintaining the social order, and consolidating the republic's security. The country has three levels of courts. The lowest level is the District Court, followed by the High Court, culminating in the country's Supreme Court. The Supreme Court exercises jurisdiction over the appeals against judgments in civil and criminal cases; appeals against judgments of high courts and their branches in criminal cases; motions to set aside rulings of high courts or their branches in civil and criminal cases; and cases of extraordinary appeal.

Taiwanese children are provided free education between the ages of six and twelve and children from poor families are given free textbooks. A three-year period in a junior middle school is also provided. Secondary education consists of three different types of schools: general high schools, normal schools, and vocational schools. These high schools have tended to be somewhat selective and each school is ranked at a particular level of prestige related to the quality of students it admits. The nation's pre-school education program attempts to provide Taiwanese children with good habits and appropriate group-living skills. Higher education includes junior colleges, colleges, universities, and research institutes.

The Ministry of Education is responsible for policy making and educational development. At the provincial level these is also a department of education. The Ministry of Education provides funding for encouraging colleges and universities to establish graduate schools and the doctoral degree is normally awarded by the Ministry of Education. The Ministry of Education also is responsible for the coordination of academic research and it also presents awards for outstanding academic achievements.

It has been argued that the educational system in the Republic of China has been deeply affected by the unique characteristics of Chinese civilization itself. The linguistics patterns, Confucianism, the examination system, and Chinese family life have all played a major role. The Chinese written language is not alphabetical and relies on thousands of characters in order to reflect meanings and ideas. This written language has been intact for about 2,000 years in an almost unchanged form which has reflected the Chinese civilization. The examination system has endured for about 1,500 years and has been relatively fair and open. Chinese family life has emphasized orderliness and tradition and has played a major role in the lives of Chinese people and their learning institutions.

MULTICULTURAL EDUCATION EFFORTS

The Ministry of Education does not have a formal multicultural education program except for some limited efforts in a few private schools. Moreover, there is nobody in the Ministry of Education who is responsible for such undertakings and no funds are allocated. The official language of instruction is Mandarin Chinese, but many high school students become bilingual in English, since the largest number of students at the university level who study abroad go to the United States.

The status of women in Taiwan has generally coincided with the family mores. Over the years, the situation has changed to the extent that many Taiwanese women are now becoming scholars, something that rarely occurred in the past. The microcultures of the country include people from the mainland China areas, and a number of aboriginal groups. During the past few decades there has been a concerted effort to have everyone in the country master the Mandarin language. Accordingly, the curriculum of the schools tends to stress cultural assimilation. There are very few attempts to teach about the historical contributions of the indigenous groups prior to 1949, and few efforts are made to ensure the exclusion of racist/sexist content in curriculum and library materials and textbooks. All of the country's schools are integrated.

During the past four decades, Taiwan's educational system, like those of many other countries, has relied on a new optimistic philosophy of a free, universal, and compulsory system of education which is based on many of the equality notions expressed by Thomas Jefferson. This philosophy tended to express the ideal that cultural integration was necessary for national unity, and that a shortage of trained manpower was the primary obstacle to growth and modernism.

SUMMARY

The new nation of Taiwan has had a short history of conflict due to its location and vulnerability. Occupied by the Japanese and being a prime target of the People's Republic of China, the country has had to rely on various kinds of assistance from other nations, such as the United States, for its very economic survival. However, in its brief history, Taiwan has emerged as a hearty nation with a robust economy, and consequently, it has not been plagued with the major problems of poverty that other developing nations have had to face.

Despite a relative lack of formal multicultural education programs, the schools have developed progressive programs, which have attempted to provide free education for all of the country's youth regardless of socio-economic status. The literacy level is high and the infant mortality level is low which indicates that, by and large, Taiwan's system of education has been quite successful.

The rapid advances of the country can perhaps be attributed to the Taiwanese people's long affection for learning and wisdom. Indeed, the strong family structure of the people has contributed to this success, as well as the nature of the written language itself. Finally, the fact that all three of these key attributes have existed throughout the years has figured into the success of this young country.

REFERENCES

Chaffee, F. et al. *Area Handbook for the Republic of China.* Washington, DC: U.S. Government Printing Office, 1969.

Chih-ping, Chen and Chih-fu, Chen. *Chinese History.* Taipei: China Publishing Company, 1963.

Halpern, A.M. *Policies Toward China.* New York: McGraw-Hill, 1965.

Kerr, George. *Formosa.* Honolulu: University of Hawaii Press, 1974.

Lynch, Patrick D. *The Changing Ideology of Educational Reform: Equality Yields to Quality.* ERIC Document No. ED 295285, 1988.

Sih, Paul K.T.S. *Taiwan in Modern Times.* New York: St. John's University Press, 1973.

Smith, Douglas C. *Theoretical Foundations of Chinese Educational and Intellectual Thought: An Occidental Interpretation.* ERIC Document No. ED 340628, 1990.

Taiwan. Government Information Office. *Republic of China: A Reference Book.* Taipei: United Pacific International, Inc., 1983.

Yang, Y.R. "Education and National Development: The Case of Taiwan." *Chinese Education and Society,* Vol. 27, No. 6 (1994), pp. 7–22.

40

Tanzania

HISTORY OF THE SYSTEM

Archaeologists believe that the first inhabitants of present-day Tanzania were hunters and gatherers. By the start of the first millennium B.C., parts of northern Tanzania were inhabited by cattle herders who used stone tools and bowls. By about A.D. 500, small groups of people who used iron implements and understood the basic principles of agriculture entered this part of Africa. It has been postulated that these people probably spoke Bantu languages.

The Bantu of the early Iron Age were limited by the types of crops which were available to them, and according to the best available evidence they had no cattle. Consequently, they tended to settle in the wetter portions of the land where it was easier to work the crops. Later, other people moved into the area, bringing cattle and cereals with them which led to an expansion of land usage. During the second half of the second millennium A.D., people began to inhabit the interior portions of the country.

During the sixteenth and seventeenth centuries, the coastal and island settlements were essentially city-states which were culturally Islamic. It is believed that the people in these coastal communities consisted of mixed Afro-Arab people, who included the ruling families, landholders, merchants, artisans, full-blooded Africans who had been enslaved and were laborers, and a few Arabs or Persians.

Even though widespread systems of formal Western education did not exist in pre-colonial Tanzania, the children were educated by living and doing. In their homes and on the farms, they were taught the important survival skills of the microculture and learned the behaviors deemed to be important. They learned the tribal history and the important mores of the tribal groups. In this context, virtually all the adult figures were "teachers." It was an education that was extremely relevant to the society.

Colonial education in Tanzania was designed to prepare young people for the service of the colonial state and to teach the values of the colonial society. The system was not designed to help young people serve "their" country. The neo-colonial country was named in 1964 when "Tanganyika" and "Zanzibar" combined to form the United Republic of Tanzania. Tanzania was originally a German colony until the end of World War I, when it was given to the British by the League of Nations.

Prior to Western intervention, the Tanzanian microcultures exhibited a number of social patterns. In general, the tribe was the unit. These tribes consisted of many different classes which were either nomadic, semi-nomadic, or pastoral. For example, the Sukuma, Tanzania's largest tribal group, have been considered to be both pastoral and agricultural. This region has always had both cattle and cotton. The Sukuma were spiritually, economically, and politically self-sufficient, and children born into this society were destined to conform to the tribal influences their entire lives. In fact, according to some Kenyans, "To the Europeans, individuality is the ideal of life, to the Africans, the ideal is the right regulations with, and behavior to, other people." Therefore, it can be seen how the early educational system tended to stress learned behavior patterns which emphasized conforming to the societal norms.

The colonial education efforts were quite different from the pre-colonial educational system which had endured for years. Instead of a system which focused on the transmission of societal values, it became more of an attempt to help promote a colonialist and capitalistic society, emphasizing the individualistic instincts of people instead of the cooperative efforts. It led to the acquisition of material wealth as the primary measure of social merit and worth. Consequently, the basic goals of the pre-colonial educational system were changed from a system of education which sought to inculcate the basic microcultural values to a system which attempted to promote the basic precepts of a colonial society.

After becoming an independent state, Tanzania introduced a policy which required complete integration of the separate racial systems. Moreover, religious discrimination was terminated. Tanzanian children could then secure admittance to any state-sponsored school, regardless of the student's race or religion.

After Tanzania acquired independent status, three primary educational goals surfaced. First, racial distinctions were abolished. Discrimination because of religious persuasion was terminated. Moreover, Tanzanian children could also be admitted to any government-aided school, regardless of race, religion, or national origin. Second, more educational facilities became available, particularly at the secondary and post-secondary levels. In the 1961/1962 school year, there were 490,000 children attending primary schools. The third action taken was an attempt to provide a more Tanzanian type of education. Children would no longer learn only British/European history, and national songs and dances would once again become a crucial part of the school curriculum. The final question became: what sort of society was the country trying to build?

It has been argued that Tanzania has tried to create a socialist society which stressed equality and respect for human dignity—sharing of the resources and work by everyone through a policy of exploitation by none. Moreover, it has been argued that the country would have an agricultural economy for many years in the future.

STRUCTURE OF THE SYSTEM

The United Republic of Tanzania became independent from England in 1961. The constitution was adapted in 1964, and the country became organized into 25 separate regions. The governmental structure of Tanzania is unicameral with a national assembly (Bunge). It is a single-party state in which presidents are elected each five years. Tanzania has universal suffrage for persons who are over 18 years of age.

Economically speaking, Tanzania is one of the poorer countries in the world. The economy is heavily dependent on agriculture which accounts for a substantial portion of the nation's gross national product. The country's industries include the production of textiles, nitrogen fertilizer, phosphate fertilizer, and cement. Other industrial pursuits include petroleum refining, brewing, and agricultural processing.

Some critics of the Tanzanian educational system have argued that, since independence, it has consisted of components which encouraged attitudes of inequality, intellectual arrogance, and the inculcation of an individualistic spirit. Moreover, the critics have said that the education provided was created for a small number of students who were intellectually superior to their peers. It induced a feeling of superiority for the successful.

Critics also felt that the educational system might even divorce its participants from a society in which the country was preparing young citizens for participation, and the schools did not mirror the basic tenets of the society. Consequently, young children might acquire attitudes which could make them unwilling to become farmers and live in the villages. The new university graduates spent a great deal of their lives separated from the typical Tanzanian. Another argument against the Tanzanian educational system has been the contention that, philosophically, it assumed that all knowledge of worth was acquired from books or from intelligent, well-read people. Many people worried that the wisdom of the elders would be wasted.

Of further concern has been the fear that some of the healthiest and strongest young men and young women were leaving the productive workforce in order to become educated. Moreover, critics of the country's educational system have argued that the only way people are judged is in terms of their passed school certificate or their degree. A final concern of some critics has been the attitude of the young regarding their parents. It has been felt that children may not value their parents if the parents do not possess these new degrees and certificates.

Tanzanian teachers are categorized at four levels. Grade C teachers have completed seven or eight years of primary school and two years of teacher education.

Grade B teachers have completed primary, have had two years of secondary education, plus two years of teacher education. They can also reach Grade B through the promotion process. Grade A teachers have completed four years of teacher education or have been promoted from level B. Grade III education officers have had six years of secondary education plus the two years of teacher education. They also can be promoted from Level A.

MULTICULTURAL EDUCATION EFFORTS

Tanzania's multicultural education efforts can perhaps be best characterized as a gallant effort to provide a meaningful education for all students, regardless of race or national origin. Responses submitted during the earlier international study indicated that Tanzania's educational system did include a multicultural education component. This program is provided through the Office of International Education. While there were no special funds for multicultural efforts, Tanzania's multicultural programs have been implemented through centers, special certification, and culturally integrated schools.

In the lower primary schools, Swahili is the language of instruction. However, some children go home to another language such as Kisukuma. Consequently, many young Tanzanian students become bilingual. Then, when the young child reaches Standard III, English is introduced, resulting in the acquisition of three languages. At times, French and German are also used for instruction. In fact, Tanzania has sometimes been used as a shining example of successful language planning in favor of an indigenous African language. While Kiswahili is the mother tongue of only about 10 percent of the Tanzanian population, it has become accepted and used as a second language by more than 90 percent of the population. However, English is still the language of instruction for post-primary education.

Since the end of the colonial period, most children attend integrated schools, and the racially segregated schools were abolished. Also, religious instruction is excluded from the school curriculum. During the colonial period, the curriculum was mostly Eurocentric. However, after the country acquired its new independent status, the schools also stressed the history of its indigenous populations. In an attempt to silence some of the education critics, the country's national songs and dances have also become an important part of the school curriculum. All curriculum materials, texts, and library holdings are inspected for possible racist or sexist language.

In-service education programs in language culture for teachers are provided by the Office of International Education. Two or three years after teachers are certified, they receive in-service instruction in different cultures, geography, ethics, and language. Cultural pluralism rather than assimilation is stressed in the curriculum and instruction.

According to Tanzania's questionnaire responses, "educational manpower" was the greatest barrier to Tanzanian educational programs. Improvements suggested by the respondent were actual visits by students through cultural exchange organizations; more exchanges with American students, particularly with Native Americans (about whom Tanzanian students are curious); and a cultural exchange of teachers.

SUMMARY

Perhaps the most interesting aspect of multicultural issues in Tanzania has been the move away from a Eurocentric education approach to a more Afrocentric position. Also interesting is the emphasis on Swahili as the primary language of instruction. As a developing nation, the country is beset with the usual economic problems, making some needed reforms quite difficult to acquire.

Additionally, the philosophical focus on the system itself is complicated. Historically an agricultural country, one of the key issues is what level of education should be provided for young people. How many of the traditional agrarian values and skills should still be taught in the schools? And how many children should have access to a more sophisticated education which will assist Tanzania in achieving an appropriate role in the international marketplace?

There is an attitude among some educators that schools should include farms which are operated by the students who would contribute to the basic upkeep of the schools. The success of these farms would depend on the skills and talents of the students and their teachers. Most important, these farms and the educational system of which they are a part need to encourage the creation of an independent citizenry which can compete successfully internationally.

Many of the educational problems faced by Tanzania are plaguing other African countries. Some of the records are inaccurate and it is often difficult to determine accurately the enrollment figures and the actual expenditures for education. Sometimes head teachers miscount their students. Some of the head counts are merely guesses, while problems of communication and transportation create further difficulties in the acquisition of accurate statistics.

REFERENCES

Cameron, John. *The Development of Education in East Africa.* New York: Teachers College Press, 1970.

Clark, Desmond, J. *The Prehistory of Africa.* New York: Praeger, 1970.

Kenyatta, Jomo. *Facing Mount Kenja.* London: Seeker and Warburg, 1961.

Mitchell, Bruce and Salsbury, Robert. *An International Survey of Multicultural Education.* Cheney, WA: Western States Consulting and Evaluation Services, 1991. (See Appendix.)

Mtonga, H. L. "Comparing the Role of Education in Serving Socioeconomic and Political Development in Tanzania and Cuba." *Journal of Black Studies,* Vol. 23, No. 3 (1994), pp. 382–402.

Nyerere, Julius. "Education in Tanzania." In A. Babs Fafunwa (Ed.), *African Education in Perspective*. London: Allen & Unwin, 1982.

Rubagumya, C.M. (Ed.). *Language in Education in Africa: A Tanzanian Perspective.* Clevedon, Avon: Multilingual Matters Ltd., 1990.

Samoff, Joel. "The Facade of Precision in Education Data and Statistics: A Troubling Example from Tanzania." *The Journal of Modern African Studies,* Vol. 29, No. 4 (December 1991), pp. 669–689.

41

Turkey

HISTORY OF THE SYSTEM

The modern-day country of Turkey is actually a very young nation on old land. The name "Turkey" had no political or geographic significance until it was founded in 1923. The Turks called the vast land area that they captured *Anatole,* which geographically is synonymous with "Asia Minor." Turkey has been viewed as a land bridge which connects Asia and Europe. In addition to the history of the Turkish nation, the history of the area includes the development of Anatolia before the arrival of the Turks, and the contributions of the Turks and Seljuks, who were responsible for bringing Islam and the Turkish language to Anatolia.

The Turkish horsemen who rode into Anatolia during the eleventh century were called *gazis* (warriors of the Islamic faith). They came with their tribal leaders to spread the word of Islam, but also to take booty and land as well. While the Ottoman Empire emerged as a result of their conquests, it was not specifically Turkish, even though it was Islamic. Under the influence of Ataturk, twentieth century Turkey linked the Turkish nation with the ancient Anatolia.

Ataturk's ideological legacy was known as Kemalism. It included the "Six Arrows" of republicanism, nationalism, populism, reformism, statism, and secularism. These concepts have become the foundation for the constitutions throughout the country's history.

Archaeological evidence strongly suggests that a neolithic culture existed about the seventh millennium B.C. in Anatolia. Perhaps the world's first urban civilization was unearthed at Catalhuyuk in the Konya Basin area. During the third millennium, a copper age was in existence and bronze weapons were used during the same time frame. Late in the third millennium B.C., hordes of Indo-European language groups crossed the Caucasus into Anatolia. Included in these groups were the bronze-working chariot-borne warriors who conquered and settled the central plain. The name of this group, Hittites, apparently was borrowed from the indigenous residents, the Hatti. This Hittite empire reached its peak of success in the fourteenth and thirteenth centuries B.C., but it collapsed about 1200 B.C. when the Phrygians rebelled and burned Hattusas. Apparently, this group of people were clients of the Hittites.

During the twelfth to the ninth centuries B.C., a time of general chaos existed in Anatolia and the Aegean world. The rise of the Assyrian empire in Mesopotamia coincided with the destruction of Troy, Hattusas, and a large number of other cities in the area. Order was finally reestablished in Anatolia by the Lydians, a Thracian warrior caste which controlled the indigenous populations and acquired enormous riches from gold which was found in the tributaries of the Hermus River.

Anatolia's Aegean coast was a critical part of the Minoan civilization which received much of its cultural impetus from Crete. Many cities were founded along the Anatolian coast during the period of Greek expansion following the eighth century B.C. One of these cities was Constantinople, which was created on the Bosporus Strait by Megara, a city-state. However, by A.D. 43, all of Anatolia except for Armenia became part of the Roman Empire.

The first actual references to the Turks appear in records of the Chinese about 200 B.C. These documents discuss tribal groups called the Hsiung-nu, which historians say is an early form of the word *hun*. These people resided in an area bounded by Lake Baikal, the northern edge of the Gobi Desert, and the Altai Mountains. They are believed to have been the ancestors of the Turks.

During the first millennium A.D., enormous population shifts were occurring in central Asia as a result of growing populations creating great strains on the agricultural infrastructure and climatic changes. The Oguz Turks split into two factions during this time, with one group going to India and the other heading west. The western group was led by descendants of Seljuk and they established a relationship with the Abbasid caliphs of Baghdad. They were known as warriors of the Islamic faith, or *gazis*. The *gazis* were Turkish horsemen who were organized into tribal bands. Each year, the *gazis* cut deeper into Byzantine territories, raiding the infidels and taking booty according to their tradition.

Armeni had been annexed by the Byzantine Empire in 1045, but religious bickering between the Armenians and Greeks prevented the two Christian groups from cooperating against the Turks on the frontier. After being defeated by the Seljuks after the Battle of Manzikert, many of the Armenians became scattered throughout the empire, some of them settling in and around Constantinople.

About ten years after the Battle of Manzikert, the Seljuks had won control of Anatolia. Finally, the successes of the Seljuks prompted a response from Europe, resulting in the First Crusade. Then, in 1097, a counteroffensive by the Byzantine emperor, with the aid of Western crusaders, resulted in a massive defeat. Konya fell to the crusaders who required the Turks to provide them with reconnaissance on their march to Jerusalem. A Turkish revival in the 1140s reversed many of the victories won by the Christians, but greater damage was done to Byzantine security by dynastic confrontations in Constantinople. In 1204, the crusaders installed Count Baldwin of Flanders in the Byzantine capital as emperor of the Latin empire.

The evidence about the early history of the Ottomons is quite sketchy. During the mid-thirteenth century, Ertugral, Khan of a tribe of the Oguz Turks, left Persia during the middle of the thirteenth century to escape the Mongols and sided with the sultan of Rum. He was granted territory in Bythynia, which faced the Byzantine at Bursa, Nicomedia, and Nicea. The leadership was handed down to his son, Osman I, who reigned from 1299 to 1326. He formed the Osmanli dynasty (better known as the Ottoman Empire) which lasted for 600 years.

Osman I's amirate attracted gazis from other amirates, robbing them of their strength and providing the Ottoman state a military stature which was much greater than its size. Osman I became a sultan and organized a politically centralized administration. His successor crossed the Dardanelles, establishing a permanent base in Gallipole in 1354. In 1389, the Ottoman gazis defeated the Serbs and Ottoman victories persisted.

However, in 1402, the Ottoman forces were defeated by the Mongols near Ankara. But after the fall of Constantinople in 1453, it became the capital of the Ottoman Empire and many Byzantine institutions were fused with Islamic and Turkish customs. Just as the Byzantine Empire had been Christian, the Ottoman Empire was Islamic. In order to be accepted into the ruling class, persons were required to be loyal to the Islamic faith and the sultan, and to comply with the behavior of the Ottoman Court.

While the Ottoman Empire had Turkish and Islamic roots, it was also a mixture of heterogeneous ethnic groups and religious creeds. Religious preference determined ethnicity. As a result, Muslims were lumped together in spite of language or ethnic background. At that time, the Turks were Turkish-speaking Sunni Muslims.

The Ottoman Empire expanded its maritime influence under the rule of Bayezid II from 1418 to 1512. The Sultan's new navy was reinforced by corsairs and managed to displace the naval might of Venice and Genoa in the eastern and central Mediterranean. However, in 1571, the Ottoman fleet was defeated by Spanish and Venetian naval forces.

During the 1700s, the Ottoman Empire was nearly always involved in a conflict with either Persia, Poland, Austria, or Russia. The Treaty of Kuchuk-Koynarja ended the Russo-Ottoman war of 1768/74, and Russian ships had free access to Ottoman waters. The empire was in a steady decline, and by 1833, Tsar Nicholas I of Russia described the Ottoman Empire as "The Sick Man of Europe." However, two more wars with Russia were fought during the nineteenth century. The treaty of the second war resulted in a large independent Bulgarian state being created under Russian protection.

By the late 1800s, the Ottoman Empire had become more and more isolated from Europe and the only European support came from Germany. In 1902, a

Berlin-to-Baghdad rail line was approved and the Ottoman Empire became an economic and political satellite of Germany.

However, by the turn of the century, there was increasing opposition to the concept of a sultan regime among Western intellectuals and liberal members of the ruling class. Some of the opposing factions subscribed to the notion of a union of Turkish-speaking peoples both inside and outside the Ottoman Empire. Moreover, Abdul Hamid II became increasingly unpopular due to his oppressive policies. One anti-sultan group was led by Mustafa Kemal (Ataturk) who organized a dissident faction, known as the Young Turks. They were interested in restoring the constitution of 1876. By 1908 army units in Macedonia revolted, demanding a return to constitutional government. The Young Turk leaders were successful in reestablishing a constitutional government.

By 1914, World War I was approaching, and a secret treaty was drawn up with Germany which allowed the Ottoman Empire to remain neutral until provocation would make it necessary to become involved in war. At this time, Enver Pasha, one of the most authoritarian elements of the Young Turk movement, was in power. During 1914–1915, an ill-fated Ottoman offensive into Russia resulted in staggering losses. It was hoped that this failed military action might effectively rally the tsar's Turkish-speaking subjects. But the beaten Ottoman army was forced to withdraw to Lake Von.

After Ottoman Empire victories in Mesopotamia, the Ottomans were badly defeated in 1917 when the British armies captured Baghdad and drove the Ottomans out of Mesopotamia. In four years of war, an army of 2.4 million troops had been mobilized by the Ottomans. About 350,000 were killed in the battles that occurred. At the end of the war, the Young Turk leaders were exiled in Germany, and Ataturk returned to assume the leadership of the Ottomans. Ataturk adopted Napoleon as his role model and he attempted to impose Western cultural, political, and social values on the country.

After the war, the allied troops occupied Constantinople and were able to intervene whenever their interests seemed to be threatened. By 1920, the terms of a peace treaty were worked out, and during the next year the Law of Fundamental Organization proclaimed Turkey a sovereign nation, headed by Ataturk.

When Ataturk assumed office, a number of major reforms in Turkey's political, social, and economic life helped to transform the country into a modern state. Ataturk urged the citizens to adopt a posture which reflected European behaviors more closely. He forced people to cut many of their links with the past and promoted his Six Arrows of Kemalism. The six points included populism, reformism, statism, secularism, republicanism, and nationalism. These were written into the constitution which was adopted in 1924.

After Ataturk's death in 1938, Turkey tried to remain neutral during World War II. However, in 1944 the country declared war on Germany, even though they were not involved in any military actions. Turkey then became one of the original 51 members of the United Nations. In 1946, the Democrat Party was organized, becoming the primary competition for the Republican People's Party. In 1950, the Democrat Party received 408 seats compared to only 69 for the Republican People's Party. This ended the domination which the Republican People's Party had enjoyed since the founding of the Republic.

During the 1970s, three right-wing parties merged as the National Salvation Party. This was an Islamic-dominated political unit which imposed a number of demands on the Demirel government in exchange for their support. This angered the leftist wing, and a period of political unrest occurred, reaching its peak during the summer of 1980 when the parliament hardly functioned at all and Turkey had no elected president. The National Salvation Party demanded the reinstatement of Islamic law in Turkey. Finally, when anarchy threatened the country, the armed forces seized control. The Grand National Assembly was dissolved, and after the Kartelli Bank collapsed in 1982 a new constitution was approved by 90 percent of the electorate.

STRUCTURE OF THE SYSTEM

Turkey's political system is an interesting combination of democracy blended with a long history of respect for authority. As stated in the previous section, the country went through a reform movement under Mustafa Kemal (Ataturk), during which the country established a representative, parliamentary government. While most Turks seem willing to accept limits on their personal and political rights, they are also committed to the concept of a participatory democracy. Coupled with this condition, the history of reasonably compatible cooperation between military and civilian elements seems to have served the country well. In fact, military involvement saved the country from near civil war in 1980 when the country experienced a spate of political and communal violence which paralyzed the country.

Turkey has a unicameral legislature (the Grand National Assembly) elected by secret ballot every five years. Suffrage is universal and free for all citizens over the age of 20, and executive power is exercised by the president, prime minister, and a council of ministers. Participation in the national elections has been commendable, and competitive political parties are an integral part of the election system. Turkish citizens of both genders are eligible for election to the Grand National Assembly if they are over the age of 30 and have completed primary education and have not committed a serious crime or been involved in ideological and anarchistic activities. Male candidates are required to have completed military service. The president is elected by the Grand National Assembly and must have completed secondary education and be more than 40 years old.

The role of the president is to hold meetings of the Grand National Assembly, ratify international treaties, and promulgate laws. It is possible for the president to veto legislation passed by the parliament, submit constitutional amendments proposed by the parliament, and challenge the constitutionality of parliamentary legislation and cabinet decrees. The president also has the right to proclaim martial law and engage the armed forces of the country. But the president's responsibility to the people is also an issue. It is possible to impeach the president of Turkey for high treason with the approval of 75 percent of the assembly members.

Turkey's constitution provides a guarantee for judicial independence. The Grand National Assembly is unable to discuss or make statements about any case which might be in litigation. Trials are public except for those which may involve any sort of public morality issues or public security. The High Council of Judges and Public Prosecutors is responsible for ensuring judicial integrity. This body is able to render decisions pertaining to the careers of judges, including supervision, transfers, promotions, and appointments.

Turkey's constitution mandates compulsory education which is free of charge in all of the country's state schools. The Turkish language is the mother tongue and is used in instructional programs in the schools. Primary and secondary schools are required to provide religious instruction which is under the control and supervision of the state. Education is under the control of the state and is based on contemporary science and education methods. Nobody is to be coerced into worshipping or participating in religious rites or ceremonies of any kind.

Freedom of religion in the schools is guaranteed as long as the practice of this right does not impinge on the indivisible integrity of the state. The present system of Turkish education is compulsory for the elementary level. Pre-school education programs are offered for children between the ages of four and six. Primary (elementary) education is coeducational and compulsory. It is a five-year program for children between the ages of twelve and fourteen, while general, vocational, and technical high schools are also available. In order to attend these schools, students must graduate from the middle grades.

Higher education is available at several hundred institutions throughout the country. The Turkish universities are academically autonomous, as guaranteed by a law of higher education which was passed in 1881. This legislation established a number of structural, curricular, and ideological changes which impacted the higher education system in Turkey. Education has also been looked upon as a vehicle for acquiring upward mobility in recent years.

In addition to the various levels of education, Turkey's educational system also provides special education programs for children with various kinds of handicaps. Inadequate skill levels have been viewed as constituting the country's most crucial educational problem. As a result, the Ministry of National Education, Youth, and Sports has been instituting special vocational programs.

MULTICULTURAL EDUCATION PROGRAMS

As previously discussed, the language of instruction in the schools is Turkish, yet the country provides instruction in the mother tongue of Armenian, Greek, and Jewish students. However, the curriculum guides for such students follow the subject areas prescribed by Turkey's Ministry of Education. The nation's schools have attempted to provide a quality education for all of the country's ethnic groups.

The Turkish Kurds use their language on a regular basis, although it has been discouraged. There are a number of isolated Kurdish villages in addition to the large population which tends to be concentrated in the southeast. The Turkish Arabs are mostly concentrated along the Syrian border, and about 70,000 Circassian Muslim immigrants, particularly in the Adana, are mostly farmers and farm laborers. The Donme are descendants of the Jewish followers of a self-proclaimed messiah, Sebi, who converted to Islam in the seventeenth century.

Other ethnic groups in Turkey include a fairly large population of Greeks, Armenians, and Jews. In addition to the non-Muslim religions, there are Christians, Jews, and Greek Orthodox. The Armenians are mostly members of an autonomous Orthodox church.

One of the educational controversies during recent years has related to the issue of human relations education for the promotion of health and well-being among people and nations of the world. Due to the many socio-cultural changes in recent years, it has been argued that youth have been in need of education programs which foster personal growth in order to enhance Turkish society. Thus, it has been further argued that education should not be limited to the imparting of knowledge, but also should promote the development of sound interpersonal concepts in order to help students understand themselves better and become more aware of the importance of good interpersonal relations.

One of the major concerns in Turkish education has been the gender-role issues in the country's educational system. A study was undertaken to investigate gender-role influences on the self-identity process of Turkish adolescents as part of an international self-identity research project. The study attempted to examine the role gender played in the value systems of Turkish adolescents.

A questionnaire survey of 154 male and 119 female adolescents (ages fourteen to seventeen) from both urban and rural parts of the country was undertaken. The results of the study indicated that "familyness" was the dominant source of feelings of belonging for both male and female subjects. The second most prominent source was "friendships and school." Females valued friendship and school more than males. The self-identity of females was influenced by relationships and happiness, while males tended to be more heavily influenced by material items, such as house, television, and sports equipment. Sports and athletic activities were highly important in males self-validation process, while females seemed to be oriented more toward artistic and creative activities.

General affective attributes such as honesty, respect, or thoughtfulness were evaluated about the same by both males and females as important criteria for self-evaluation.

Males were more religious, patriotic, and felt stronger ties to ancestors, while females seemed to be more altruistic and tended to place a high importance on social relationships. Females were dependent on nonphysical attributes in their self-evaluation, while males emphasized physical attributes as important sources of self-evaluation.

SUMMARY

Turkey's establishment as a republic in 1923 marked the beginning of a nation which has often been characterized as being willing to have its appetites curbed by its military establishment. Throughout its history, the military has stepped in to put down major acts of civil unrest, gradually relinquishing control back to its governmental units. It is a young republic whose history grew out of the vast power of the Ottoman Empire, a world power for many years.

The educational system has gradually tried to deal with issues such as gender reform and education for minorities during recent years, but it still does not seem to be a major concern. Since the country did not respond to the authors' international survey of the multicultural education, it was difficult to determine what attempts at multicultural education were in effect. Nonetheless, the country's educational system attempts to provide a quality education for all students regardless of race or ethnicity, and attempts are being made to provide instruction in the mother tongue of students when needed.

Interesting gender differences among adolescents were noted, pertaining to the different attitudes of young men and young women regarding such things as affective attributes and self-identity issues.

REFERENCES

Ahmod, Feroz. *The Making of Modern Turkey.* London: Routlege, 1993.

Baymur, Feriba. "The Importance of Human Relations for Promotion of Health and Well-Being Among People and Nations of the World." Paper presented at the International Council of Psychologists, Singapore, 1988.

Cahen, Claude. *Pre-Ottoman Turkey.* New York: Taplinger, 1968.

Ceram, C.W. *The Secret of the Hittites: The Discovery of an Ancient Empire.* New York: Knopf, 1956.

Karpat, Kemal H. "Political Developments in Turkey." *Middle Eastern Studies,* Vol. 8, No. 3 (October 1972), pp. 349–375.

Pittman, Paul M., III. *Turkey: A Country Study.* Washington, DC: U.S. Government Printing Office, 1988.

Shaw, Stanford J. *History of the Ottoman Empire and Modern Turkey.* Cambridge: Cambridge University Press, 1977.

Tildirim, Ali. *Sex-Role Influences on Turkish Adolescents' Self Identity.* Annual Meeting of the American Educational Research Association, Atlanta, 1983.

Vali, Ferenc A. *Bridge Across the Bosporus.* Baltimore, MD: The Johns Hopkins Press, 1971.

42

The United States

HISTORY OF THE SYSTEM

Prior to the arrival of the Europeans, educational pursuits in the present-day boundaries of the United States were carried on by hundreds of Native American tribes and bands. The purpose of such efforts was to help young people become contributing members of the numerous microcultural groups which inhabited the country. The curricula did not include subjects such as reading, since none of the Native Americans had a written language until Sequoia wrote one for the Cherokee tribe in 1846. However, during the post-Columbian era, all that would change.

Leading figures during the post-revolution/constitution-creation period argued the importance of establishing educational systems which ensured the free education of all children as a means of perpetuating the basic principles of a participatory democracy. The argument (by Jefferson and others) was that such an educational effort was necessary if the citizens were to become able to make valid, intelligent decisions in the voting booth. However, early in the country's history, it was decided that the nation should not make education a major federal function.

Thus, from the early post-Columbian days until the present, a number of major differences in the educational systems of the 50 states have become one of the trademarks of American education. For example, some states (such as Texas and California) have "statewide adoptions" for school textbooks, while others allow individual school districts to make their own decisions about what textbooks to use with children. Moreover, a great disparity exists from state to state regarding the funding of public education. Wealthier states have been able to spend much more on education compared to poorer states.

Originally, many American schools were created along religious lines, and the powerful religious traditions required that schools provide a strong reading curriculum in order to ensure that the faith was perpetuated through Bible reading. For example, the Puritans, who established an early Massachusetts Bay colony, built a printing press, established schools, and developed a college.

Following the American Revolution, the old notion of the child as a "miniature adult" gradually disappeared, giving way to newer philosophies of pedagogy based more extensively on the ideas of Rousseau and Pestalozzi, which emphasized a more "child-centered" approach. These notions, coupled with the Jeffersonian precepts of tax-supported schools with free instruction, gradually led to the creation of schools which initially were available to European-American boys and later for European-American girls as well. Education was not mentioned in the U.S. Constitution.

America's slavery system created a major barrier to the education of African-American children throughout the country's history. Indeed, due to repressive laws and plantation policies, literacy was something that many African-American children were not able to acquire. Consequently, at the end of the Civil War in 1865, a nation of largely illiterate African-American people was finally granted citizenship with the passage of the fourteenth amendment. This partially overturned the Dred Scott decision of the U.S. Supreme Court in 1857, which denied citizenship to all African-American people. The segregated southern school system for African-American children which followed the Civil War was one of decidedly inferior quality, and it failed miserably to meet the needs of these youth.

During the nineteenth century, the common school movement became well accepted. The Kalamazoo case of 1872 provided a legal lever for local school boards to levy taxes for the operation of public high schools. Thus, by the late 1800s, the concept of American education became a critical cornerstone in the nation's history from that time on.

However, the issue of educational equality did not surface in U.S. courts until the 1896 *Plessy v. Ferguson* Supreme Court decision. While the Louisiana case pertained to the segregation of railway cars, it directly affected the schools because the "separate but equal" ruling applied to all American institutions, the schools in particular. The impact of the Plessy case was felt for nearly six decades, until the 1954 *Brown v. Board of Education* decision which declared the segregated schools of Topeka, Kansas, to be unconstitutional. The decision was rendered by the U.S. Supreme Court, the nation's highest judicial body. The case helped trigger the American Civil Rights Movement, which constituted the largest social revolution in the nation's history.

American education was heavily influenced by the European systems which were much older. During the twentieth century, the ideas of Jean Piaget and Jean Jacques Rousseau impacted most American schools in one way or another. Piaget's work on the developmental stages is well known. The first of his stages was the sensorimotor period from birth to age two. During this stage, infants are primarily egocentric, having difficulty distinguishing between the immediate environment and their own bodies. Stage two, preoperational thought, occurs from ages two to seven. Children learn to use language, develop mental images, and acquire rudimentary number concepts.

Stage three is called concrete operations, and extends from ages 7 to 11. During this time, children can learn to think deductively, and an increase in logic and objectivity occurs. Also, children learn to understand concepts of time and space and to classify objects. The fourth stage is called formal operations, which is a period of increasing ability to engage in abstract thinking. Starting at age 12, children become more able to solve problems and become increasingly adept at higher level thought production. American curriculum placement has been greatly influenced by these four stages.

The ideas of Rousseau have also been greatly influential. He took issue with the notion that human nature was inherently evil and that people were born in sin. Based on his book *Emile, ou Traite de l'Education,* he developed the idea that children were born with good tendencies. They were not miniature adults. Rather, they were unique entities who needed to be understood if teachers were to be successful with them. This was the way to develop good people. Also, children themselves should have a major role in the education process. His influences helped shift the center of education from the church to the child. Moreover, his avant-garde ideas would later influence many important educators, such as John Dewey and Carl Rogers.

During the 1900s, the so-called "factory system" of U.S. education became quite well solidified. Most states created graded systems which consisted of kindergarten to twelfth grade programs. Compulsory education laws and school board policies mandated that children would attend school from roughly age 8 to 16. Strong teacher certification requirements were implemented, and all 50 states would eventually require a minimum bachelor of arts degree for full certification.

World War II ushered in a period of increased business involvement in school matters. The National Chamber of Commerce championed an emerging partnership between business and education. The National Education Association and later the American Federation of Teachers would become powerful union voices for the welfare of American teachers.

The Commission on Reorganization of Secondary Education helped create a major shift in educational goals in 1918 in its important "Seven Cardinal Principles of Secondary Education." The seven principles were health, command of fundamental processes, worthy home membership, vocational efficiency, civic participation, worthwhile use of leisure time, and ethical character. Eventually, the concept of secondary education was expanded so the common view was that both boys and girls were entitled to attend a comprehensive secondary school.

This century saw the practice of testing expand to the extent that intelligence testing became a common practice for many school districts. The work of Lewis Terman in his refinement of the Binet measurement instruments would help lead the way to an increased measurement of human intelligence as it affected school children. The national testing movement, influenced by Ralph Tyler and others, would lead to the mass testing of American school children, an unprecedented phenomenon in American education.

The twentieth century also saw the United States create numerous special education programs for the "exceptional child." In the beginning, special schools and classes were established to meet the unique needs of such youth. However, legal changes such as Public Law 94-142 would result in "mainstreaming" programs which would allow special-needs children to participate in heterogeneous classes if they so chose.

For the first time in history, the nation had a secretary of education during the Carter administration. The position survived a major attempt to recreate the Department of Health, Education, and Welfare during the Reagan years. However, the effort failed, partly because the first Reagan appointee to the Office of Education, Terrell Bell, recognized the importance of having a separate office for American education.

Perhaps the most dramatic change during this century centered around the development of computer-assisted instruction. Sophisticated computer-assisted programs, such as the SMART Classroom in Oxnard, California, made it possible for teachers to become facilitators of learning through increased interaction with students on a one-to-one basis. In this manner, it has been argued that individual needs could be met more effectively.

STRUCTURE OF THE SYSTEM

The American system of education has been said to consist of 50 separate school systems—one for each state. All have a state superintendent who is responsible for the operation of both public and private schooling. The various superintendents' offices are responsible for funding, certification of teachers, and the development of local programs. Presently, as well as historically, the American educational system has been considered to be a federal interest, a state responsibility, and a local function.

As a federal interest, the government tends to focus on special "compensatory" education programs which try to guarantee an equal educational opportunity for all students. One example is the Head Start program for low-income students who may not receive a constitutionally guaranteed equal education opportunity. Thus, the primary budgetary needs of individual school districts must be met at the local and state levels. Also, the federal government enforces legal edicts, such as decisions rendered by the U.S. Supreme Court. Local school districts must adhere to the rulings of court cases, such as *Brown v. Board of Education,* which disallows racially segregated schools around the country.

On the other hand, individual states historically have been responsible for seeing that all children receive an education. This has meant that in the absence of a central ministry of education, individual states have selected a superintendent who must see that a quality education effort exists. This also means that states must provide adequate funding in order to ensure that effective programs are carried out. Among other things, the American model demands an adequate level of funding which enables schools to function properly, meeting the needs of all students.

State legislatures also must determine certification standards for classroom teachers. Public and private teacher education institutions must comply with the various state demands which pertain to the certification process. Such institutions are subject to evaluation visitations which examine the quality of college/university instruction, the content of pedagogical classes, and the suitability of various in-service efforts. State superintendents' offices ensure that all legal state mandates pertaining to education are carried out in the schools.

Local education agencies are responsible for the function of American education. Local boards of education are elected by the people and are responsible for hiring a superintendent of schools, who in turn is responsible for implementing suitable education programs. Thus, personnel are employed in order to provide direct instructional services to students, and to supply the necessary support services. All local education efforts must comply with federal, state, and local laws.

During the last half of the twentieth century, American schools received major criticisms from such adversaries as Hyman Rickover, John Holt, and Rudolph Flesch. The criticisms dealt with such issues as the proper approaches to reading instruction, discipline in the schools, the role of testing in the schools, prayer in schools, student rights and responsibilities, professionalism of teachers, dismissal of professional personnel, teacher certification, censorship, and many others.

Criticisms from the political left and right, along with an increasing level of irritation from the religious right, have resulted in a proliferation of private schools and home-schooled students all over the country. Since the students attending these schools often come from relatively affluent families, the performance of private school students as measured by test scores has created a perception in the eye of the public schools are decreasing in quality.

Thus, as the nation approaches the beginning of the twenty-first century, an increasing number of school reform programs have been initiated in various parts of the country. Many of them have been built around the use of performance criteria and/or behavioral objectives. However, the studies have been shown that such efforts have failed to generate the kinds of improvements which have been predicted. Other reform efforts, such as the Palmdale, California, Plaza Learning Center, have empowered teachers to become decision makers in unique school programs.

Special programs for exceptional children can be found all over the country. Exceptionality in America can be defined as extreme physical, psychological, behavioral, emotional, or intellectual deviation from the norm. The programs are sometimes expensive, especially for students with extreme intellectual limitations who are sometimes in classrooms of seven or eight students, one teacher, and a classroom aide. Also, the public schools are frequently the recipients of exceptional children for whom there are no special programs in the private schools.

MULTICULTURAL EDUCATION EFFORTS

Similar to the nations of Western Europe, the United States has been a world leader in per-capita income, enjoying an unusually high standard of living. Historically, it has been a haven for the oppressed and an attraction for opportunists. Moreover, there has been a continuous need for cheap labor. All of these factors resulted in a highly pluralistic society. Due to its unique constitutional guarantees, the efforts to provide equal educational opportunities for children from all American microcultures has presented a monumental challenge for the educational system. However, in spite of these guarantees, the nation has sometimes failed to provide equal education opportunities for all American students, regardless of gender, race, or ethnicity.

Supreme Court decisions have made the racial segregation of schools illegal and have required special bilingual programs for guaranteeing equal educational opportunities for students with limited English-speaking ability. "Chapter 1" programs have been established for economically disadvantaged children even though the funding was drastically cut during the 1980s. Through these and other national mandates, American schools have begun to address rather seriously the concept of educational equity for all children, regardless of gender, race, ethnicity, or economic circumstances.

Many of these efforts were motivated by the social revolutions of the 1960s. Educators, worried about a history of manifest destiny, racial exploitation, and white supremacy, sought ways to restructure the curriculum and instruction efforts in order to help children acquire more positive attitudes about the racial and ethnic diversity which exists in the country. However, only a fragmented national effort in multicultural education programs has resulted.

A majority of America's 50 states now have formal multicultural education programs, and 28 states have a person who is responsible for such efforts; 20 states also require that prospective teachers meet various types of requirements in multicultural education prior to certification. The state of Michigan has taken a strong stand which requires post-secondary institutions to ensure that certificated teachers participate in preparation sequences which include 17 multicultural elements, such as understanding the cultures, communication styles, beliefs, and social conditions of various racial groups, ethnic groups, males, females, and religions of the United States.

Since the Civil Rights years, major controversies have ensued regarding the multicultural content of textbooks and curriculum materials. Many school districts have devised screening procedures in order to ensure that such materials are free of racist/sexist content: 24 states have a statewide process for screening textbooks, while 26 have a procedure for subjecting curriculum materials to screening for racist/sexist content.

About half of the states have established programs which address several key issues related to multicultural education. Alaska, Texas, Florida, Connecticut, Nebraska, Iowa, Ohio, South Carolina, Washington, and Wisconsin have a state multicultural program, a state director for such enterprises, multicultural education certification requirements, screening procedures for evaluating textbooks and curriculum materials for racist/sexist content, and state policies or laws regarding multicultural education. When queried by the authors, Idaho, Indiana, Maine, Mississippi, Missouri, Rhode Island, and Wyoming responded negatively to these six key multicultural issues.

Several states have taken strong stands which require teachers to acquire high levels of understanding regarding American pluralism as a prerequisite for helping their own students develop better multicultural attitudes. In order to achieve that goal, some have adopted strong policy statements. Washington has created the following multicultural education goals: "The process of education should emphasize that cultural, ethnic, and racial differences contribute positively to our nation's future"; and "As a result of the process of education each student should interact with people of different cultures, races, generations, and life styles with significant rapport." Moreover, the state has developed a list of 26 multicultural competencies which must be demonstrated by certificated teachers.

New Jersey is another state which has made a strong statement about multicultural education. These requirements stipulate that 90 hours of preparation programs include: (1) the cultural/historical background of students with limited English proficiency; (2) specialized instructional content; and (3) specialized teaching techniques and curriculums.

Iowa has mandated a multicultural/nonsexist focus for all programs, curricula, and teaching perspectives. The state philosophy conveys a strong pluralistic thrust, and there is a human relations requirement for teacher certification. Iowa feels that it is important for students to recognize the contributions and perspectives of all races and cultural groups. The State Department of Education values the notion of cultural pluralism, which is an idea that celebrates America's cultural diversity. This notion applies to all areas of the curriculum, including such subject areas as math and science which have been dominated by European-American males. The state also has mandated that the curriculum structure, content, instructional materials, and teaching strategies shall reflect the contributions and perspectives of women, men, and all racial/ethnic groups.

In Ohio, the State Board of Education Teacher Education and Certification Standards requires that the professional education program shall provide: the acquisition of knowledge, skills, attitudes, and values as they relate to the cultural, psychological, and sociological bases of human diversity; effective instructional practices which will include promoting individual student learning in culturally, racially, and socio-economically diverse settings that address the needs of pupils, including those with exceptionalities and different learning styles; and clinical and field-based experiences for classroom teachers that are conducted in culturally, racially, and socio-economically diverse settings. Other states are starting to mandate similar precertification requirements.

Pennsylvania has a preamble which states: "Educational development is possible when the school environment and curriculum are multiethnic and multicultural." The Ohio State Board of Education also has a list of goals entitled: "Goals of Quality Education." One of these goals states that: "A quality education shall help each student acquire knowledge of different cultures and an appreciation of the worth of all peoples."

Nebraska's policy statement requires that in order for the state's schools to pass the accreditation requirement, multicultural education and cultural pluralism must be integrated into the curriculum. This mandate is quite encouraging in that it seems to provide the strongest possible message that American pluralism is to be taken seriously; and if people wish to teach, they must give the issue more than lip service.

Since the *Brown v. Board of Education* Supreme Court decision of 1954, American educators have dealt with the issue of racially segregated schools which are still unconstitutional and illegal. Indeed, in its 9–0 decision, the high court declared that racially segregated schools were inherently unequal. The subject of school desegregation has been one of the most controversial issues of American schools. The topic is often highly politicized, with those favoring desegregation tending to come from the political left, while those from the right have often opposed school efforts to create racially integrated schools.

Many school districts have lost large numbers of European-American students as a result of desegregation efforts. Some families moved away to suburban areas in order to thwart the desegregation efforts. This "white flight" phenomenon has made it more difficult for some school districts to remain desegregated.

Attempts to "pair" schools for integration purposes have sometimes resulted in physical confrontations between parents and law enforcement officials. Since this procedure requires "swapping" students according to racial backgrounds, the technique has been widely criticized and the yellow school bus often was viewed as the key scapegoat.

Other desegregation efforts have met with less opposition. For example, in communities where older schools have been located in inner-city areas populated with low-income persons of color, the school districts have sometimes closed the school rather than rebuilding. Thus, the children could be reassigned to other schools, and more acceptable levels of racial integration resulted.

Another successful school desegregation strategy has been the grade level redistribution attempts. One school might be designated as a kindergarten or first grade school. All of the children in the school district would go to the designated place for their age. Thus, children from all racial and ethnic backgrounds become forcefully integrated because of the age issue. Moreover, educators can craft special program offerings and meet the specific needs of children quite effectively.

A final approach particularly effective for grades seven to twelve, has been the special-emphasis school. Schools can be designated for specialty programs in a particular topic or subject area. For example, one school might become a math/science specialty school. All students with that particular aptitude could opt to attend. A second school might stress fine arts. So the specialty programs could attract students from quite large attendance areas, thus ensuring a more satisfactory level of integration.

Many children of color in America who were isolated in the nation's inner cities found themselves in segregated schools during the 1980s. Typically, such schools have large percentages of children from the culture of poverty. As is so often the case, such American school children suffer from low test scores and poor school performance compared to students from more affluent backgrounds. Sadly, the numbers of low-income children from minority backgrounds who attend racially segregated schools seem to be increasing.

In order to deal with the problem, some school districts have attempted to upgrade the programs in segregated inner-city schools because of the many barriers to desegregation. One example of such an effort is the "Ten Schools Program" in the Los Angeles Unified School District. The project has involved ten elementary schools with extremely low test scores. The ten school sites are located in south central Los Angeles, an area with high unemployment, an immense drug-gang problem, extremely poor school performance, and an inordinately high crime rate. The area was formerly an African-American enclave, but has changed in recent years because of a rapidly growing Latino-Chicano population.

A number of special programs have been in evidence, including special tutoring and counseling, strong parent-involvement activities, drug and alcohol instruction, and solid bilingual education programs for students who have a mother tongue other than English. Other features include "Writing to Read" programs, improved library services, cooperative learning efforts, multicultural education curriculum components, and committed teachers who truly care about improving the educational fortunes of poor children.

Starting during the Civil Rights era of the 1960s, and buoyed by the *Lau v. Nichols* Supreme Court decision of 1974, some American schools have attempted to provide basic instruction in the native language of the child in order to increase the probability that each child will experience early success in the American education enterprise. Typically, such programs attempt to provide instruction in the child's native language when needed. At the same time, the student receives instruction in English (usually in English as a Second Language [ESL] programs) in order to hasten the day when the person is truly bilingual, and the need for special bilingual programs disappears. The rationale is that if children are able to work in their native language first, they have a greater likelihood of achieving success.

The state of New Jersey provides an excellent example of a strong bilingual education program. It is defined by law as "a full-time program of instruction in all those grade levels served by the school district and which "offers all courses and subjects required by law and regulation; develops skills in both the native language of the child and English; and addresses both the cultural background of the children enrolled and that of the United States." New Jersey feels that English as a Second Language (ESL) programs go hand in hand with the state's transitional bilingual education programs. They are used in all areas of instruction when appropriate. Bilingual programs must be provided whenever there are twenty or more students of limited English proficiency from the same language identified in the district. Such programs also allow for the voluntary enrollment of English-speaking students in the program, provided they do not comprise a majority of the students enrolled.

There is some evidence that racism is on the rise in America. The white supremacy and militia exploits in Montana, northern Idaho, Michigan, and other states have widened the territory in which organizations such as the Ku Klux Klan, American Nazi Party, the Aryan Nations "church," and the Posse Comitatus have thrived. Ugly incidents such as the murder of a Provo, Utah, boy in New York City, the skinhead murder of a young African in Portland, and the Brighton Beach incident have provided verification of the deep racial hostilities which still run rampant throughout the country. American educators have sought ways to help students acquire more positive attitudes about the value of American pluralism. Some have argued that multicultural themes should be incorporated into the lesson plans used with students on a continuous basis. Others have provided excellent guidelines for creating various types of multicultural planning. Most authors seem to agree that no matter the philosophical approach, *all* students, regardless of race, religion, or socio-economic status, need to acquire an appreciation for American pluralism. It is definitely a part of the school's responsibility.

SUMMARY

It can be seen that multicultural education in the United States has made a solid beginning. Because of the country's historical reliance on cheap labor from various parts of the world, the nation has a pluralistic society which is unique. Its constitution, originally written for Europeans, has been interpreted as a document which applies to everyone, regardless of race, ethnicity, gender, or national origin.

For the schools, this phenomenon has required the implementation of educational programs which ensure that all American students have access to equal educational opportunities. Thus, the first role of multicultural education programs is to help the educational establishment create instructional sequences which address the various issues of equity for *all* students.

However, the second goal of multicultural education programs is perhaps even more difficult to achieve. The United States, like the rest of the world, is currently experiencing major increases of racial and ethnic violence. The ever-increasing gang activity and a proliferation of hate groups has escalated the number of violent confrontations between the various factions. Consequently, an important element of good multicultural programs is teaching tolerance. In order to achieve that goal, teachers have taken a more pluralistic view of American history—moving away from the traditional Eurocentric approach which flourished during the first 200 years of the country's history. Many multicultural education programs have adapted a "stew" or "salad" theory as opposed to the old notion of the "melting pot."

REFERENCES

Banks, James. *Teaching Strategies for Ethnic Studies.* Boston: Allyn & Bacon, 1992.

Banks, James and McGee, Cherry. *Multicultural Education.* Boston: Allyn & Bacon, 1993.

Bates, Percy. "Desegregation: Can We Get There from Here?" *Phi Delta Kappan* (September 1990), pp. 8–17.

Bennett, Christine. *Multicultural Education: Theory and Practice.* Boston: Allyn & Bacon, 1995.

Brown v. Board of Education. 347 U.S. 483, 1954.

Grant, Carl A. *Educating for Diversity.* Boston: Allyn & Bacon, 1995.

Lau v. Nichols. 414 U.S. 563, 1974.

Mitchell, Bruce and Salsbury, Robert. *A National Survey of Multicultural Education.* Cheney, WA: Western States Consulting and Evaluation Services, 1988.

Mitchell, Bruce et al. *The Dynamic Classroom: A Creative Approach to the Teaching/ Evaluation Process.* Dubuque, IA: Kendall/Hunt Publishing Company, 1995.

More than Bows and Arrows. A film narrated by Scott Momaday, Pulitzer Prize-winning author, university professor, and member of the Kiowa tribe, 1983.

New Jersey. State Department of Education. *Guidelines for Development of Program Plan—Bilingual/ESL Education Programs.* New Jersey Department of Education, 1989.

Rippa, Alexander S. *Education in a Free Society.* New York: Longman, 1988.

Slavin, Robert. "PET and the Pendulum: Educational Faddism and How to Stop It." *Phi Delta Kappan* (June 1989).

Superintendent of Public Instruction. *Position Statement on Multicultural Education.* Lansing: Michigan Department of Education, 1981.

Tiedt, Pamela and Tiedt, Iris. *Multicultural Teaching.* Boston: Allyn & Bacon, 1995.

Washington Department of Public Instruction. *Handbook for Goal-Based Curriculum Planning and Implementation.* Olympia, WA: State Department of Education, 1975.

Appendix:
An International Survey
of Multicultural Education

In recent years, educators the world over have attempted to address the issue of multicultural education in teaching and learning. Multicultural education is a concept which is rather difficult to define. However, the notion does encompass a number of key issues regarding American pluralism which have been addressed recently in connection with the preparation of teachers around the world.

Recently, one of the authors published several articles which reported on the results of some American studies in multicultural education (Mitchell, 1985 and 1987). These surveys of the 50 state departments of public instruction have provided valuable insights regarding the state of the multicultural education "art" in the United States. As an outgrowth of these investigations, the authors recently expanded on this notion by conducting an international survey of multicultural education. It was hoped that such an undertaking would provide important information regarding educational attempts to deal with issues pertaining to cultural pluralism.

In order to acquire the data, questionnaires were sent to appropriate contact persons within the various ministries of education in the United Nations countries. Several non-U.N. countries, such as South Africa, were also included in the survey. After the usual pleading and cajoling, a total of 42 usable responses were received. Obviously, for standard research purposes, such a return percentage is not acceptable (we assume that this was due to political reasons). However, in spite of these shortcomings, we feel that the responses were useful in providing educators with some valuable global insights on the issues.

In structuring the questionnaires, thirteen basic issues were dealt with, as follows:

1. central direction for multicultural programs;
2. funding levels for multicultural education;

3. leadership in multicultural education programs provided by the central education offices;

4. cultures which exist in the country;

5. the nature of multicultural certification requirements for school teachers in the country;

6. the extent to which the official state position stresses a culturally pluralistic versus an assimilationist perspective in the educational curriculum;

7. official languages of instruction in the country's school system;

8. racial integration/segregation of the nation's schools;

9. whether the history of indigenous peoples is consciously stressed in the curriculum of the schools;

10. national efforts to include bilingual/bicultural instruction in the schools;

11. procedures for evaluating curriculum materials, library materials, and textbooks for racist and/or sexist content;

12. the biggest problems facing the country in the area of multicultural programs in the schools; and

13. the most important improvements needed in the country's multicultural education programs.

In the summary to follow, we will attempt to provide a synthesis of our findings. Obviously, in a rather brief summary, it will not be possible to share the responses from all participating countries for each of the thirteen issues. Consequently, the report to follow will convey our perception of the more important information available in our data analysis.

CENTRAL DIRECTION

Several countries, such as Australia, Canada, and the United States, do not provide any central direction for multicultural education programs. Such enterprises tend to emanate from the states, territories, and provinces. In Australia, this is a shared responsibility of the territories and the commonwealth government. In the United States, this function is left to the individual states. For example, the state of Washington has a director for multicultural education and gender equity. This office assists local school districts in establishing their own programs. The same office is also responsible for working with colleges and universities in creating appropriate teacher-preparation activities which stress multicultural education principles.

Other countries, such as Austria, Colombia, Denmark, Ecuador, El Salvador, Israel, the Netherlands, Paraguay, the Philippines, Spain, and Tanzania, all reported having multicultural education programs with some sort of central direction provided. Several countries reported that such programs existed, but with no central control. Austria's efforts to deal with multicultural education have resulted in the creation of the Department of International Contacts and Intercultural Learning (Department I/13).

Denmark has the UNESCO Associated Schools Project in the Ministry of Education, which is responsible for multicultural education. In the Philippines, the Office of the Deputy Minister for Higher Education is responsible for multicultural education. That office provides leadership in specific kinds of multicultural programs, and works with the cultural center of the Philippines and other agencies involved in cultural programs.

TEACHER CERTIFICATION

Only five nations reported any sort of multicultural education requirements in the teacher certification process, with Colombia, Kuwait, Paraguay, Tanzania, and the United States claiming such programs. The chief difference among these certification requirements seemed to be based on the various political systems of the five nations. The first four countries have strong central direction in their educational programs. However, in the United States, that direction emanates from the 50 states. Consequently, such ventures are fragmented at best. For example, in the Mitchell (1987) study, sixteen states and the District of Columbia reported multicultural certification requirements, while 32 did not. The state of Washington includes multicultural education as part of its "basic education" approach. Utah's State Board of Education maintained that since America is a culturally diverse society, its educational system demands teachers who are prepared in the understanding of this diversity and who have skills which will make them capable of providing the most valuable learning experiences for children of all cultures. The states reporting multicultural certification components were Alabama, Connecticut, Illinois, Iowa, Massachusetts, Minnesota, Nevada, New Jersey, North Dakota, Ohio, South Dakota, Tennessee, Texas, Utah, Washington, Wisconsin, and the District of Columbia.

PLURALISM VERSUS ASSIMILATION

Fifteen countries responded that they subscribed to a philosophy which stressed a pluralistic perspective in educational programs. This meant that the educational system tended to adhere to a notion that many social scientists have referred to as the "stew theory." This concept implies that the strength of an organization rests in the diversity of its people. The analogy to the stew is obvious. Each of the ingredients offers something special to the total flavor while still retaining its individual identity. On the other hand, an assimilationist emphasis means that the microcultures of a country must rid themselves of their basic cultural integrities and adopt the cultural value system of the dominant culture, whatever that might be. This is often referred to as the "melting-pot theory."

Pluralistic countries included Australia, Colombia, Guinea, India, Israel, Japan, Liberia, the Netherlands, Norway, Paraguay, Singapore, Spain, Sri Lanka, and the United States (a majority of states indicated this to be their approach in the 1987 study). Assimilationist countries were Bahrain, Canada, People's Republic of China, Congo, Austria, El Salvador, Guyana, Kenya, Taiwan, and Thailand. The Malaysian respondent indicated that their country stressed integration within the Islamic/Malay culture. Many respondents simply did not answer this question. We assume that since this question partially requires a value judgment, some persons chose not to state an opinion. We found a similar situation when the same question was asked in the United States study (Mitchell, 1987) and fifteen responding states did not answer that question.

LANGUAGES OF INSTRUCTION

The question of what is to be a nation's official language of instruction has been a highly emotional issue throughout the history of education. For example, in the United States, there is presently a strong national movement advocating the use of "English only" throughout American institutions. However, in the field of education, such a practice would be contrary to the 1974 *Lau v. Nichols* Supreme Court decision which legalized bilingual instruction in American schools. The rest of the world's educational systems have encountered similar problems relating to the official languages of instruction.

Most countries surveyed reported an official language or languages of pedagogy, but several allowed for the use of other languages in teaching "language different" students. The ultimate questions were: "What is the best language approach for school children who are not native speakers? Do bilingual programs work best? Is it possible for the educational system to provide them?" Our responses showed that sixteen countries made use of bilingual instruction programs. In addition to the United States, the countries of Australia, Austria, Belgium, Brazil, Canada, People's Republic of China, Colombia, Ecuador, Finland, India, Kenya, Malaysia, Norway, Paraguay, the Philippines, Sri Lanka, and Tanzania all reported the inclusion of bilingual instruction programs.

Four countries described the use of two "official" languages of instruction. These were Canada (English and French), Finland (Finnish and Swedish), the Philippines (Filipino and English), and Sri Lanka (Sihala and Tamil). Australia has a number of programs that provide schooling for children in their ethnic language, including English as a Second Language (ESL) programs. In Austria, even though German is the official language, mother-tongue programs are provided in the curriculum. In Belgium, students of migrant parents receive instruction in the Dutch language and, at the same time, in the language and culture of their country of origin. In Ecuador, the language of instruction is basically Spanish, but Shuar and Awa-Kuaiker are also used. Special programs have been developed to teach immigrant and indigenous children in their native language through a bilingual/intercultural program (EBI). In Kenya, while English is the official language of instruction, for the first three years of primary education children are taught in their mother tongue. Finally, in Tanzania, Swahili, English, French, and German are all languages of instruction.

SCHOOL INTEGRATION

In regard to policies of school segregation by race and ethnicity, only five countries reported the existence of such requirements. Students from Israel and Papua New Guinea do not attend culturally and racially integrated schools. South Africa's apartheid policies prevent racial integration (of course, this has changed since the study). In Sri Lankan schools there are special schools for Sinhalas and Tamils.

Several countries, such as Ireland, reported that the segregation/integration issue did not apply due to a dearth of pluralistic microcultures. Other countries, such as Malaysia, described political issues which overshadowed the problem of ethnic/racial desegregation or integration. While no official anti-integration policies exist, many children attend segregated schools due to distances or cultural/religious preferences. Thus, in countries where children have relative freedom in school selection, segregated schools sometimes exist in the absence of official desegregation programs mandated by the state.

By contrast, the United States employs a legal policy making either de facto or de jure segregation by race or ethnicity illegal. However, this is sometimes not enforced aggressively.

HISTORY OF INDIGENOUS PEOPLE

Thirty-two of the responding nations reported that they included the history of indigenous peoples in the curriculum. As is the case in the United States, many have argued that in order for such children to become good learners, it is first necessary for them to become proud of their cultural heritage. In much of the world, the various colonial schools taught quite the opposite, and the indigenous peoples were forced to assimilate (if they were even allowed to do that) and to give up their native language and culture in the process. The vigor with which this policy is pursued seemed to vary a great deal from country to country. For example, the Israeli respondent reported that this type of instruction was undertaken on an optional basis. On the other hand, Tanzania requires that all teachers provide instructional sequences addressing the history of indigenous peoples.

Seven countries responded that such instruction was not a formal part of their educational sequences. These nations included Canada, Guyana, Liberia, Mauritius, Norway, Papua New Guinea, South Africa, and Spain. Mauritius reported that there were no indigenous people in the country.

SCREENING MATERIALS FOR RACIST/SEXIST CONTENT

Austria, Bahrain, Bangladesh, Barbados, Belgium, Cuba, Ecuador, El Salvador, England, Finland, Guyana, India, Kenya, Liberia, Malaysia, Mauritius, Norway, the Philippines, Singapore, Tanzania, and the United States all reported that textbooks and other materials were screened for racist and sexist content. However, there seemed to be a great deal of variation in the manner in which this was accomplished. For example, in the United States, only sixteen states had no procedures for carrying this out at the state level. But even in the sixteen nonscreening states, many of the local educational agencies had such a requirement.

PROBLEMS PERTAINING TO MULTICULTURAL EDUCATION

Of course, no survey would be complete without allowing the respondents to stipulate the major problems and needed improvements. Obviously, open-ended questions of this nature usually do not elicit consistent responses. However, in the area of multicultural education, some interesting ideas emerged. Guinea reported that no multicultural education programs existed, and Canada responded that many people could not understand the need for multicultural education programs. Guyana reported that the biggest problem was a suspicion on the part of some ethnic groups that they might lose their identity. Belgium identified problems of language barriers between children of immigrant parents and teachers, and similar language barriers between teachers and the parents of this group of children. Belgium also reported that certain teachers were not sensitized or had a lack of education to plan and implement programs in multicultural education.

The Italian respondent replied that Italy's biggest problem was the strong monolithic national identity and culture; whereas Spain reported that their main problem was the large number of isolated communities which maintained their identity within the framework of the uniform politics of earlier times which had isolated their views. Taiwan argued that their disadvantaged students received an inferior education. While they were the only country to make this statement, the authors had the feeling that, if pressed, many others would have shared this view. Tanzania referred to a lack of manpower, a problem shared by many developing nations. Interestingly, the Philippines identified their largest problem as negative influences from the Western cultures (i.e., sexual permissiveness, and inadequate appreciation of the cultural heritage). India professed a difficulty in maintaining a proper balance between unity and diversity, while El Salvador felt that the poverty in the country was the major problem.

IMPROVEMENTS NEEDED

Finally, the question regarding most important improvements needed in multicultural education programs provided some stimulating responses. Sri Lanka and the South Africa respondents felt that their segregated school systems must become integrated. Several countries, including Canada, the People's Republic of China, Spain, and Japan, described a need for helping students to better understand and appreciate the cultural diversity within their midst. Guinea, Malaysia, and South Africa felt that their countries needed to create multicultural education programs, while Ireland and Israel felt that in-service training in multicultural education should be provided for their teachers. Belgium articulated a need for improved home/school relationships, breaking language barriers, and solid research in multicultural education. The Philippines wanted to make their educational programs more Filipino-oriented, Spain felt a need for bilingual education programs, while Taiwan wished to improve the status of disadvantaged students. The United States respondent expressed a need for more aggressive leadership in multicultural education through the Office of Education.

SUMMARY

In attempting to summarize the findings, they might best be characterized as a modest beginning. Certainly, far too few countries have aggressively addressed the growing national and international problems of racism, sexism, stereotyping, and ethnocentrism. The world community seems to be taking a look at the issues, and, as the report shows, a few countries seem dedicated to addressing such problems through the educational process. Perhaps the lack of priority given to this topic is reflected in the actual number of responses. An earlier *Kappan* article by one of the authors (Mitchell, 1987) related to a world study of gifted/talented education. Just under 60 percent of the world's nations responded to the survey requests. The fact that only 36 percent of the countries surveyed responded to the multicultural education requests seems to indicate that such an educational topic may be of low priority or of high political sensitivity.

The problem seems to have escalated in recent years, particularly in countries such as the United States and South Africa. It may well continue to do so unless the educational systems of the world unite to address these issues. Based on these data, it would appear that several things are needed. First, teacher preparation programs must help instructors understand and appreciate more fully the pluralistic nature of their country and the world. Moreover, teachers must learn to plan instructional programs in which multicultural instruction strands become an integral part of the regular curricular topics. Second, educational systems must find ways to integrate student populations. Segregation by races creates first- and second-class school systems which simply must not be a part of the twenty-first century. Third, nations must provide bilingual/bicultural programs which allow children to learn in their native language first, thus counteracting the devastating failure rates which often occur when young children are required to learn basic concepts and a new language at the same time. Fourth, the history and contributions of indigenous populations must become an important part of the curriculum. The world must not allow such persons to be viewed as second-class citizens. Finally, all curriculum materials and reading matter must be screened for racist and sexist content. The literature of too many countries continues to promulgate such negative attitudes in the minds of young children.

In summary, multicultural education should be a major undertaking for the school systems of the world—beginning at once. Otherwise, the world might fall victim to racism long before it is vaporized in a nuclear holocaust.

REFERENCES

Mitchell, Bruce. "Multicultural Education: A Second Glance at the Present American Effort." *Educational Research Quarterly,* Vol. 11, No. 4 (1987), pp. 8–12.

Mitchell, Bruce and Williams, William. "Education of the Gifted and Talented in the World Community." *Phi Delta Kappan,* Vol. 68, No. 7 (1987), pp. 531–534.

Bibliography

Abba Eban, Solomon. *Personal Witness: Israel Through My Eyes.* New York: G.P. Putnam's Sons, 1992.

Adult Education: A Plan for Development. London: HMSO, 1973.

Agrawal, D.P. *The Copper Bronze Age in India: An Integrated Archaeological Study of the Copper Bronze Age in India in the Light of Chronological Technological and Ecological Factors.* New Delhi: Munshiram Manoharlal, 1971.

Ahmod, Feroz. *The Making of Modern Turkey.* London: Routlege, 1993.

Akenson, Donald H. *A Mirror to Kathleen's Face. Education in Independent Ireland, 1922–1960.* Montreal: McGill-Tweens, University Press, 1975.

Alawiye, Osman and Alawiye, Catherine. "Comparative Self-Concept Variances of School Children in Two English-Speaking West African Nations." *The Journal of Psychology,* Vol. 124, No. 2 (1990), pp. 169–176.

Aldred, Cyril. *The Egyptians.* London: Thames and Hudson, 1984.

Andam, A.A.B. "Towards a Gender-Free Science Education: A Situational Analysis from Ghana." *Discovery and Innovation,* Vol. 6, No. 1 (1994), pp. 25–28.

Andaya, Barbara Watson and Andaya, Leonard V. *A History of Malaysia.* Kuala Lumpur: Oxford University Press, 1975.

Ansah, P.A.V. "Broadcasting and Multilingualism." In E.G. Wedell (Ed.), *Making Broadcasting Useful: The African Experience: The Development of Broadcasting in Africa in the 1980s.* Manchester: Manchester University Press, 1986.

Ansu-Kyeremeh, Kwasi. "Cultural Aspects of Constraint on Village Education by Radio." *Media, Culture, and Society,* vol. 14. London, Newbury Park, CA, and New Delhi: Sage, 1992, pp. 111–128.

Antonouris, George. "Multicultural Perspectives." *Times Educational Supplement,* Vol. 30, No. 9 (1988).

Antwi, Moses. *Education, Society and Development in Ghana.* Accra, Ghana: Unimax Publishers Ltd., 1992.

Anzovin, Steven. *South Africa: Apartheid and Divestiture.* New York: H.W. Wilson, 1987.

Ardlagh, John. *France in the 1980s.* New York: Penguin, 1983.

Asiedu, Akrofi. "Education in Ghana." In A. Babs Fafunwa and J.V. Aisiku (Eds.), *Education in Africa.* London: George Allen & Unwin, 1982.

Asiedu, Akrofi A. *Ghana, The New Structure and Content of Education for Ghana.* Accra: Ministry of Education, 1974.

Austin, D. *Politics in Ghana.* London: Oxford University Press, 1964.

Australian Deputy Chairperson, National Advisory and Coordinating Committee on Multicultural Education (NACCME), 1992. (Survey responses.)

Aznam, Suhairi. "The Women's Burden." *Far Eastern Economic Review* (June 1990), p. 18.

Balakrishnan, N. "A Broad Education." *Far Eastern Economic Review* (January 1991), p. 18.

Balakrishnan, N. "Speak Singaporean." *Arts and Society* (February 1989), pp. 40–41.

Banerjee, N.R. *The Iron Age in India.* Delhi: Munshiram Manoharlal, 1965.

Banks, James. "Multicultural Education and Its Critics: Britain and the United States." In S. Modgil et al. (Eds.), *Multicultural Education: The International Debate.* Lewes: Palmer Press, 1990.

Banks, James. *Teaching Strategies for Ethnic Studies.* Boston: Allyn & Bacon, 1992.

Banks, James and McGee, Cherry. *Multicultural Education.* Boston: Allyn & Bacon, 1993.

Barker, Elisabeth. *Austria 1918–1972.* Coral Gables: University of Florida Press, 1973.

Barnard, H.C. *Education and the French Revolution.* Cambridge, MA: Harvard University Press, 1969.

Barnett, Clifford R. *Poland: Its People, Its Society, Its Culture.* New Haven, CT: HRAF Press, 1958.

Barry, Tom and Norsworthy, Kent. *Honduras.* Albuquerque, NM: The Inter-Hemispheric Education Resource Center, 1990.

Bartels, F.L. *The Roots of Ghana Methodism.* Cambridge: Cambridge University Press, 1965.

Bartnicka, K. "Education in Poland: Past, Present, and Future." *History of Education Quarterly,* Vol. 34, No. 3 (1994), pp. 370–372. (Book Review)

Bastenier, A. et al. *Vocational Training of Young Migrants in Belgium.* Berlin: European Centre for the Development of Vocational Training, 1986.

Bates, Percy. "Desegregation: Can We Get There from Here?" *Phi Delta Kappan* (September 1990), pp. 8–17.

Bayly, C.A. "Local Control in Indian Towns—The Case of Allahabad: 1880–1920." *Modern Asian Studies,* Vol. 5, No. 4 (1971), pp. 289–311.

Baymur, Feriba. "The Importance of Human Relations for Promotion of Health and Well-Being Among People and Nations of the World." Paper presented at the International Council of Psychologists, Singapore, 1988.

Belgium. Ministry of Education. *Education in Belgium.* Brussels: Ministry of Education, 1984.

Bennett, Christine. *Multicultural Education: Theory and Practice.* Boston: Allyn & Bacon, 1995.

Bethell, Leslie (Ed.). *The Cambridge History of Latin America.* Cambridge: Cambridge University Press, 1991.

Birch, de Gray. *The Commentaries of the Great Affonso d'Albuquerque, Second Viceroy of India.* London: Hakluyt Society, 1884.

Blood, Peter. *Bangladesh: A Country Study.* Washington, DC: Department of the Army (D.A. Pam. 550-175, Headquarters, Department of the Army), 1992.

Blutstein, Howard et al. *Area Handbook for Honduras.* Washington, DC: U.S. Government Printing Office, 1971.

Bollay, Burton. "Enrollment Boom, Rise of Fundamentalism Put Egypt's Universities Under Pressure." *The Chronicle of Higher Education* (June 12, 1991), pp. 31–33.

Brady, T. *Turning Swiss: Cities and Empire, 1450–1530.* Cambridge: Cambridge University Press, 1985.

Bramsted, Ernest K. *Germany.* Englewood Cliffs, NJ: Prentice-Hall, 1972.

Brinton, Crane. *The Americans and the French.* Cambridge, MA: Harvard University Press, 1968.

Bronwojciechowska, A. "Education and Gender in Sweden: Is There Any Equality?" *Women's Studies International Forum,* Vol. 18, No. 1 (1995), pp. 51–60.

Brown, Larry. "Hunger in the U.S." *Scientific American* (February 1987).

Brown, M.A.G. "Education and National Development in Liberia." Unpublished Doctoral Dissertation, Ithaca, NY, 1967.

Brown v. Board of Education. 347 U.S. 483, 1954.

Bulgaria. Ministry of Education. *Law for Closer Ties Between School and Life.* Sofia: Ministry of Education, 1954.

Burnstein, Stanley M. "Introducing Kush: A Mini-Guide to an Ancient African Civilization." *Social Studies Review* (Fall 1993), pp. 22–30.

Busskohl, Tordis. This information is based on conversations with Busskohl, prominent educator of pre-school children in Norway and the United States. Spokane, WA, 1994.

Butler, Ewan. *The Concise History of Scandinavia.* New York: American Heritage Publishing Company, 1973.

Bykov, R. *Slova i tribuny-ekonomika nashego detstva.* Moscow: Current Digest of the Soviet Press, 1989.

Cahen, Claude. *Pre-Ottoman Turkey.* New York: Taplinger, 1968.

Cameron, John. *The Development of Education in East Africa.* New York: Teachers College Press, 1970.

Cammaert, Marie France. *Interculturalism: Theory and Practice.* Seminar on the Education and Cultural Development of Migrants, Limbourg, Belgium, April 1987. (Council for Cultural Cooperation, Strasbourg, France.)

Capper, Phillip (Ed.). *Proceedings of the Post Primary Teachers Association Curriculum Conference.* Christchurch: Post Primary Teachers Association, 1991.

Carlgren, W.M. *Swedish Foreign Policy During the Second World War.* New York: St. Martin's Press, 1971.

Carnoy, Martin and Werthein, Jorge. *Cuba's Economic Change & Educational Reform.* Washington, DC: World Bank, 1979.

Carr, W. *A History of Germany 1815–1985.* London: Edward Arnold, 1987.

Carter, Jeanette. "Liberian Women: Their Role in Food Production and Their Educational and Legal Status." Unpublished Paper, University of Idaho, Moscow, 1982.

Ceram, C.W. *The Secret of the Hittites: The Discovery of an Ancient Empire.* New York: Knopf, 1956.

Chaffee, F. et al. *Area Handbook for the Republic of China.* Washington, DC: U.S. Government Printing Office, 1969.

Chang, M.C. "Teacher Training." Paper presented to the World Bank Conference on School Quality, Harper's Ferry, WV, 1983.

Chapman, Ruth. *Social Engineering in the Curriculum.* Workshop conducted at the Post Primary Teachers Association Curriculum Conference, Christchurch, 1991.

Chevalier, Francois. *Land and Society in Colonial Mexico: The Great Hacienda.* Berkeley: University of California Press, 1963.

Chih-ping, Chen and Chih-fu, Chen. *Chinese History.* Taipei: China Publishing Company, 1963.

Ching, Julia. *Probing China's Soul.* San Francisco, CA: Harper and Row, 1990.

Chung, J.S. "Women's Unequal Access to Education in South Korea." *Comparative Education Review,* Vol. 38, No. 4 (November 1994), pp. 487-505.

Clark, Desmond J. *The Prehistory of Africa.* New York: Praeger, 1970.

Clark, Steve (Ed.). *Nelson Mandela Speaks.* New York: Pathfinder Press, 1993.

Cochrane, Eric. "Disaster and Recovery: 1527–1750." In John Julius Norwich (Ed.), *The Italians: History, Art, and the Genius of a People.* New York: Abrams, 1983.

Cohen, Mitchell. *Zion and State: Nation, Class, and the Shaping of Modern Israel.* New York: Basil Blackwell, 1987.

Cole, Johnetta. "Race Toward Equality: The Impact of the Cuban Revolution on Racism." *The Black Scholar* (November/December 1980).

Comision Economica para America Latina (CEPAL). *La evolucion de America,* 1980.

Committee of Experts. *Edukacja—narodowym autorytetem (Education—a National Priority).* Warszawa: Panstwowe Wydawnictwo Naukowe (Scientific Publishing House of State), 1989.

Constitution of the Federation of Malaya, Article 160–2.

Contreras, Maxmilliano. "The Binational Student." *Equity and Excellence,* Vol. 23, Nos. 1 & 2 (1986), pp. 77–80.

Conversation with employees at Cape Coast University, Cape Coast, Ghana, May 1994.

Conversations with Francis Kazemek and William Williams, Professors of International Education, University of Eastern Washington, August 1994.

Conversations with Dr. James Cowan, Ventura County (California). Spokane, WA, 1994.

Conversations with Dr. J.T. Nelson, a professor of Education at Gonzaga University, and an expert on South African Education. Spokane, WA, 1994.

Conversations with school administrators at a USAID Grant meeting at Cape Coast University, Cape Coast, Ghana, May 1994.

Coolahan, John. *Irish Education: Its History and Structure.* Dublin: Institute of Public Administration, 1990.

Craig, Gordon. *The Germans.* New York: Putnam's Sons, 1982.

Crecelius, Daniel. *The Roots of Modern Egypt.* Minneapolis: Bibliotheca Islamica, 1981.

Crow, John A. *Italy: A Journey through Time.* New York: Harper & Row, 1965.

Cummings, William K. *Education and Equality in Japan.* Princeton, NJ: Princeton University Press, 1980.

Currie, Annie. "A Class of Their Own." *Times Educational Supplement* (November 6, 1992).

Curtis, Glenn E. (Ed.). *Bulgaria: A Country Study.* Washington, DC: Library of Congress, 1989.

Davies, Norman. *Heart of Europe: A Short History of Poland.* Oxford: Clarendon Press, 1984.

Dayan, Moshe. *Breakthrough: A Personal Account of the Egypt-Israel Peace Negotiations.* New York: Knopf, 1981.

de Cuellar, Javier Perez. Statement made through the United Nations Department of Public Information, May 21, 1991.

Delaney, Brian and Paine, Lynn. "Shifting Patterns of Authority in Chinese Schools." *Comparative Education Review* (February 1991), p. 33.

Dent, N.C. *Education in England & Wales.* Great Britain: Linnett Books, 1977.

Derry, T.K. *A History of Modern Norway.* Oxford: Clarendon Press, 1973.

Derry, T.K. *A History of Scandinavia.* Minneapolis: University of Minnesota Press, 1919.

Desai, L.P. "Western Educated Elites and Social Change in India." *Economic and Political Weekly* (Bombay), vol. 19 (April 14, 1984), pp. 639–647.

Din'o Koev, Za. *Concerning Party Partisanship in Education and Instruction.* Sofia: Narodna Prosveta, 1964.

Directives of the Eighth Congress of the Bulgarian Communist Party for the Development of the People's Republic of Bulgaria During the Period 1961–1980. Sofia, 1961.

Dolan, Ronald E. (Ed.). *Philippines: A Country Study.* Washington, DC: Department of the Army, 1993.

Donohue-Clyne, Irene. " 'Children Only Go to School to Colour In. . . . ' Overseas Educated Teachers' Perception of Australian Schools." *Multicultural Teaching to Combat Racism in School and Community,* Vol. 11, No. 3 (1993).

Dossantos, J.C. "The Recent Process of Decentralization and Democratic Management in Brazil." *International Review of Education,* Vol. 39, No. 5 (1993), pp. 391–403.

Dunn, D. "Gender Inequality in Education and Employment in the Scheduled Castes and Tribes of India." *Populations Research and Policy Review,* Vol. 12, No. 1 (1993), pp. 53–70.

Dunstan, John. *Soviet Education Under Perestroika.* London: Routledge Publishing Co., 1992.

Dupree, Louis. *Afghanistan.* Princeton, NJ: Princeton University Press, 1932.

Dupuy, Trevor N. *Elusive Victory: The Arab-Israeli Wars, 1947–1974.* New York: Harper and Row, 1978.

Easton, Stephen. *An Analysis of Elementary, Secondary, and Vocational Schooling.* Vancouver, BC: The Frasier Institute, 1988.

Education Act of 1944, Section 5. London, England. Original regulations are from Section 33(2) of the Education Act of 1944 and Circular 276, Provision of Special Schools, dated June 25, 1954, London, England.

The Education of the Adolescent. London: HMSO, 1926.

Ehteshami, Soraya. "The Role of Radio and Television in the Improvement of Education in Iran." Master's Thesis, Eastern Washington University, Spokane, WA, 1977.

Eisemon, T.O. *Benefitting from Basic Education, School Quality and Functional Literacy in Kenya.* Oxford: Pergamon Press, 1988.

Eisikovits, Rivka and Beck, Robert H. "Models Governing the Education of New Immigrant Children in Israel." *Comparative Education Review* (May 1990), pp. 177–178.

Ekstrand, Lars. *Children in India and Sweden.* Lund, Sweden: University Center for Multicultural Studies, 1990.

Elementary Education Act of 1870, Section 14(2). London, England.

Elon, Amos. "Report from Vienna." *The New Yorker,* Vol. 67 (May 13, 1991).

Emerson, Rupert. *Malaysia: A Study in Direct and Indirect Rule.* New York: Macmillan, 1937.

Erickson, T. et al. *Characteristics and Relationships in Public and Independent Schools, COFIS Baseline Survey Interim Report.* British Columbia: Center for Research in Private Education, 1979.

Eurich, Nell P. *Systems of Higher Education in Twelve Countries.* New York: Praeger, 1981.

Fafunwa, A. Babs and Aisiku, J.V. (Eds.). *Education in Africa.* London: George Allen & Unwin, 1982.

Fage, J.D. *Ghana: A Historical Interpretation.* Madison: University of Wisconsin Press, 1959, p. 106.

Fagen, Richard. *Cuba: The Political Content of Adult Education.* Stanford, CA: Hoover Institution, 1964.

Fitch, B. and Oppenheimer, M. "Ghana, End of an Illusion." *Monthly Review* (July–August 1966).

Fitzmaurice, John. *The Politics of Belgium: Crisis and Compromise in a Plural Society.* New York: Martens, 1983.

Fleisher, Frederic. *The New Sweden.* New York: David McKay Inc., 1967.

Fletcher, Nancy. "The Separation of Singapore from Malaysia." Ithaca, NY: Cornell University Southeast Asia Program, Data Paper No. 37, 1969.

Foner, Philip S. *A History of Cuba.* New York: International Publishers, 1962.

Foster, P. *Education and Social Change in Ghana.* Chicago: University of Chicago Press, 1965.

Fraser-Tyler, Kerr W. *Afghanistan: A Study of Political Developments in Central and Southern Asia.* New York: Paragon Books, 1967.

Freedman, Darlene. "There Aren't Many of Them Here So There Isn't a Problem." Unpublished Paper, Eastern Washington University, 1990.

Freire, Paulo. *Pedagogy of the City.* New York: Continuum Press, 1993.

Fris, Ann-Margaret. "Policies for Minority Education. A Comparative Study of Britain and Sweden." Unpublished Doctoral Dissertation, University of Stockholm, 1982.

Frish, G. *Kogda, Partii Postuchatsya v Shkoly.* Moscow: Current Digest of the Soviet Press, 1990.

Frye, Richard N. *The Heritage of Persia.* London: Weidenfeld and Nicholson, 1961.

Fulbrook, Mary. *A Concise History of Germany.* Cambridge: Cambridge University Press, 1990.

Furre, B. "Norske Historie." In T.K. Derry, *A History of Modern Norway.* Oxford: Clarendon Press, 1973.

Futu'hu-l, Bulda'n in, Elliott, H.M., and Dowson, J. (Eds). *The History of India, As Told by Its Own Historians: The Muhammadan Period: Historians of Sind, 1,* Vol. 25. Calcutta: Susil Gupta Ltd., 1955.

Galbally, F. *Review of Post-Arrival Services and Programs.* Canberra: Australian Government Printing Service, 1978.

Gardner, Howard. *To Open Minds: Chinese Clues to the Dilemma of Contemporary Education.* New York: Basic Books, 1989.

Gayfer, Margaret. *An Overview of Canadian Education.* Toronto: The Canadian Education Association, 1974.

Georgeoff, Peter. *The Social Education of Bulgarian Youth.* Minneapolis: University of Minnesota Press, 1968.

Gerson, Noel. *Belgium.* New York: The Macmillan Company, 1964.

Ghana. *One-Year Development Plan.* Accra: Publishing Corporation, 1970, p. 159.

Ghana. *Report of the Commission on University Education.* Government Printing Department, 1961.

Ghana. Ministry of Information. *Report of the Educational Review Committee.* Accra: Tema, State Publishing Corporation, 1967.

Ghirshman, R. *Iran: From the Earliest Times to the Islamic Conquest.* London: Pelican Press, 1954.

Gibb, H.A.R. *Ibn Battuta's Travels in Asia and Africa, 1325–1354.* New York: Robert M. McBride & Co., 1929.

Gill, Anton. *A Dance Between Flames.* New York: Carroll & Graff Publishers, 1993.

Goldbloom, Victor. "The New Language Czar." *Macleans* (July 8, 1991).

Goldschmidt, Arthur, Jr. *Modern Egypt: The Formation of a Nation State.* Boulder, CO: Westview Press, 1988.

Gollnick, Donna and Chinn, Philip. *Multicultural Education in a Pluralistic Society.* New York: MacMillan College Publishing Company, 1994.

Gonen, Amiram. *The Encyclopedia of the Peoples of the World.* New York: Henry Holt Publishing Co., 1993.

Gordon, L. "Controlling Education: Agency Theory and the Reformation of New Zealand Schools." *Educational Policy,* Vol. 9, No. 1 (March 1995), pp. 54–74.

Gordon, Tuula. "Citizens and Others: Gender, Democracy and Education." Unpublished Paper, University of Helsinki, 1992.

Gotchev, A. "Education and Research in the Social Sciences: Transition Dilemmas in Bulgaria." *East European Politics and Societies,* Vol. 7, No. 1 (1993), pp. 43–58.

Graham, T. "The Fourth Republic?" *West Africa* (March 16, 1987), p. 507.

Grant, Carl A. *Educating for Diversity.* Boston: Allyn & Bacon, 1995.

Gregorian, Vartan. *The Emergence of Modern Afghanistan.* Stanford, CA: Stanford University Press, 1969.

Grert, Tim. *Haakon VII of Norway.* New York: Hippocrene Books, 1983.

Grousset, Rene. *In the Footsteps of the Buddha.* London: George Routledge & Sons Ltd., 1932.

Groves, C.P. *The Planting of Christianity in Africa. Vol. 1.* London: Lutterworth Press, 1958, p. 152.

Grunberger, Richard. *A Social History of the Third Reich.* Harmondsworth: Penguin, 1979.

Guerard, Albert. *France, A Short History.* New York: W.W. Norton, 1946.

Gunther, John. *Inside Australia.* New York: Harper and Row, 1972.

Hale, J.R. "Humanism and Renaissance: 1350–1527." In John Julius Norwich (Ed.), *The Italians: History, Art, and the Genius of a People.* New York: Abrams, 1983.

Halecki, Oscar (Ed.). *Poland.* New York: Praeger, 1957.

Hall, D.G.E. *A History of South East Asia,* 3rd ed. London: Macmillan & Co., 1968.

Halpern, A.M. *Policies Toward China.* New York: McGraw-Hill, 1965.

The Handicapped Pupils and Special Schools Regulations (SI 1959, No. 365). London, England, 1959.

Hanratty, Dennis M. and Meditz, Sandra W. (Eds.). *Colombia, A Country Study.* Washington, DC: Department of the Army, 1990.

Hart, Gary. *Russia Shakes the World.* New York: HarperCollins Publishers, 1991.

Hauner, Milan. *The Soviet War in Afghanistan.* Philadelphia: University Press of America, 1991.

Havighurst, Robert and Moreira, Roberto. *Society and Education in Brazil.* Pittsburgh: University of Pittsburgh Press, 1965.

Hawkins, John N. "Japan." *Education and Urban Society* (August 1986), pp. 412–422.

Helg, Aline. *La educacion en Colombia, 1918–1957: Una historia social, economica y politica.* Bogota: Fondo Editorial CEREC, 1987.

Helmreich, Jonathan E. *Belgium and Europe: A Study in Small Power Diplomacy.* The Hague: Mouton, 1976.

Heston, Alan. *Poverty in India: Some Recent Policies.* India Briefing, 1990.

Hillgarth, J.N. *The Spanish Kingdoms.* Oxford: Clarendon Press, 1976.

Hindley, Reg. *The Death of the Irish Language.* London: Routledge Publishing Company, 1990.

Hinkle, Pia. "A School Must Rest on the Idea that Children Are Different." *Newsweek* (December 2, 1992).

Hogan, John. "Education in the Republic of Ireland." In Robert Bell et al., *Education in Great Britain and Ireland.* London: Open University Press, 1973.

Hooper, John. *The Spaniards: A Portrait of New Spain.* New York: Penguin Books, 1987.

Hunter, Shireen T. *Iran After Khomeini.* New York: Praeger, 1992.

Hutchinson, Bertram. *Trabalho, Status, e Educacao.* Rio de Janeiro: Centro Brazileiro de Pesquaisas Educacionais, Ministry of Education and Culture, 1989.

India. Ministry of Information and Broadcasting, Research and Reference Division. *Statistical Outline of India.* Bombay: Ministry of Information and Broadcasting, 1984.

Indire, Filomina. "Education in Kenya." Cited in A. Babs Fafunwa and J.V. Aisiku (Eds.), *Education in Africa.* London: George Allen & Unwin, 1982.

Interviews between the author and advanced education students (graduate level) at University College of Education of Winneba, 1994.

Ireland. Department of Education. *Dail Eireann Proceedings.* Dublin: Department of Education, May 1941.

Ireland. Department of Education. *Report of the Commission on Technical Education.* Dublin: Department of Education, 1927.

Ireland. Department of Education. *Report of the Department of Education.* Dublin: Department of Education, 1924.

Ireland. Department of Education. *Vocational Continuation Schools and Classes, Memorandum for the Information of Committees.* Dublin: Department of Education, 1931.

Ireland. Department of Education. *Vocational Education Act of 1930.* Dublin: Public Statutes of the Direchtas, 1930.

Iwao, Sumiko. "Skills and Life Strategies of Japanese Businesswomen." In Merry White and Susan Pollak (Eds.), *The Cultural Transition: Human Experience and Social Transformation in the Third World and Japan.* London: Routledge & Kegan Paul, 1986.

James, H. *The German Slump.* Oxford: Clarendon Press, 1986.

Janietz, Patricia L. "Developing Collaboratively on International School Special Needs Plan for Multicultural, Multilingual, and Multinational Secondary Students." Paper presented at the Council for Exceptional Children Symposium on Culturally Diverse Exceptional Children. Albuquerque, NM, Oct. 18–20, 1990.

Jelavich, Barbara. *Modern Austria: Empire and Republic 1815–1986.* Cambridge: Cambridge University Press, 1987.

Jeong, I. and Amer, J.M. "State, Class & Expansion of Education in South Korea: A Comparative Review." *Comparative Education Review,* Vol. 38, No. 4 (1994), pp. 531–545.

Jiaoyu, Zhongguo. *Beijing: Chinese Education Yearbook,* 1984, vol. 1.

Jinfang, Qian and Kexiao, Huang. "On the Contemporary Reform of Secondary Education in the Eighties." *Canadian and International Education,* Vol. 16, No. 1 (1987), pp. 86–102.

Johnson, Kristi-Planck. *The Nordic Council and Immigrant Education Policy.* Oslo: EDRS Price, 1989.

Joseph, George. "The Multicultural Dimension." *Times Education Supplement,* Vol. 30, No. 9 (1988).

Joshi, Barbara R. *Untouchable! Voices of the Dalit Liberation Movement.* London: Zed Books, 1986, p. 14.

Kabeer, Naila. "The Quest for National Identity: Women, Islam, and the State in Bangladesh." *Feminist Review,* No. 37 (1991), pp. 38–56.

Kamaluddin, S. "Malthusian Nightmare." *Far Eastern Economic Review,* Vol. 51, No. 20 (1991), p. 12.

Kamaluddin, S. "Top Degree, Top Dollar." *Far Eastern Economic Review,* Vol. 55, No. 21 (1992), p. 27.

Kamil, Jill. *The Ancient Egyptians.* Cairo: American University in Cairo Press, 1984.

Karpat, Kemal H. "Political Developments in Turkey." *Middle Eastern Studies,* Vol. 8, No. 3 (October 1972), pp. 349–375.

Katz, Joseph. *Society, Schools, and Progress.* Oxford: Pergamon Press, 1969.

Katzenstein, Peter J. *The Political Economy of Austria.* Washington, DC: American Enterprise Institute, 1982.

Kee, Francis Wong Hoy. *Comparative Studies in Southeastern Asian Education.* Singapore: Heinemann Educational Books, 1973.

Kee, Francis Wong Hoy and Hong, Ee Tiang. *Education in Malaysia.* Hong Kong: Heinemann Educational Books (Asia) Ltd., 1975.

Kelly, G. and Altbach, P. *Education and the Colonial Experience.* New Brunswick, NJ: Transaction Books, 1984.

Kennedy, Kerry J. and McDonald, Gilbert. "Designing Curriculum Materials for Multicultural Education: Lessons from an Australian Development Project." *Curriculum Inquiry,* Vol. 16, No. 3 (1986).

Kenyatta, Jomo. *Facing Mount Kenja.* London: Seeker and Warburg, 1961.

Kerr, George. *Formosa.* Honolulu: University of Hawaii Press, 1974.

Kindler, Anna M. "Children and the Culture of a Multicultural Society." *Art Education,* Vol. 47, No. 4 (July 1994), pp. 54–60.

Koht, H. "In Place of Almueskole; School for the Common Person." In T.K. Derry, *A History of Modern Norway.* Oxford: Clarendon Press, 1973.

Kosonen, Liisa. The Teacher Bursaries Scheme. A European Teacher's Seminar on the Teaching of Linguistic and Cultural Minorities. Vaaksey, Finland, 1990.

Kossman, E.H. *The Low Countries: 1780–1940.* Oxford: Clarendon Press, 1993.

Kovacs, M.L. and Cropley, A.J. *Immigrants and Society.* New York: McGraw-Hill, 1975.

Kozakiewicz, Mikola. "Educational Transformation Initiated by the Polish Perestroika." *Comparative Education Review,* Vol. 36, No. 1 (1992), pp. 91–101.

Kozol, Jonathon. *Children of the Revolution.* New York: Delacorte Press, 1978.

Kuehn, Larry. "Education vs. Melting Pot." *School Policy* (Summer 1992), pp. 65–68.

Kurian, George. *Encyclopedia of the Third World,* 3rd. ed. New York: Facts on File, 1987.

Lange, David. *Tomorrow's Schools.* Auckland: Ministry of Education, 1990.

Larsen, Karen. *A History of Norway.* Princeton, NJ: Princeton University Press, 1948.

Lau v. Nichols. 414 U.S. 563, 1974.

Lebovics, Herman. *True France.* Ithaca, NY: Cornell University Press, 1992.

Legge, Eric. "Beyond Two Languages." *Macleans* (April 22, 1991).

Leitch-LePoer, Barbara (Ed.). *Singapore: A Country Study.* Washington, DC: Department of the Army (DA Pam 550-184), 1991, pp. xiii–xvii.

Leslav, A., Krausz, E., and Nussbaum, S. "The Education of Iraqi and Romanian Immigrants in Israel." *Comparative Education Review,* Vol. 33, No. 2 (1995), pp. 178–194.

Lewis, H.D. *The French Education System.* New York: St. Martin's Press, 1985.

Liberia. *Annual Report of the Minister of Education to the National Legislature.* Monrovia: Ministry of Education, 1988.

Lie, Suzanna. "Linguistic Minority Children's Comprehension of Language in the Classroom and Teachers' Adjustment to Their Pupils' Performance: A Norwegian Case Study." *Journal of Multilingual and Multicultural Development,* Vol. 12, No. 5 (1991).

Lindblad, S. and Wallin, E. "On Transitions of Power, Democracy, and Education in Sweden." *Journal of Curriculum Studies,* Vol. 25, No. 1 (1993), pp. 77–78.

Lingard, John. "Multicultural Education: Perception and Implementation at the School Division Level in Saskatchewan." Unpublished Paper, Saskatoon, Saskatchewan, 1987.

Lord Swann. *Education for All London.* London: Department of Education and Science, HMSO, 1988.

Lovett, Clara. *The Democratic Movement in Italy, 1830–1876.* Cambridge, MA: Harvard University Press, 1982.

Lovett, T., Gunn, D., and Robson, T. "Education, Conflict, and Community Development in Northern Ireland." *Community Development Journal,* Vol. 29, No. 2 (1994), pp. 177–186.

Lowe, Armin. "Early Intervention Programs in Bangladesh." *The Volta Review,* Vol. 95, No. 5 (1993), p. 137.

Lucio, Ricardo and Serrano, Mariana. "The State and Higher Education in Colombia." *Higher Education,* Vol. 25, No. 1 (January 1993), pp. 61–72.

Lundquist, Sven. "Experience of an Empire: Sweden as a Great Power." In Michael Roberts (Ed.), *Sweden's Age of Greatness.* New York: St. Martin's Press, 1973.

Lynch, James. "Community Relations and Multicultural Education in Australia." *Comparative Education,* Vol. 18, No. 1 (1982).

Lynch, Patrick D. *The Changing Ideology of Educational Reform: Equality Yields to Quality.* ERIC Document No. ED 295285, 1988.

Mackay, Angus. *Spain in the Middle Ages: From Frontier to Empire, 1000–1500*. New York: St. Martin's Press, 1977.

Malcolm, J. *Life of Clive, vol. 2*. Manchester: Manchester University Press, 1923.

Manoukian, M. *The Akon and Ga-Adangme Peoples of the Gold Coast*. London: Oxford University Press, 1950, p. 21.

Marks, Richard. *Cortes*. New York: Alfred A. Knopf, 1993.

Marsot, Afaf Lutfi Al-Sayyid. *Egypt in the Reign of Muhammad Ali*. Cambridge: Cambridge University Press, 1984.

Marsot, Afaf Lutfi Al-Sayyid. *A Short History of Modern Egypt*. Cambridge: Cambridge University Press, 1985.

Maurois, Andre. *A History of France*. New York: Farrar, Strauss, & Cudahy, 1956.

Mayall, James and Navari, Cornelia. *The End of the Post War Era: Documents on Great Power Relations, 1968–1975*. Cambridge: Cambridge University Press, 1980.

Mayerson, Paul and Alimi, M. Zaher. "Developing a Language Curriculum in Afghanistan." Conference Presentation. ERIC No. ED 140232, August 1976.

Mayhoe, Ruth (Ed.). *Education and Modernization: The Chinese Experience*. Oxford: Pergamon Press, 1984.

McConaghy, Tom. "French Education Rights Upheld by Supreme Court." *Phi Delta Kappan* (October 1990).

McGinn, Noel et al. *Education and Development in Korea*. Cambridge, MA: Harvard University Press, 1980.

McInerney, Dennis. "Teacher Attitudes to Multicultural Curriculum Development." *Australian Journal of Education*, Vol. 31, No. 2 (1987).

Metz, Helen Chapin. *Iran: A Country Study*. Washington, DC: U.S. Government Printing Office, 1989.

Metz, Helen Chapin (Ed.). *Egypt: A Country Study*. Washington, DC: Department of the Army, 1991.

Metz, Israel and Metz, Helen Chapin. *Israel: A Country Study*. Washington, DC: Library of Congress, 1990.

Meyer, Michael C. and Sherman, William. *The Course of Mexican History*, 2nd ed. New York: Oxford University Press, 1983.

Meyer, W.D. "Remnants of Eastern Europe's Totalitiarian Past: The Example of Legal Education in Bulgaria." *Journal of Legal Education*, Vol. 7, No. 1 (1993), pp. 43–58.

Mezerik, A.G. (Ed.). *Congo and the United Nations* (3 vols.). New York: International Review Service, 1960–1963.

Michener, William. *Iberia*. New York: Random House, 1968.

Mitchell, Bruce. "Multicultural Education: A Second Glance at the Present American Effort." *Educational Research Quarterly*, Vol. 11, No. 4 (1987), pp. 8–12.

Mitchell, Bruce. Visits to Ghanaian libraries were conducted in 1994 through participation in a USAID grant with Eastern Washington University and the University of Cape Coast.

Mitchell, Bruce et al. *The Dynamic Classroom: A Creative Approach to the Teaching/Evaluation Process*. Dubuque, IA: Kendall/Hunt Publishing Co., 1995.

Mitchell, Bruce and Salsbury, Robert. *A National Survey of Multicultural Education*. Cheney, WA: Western States Consulting and Evaluation Services, 1988.

Mitchell, Bruce and Salsbury, Robert. *An International Survey of Multicultural Education*. Cheney, WA: Western States Consulting and Evaluation Services, 1991. (See Appendix.)

Mitchell, Bruce and Salsbury, Robert. *Multicultural Education in the World Community.* Cheney, WA: Western States Consulting and Evaluation Services, Publication Division, 1991. (See Appendix.)

Mitchell, Bruce and Salsbury, Robert. Responses received from the authors' international multicultural education study. Cheney, WA: Eastern Washington University. Unpublished Monograph, 1991. (See Appendix.)

Mitchell, Bruce and Williams, William. "Education of the Gifted and Talented in the World Community." *Phi Delta Kappan,* Vol. 68, No. 7 (1987), pp. 531–534.

Momatey, Victor. *Rise of the Habsburg Empire, 1526–1815.* New York: Holt, Rinehart and Winston, 1971.

Moodie, T. Dunbar. *The Rise of Afrikanerdom: Power, Apartheid, and the Afrikaner Civil Religion.* Berkeley: University of California Press, 1975.

More than Bows and Arrows. A film narrated by Scott Momaday, Pulitzer Prize-winning author, university professor, and member of the Kiowa tribe, 1983.

Mtonga, H.L. "Comparing the Role of Education in Serving Socioeconomic and Political Development in Tanzania and Cuba." *Journal of Black Studies,* Vol. 23, No. 3 (1994), pp. 382–402.

"The Multicultural Dimension." *Times Educational Supplement,* Vol. 3562 (October 5, 1984), pp. 45–46.

Naamani, Israel T. *The State of Israel.* New York: Praeger, 1980.

Neilsen, Jorgen S. "The Training of Teachers of the Children of Migrant Workers: Cultural Values and Education in a Multicultural Society." Report of the European Teachers 13th Seminar, Federal Republic of Germany, 1981.

Nelson, Harold. *South Africa: A Country Study.* Washington, DC: U.S. Government Printing Office, 1981.

Nelson, Harold D. *Kenya: A Country Study.* Washington, DC: The American University, 1984.

Nelson, Harold D. (Ed.). *Liberia: A Country Study.* Washington, DC: Department of the Army (Foreign Area Studies), 1985.

Nelson, Murray. "Learning from and in Norwegian High Schools." *Social Education,* Vol. 55, No. 5 (September 1991), p. 294.

Neville, Liddy. "The Sunrise Experience: Theory and Practice in an Australian Educational Community." *Education,* Vol. 110, No. 4 (1990).

New Jersey. State Department of Education. *Guidelines for Development of Program Plan—Bilingual/ESL Education Programs.* New Jersey Department of Education, 1989.

"New Zealand." In *The Cambridge History of the British Empire.* London: Cambridge University Press, 1933.

New Zealand. Ministry of Education. *Education in New Zealand.* Wellington: Ministry of Education, 1992.

Nicholson, Rangi and Garland, Ron. "New Zealanders' Attitudes to the Revitalization of the Maori Language." *Journal of Multilingual and Multicultural Development,* Vol. 12, No. 5 (1991).

Nimako, S.G. *Ghana Today: Education in Ghana 1930–1973.* Accra, Ghana: Information Services Department, 1976, pp. 5–6.

Noakes, J. and Pridham, G. (Eds.). *Nazism* (3 vols.). Exeter: Exeter Studies in History, 1988.

Nyerere, Julius. "Education in Tanzania." In A. Babs Fafunwa (Ed.), *African Education in Perspective.* London: Allen & Unwin, 1982.

Nyrop, Richard F. and Seekins, Donald M. *Afghanistan: A Country Study.* Washington, DC: U.S. Government Printing Office, 1986.

Nyrop, Richard et al. *India, A Country Study.* Washington, DC: Department of the Army, 1986.

O'Donnell, Michael. "Irish Education Today." *Iris Hibernia,* Vol. 1, No. 1 (1962), p. 20.

Oliver, W.H. and Williams, B.R. (Eds.). *The Oxford History of New Zealand.* Wellington: Oxford University Press, 1981.

Omer-Cooper, J.D. *The Cambridge History of Africa.* Cambridge: Cambridge University Press, 1976.

Oskaar, Elis. *Language—Integration—Identity: Socio-Cultural Problems of New Minorities.* ERIC No. ED 269485, 1982.

Paek, Young-ok. "A Woman's Place." *News Review* (December 1992), p. 30.

Papanek, Hanna. "Class and Gender in Education-Employment Linkages." *Comparative Education Review* (August 1985), p. 317.

Parkhurst, H. *Education on the Dalton Plan.* London: Bell Publishing Co., 1922.

Paul, Bimal Kanti. "Female Activity Space in Rural Bangladesh." *The Geographical Review,* Vol. 82, No. 1 (1992), pp. 1–12.

Pearse, Patrick. "The Murder Machine." In *Political Writings and Speeches.* Dublin: Talbot Press, 1966.

Peasley, Amos J. (Ed.). *Constitutions of Nations,* vol. I. The Hague: Martinus Nijhoff, 1956.

Perlmutter, Amos. *Israel: The Partitioned State.* New York: Charles Scribner's Sons, 1985.

Peyrefitte, Alain. *The Trouble with France.* Tom Bishop and Nicholas Wahl (Eds.), trans. William R. Bryan. New York: NYU Press, 1986.

Pietila, Asta (Ed.). *Education of the Samis in Finland.* Helsinki National Board of General Education Research and Development Bureau, 1981.

Pittman, Paul M., III. *Turkey: A Country Study.* Washington, DC: U.S. Government Printing Office, 1988.

Planck, Max. *Between Elite and Mass Education.* Albany, NY: SUNY Press (Institute for Human Development and Education), 1983.

Popovych, Erika and Levin-Stankevich, Brian. *The Soviet System of Education.* Washington, DC: American Association of Collegiate Registrars and Admission Officers and NAFSA, Association of International Educators, 1992.

Porter, Ed. "Foreign Involvement in China's Colleges and Universities." *International Journal of Intercultural Relations,* Vol. 11, No. 4 (1987), pp. 369–370.

Portera, Agostino. "Is an Interactive Integration of the European Peoples Possible? An Example of Italian Youth in the West German Republic." *Journal of Multilingual and Multicultural Development,* Vol. 12, No. 4 (1991), pp. 271–276.

Price, R.F. *Chinese Intellectuals and the West.* London: Oxford University Press, 1970.

Pridmore, F. *Memoirs of the Raffles Museum.* Singapore, 1955.

Procacci, Giuliano. *History of the Italian People.* New York: Harper and Row, 1968.

Program Nauczania: Historia Dla Szkoly Sredniej (Program for Teaching History in High Schools). Warszawa: Ministerstwo Edukacji Narodowej (Ministry of National Education), 1990.

Psacharopoulos, George and Velez, Eduardo. "Schooling, Ability, and Earnings in Colombia, 1988." In *Economic Development and Cultural Change.* Chicago: University of Chicago Press, 1992.

Rahim, Enayetur. *Bangladesh: A Country Study.* Washington, DC: Department of the Army (D.A. Pam. 550-175, Headquarters, Department of the Army), 1992.

Ramsey, John F. *Spain: The Rise of World Power.* Birmingham: The University of Alabama Press, 1980.

Republic of Kenya. *Report of the Presidential Working Party on Education and Manpower Training for the Next Decade and Beyond.* Nairobi: Government Printer, 1988.

Rey-von-Allmen, Micheline. *The Education of Migrant Workers' Children—The Training of Teachers.* Lisbon: Council for Cultural Cooperation, 1981.

Rezun, Miron. *Iran at the Crossroads.* Boulder, CO: Westview Press, 1990.

Rippa, Alexander S. *Education in a Free Society.* New York: Longman, 1988.

Rix, R. "Education for the New Spain." *Bulletin of Hispanic Studies,* Vol. 71, No. 2 (1994), pp. 291–292. (Book Review.)

Robertson, Neville L. and Barbara, L. *Education in South Africa.* Bloomington, IN: PDK Fastback Series, #90, Phi Delta Kappa, 1977.

Roger, Hans. *Russia in the Age of Modernization and Revolution.* Burat Mill, England: Longman Co., 1980.

Rosen, Stanley. "Editor's Introduction." *Chinese Education,* Vol. XVII, No. 2 (1984).

Rubagumya, C.M. (Ed.). *Language in Education in Africa: A Tanzanian Perspective.* Clevedon, Avon: Multilingual Matters Ltd., 1990.

Rubin, Barnett R. "Post–Cold War State Disintegration: The Failure of International Conflict Resolution in Afghanistan." *Journal of International Affairs* (Winter 1993).

Rudolph, David. *Honduras, A Country Study.* Washington, DC: U.S. Government Printing Office, 1984.

Rudolph, James. *Mexico, A Country Study.* Washington, DC: Department of the Army, 1985.

Ruiz, Ramon Eduardo. *Triumphs and Tragedy.* New York, W.W. Norton & Company, 1992.

Rust, Val D. "Reforms in East Germany, Czechoslovakia, and Poland." *Phi Delta Kappan,* Vol. 73, No. 5 (1992), p. 389.

Sabzalian, Ali. *Iran.* Berne, Switzerland: Embassy of the Islamic Republic of Iran, 1987.

Saini, Shiv Kumar. *Development of Education in India: Socioeconomic and Political Perspectives.* New Delhi: Cosmo, 1980.

Samoff, Joel. "The Facade of Precision in Education Data and Statistics: A Troubling Example from Tanzania." *The Journal of Modern African Studies,* Vol. 29, No. 4 (December 1991), pp. 669–689.

Sampson, Anthony. *Black and Gold.* New York: Pantheon Books, 1987.

Sarkar, Judanath. *History of Aurangzeb.* Calcutta: M.C. Sarkar and Sons, 1952.

Savada, Andrea and Shaw, William. *South Korea: A Country Study.* Washington, DC: Department of the Army, 1992.

Schlesinger, Philip. "On National Identity: Some Conceptions and Misconceptions Criticized." *Social Science Information,* Vol. 26 (1987), pp. 219–264.

Schluter, Ragnhild. "The Immigrant Project, 1980–1981." *European Journal of Teacher Education,* Vol. 9, No. 2 (1986), pp. 153–168.

The Schools Regulations (SI 1959, No. 365). London, England, 1959.

Scott, Margaret. "Confusion of Tongues." *Far Eastern Economic Review* (July 6, 1989), pp. 44–46.

Seoul Ministry of Education. *Statistical Yearbooks of Education.* Seoul: Ministry of Education, 1953.

Shaw, Stanford J. *History of the Ottoman Empire and Modern Turkey.* Cambridge: Cambridge University Press, 1977.

Shigaki, Irene. "Child Care Practices in Japan and the U.S." *Young Children,* No. 29 (1993), p. 38.

Shindu, J. "Self Employment Efforts Among Primary School Leavers in Kenya." Unpublished Doctoral Dissertation, University of Nairobi, Kenya, 1977.

Shinn, Rinn-Sup. *Italy: A Country Study.* Washington, DC: U.S. Government Printing Office, 1985.

Siemaktylikowska, A. "Curriculum Development in Secondary Schools in Poland." *Journal of Curriculum Studies,* Vol. 25, No. 1 (1993), pp. 89–93.

Sierro, Justo. *The Political Evolution of the Mexican People.* Austin: University of Texas Press, 1988.

Sifuna, D.N. *Revolution in Primary Education: The New Approach in Kenya.* Nairobi: East African Literary Bureau, 1986.

Sih, Paul K.T.S. *Taiwan in Modern Times.* New York: St. John's University Press, 1973.

Sinari, R.A. *The Structure of Indian Thought.* New York: Oxford University Press, 1989.

Singapore. Ministry of Communication and Information, Information Division. *Governmental Structure.* Singapore: Ministry of Communication and Information, 1989.

Singh, M. Garbutcheon. "Issues in Cross-Cultural Education: Inverting the Education Studies Curriculum." *Teaching Education,* Vol. 4, No. 1 (1991).

Slavin, Robert. "PET and the Pendulum: Educational Faddism and How to Stop It." *Phi Delta Kappan* (June 1989).

Smerling, Louis. "Admissions." In Jay Henderson and Ronald N. Montaperto (Eds.), *China's Schools in Flux.* White Plains, NY: M.E. Sharpe, 1979.

Smith, Douglas C. *Theoretical Foundations of Chinese Educational and Intellectual Thought: An Occidental Interpretation.* ERIC Document No. ED 340628, 1990.

Smith, Graham H. *Reform and Maori Educational Crisis: A Grand Illusion.* Keynote Speech at the Post Primary Teachers Association Curriculum Conference, Christchurch, 1991.

Solsten, Eric and Meditz, Sandra (Eds.). *Finland: A Country Study.* Washington, DC: U.S. Government Printing Office, 1990, pp. xxiii–26.

Solsten, Eric D. *Spain: A Country Study.* Washington, DC: Department of the Army, 1990.

Somerset, A. "Examinations Are an Instrument to Improve Pedagogy." Cited in S.P. Heyneman and I. Fagerlind (Eds.), *University Examinations and Standardized Testing.* Washington, DC: World Bank, 1988.

Stahl, Abraham. "Introducing Ethnic Materials to the Classroom." *Urban Education* (October 1985), pp. 257–271.

Steinberg, Joseph. *The Philippines: A Singular and a Plural Place.* Boulder, CO: Westview Press, 1990.

Stenberger, Marten. *Sweden.* New York: Praeger, 1962.

Strukelj, I. *Socio-Cultural and Linguistic Intergration of the Children of Migrant and Farmer Migrant Workers.* Meeting of Specialists, Final Report. Proceedings, Bled, Yugoslavia: Sponsored by the U.N. Education Scientific and Cultural Organization, June 1989.

Sundquist, J. "Ethnicity, Migration, and Health: A Population-Based Study of 338 Refugees from Latin America, 396 Non-Refugee Immigrants from Finland, and 161 from Southern Europe and 996 Age-Matched, Sex-Matched.'' *Scandinavian Journal of Social Welfare,* Vol. 4, No. 1 (1995), pp. 2–7.

Superintendent of Public Instruction. *Position Statement on Multicultural Education.* Lansing: Michigan Department of Education, 1981.

Swick, Thomas. *Unquiet Days: At Home in Poland.* New York: Ticknor & Fields Publishers, 1991.

Sykes, Percy M. *A History of Afghanistan.* London: MacMillan, 1940.

Szebenyi, Peter. ''Change in the Systems of Public Education in East Central Europe.'' *Comparative Education,* Vol. 28, No. 1 (1992), pp. 19–31.

Taiwan. Government Information Office. *Republic of China: A Reference Book.* Taipei: United Pacific International, Inc., 1983.

Talbott, John E. *The Politics of Educational Reform in France, 1918–1940.* Princeton, NJ: Princeton University Press, 1969.

Tan, E.T. ''Language, Society, and Education in Singapore: Issues and Trends.'' *International Journal of Educational Development,* Vol. 15, No. 1 (1995), pp. 95–96.

Tannenbaum, Edward R. and Noether, Emiliana P. *Modern Italy: A Topical History Since 1861.* New York: NYU Press, 1974.

Taskforce to Review Education Administration. *Administering for Excellence.* Wellington: Taskforce to Review Education Administration, 1988.

Taskforce to Review Education Administration. *Administering for Excellence.* Wellington: Taskforce to Review Education Administration, 1990.

Taylor, Robert. *China's Intellectual Dilemma.* Vancouver: University of British Columbia Press, 1981.

Tent, James F. *Mission on the Rhine.* Chicago: University of Chicago Press, 1982.

Thomas, Murray. ''Malaysia.'' *Education and Urban Society* (August 1986), pp. 399–400.

Tiedt, Pamela and Tiedt, Iris. *Multicultural Teaching.* Boston: Allyn & Bacon, 1995.

Tildirim, Ali. *Sex-Role Influences on Turkish Adolescents' Self Identity.* Annual Meeting of the American Educational Research Association, Atlanta, 1983.

Tinker, Hugh. *A New System of Slavery: The Export of Indian Labour Overseas, 1830–1920.* London: Oxford University Press, 1974.

Tomiak, J.J. (Ed.). *Soviet Education in the 1980s.* New York: St. Martin's Press, 1987.

Troyna, Barry. ''Beyond Multiculturalism Towards the Enactment of Anti-Racist Education in Policy and Pedagogy.'' *Oxford Review of Education,* Vol. 13, No. 3 (1987).

Tura, Jordi Sole. ''The Spanish Transition to Democracy.'' In Robert P. Clark and Michael H. Haltzel (Eds.), *Spain in the 1980s.* Cambridge, MA: Ballinger Publishers, 1987, pp. 25–34.

Turnbull, C.M. *A History of Singapore.* London: Oxford University Press, 1977.

Tutu, Desmond. *The Rainbow People of God.* New York: Doubleday, 1994.

UNESCO. *Bulletin of the UNESCO Regional Office for Education in the Asian Region,* Vols. 1, 2, 1965.

UNESCO. *Metodos y medios utilizados en Cuba para la superacion del analfabetismo.* Havana: Editora Pedogogica, 1965.

UNESCO. *Primary Education for Girls.* Bangkok: UNESCO Principal Regional Office for Asia and the Pacific, 1987.

UNESCO. *Republic of Korea: Educational Services in a Rapidly Growing Economy.* Paris: UNESCO, 1974.

UNESCO. *UNESCO Korean Survey.* Washington, DC: UNESCO, 1960.

United Nations. *Compendium of Social Statistics,* New York: United Nations, 1963.

United Nations. *Official Records of the General Assembly, Fifteenth Session, Part 1,* Plenary Meetings, Vol. 3, Verbatim Records, New York (September–October 17, 1960).

United Nations. "South Africa." *UN Chronicle,* Vol. XXXI, No. 2 (September 1994).

Urusov, S.D. *Memoirs of a Russian Governor.* London: Oxford University Press, 1908.

U.S. Department of Education. *The Educational System of New Zealand.* Education Around the World, No. 80-14016. Washington, DC: U.S. Government Printing Office, 1980.

U.S. Department of Health, Education, and Welfare, Office of Education. *Education in Japan: A Century of Modern Development,* by Ronald S. Anderson, No. 74-19110. Washington, DC: U.S. Government Printing Office, 1979.

U.S. News and World Report (June 1, 1992).

Valdez, Nelson. *The Cuban Revolution: A Research Study Guide (1959–1949).* Albuquerque: University of New Mexico Press, 1971.

Vali, Ferenc A. *Bridge Across the Bosporus.* Baltimore, MD: The Johns Hopkins Press, 1971.

Vander Linden, H. *Belgium: The Making of a Nation,* trans. Sybil Jane. Oxford: Clarendon Press, 1920.

Vatikiotis, Michael. "Purity and Perception." *Far Eastern Economic Review* (December 1991), p. 30.

Vogel, Ezra F. *Japan as Number One: Lessons for America.* Cambridge, MA: Harvard University Press, 1979.

Von Schuschnigg, Kurt. *The Brutal Takeover.* New York: Weidenfeld & Nicholson, 1971.

Voslou, W.B. "The Coloured Policy of the National Party." In N.J. Rhoudie, *South African Dialogue.* Philadelphia: Westminister Press, 1972, pp. 265–366.

Vreeland, Nena. *Area Handbook for Singapore.* Washington, DC: American University Foreign Area Studies, 1977.

Vreeland, Nena et al. *Area Handbook for Malaysia.* Washington, DC: U.S. Government Printing Office, 1980.

Wang, Y.C. *Chinese Intellectuals and the West, 1872–1949.* Chapel Hill: University of North Carolina Press, 1966.

Washington Department of Public Instruction. *Handbook for Goal-Based Curriculum Planning and Implementation.* Olympia, WA: State Department of Education, 1975.

Waterbury, John. *The Egypt of Nasser and Sadat: The Political Economy of Two Regimes.* Princeton, NJ: Princeton University Press, 1983.

Weaver, Mary Anne. "Letter from Bangladesh: A Fugitive from Justice." *The New Yorker* (September 14, 1994), pp. 48–60.

Weil, Thomas E. (Ed.). *Brazil, A Country Study.* Washington, DC: Department of the Army, 1983.

Welch, A.J. "Aboriginal Education as Internal Colonialism: The Schooling of an Indigenous Minority in Australia." *Comparative Education,* Vol. 24, No. 2 (1988).

Wellington, Stanley. *Balaysia and Singapore: The Building of New States.* Ithaca, NY: Cornell University Press, 1978.

Wellington, Stanley. *Colombia: A Study of the Educational System of Colombia and a Guide to the Academic Placement of Students from Colombia in Educational Institutions of the United States.* Stockton, CA: National Council on the Evaluation of Foreign Education Credentials, 1984.

Westwood, J.N. *Endurance and Endeavor.* Suffolk, England: Bungay, 1973.

Wheatley, Paul. *The Golden Khersonese.* Kuala Lumpur: University of Malaya Press, 1961.

Whitaker, Donald. *Area Handbook for Australia.* Washington, DC: Foreign Area Studies of the American University, 1978.

Whitcombe, Elizabeth. *Agrarian Conditions in Northern India.* Berkeley: University of California Press, 1922.

White, Merry. *The Japanese Educational Challenge.* New York: The Free Press, 1987.

Wickman, Stephen B. *Belgium: A Country Study.* Washington, DC: Department of the Army, 1984.

Wilber, Donald N. *Iran.* Princeton, NJ: Princeton University Press, 1976.

Wilkinson, Bruce W. "Elementary and Secondary Education Policy in Canada." *A Survey, Canadian Public Policy* (December 1986).

Williams, B.R. *The United States and the Philippines.* Garden City, NY: Doubleday & Co., 1925.

Williams, T.D. "Sir Gordon Guggisberg and Education Reform in the Gold Coast 1919–1927." *Comparative Education Review* (December 1964), pp. 290–306.

Williams, W.G. and Mitchell, B. *From Afghanistan to Zimbabwe: Gifted Education Efforts in the World Community.* New York: Peter Lang Inc., 1989.

Williamson, Edwin. *The Penguin History of Latin America.* London: Penguin Books, Ltd., 1992.

Williamson, Graham. "A New Approach to Teacher Education in England." *Educational Leadership,* Vol. 49, No. 3 (1991), pp. 61–62.

Wilson, Monica. "The Hunters and the Herders." *Oxford History of South Africa.* New York: Oxford University Press, 1969.

Winstedt, Richard O. *The Malays: A Cultural History* (rev. ed.). London: Routledge & Kegan Paul, 1950.

Wirth, John (Ed.). *State and Society in Brazil: Continuity and Change.* Boulder, CO: Westview Press, 1992.

Wolpert, Stanley. *A New History of India.* New York: Oxford University Press, 1982.

Wolters, O.W. *Early Indonesian Commerce: A Study of the Origins of Srivijaya.* Ithaca, NY: Cornell University Press, 1967.

Wong, P.L. "Constructing a Public Popular Education in Sao Paulo, Brazil." *Comparative Education Review,* Vol. 39, No. 1 (1995), pp. 120–141.

Wong, Soon Teck. *Singapore's New Education System: Education Reform for National Development.* Singapore: Institute of Southeast Asian Studies, 1988.

Wuorinen, John H. *Scandinavia.* Englewood Cliffs, NJ: Prentice-Hall, 1965.

Ximin, Pan. "A Preliminary Discussion of Problems Involving Several Aspects of Key Schools." *Chinese Education,* ed. and trans. Stanley Rosen, Vol. XVII, No. 2 (1984).

Yaacov, Inam. "Israel." *Education and Urban Society* (August 1986).

Yang, Y.R. "Education and National Development: The Case of Taiwan." *Chinese Education and Society,* Vol. 27, No. 6 (1994), pp. 7–22.

Yergin, D. and Gustafson, T. *Russia, 2010.* New York: Random House, 1993.

Zachariah, Mathew. "India." *Education and Urban Society,* Vol. 18, No. 4 (August 1986), pp. 487–499.

Zhongguo, Xingzheng. "Should a Government Be 'Large' or 'Small?' " *Beijing Review* (April 8–14, 1991).

Zickel, Raymond E. (Ed.). *Soviet Union, A Country Study.* Washington, DC: Department of the Army, 1991.

Zureik, E. "Education and Social Change Among the Arabs in Israel." *Journal of Palestine Studies,* Vol. 23, No. 4 (1993), pp. 73–93.

Index

About the Authors

BRUCE M. MITCHELL is Professor of Education at Eastern Washington University, where he specializes in multicultural education, gifted education, sociology of education, and history of education. He has published extensively in journals such as *Urban Education, Educational Research Quarterly,* and *Equity & Excellence,* and his books include *From Afghanistan to Zimbabwe: Gifted Education in the World Community* (1989).

ROBERT E. SALSBURY is Professor of Education at Eastern Washington Univeristy. He has published several monographs, and his articles have appeared in journals such as *Your Public Schools* and *Excellence in Teacher Education.*

ISBN 0-313-28985-9

90000>

EAN

9 780313 289859

HARDCOVER BAR CODE